Life on B-Dash! WAH WAH

Ken-ichi Sakura

What's this?! The third volume! That was quick! What? You mean my brain is running slow?! Even though my stomach is running right on time?! This is why I can never take out the trash on time?!! Idiot!

Ken-ichi Sakura's manga debut was *Fabre Tanteiki*, which was published in a special edition of *Monthly Shonen Jump* in 2000. Serialization of *Dragon Drive* began in the March 2001 issue of *Monthly Shonen Jump* and the hugely successful series has inspired video games and an animated TV show. Sakura's latest title, *Kotokuri*, began running in the March 2006 issue of *Monthly Shonen Jump*. *Dragon Drive* and *Kotokuri* have both become tremendously popular in Japan because of Sakura's unique sense of humor and dynamic portrayal of feisty teen characters.

DRAGON DRIVE

DRAGON DRIVE
VOLUME 3

The SHONEN JUMP Manga Edition

STORY AND ART BY
KEN-ICHI SAKURA

Translation/Martin Hunt, HC Language Solutions, Inc.
English Adaptation/Ian Reid, HC Language Solutions, Inc.
Touch-up Art & Lettering/Jim Keefe
Design/Sam Elzway
Editors/Urian Brown & Shaenon K. Garrity

VP, Production/Alvin Lu
VP, Sales & Product Marketing/Gonzalo Ferreyra
VP, Creative/Linda Espinosa
Publisher/Hyoe Narita

Published by VIZ Media, LLC
P.O. Box 77010
San Francisco, CA 94107

10 9 8 7 6 5 4 3
First printing, August 2007
Third printing, May 2010

SHONEN JUMP MANGA EDITION

DRAGON DRIVE

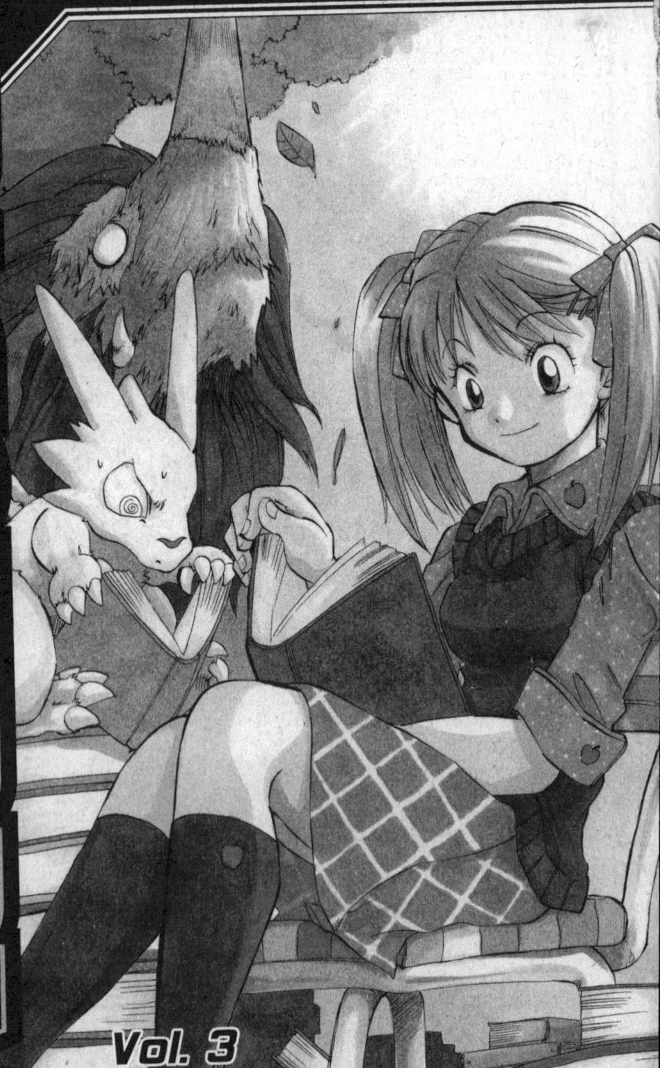

Vol. 3
BELIEVE

STORY & ART BY
KEN-ICHI SAKURA
IN COLLABORATION WITH BANDAI • CHAN'S • ORG

CHARACTERS

Reiji Ozora

A JUNIOR HIGH SCHOOL STUDENT WHO NEVER APPLIED HIMSELF, BUT HE'S TOTALLY GETTING INTO DRAGON DRIVE.

Maiko Yukino

SHE'S ALWAYS GETTING TICKED OFF BY HER UNRELIABLE CHILDHOOD PAL REIJI, BUT SHE SECRETLY CARES ABOUT HIM.

Chibi

PUZZLING DRAGON CHOSEN BY REIJI. CONCEALS AMAZING POWER.

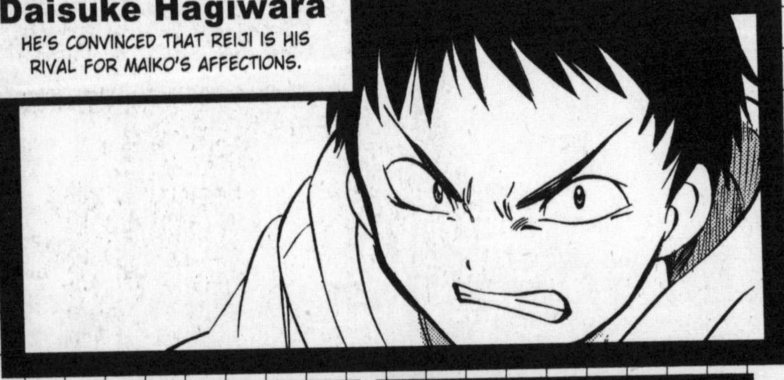

Daisuke Hagiwara

HE'S CONVINCED THAT REIJI IS HIS RIVAL FOR MAIKO'S AFFECTIONS.

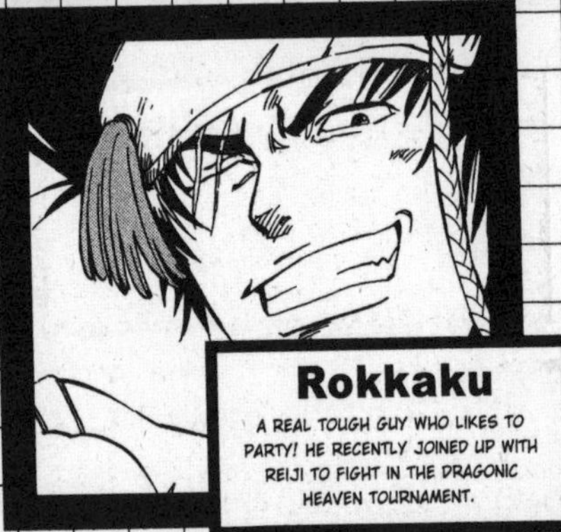

Rokkaku

A REAL TOUGH GUY WHO LIKES TO PARTY! HE RECENTLY JOINED UP WITH REIJI TO FIGHT IN THE DRAGONIC HEAVEN TOURNAMENT.

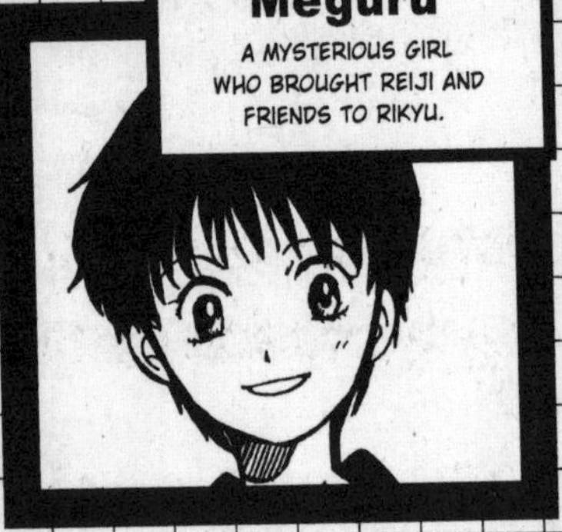

Meguru

A MYSTERIOUS GIRL WHO BROUGHT REIJI AND FRIENDS TO RIKYU.

STORY

DRAGON DRIVE IS A VIRTUAL REALITY GAME THAT ONLY KIDS CAN PLAY. THE THRILL OF THE GAME GRIPS REIJI, A BOY WHO WAS NEVER REALLY GOOD AT ANYTHING. HE BEGINS TRAINING HARD, AND HIS ENTHUSIASM FOR THE GAME IS INCREASED EVEN FURTHER IN A BATTLE WITH HIKARU HIMURO, THE INVINCIBLE TOP-RANKED D.D. PLAYER. WHILE TRAINING IN A SPECIAL ROOM ONE DAY, REIJI AND HIS FRIENDS ARE WHISKED AWAY TO RIKYU, AN ALTERNATE EARTH. THERE, THEY LEARN THAT RI-ON, THE ORGANIZATION RUNNING D.D., IS PLOTTING TO CONQUER BOTH RIKYU AND EARTH. RI-ON IS USING CHILDREN TO GET THE JINRYU STONE, WHICH HAS THE POWER TO CONTROL DRAGONS. TO SAVE HIS HOME PLANET, AS WELL AS THE ONE HE HAS JUST DISCOVERED, REIJI JOINS ROKKAKU TO ENTER THE DRAGONIC HEAVEN COMPETITION IN RIKYU, IN THE HOPES OF WINNING THE JINRYU STONE.

Vol. 3 BELIEVE
CONTENTS

DRAGON DRIVE

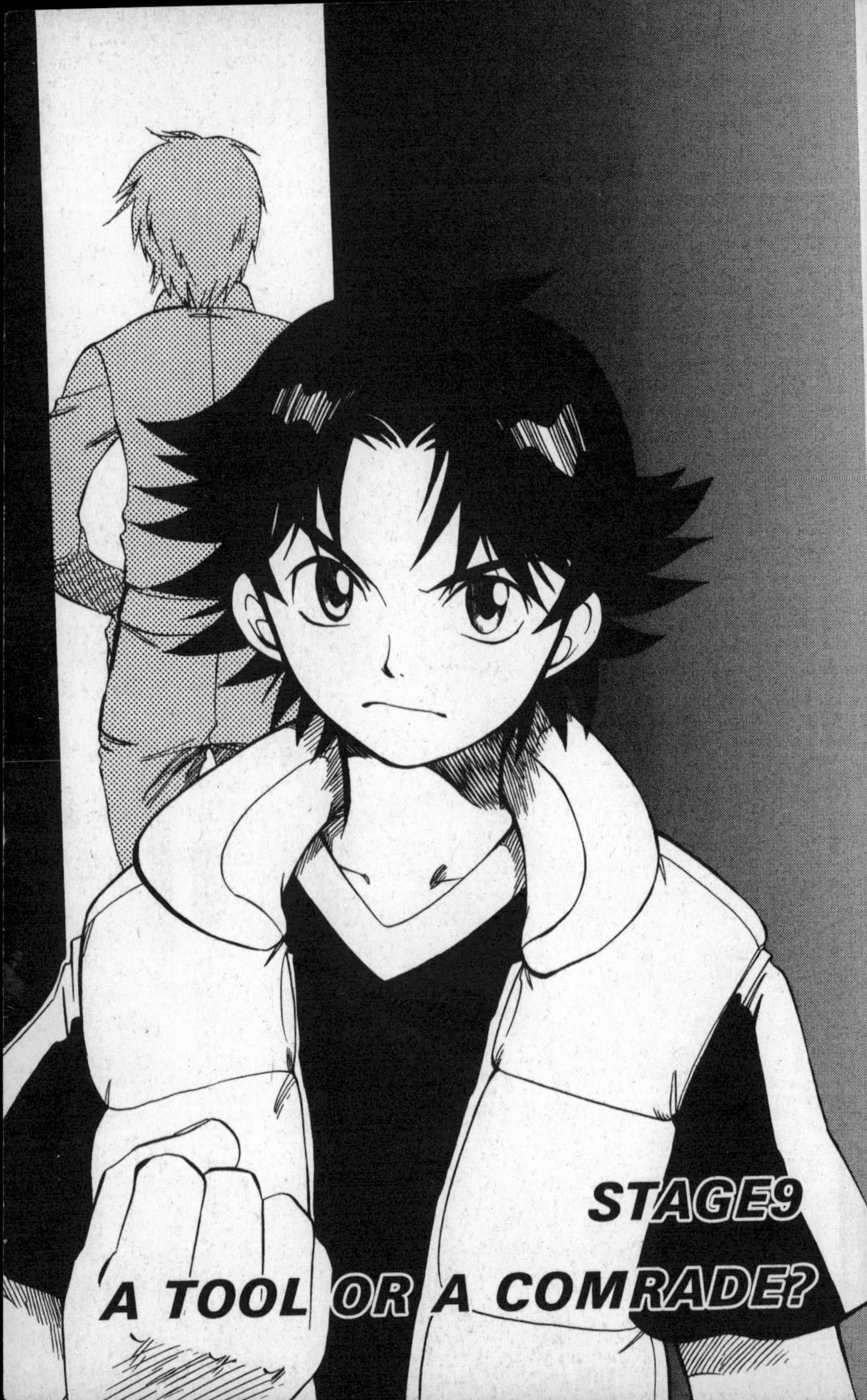
STAGE9
A TOOL OR A COMRADE?

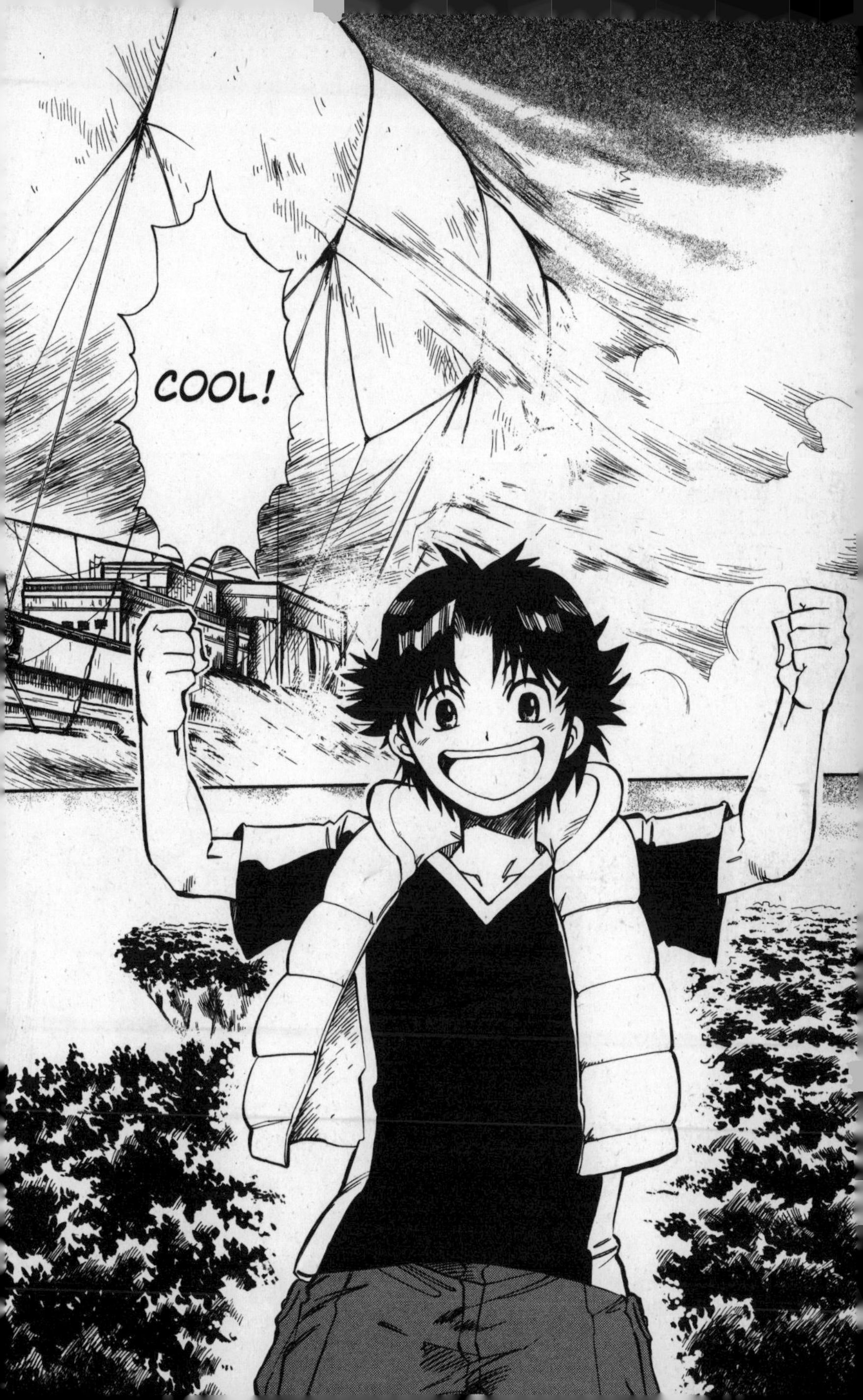
COOL!

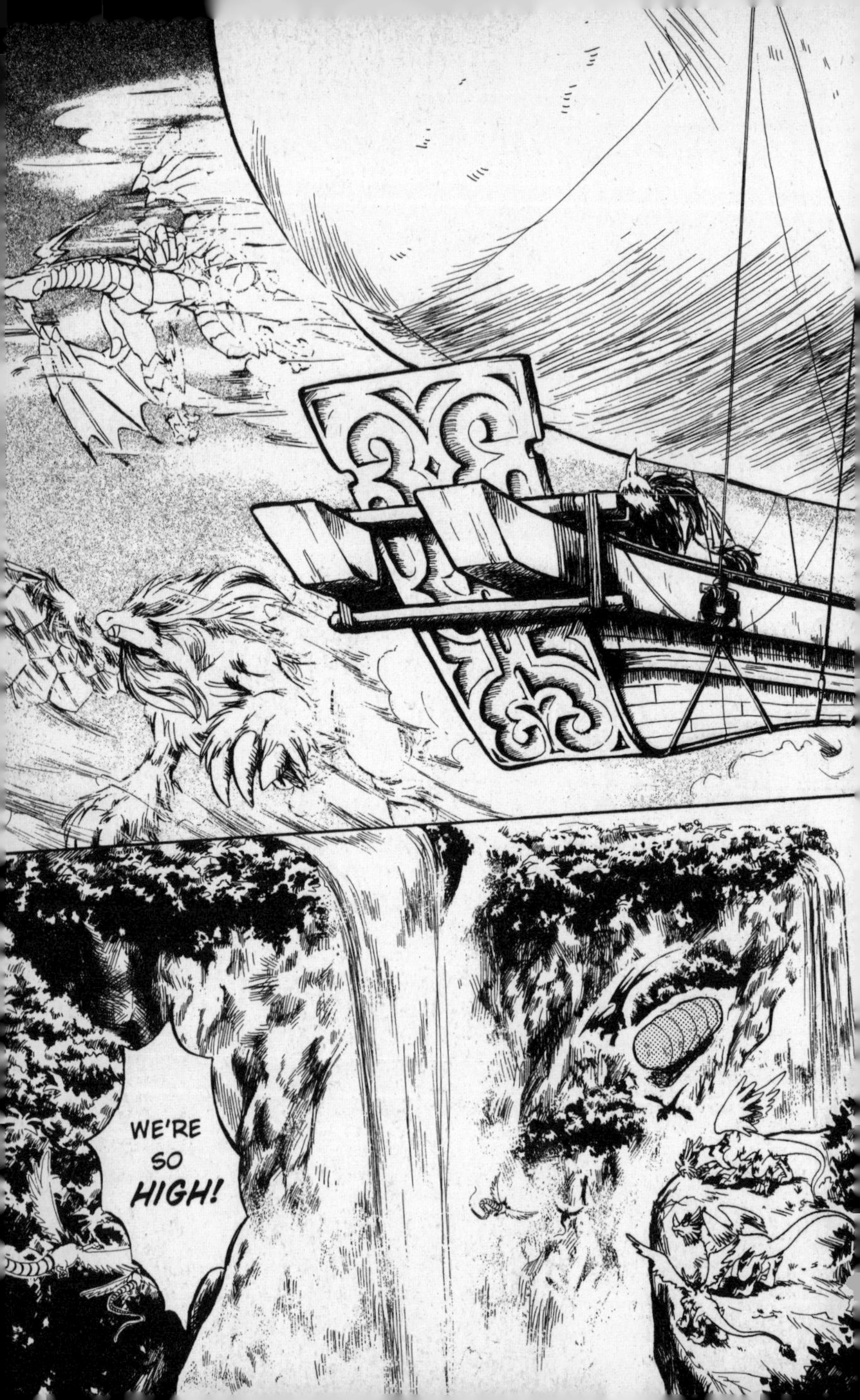
WE'RE SO HIGH!

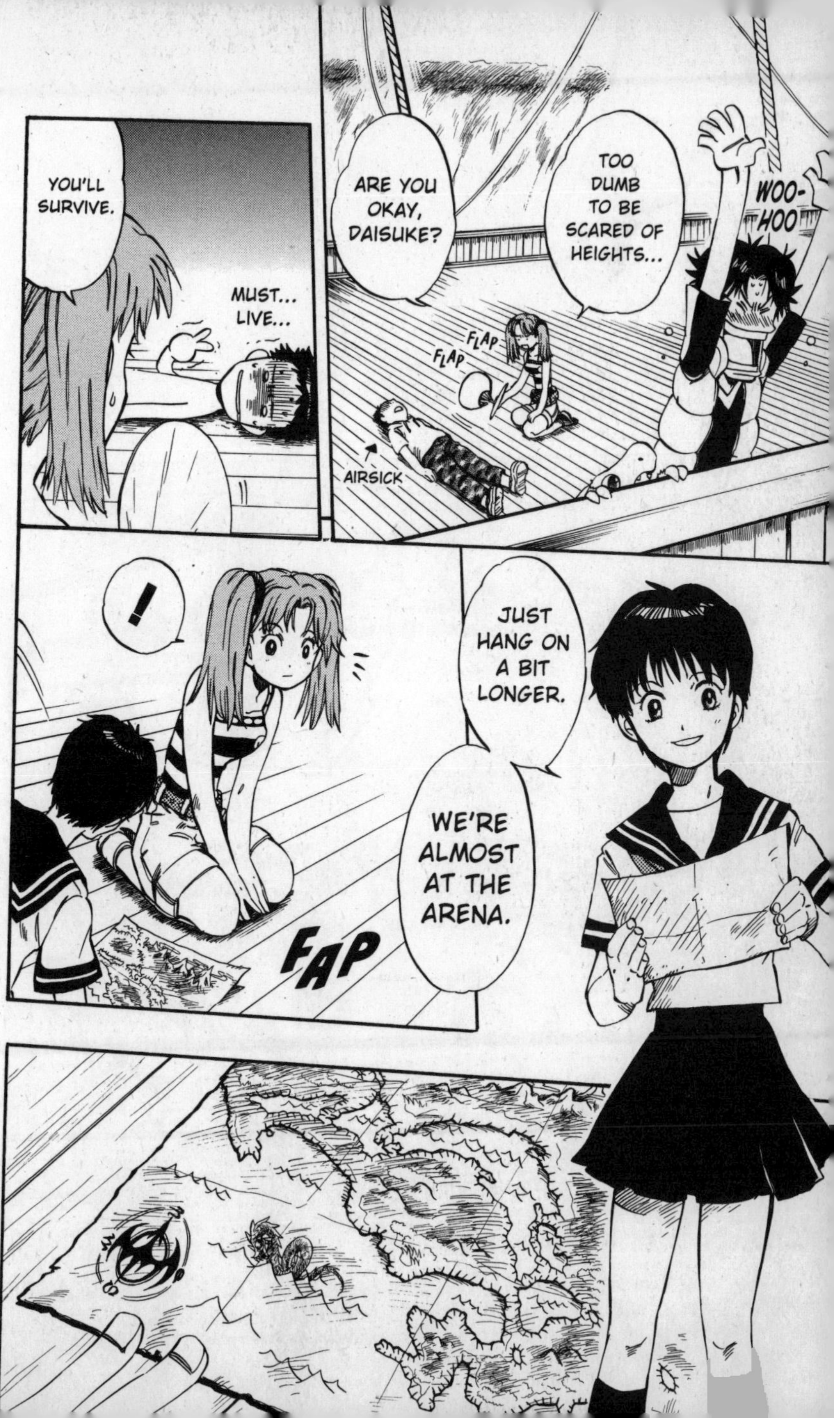
WOO-HOO
TOO DUMB TO BE SCARED OF HEIGHTS...
ARE YOU OKAY, DAISUKE?
FLAP
FLAP
AIRSICK
MUST... LIVE...
YOU'LL SURVIVE.
JUST HANG ON A BIT LONGER.
WE'RE ALMOST AT THE ARENA.
!
FAP

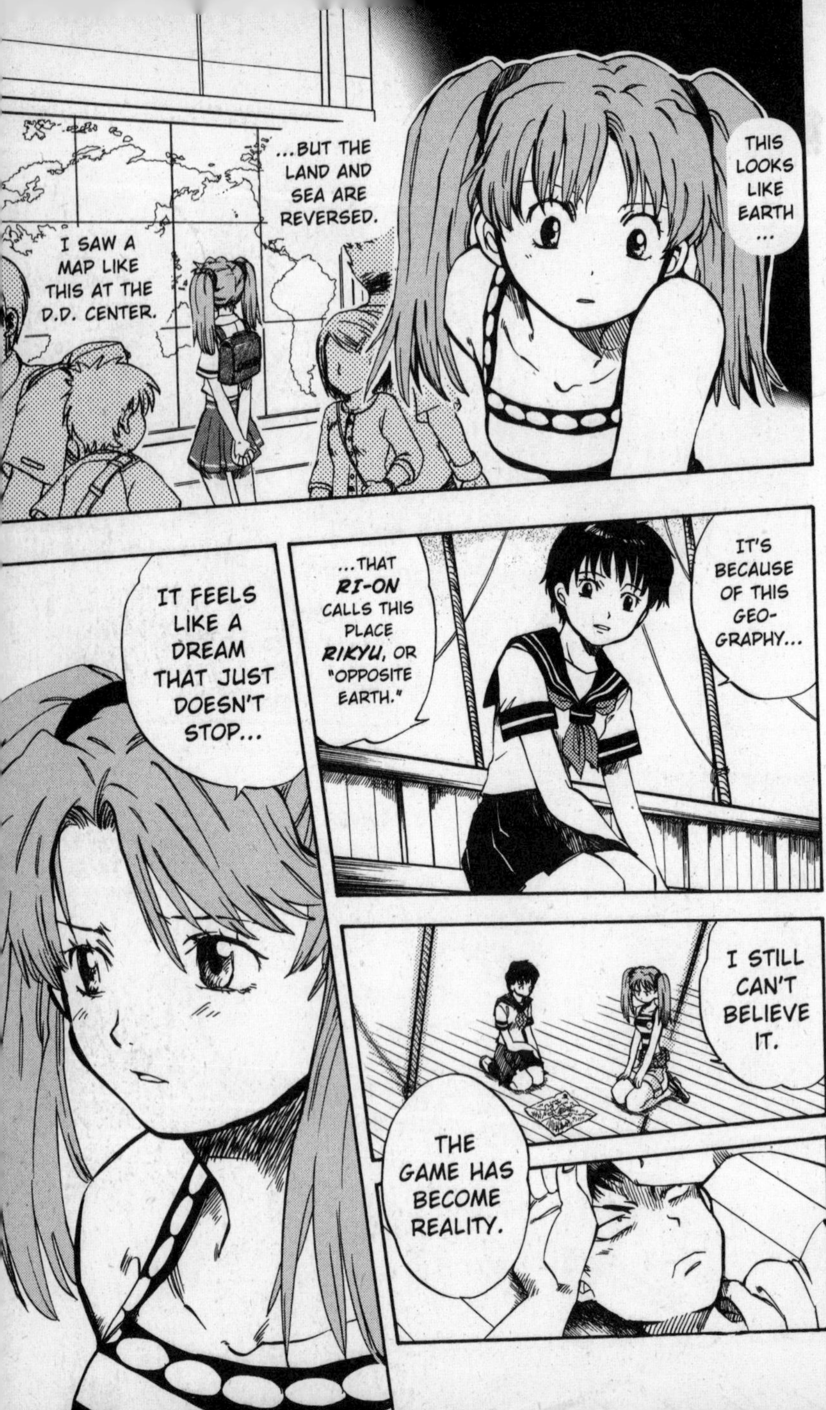
THIS LOOKS LIKE EARTH ...
...BUT THE LAND AND SEA ARE REVERSED.
I SAW A MAP LIKE THIS AT THE D.D. CENTER.
IT'S BECAUSE OF THIS GEO-GRAPHY...
...THAT RI-ON CALLS THIS PLACE RIKYU, OR "OPPOSITE EARTH."
I STILL CAN'T BELIEVE IT.
THE GAME HAS BECOME REALITY.
IT FEELS LIKE A DREAM THAT JUST DOESN'T STOP...

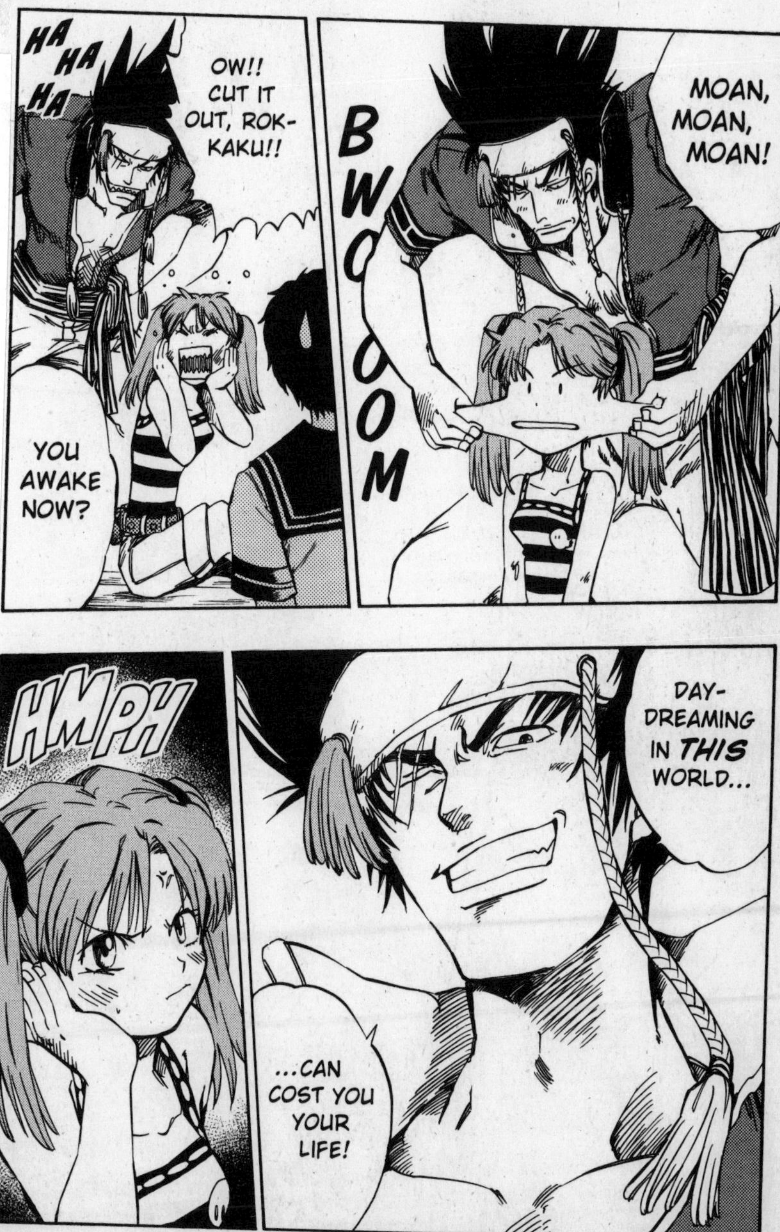
MOAN, MOAN, MOAN!
BWOOOOM
OW!! CUT IT OUT, ROK-KAKU!!
HA HA HA
YOU AWAKE NOW?
DAY-DREAMING IN *THIS* WORLD...
...CAN COST YOU YOUR LIFE!
HMPH

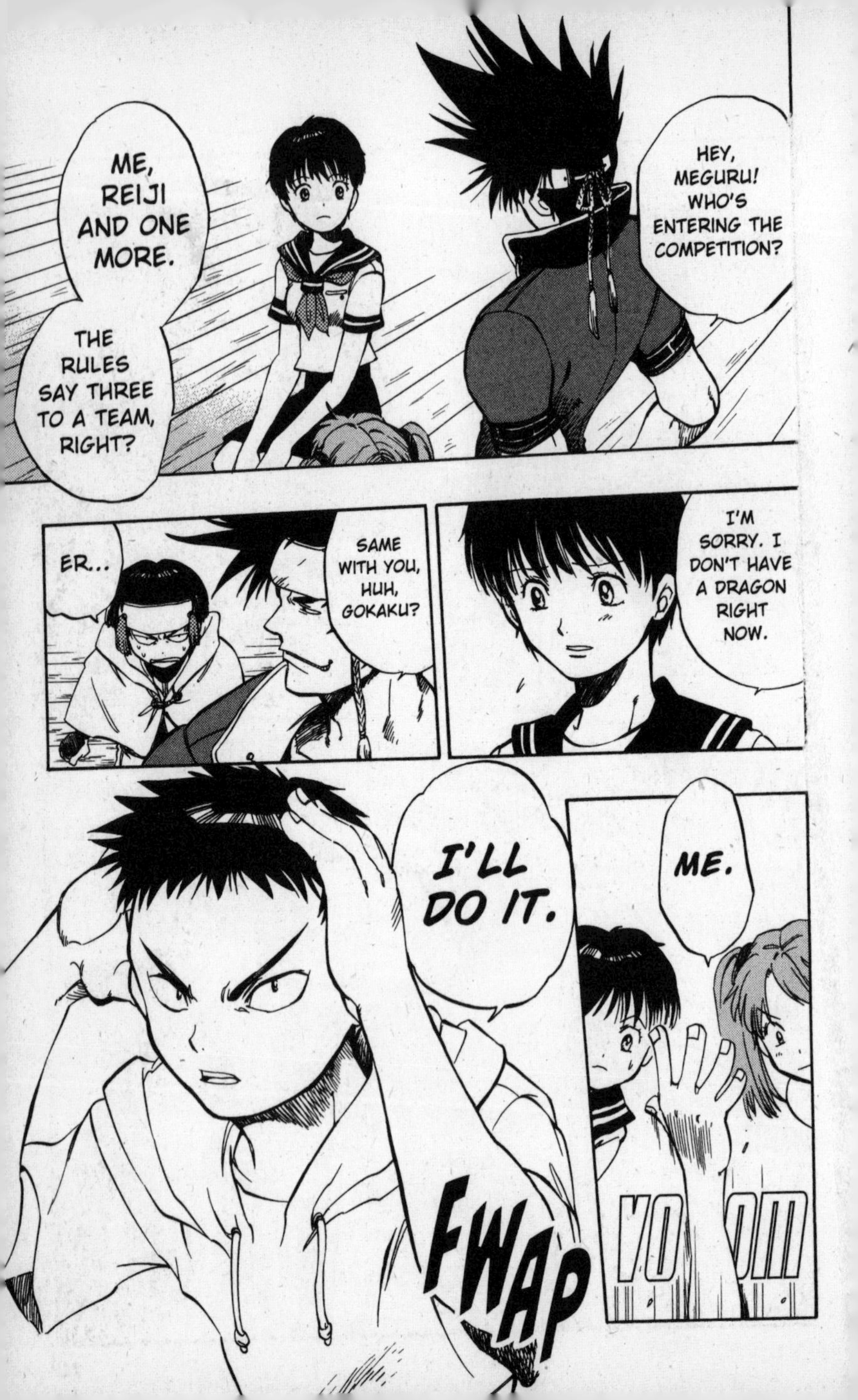
HEY, MEGURU! WHO'S ENTERING THE COMPETITION?
ME, REIJI AND ONE MORE.
THE RULES SAY THREE TO A TEAM, RIGHT?
I'M SORRY. I DON'T HAVE A DRAGON RIGHT NOW.
SAME WITH YOU, HUH, GOKAKU?
ER...
ME.
VO OM
I'LL DO IT.
FWAP

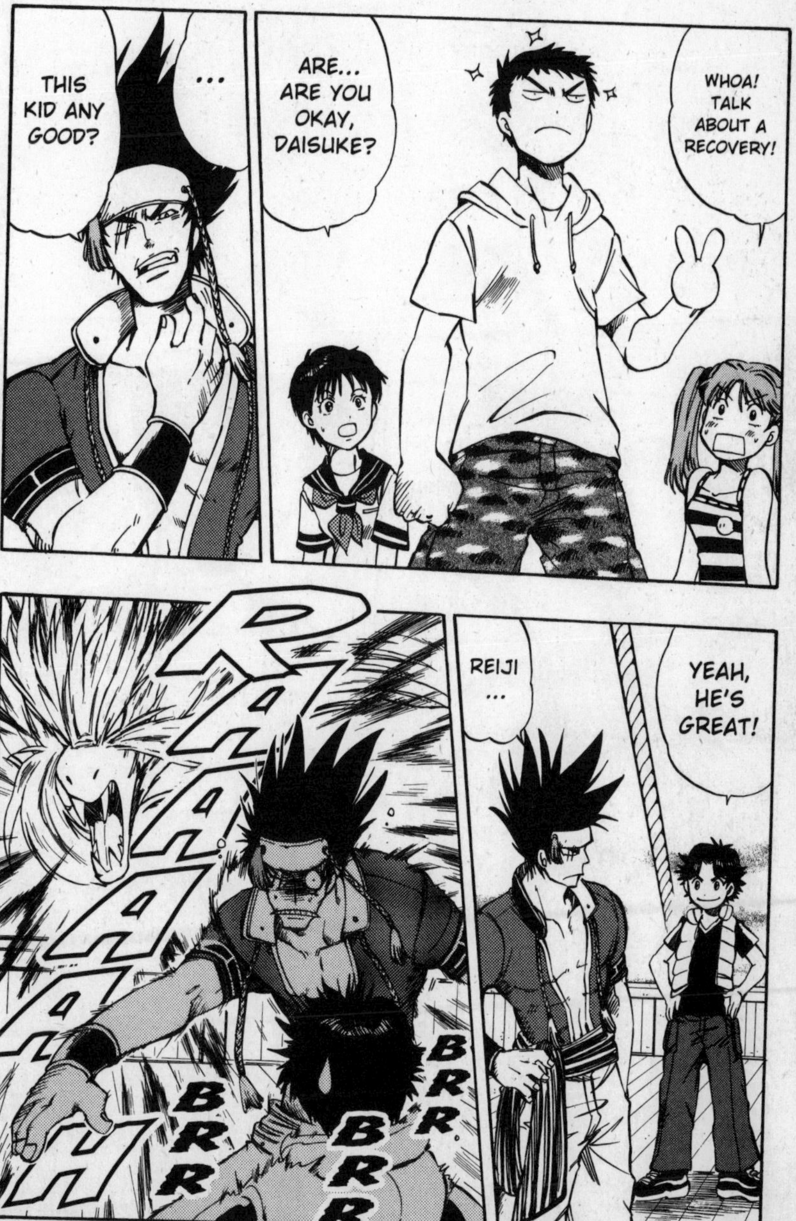
WHOA! TALK ABOUT A RECOVERY!
ARE... ARE YOU OKAY, DAISUKE?
...
THIS KID ANY GOOD?
YEAH, HE'S GREAT!
REIJI ...
RAAAAAH
BRR
BRR
BRR

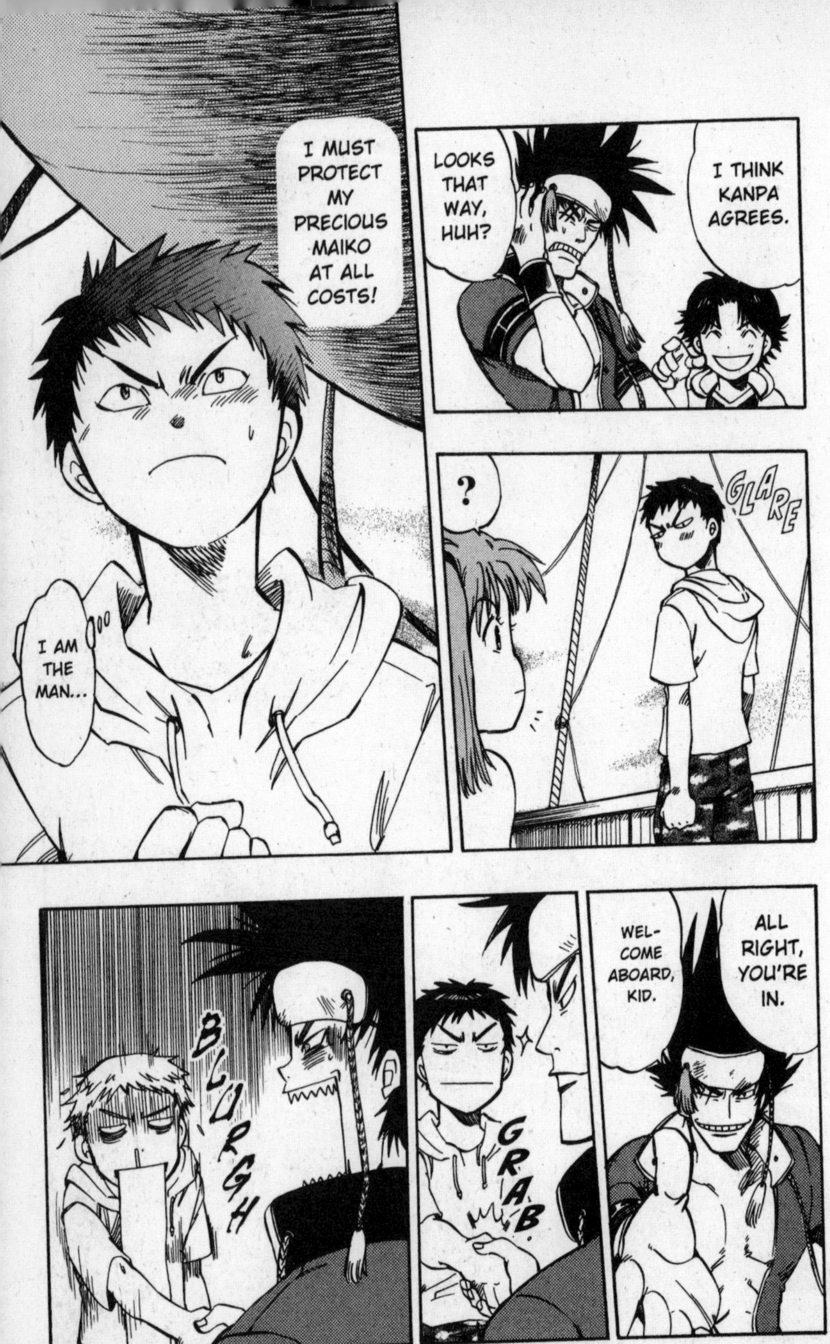
I THINK KANPA AGREES.
LOOKS THAT WAY, HUH?
?
GLARE
I MUST PROTECT MY PRECIOUS MAIKO AT ALL COSTS!
I AM THE MAN...
ALL RIGHT, YOU'RE IN.
WEL-COME ABOARD, KID.
GRAB
BLURGH!

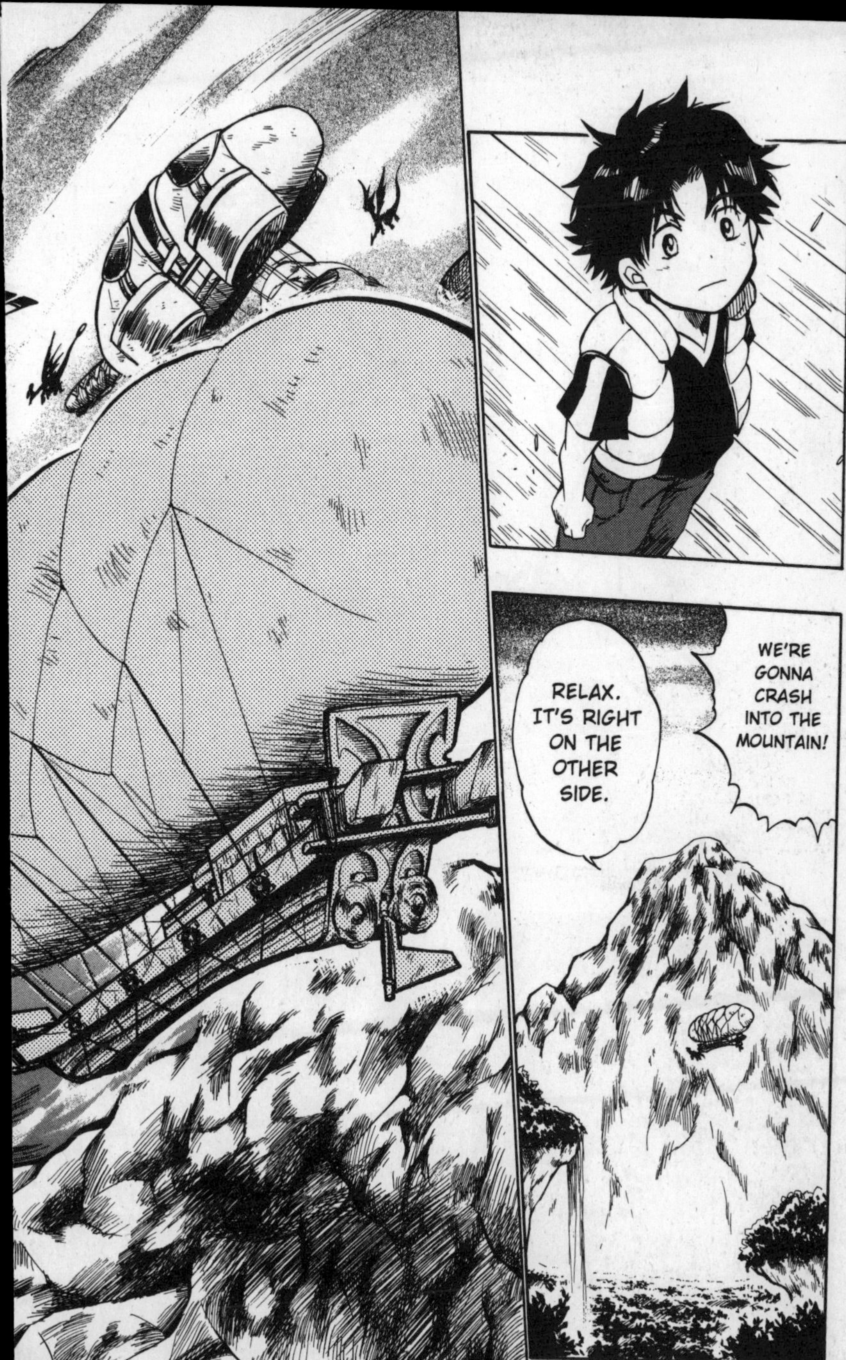
WE'RE GONNA CRASH INTO THE MOUNTAIN!
RELAX. IT'S RIGHT ON THE OTHER SIDE.

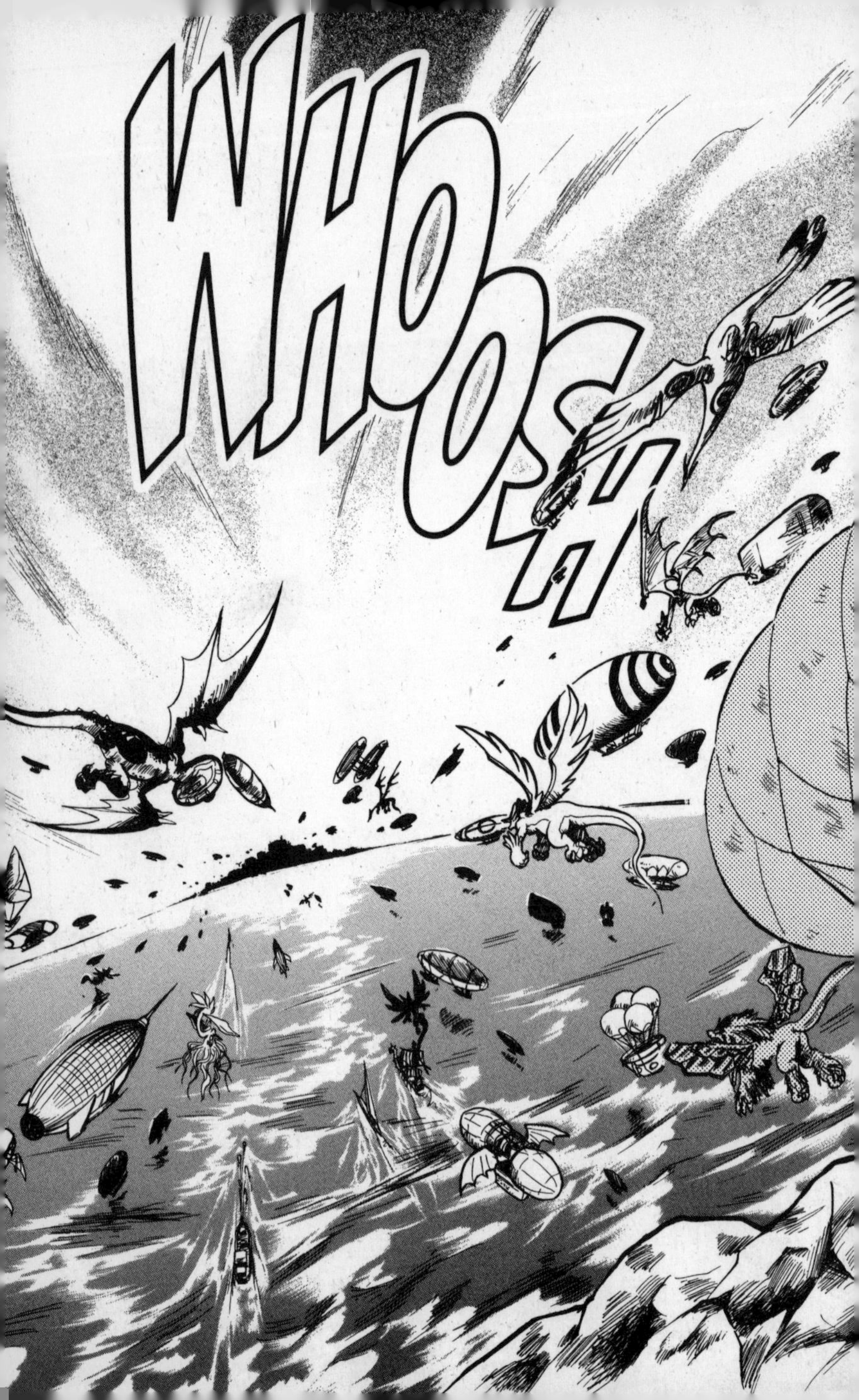
WHOOSH

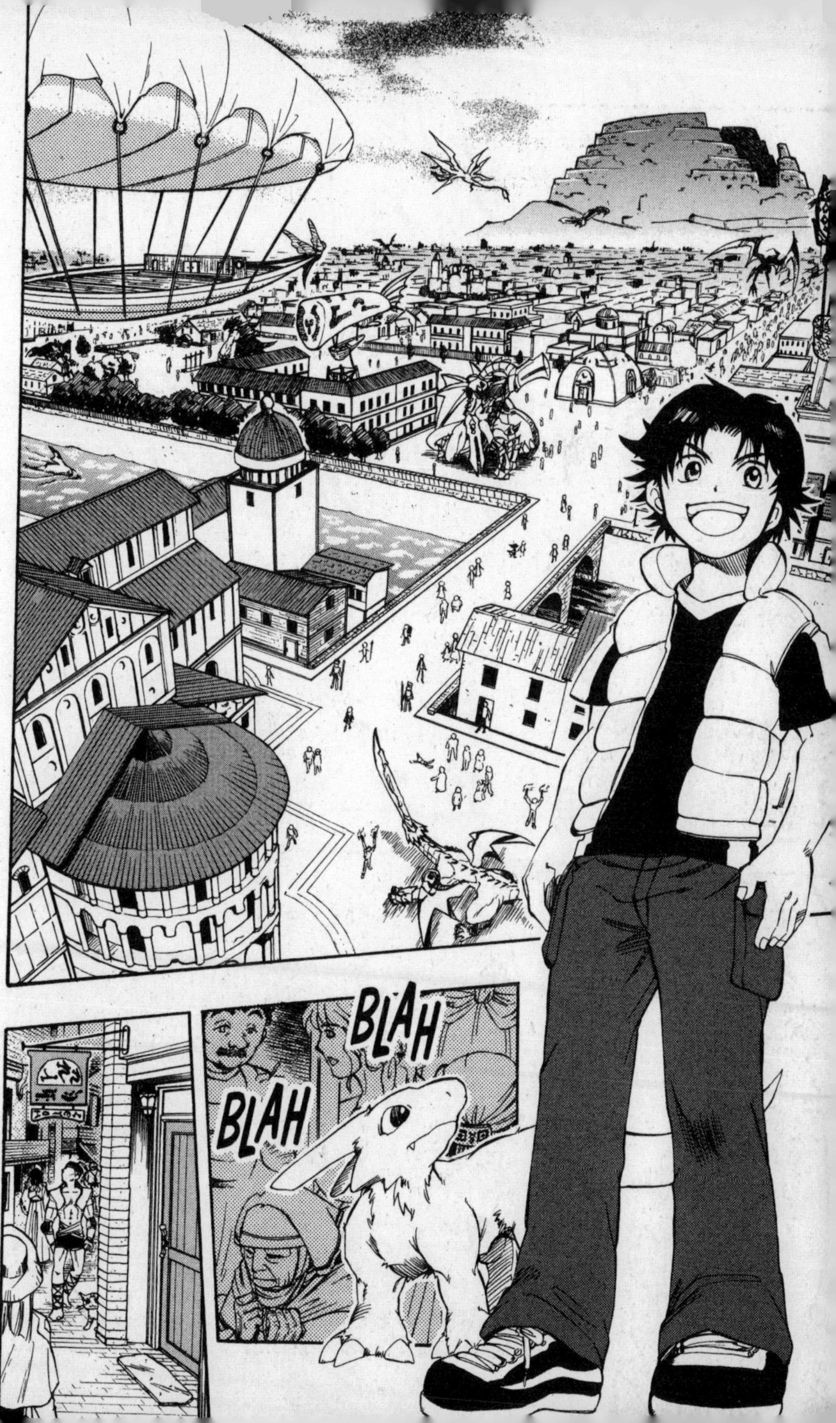
BLAH
BLAH

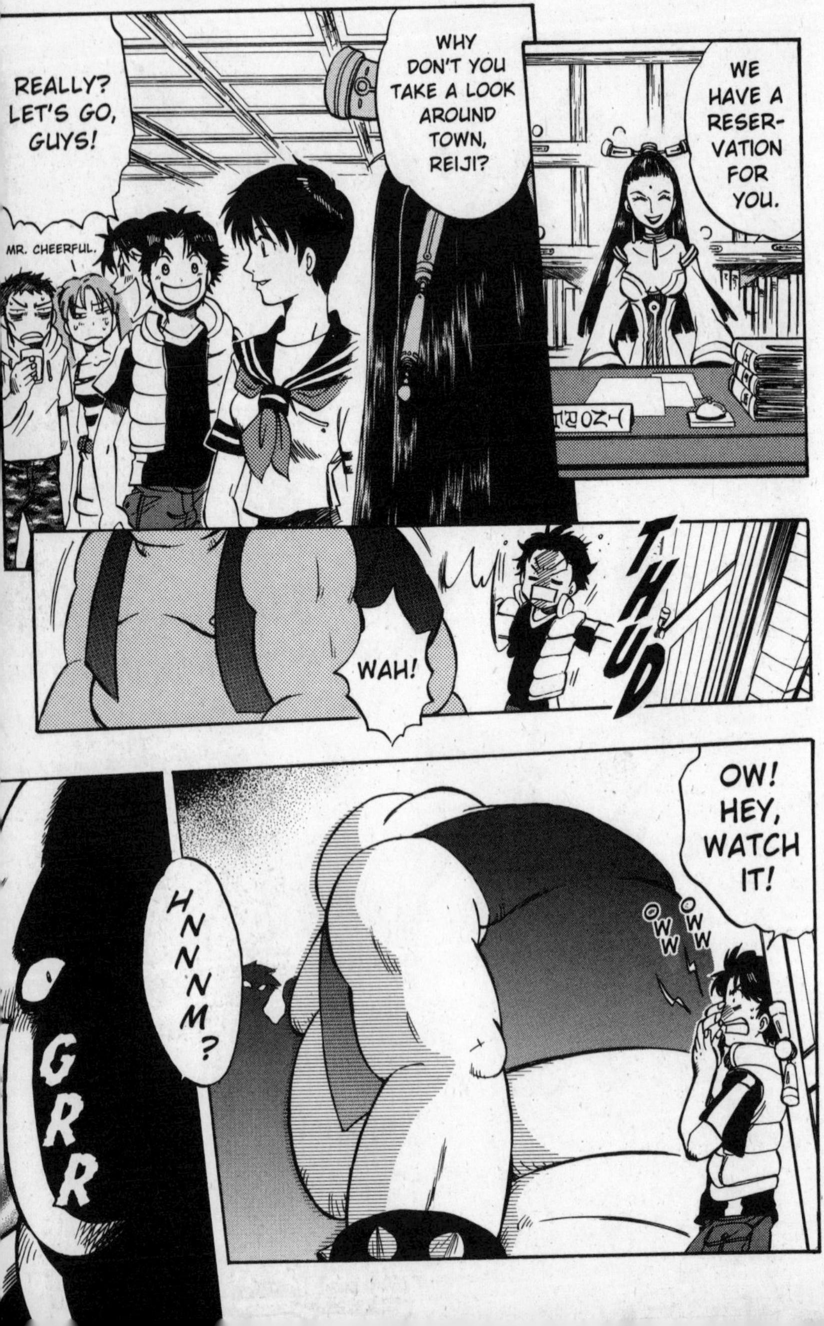
WE HAVE A RESERVATION FOR YOU.
WHY DON'T YOU TAKE A LOOK AROUND TOWN, REIJI?
REALLY? LET'S GO, GUYS!
MR. CHEERFUL.
THUD
WAH!
OW! HEY, WATCH IT!
OWW OWW
HNNNM?
GRR

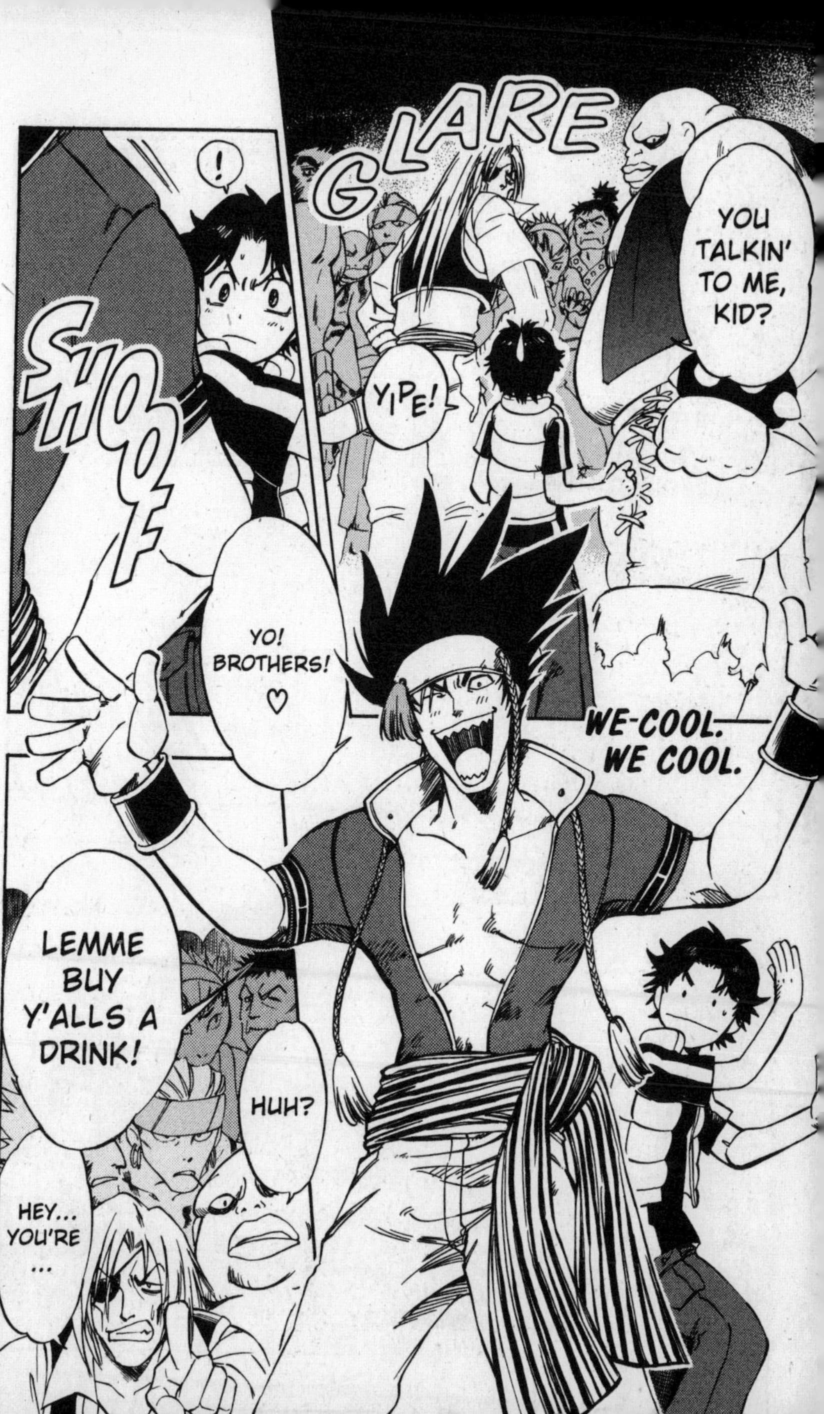
GLARE
YOU TALKIN' TO ME, KID?
YIPE!
!
SHOOOF
YO! BROTHERS! ♡
WE-COOL. WE COOL.
LEMME BUY Y'ALLS A DRINK!
HUH?
HEY... YOU'RE ...

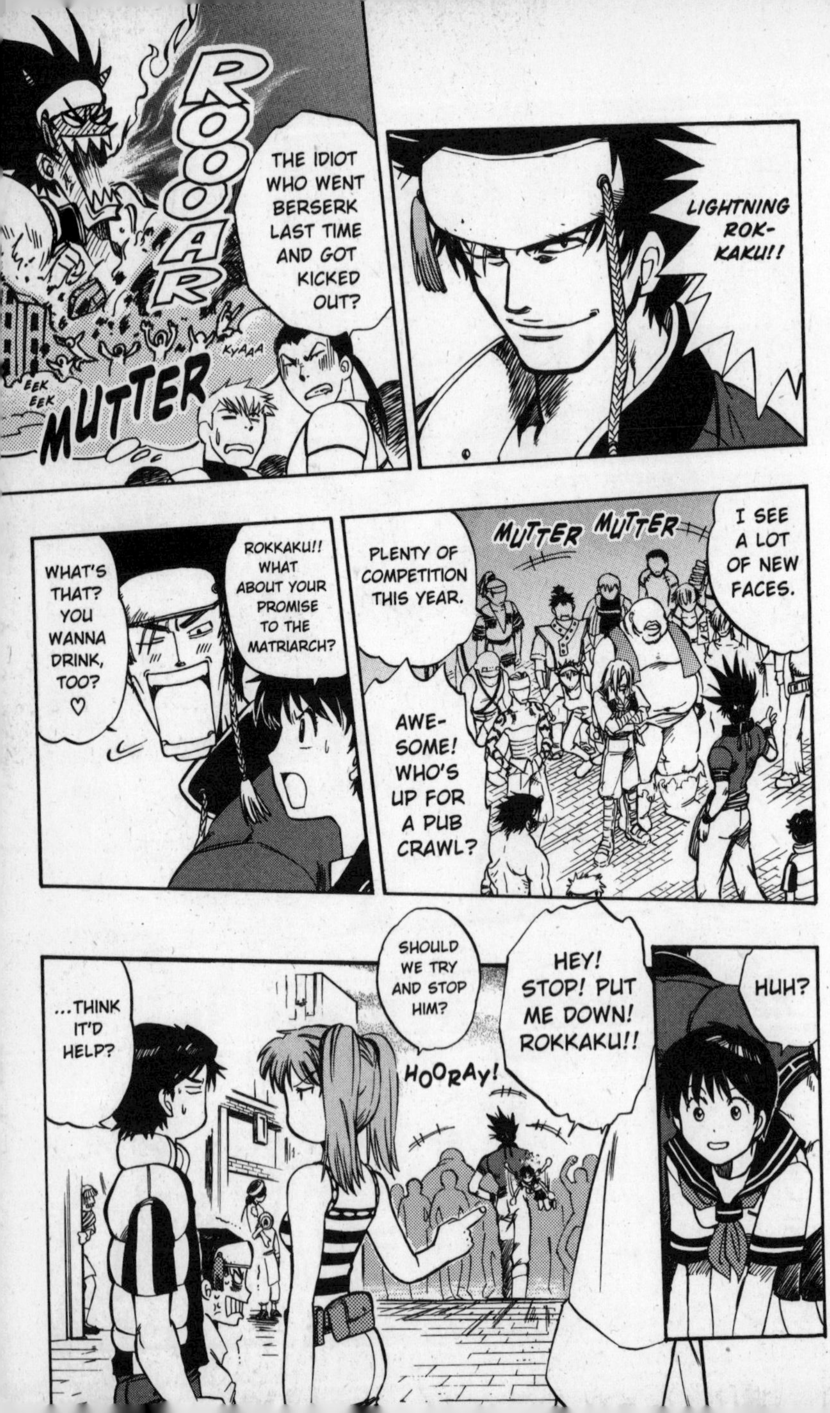
LIGHTNING ROK-KAKU!!
THE IDIOT WHO WENT BERSERK LAST TIME AND GOT KICKED OUT?
ROOOAR
KYAAA
EEK EEK
MUTTER
I SEE A LOT OF NEW FACES.
MUTTER MUTTER
PLENTY OF COMPETITION THIS YEAR.
AWE-SOME! WHO'S UP FOR A PUB CRAWL?
ROKKAKU!! WHAT ABOUT YOUR PROMISE TO THE MATRIARCH?
WHAT'S THAT? YOU WANNA DRINK, TOO? ♡
HUH?
HEY! STOP! PUT ME DOWN! ROKKAKU!!
SHOULD WE TRY AND STOP HIM?
HOORAY!
...THINK IT'D HELP?

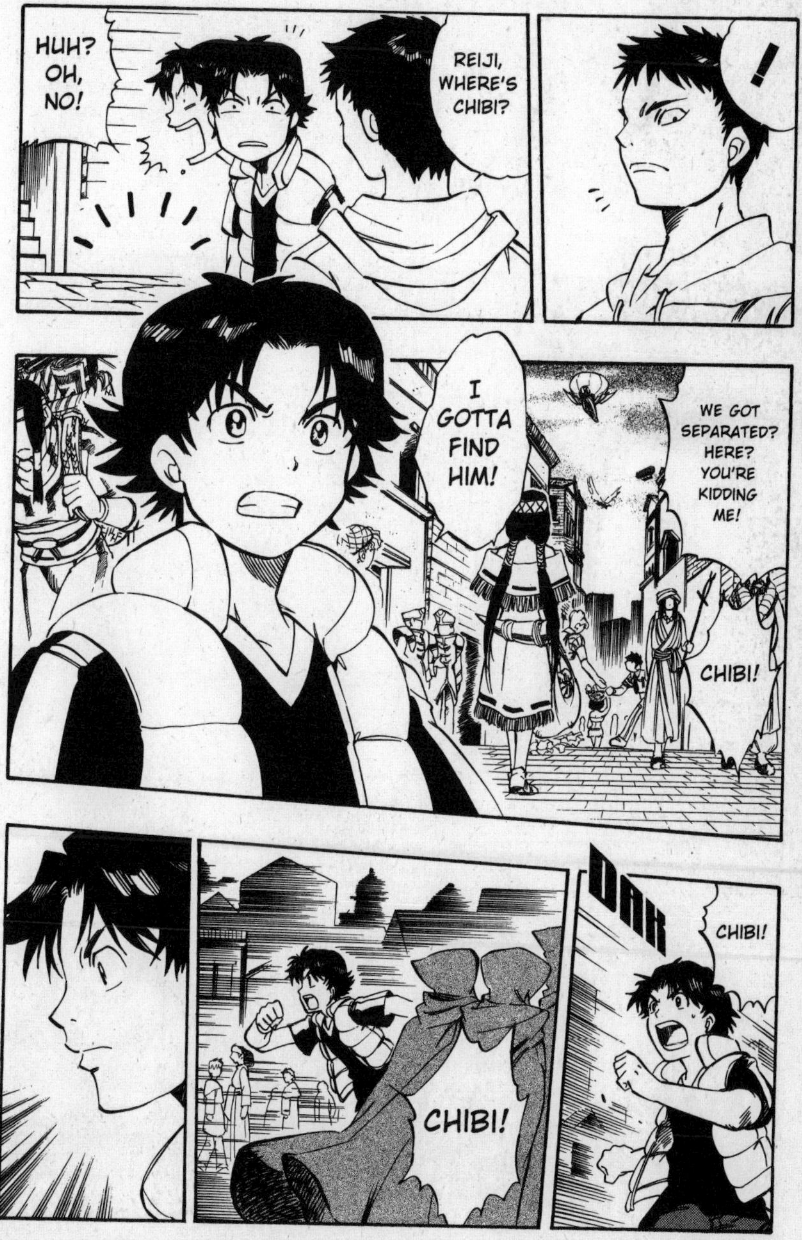
!
REIJI, WHERE'S CHIBI?
HUH? OH, NO!
WE GOT SEPARATED? HERE? YOU'RE KIDDING ME!
CHIBI!
I GOTTA FIND HIM!
DAK
CHIBI!
CHIBI!

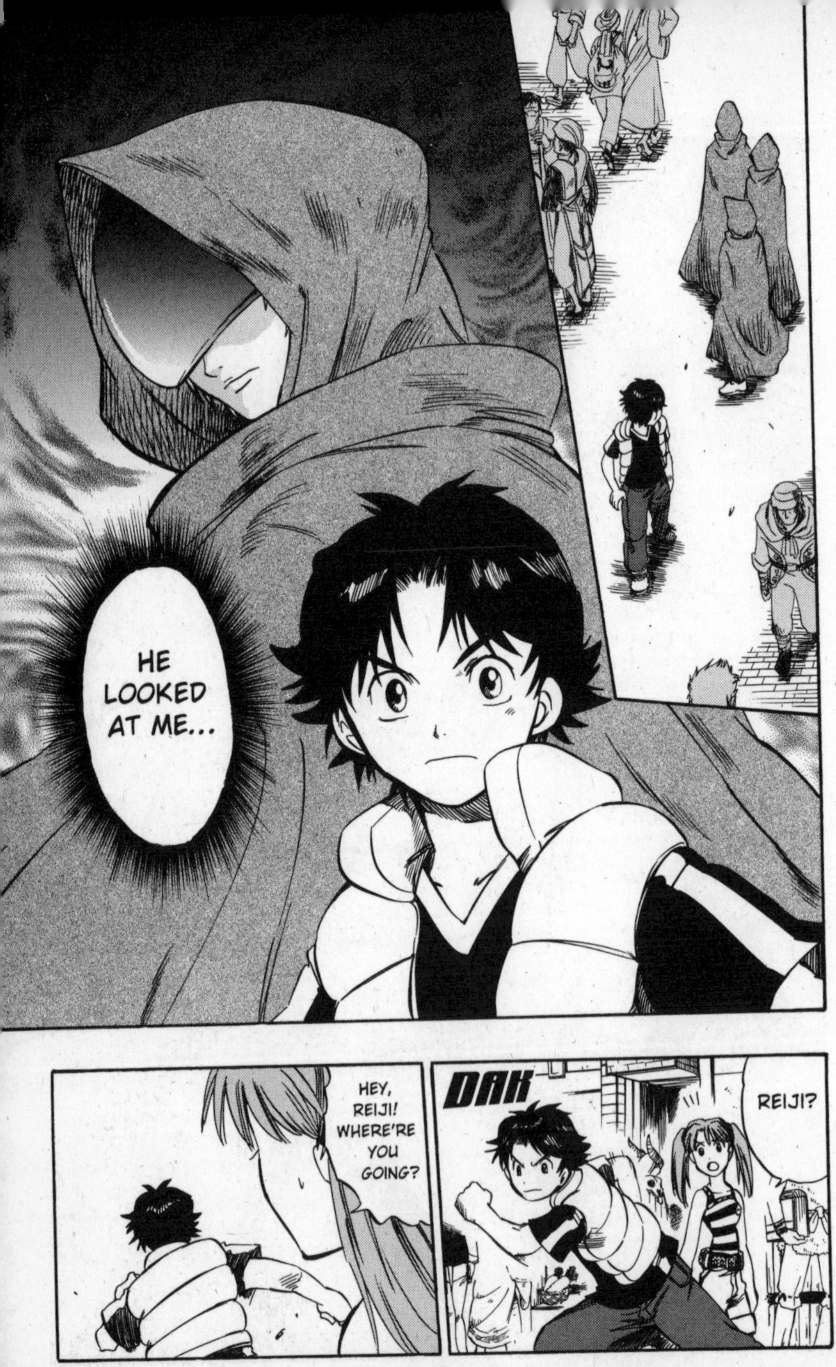
HE LOOKED AT ME...
DAK
REIJI?
HEY, REIJI! WHERE'RE YOU GOING?

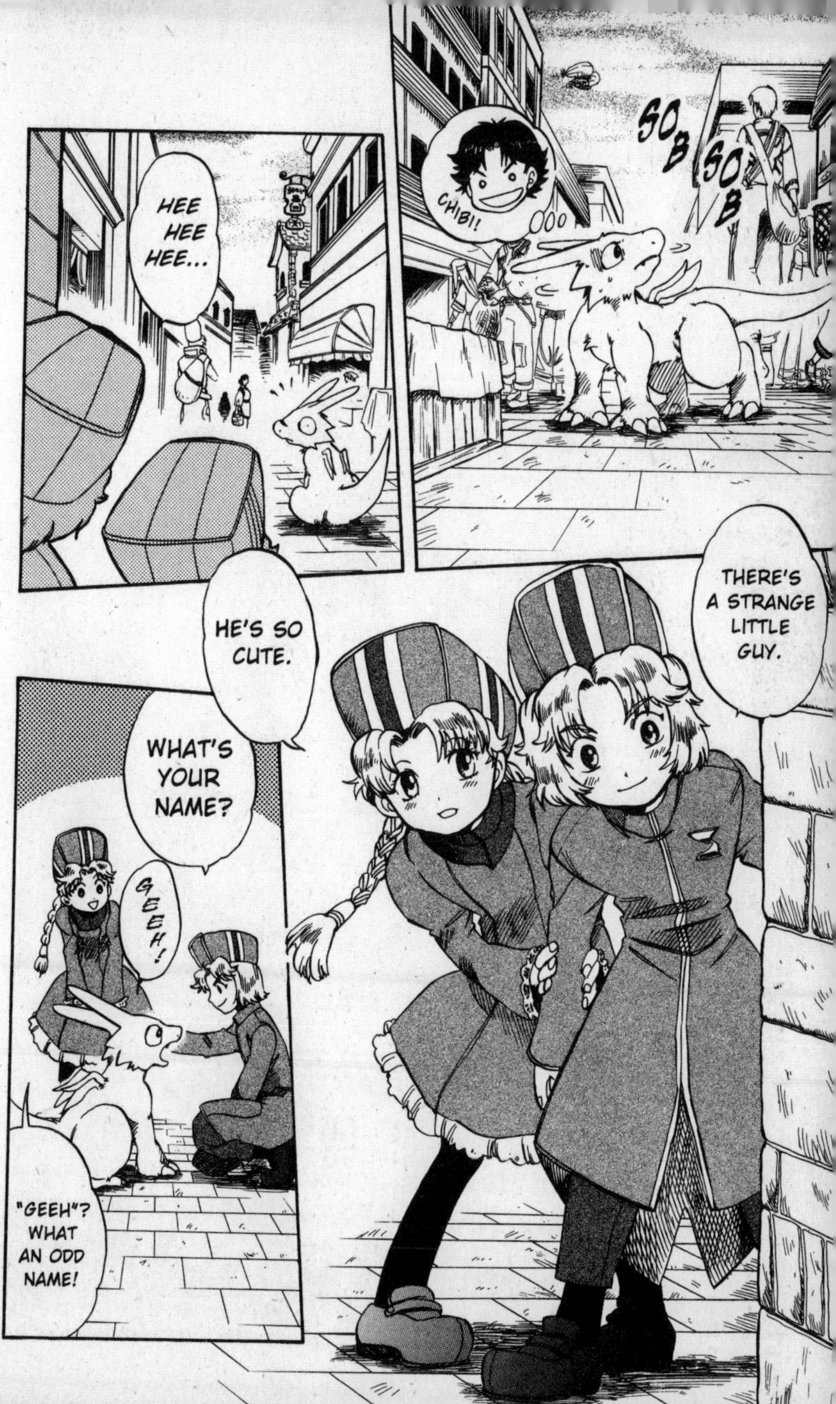
SOB
SOB
CHIBI!
HEE HEE HEE...
THERE'S A STRANGE LITTLE GUY.
HE'S SO CUTE.
WHAT'S YOUR NAME?
GEEH!
"GEEH"? WHAT AN ODD NAME!

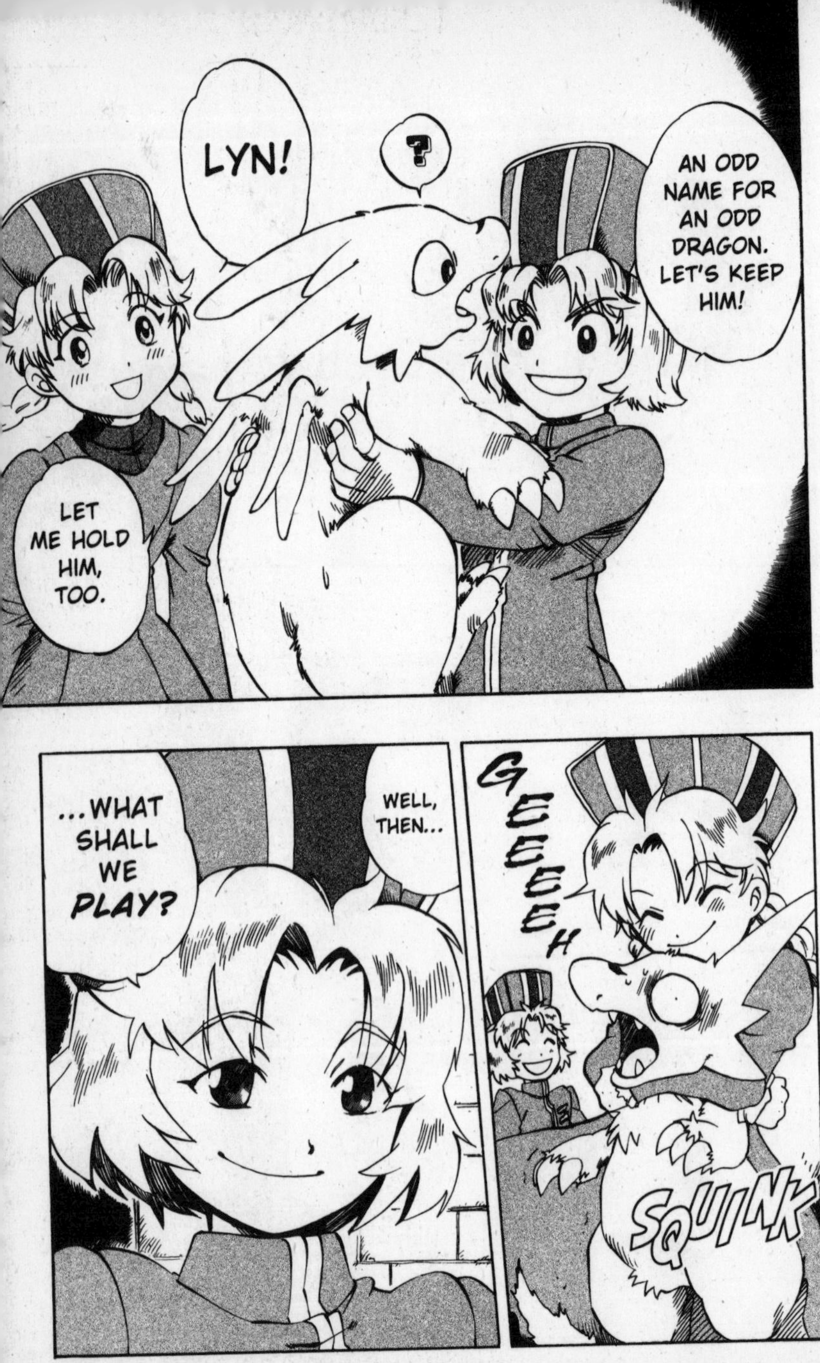
AN ODD NAME FOR AN ODD DRAGON. LET'S KEEP HIM!
?
LYN!
LET ME HOLD HIM, TOO.
GEEEEH
SQUINK
WELL, THEN...
...WHAT SHALL WE **PLAY?**

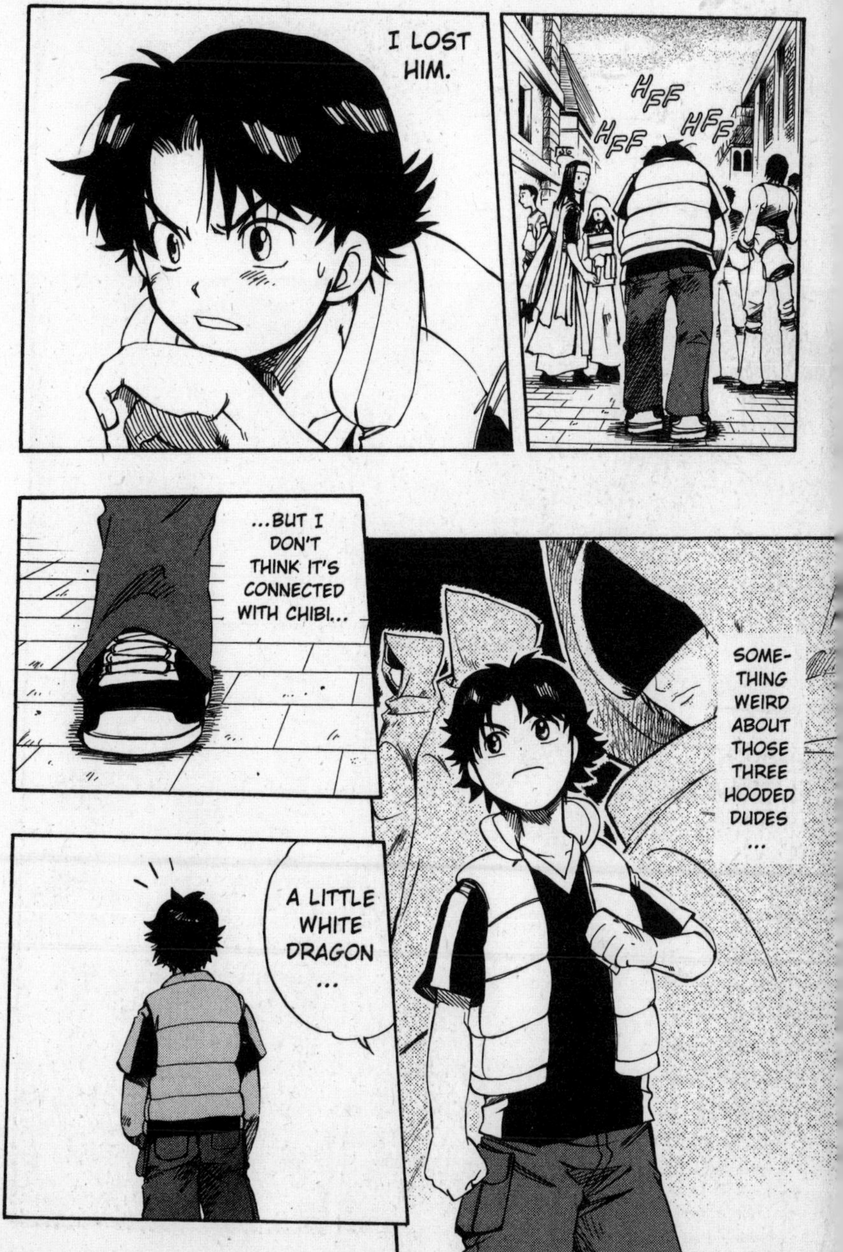
HFF
HFF
HFF
I LOST HIM.
SOME-THING WEIRD ABOUT THOSE THREE HOODED DUDES ...
...BUT I DON'T THINK IT'S CONNECTED WITH CHIBI...
A LITTLE WHITE DRAGON ...

READ THIS WAY

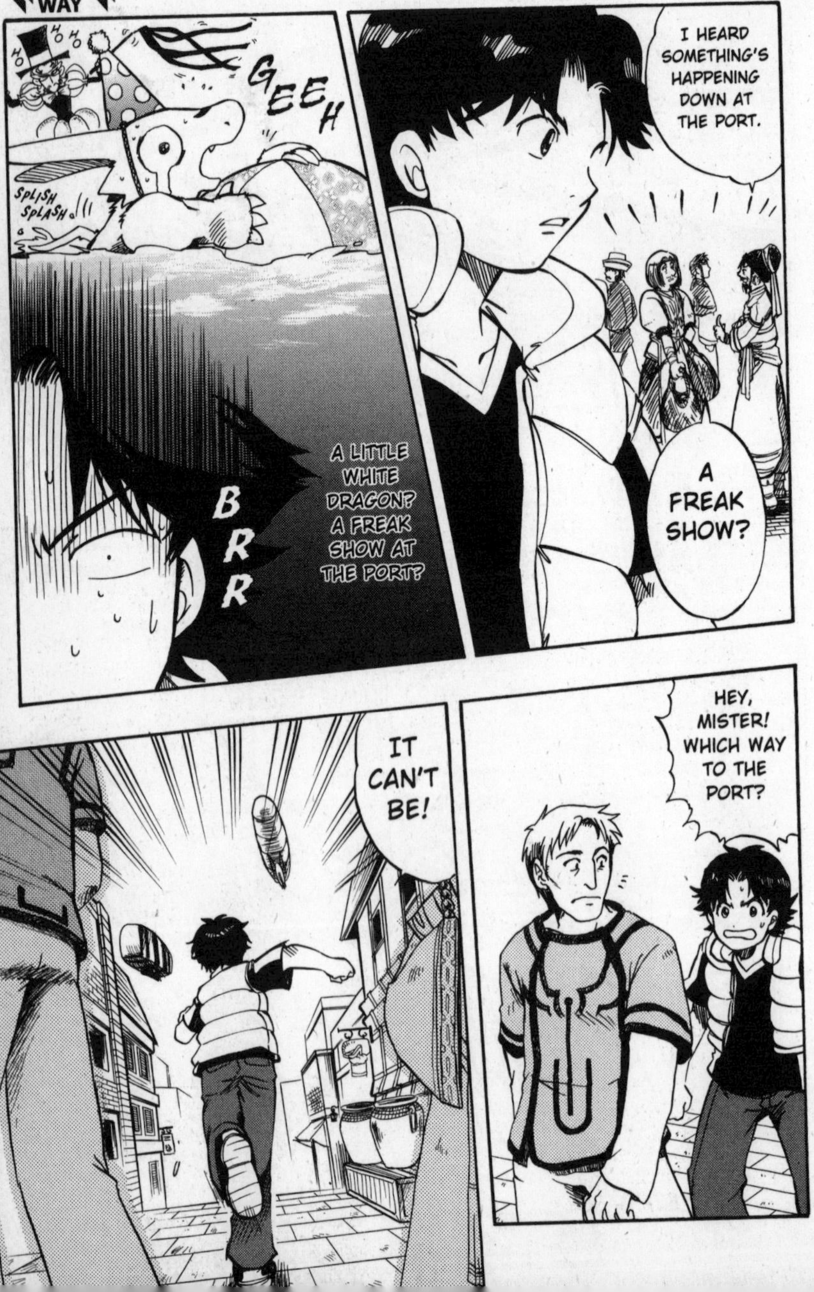
I HEARD SOMETHING'S HAPPENING DOWN AT THE PORT.
A FREAK SHOW?
GEEH
HO HO HO
SPLISH SPLASH
A LITTLE WHITE DRAGON? A FREAK SHOW AT THE PORT?
BRR
HEY, MISTER! WHICH WAY TO THE PORT?
IT CAN'T BE!

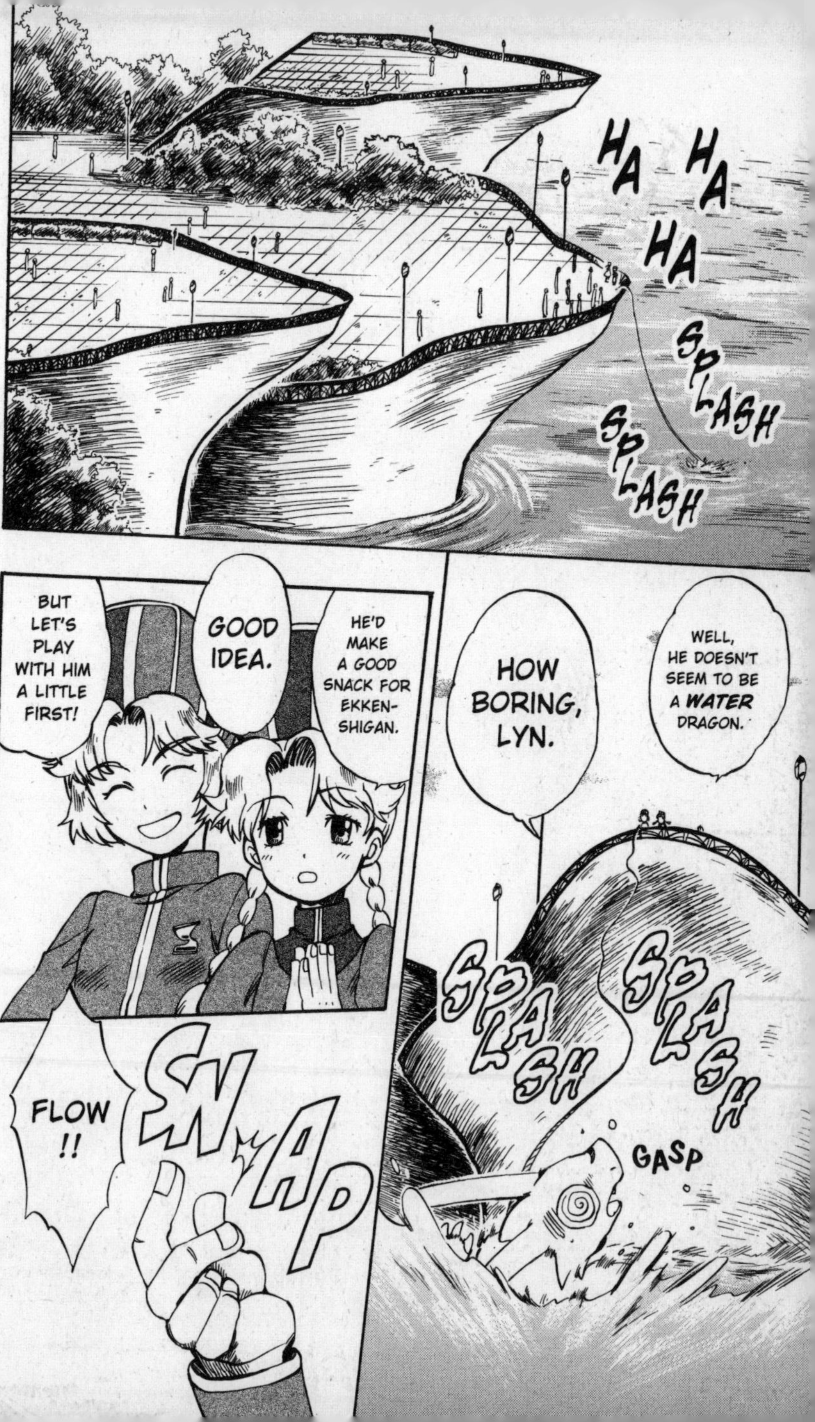
HA HA HA
SPLASH
SPLASH
WELL, HE DOESN'T SEEM TO BE A WATER DRAGON.
HOW BORING, LYN.
SPLASH
SPLASH
GASP
HE'D MAKE A GOOD SNACK FOR EKKEN-SHIGAN.
GOOD IDEA.
BUT LET'S PLAY WITH HIM A LITTLE FIRST!
FLOW !!
SNAP

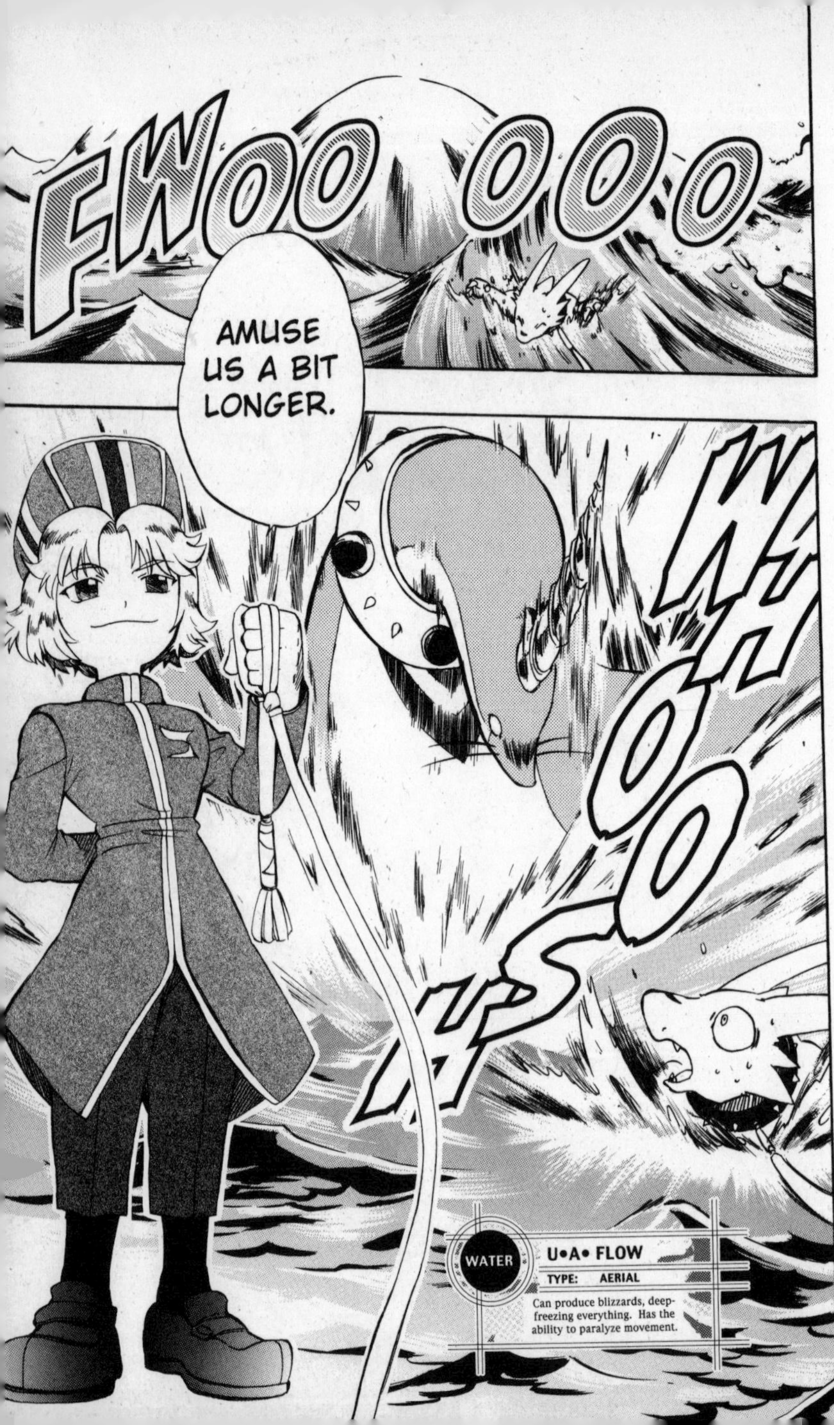
FWOO OOOO
WHOOOSH
AMUSE US A BIT LONGER.
WATER
U•A• FLOW
TYPE: AERIAL
Can produce blizzards, deep-freezing everything. Has the ability to paralyze movement.

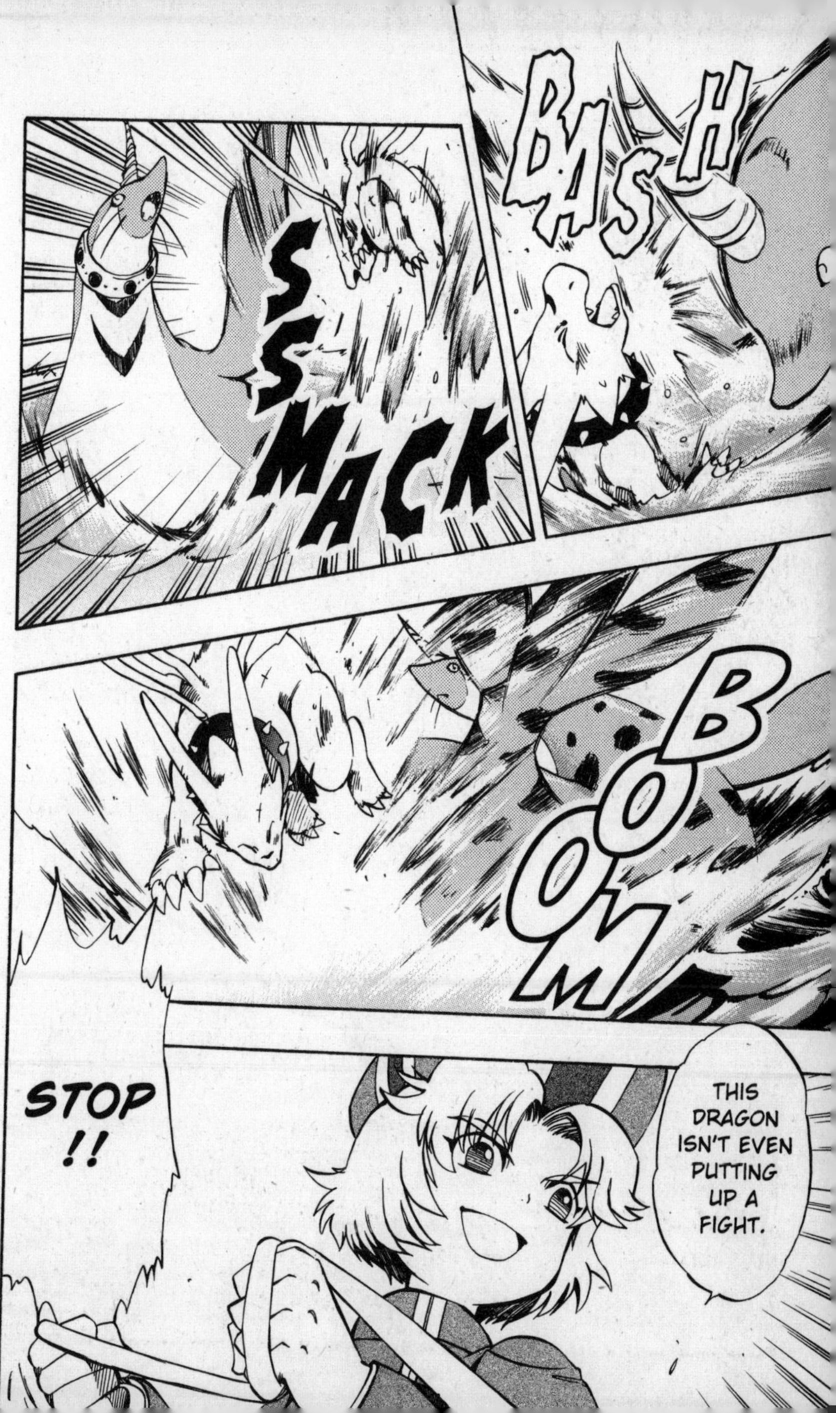
BASH
SMACK
BOOM
THIS DRAGON ISN'T EVEN PUTTING UP A FIGHT.
STOP!!

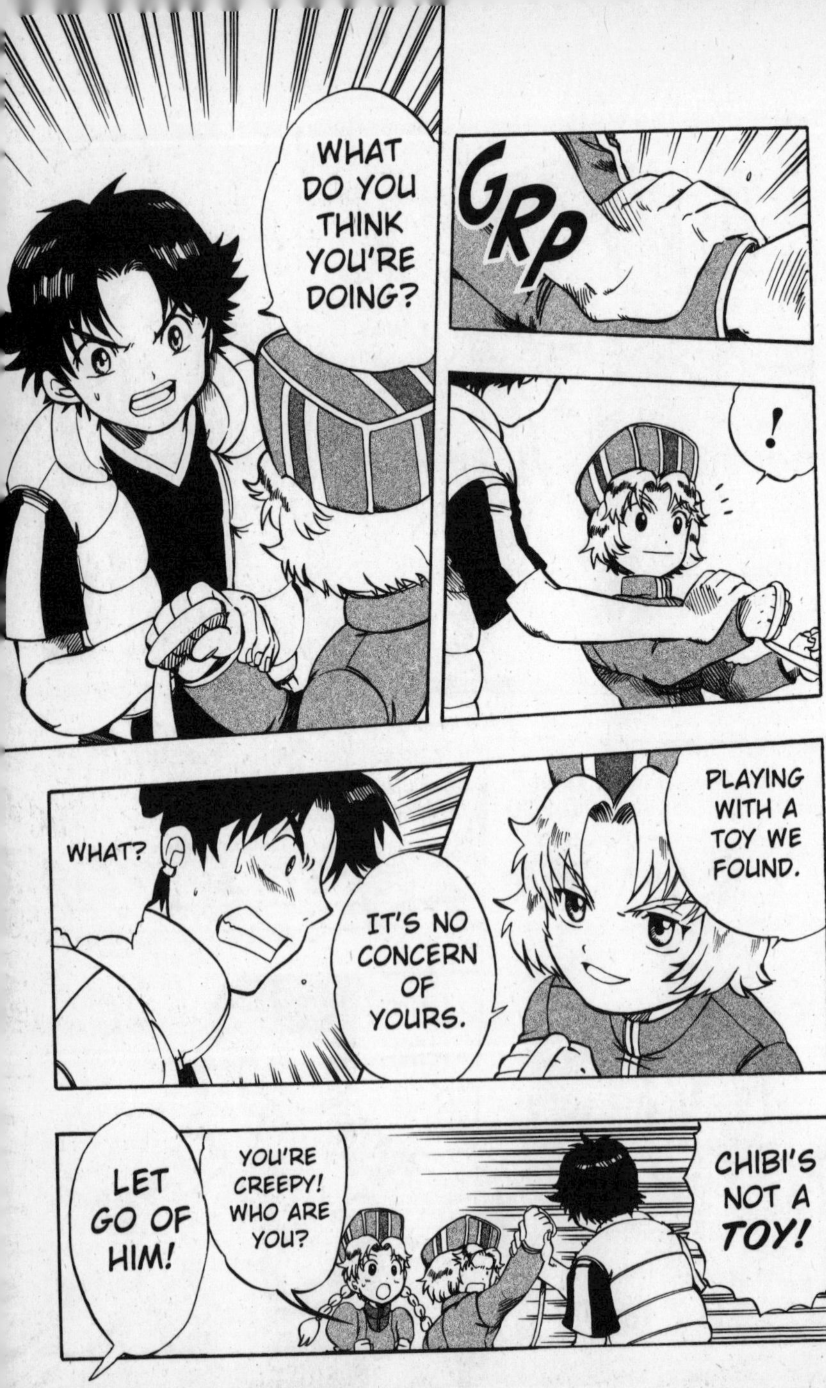
GRP
!
WHAT DO YOU THINK YOU'RE DOING?
PLAYING WITH A TOY WE FOUND.
IT'S NO CONCERN OF YOURS.
WHAT?
CHIBI'S NOT A *TOY*!
YOU'RE CREEPY! WHO ARE YOU?
LET GO OF HIM!

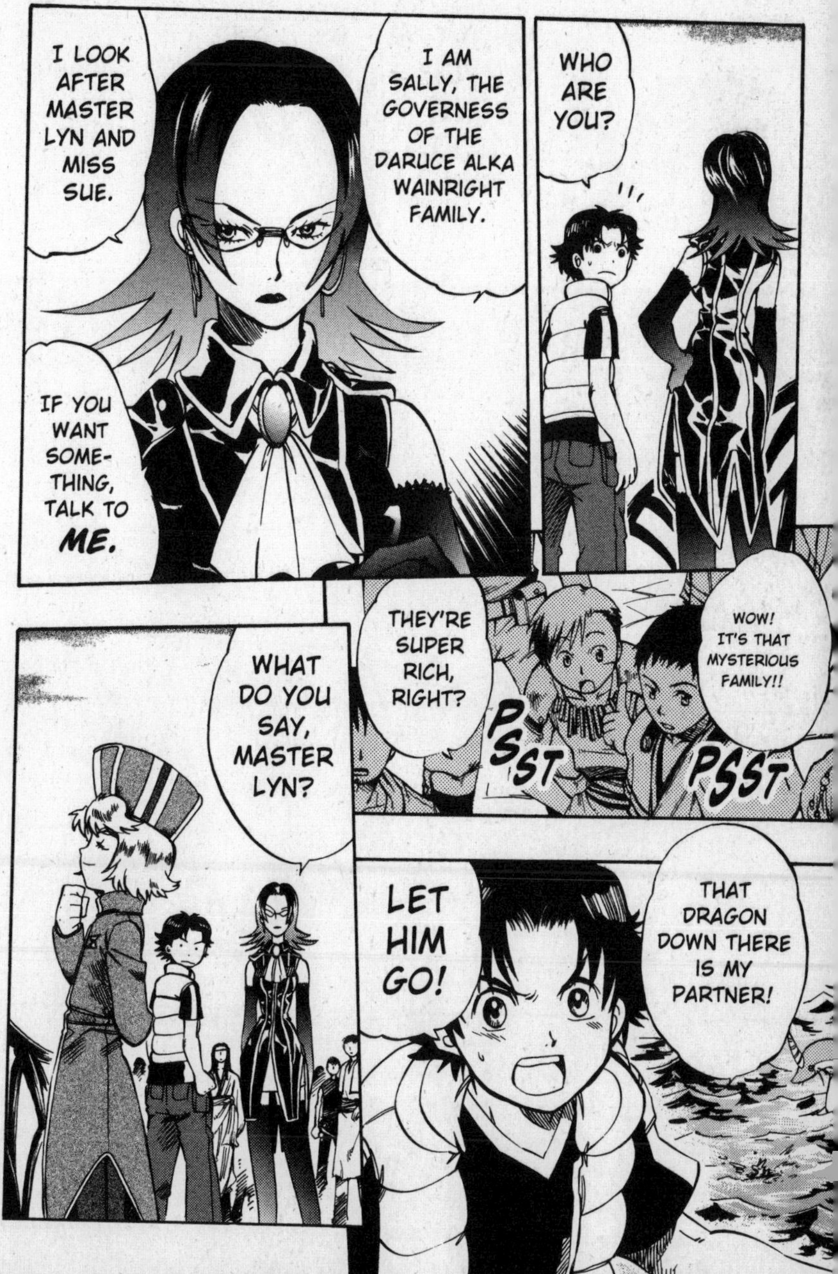
WHO ARE YOU?
I AM SALLY, THE GOVERNESS OF THE DARUCE ALKA WAINRIGHT FAMILY.
I LOOK AFTER MASTER LYN AND MISS SUE.
IF YOU WANT SOME-THING, TALK TO ME.
WOW! IT'S THAT MYSTERIOUS FAMILY!!
THEY'RE SUPER RICH, RIGHT?
PSST
PSST
THAT DRAGON DOWN THERE IS MY PARTNER!
LET HIM GO!
WHAT DO YOU SAY, MASTER LYN?

READ THIS WAY

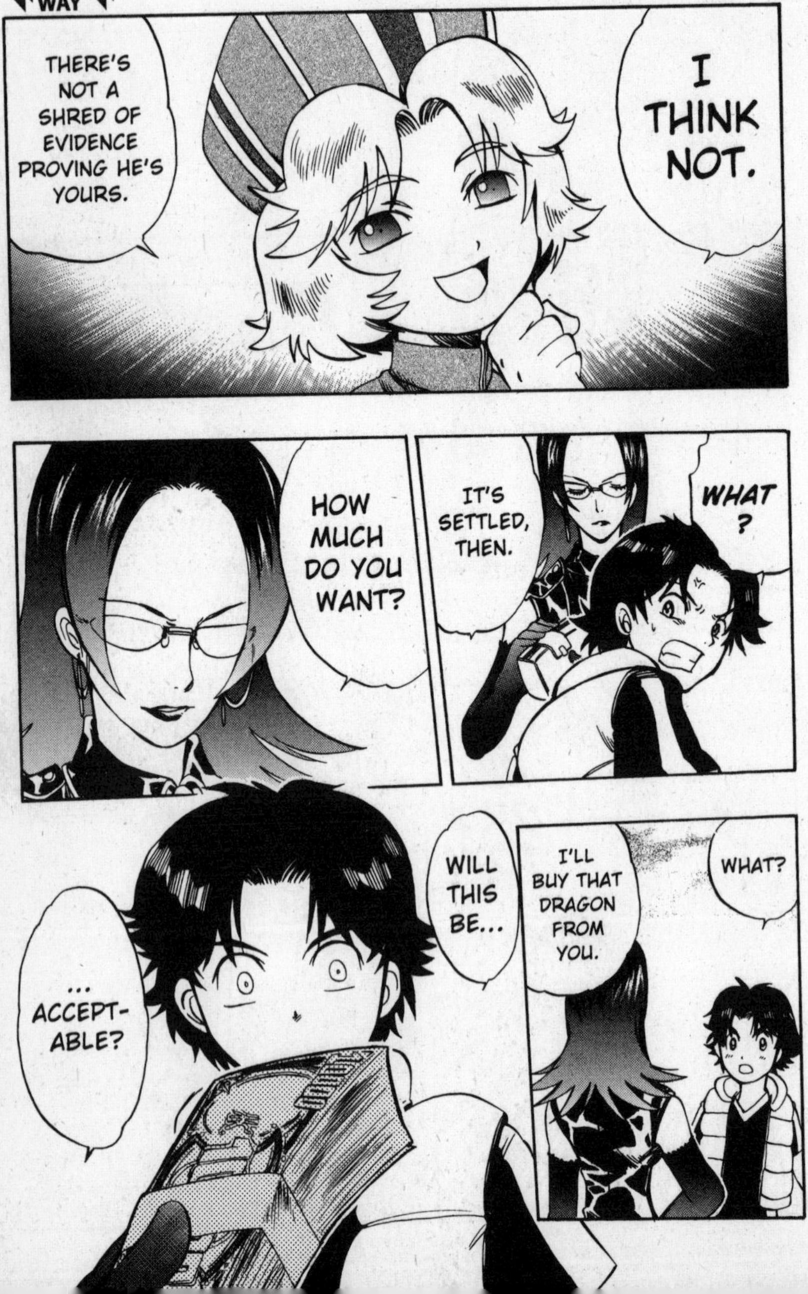
I THINK NOT.
THERE'S NOT A SHRED OF EVIDENCE PROVING HE'S YOURS.
WHAT?
IT'S SETTLED, THEN.
HOW MUCH DO YOU WANT?
WHAT?
I'LL BUY THAT DRAGON FROM YOU.
WILL THIS BE...
...ACCEPT-ABLE?

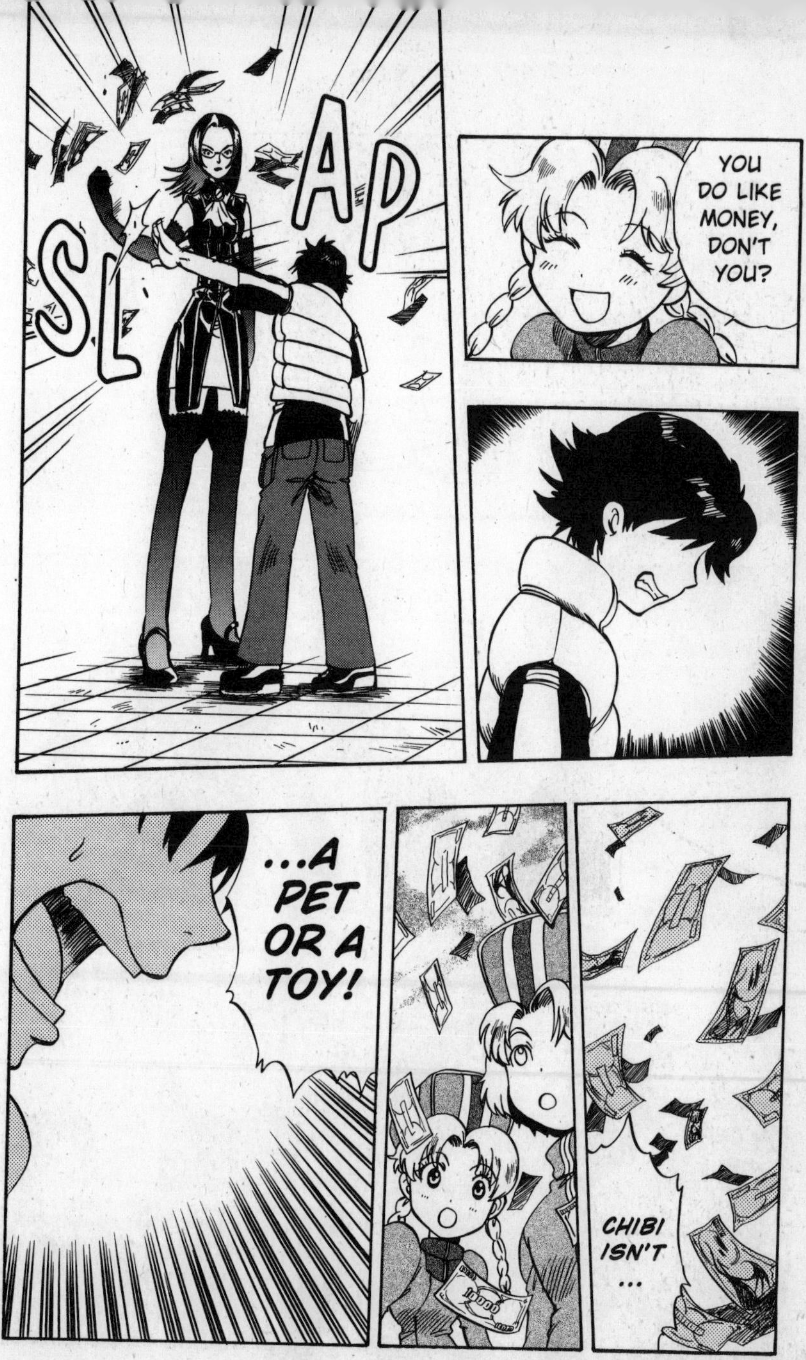
YOU DO LIKE MONEY, DON'T YOU?
SLAP
CHIBI ISN'T ...
...A PET OR A TOY!

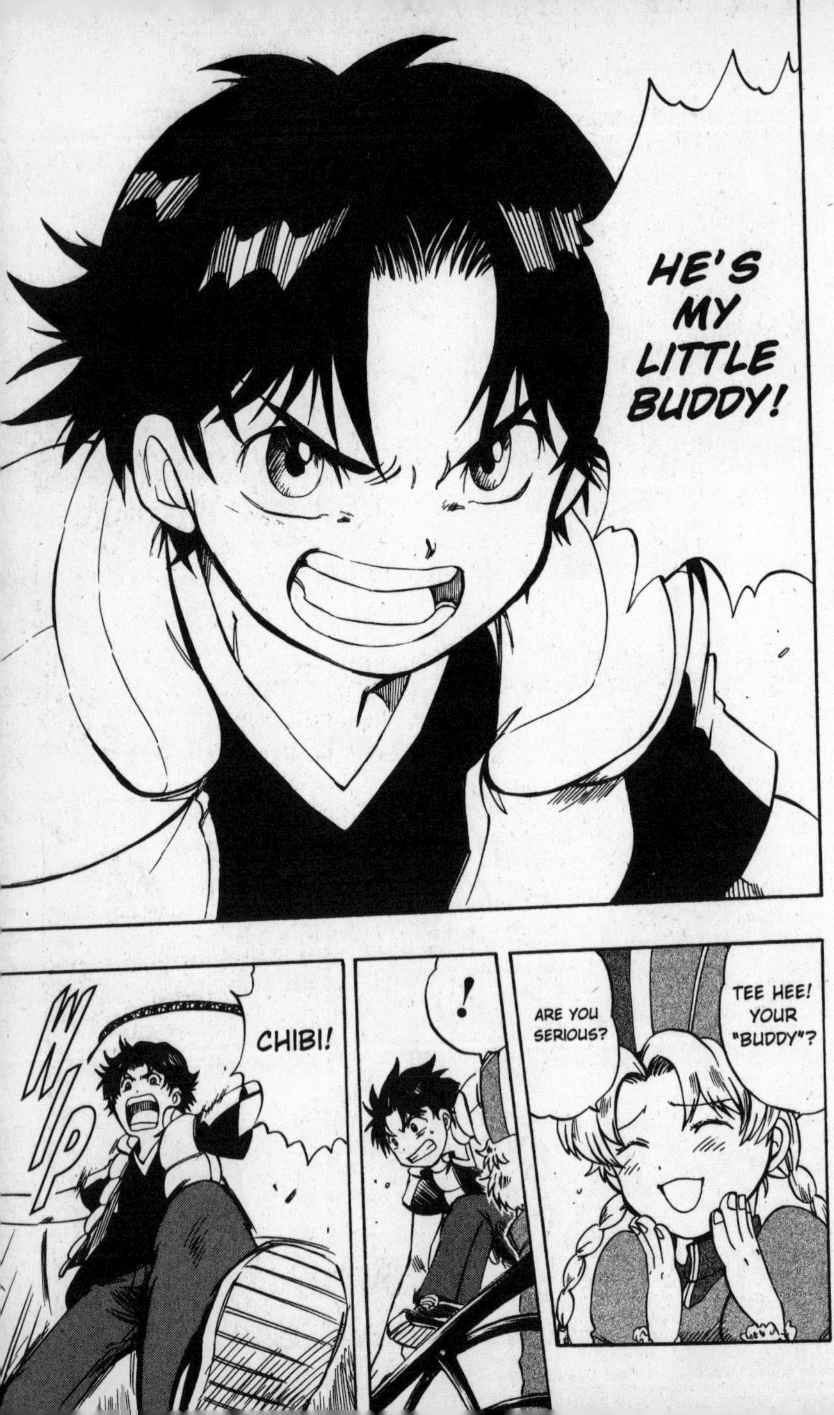
HE'S MY LITTLE BUDDY!
TEE HEE! YOUR "BUDDY"?
ARE YOU SERIOUS?
!
CHIBI!
WHIP

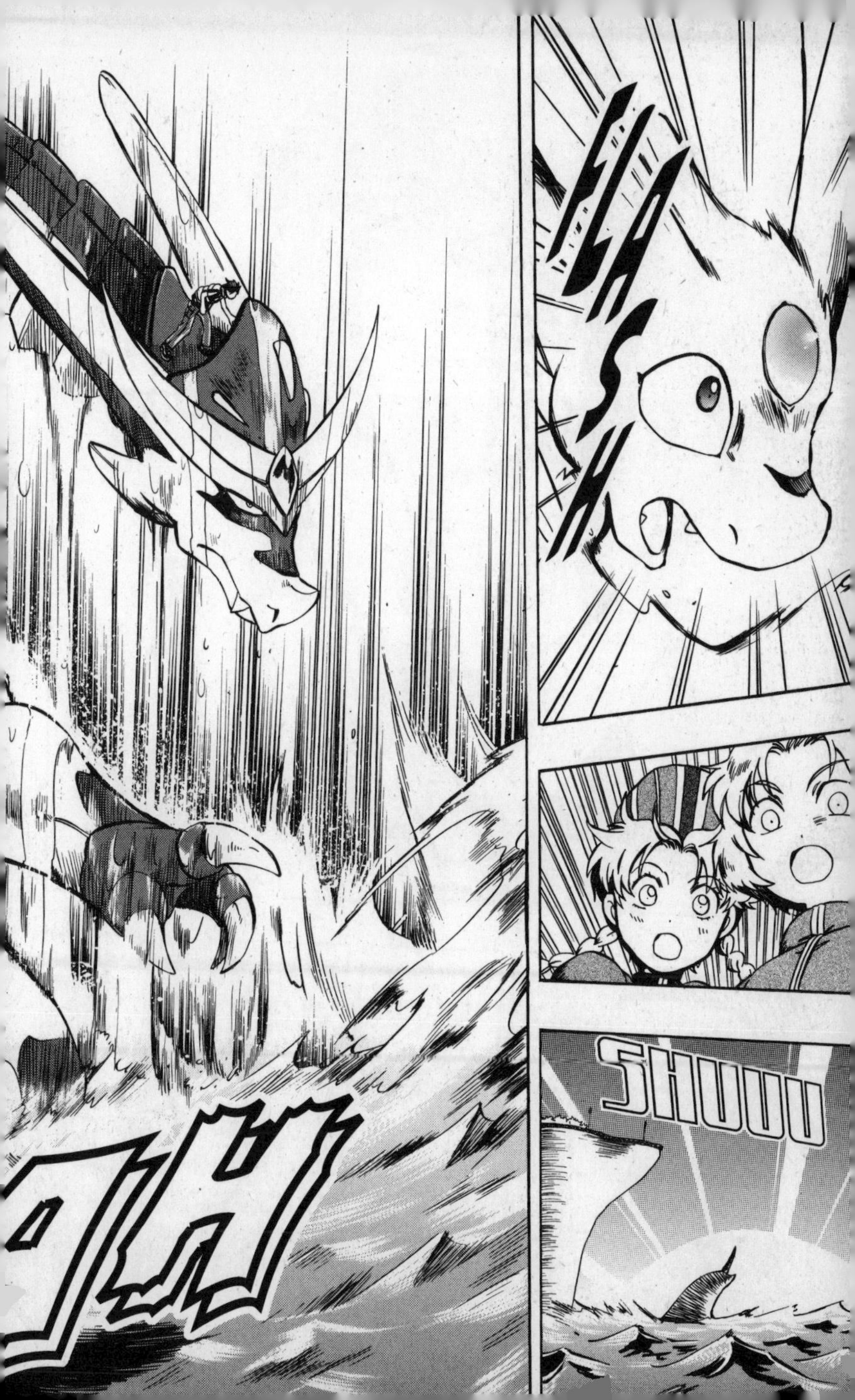
SHUUU

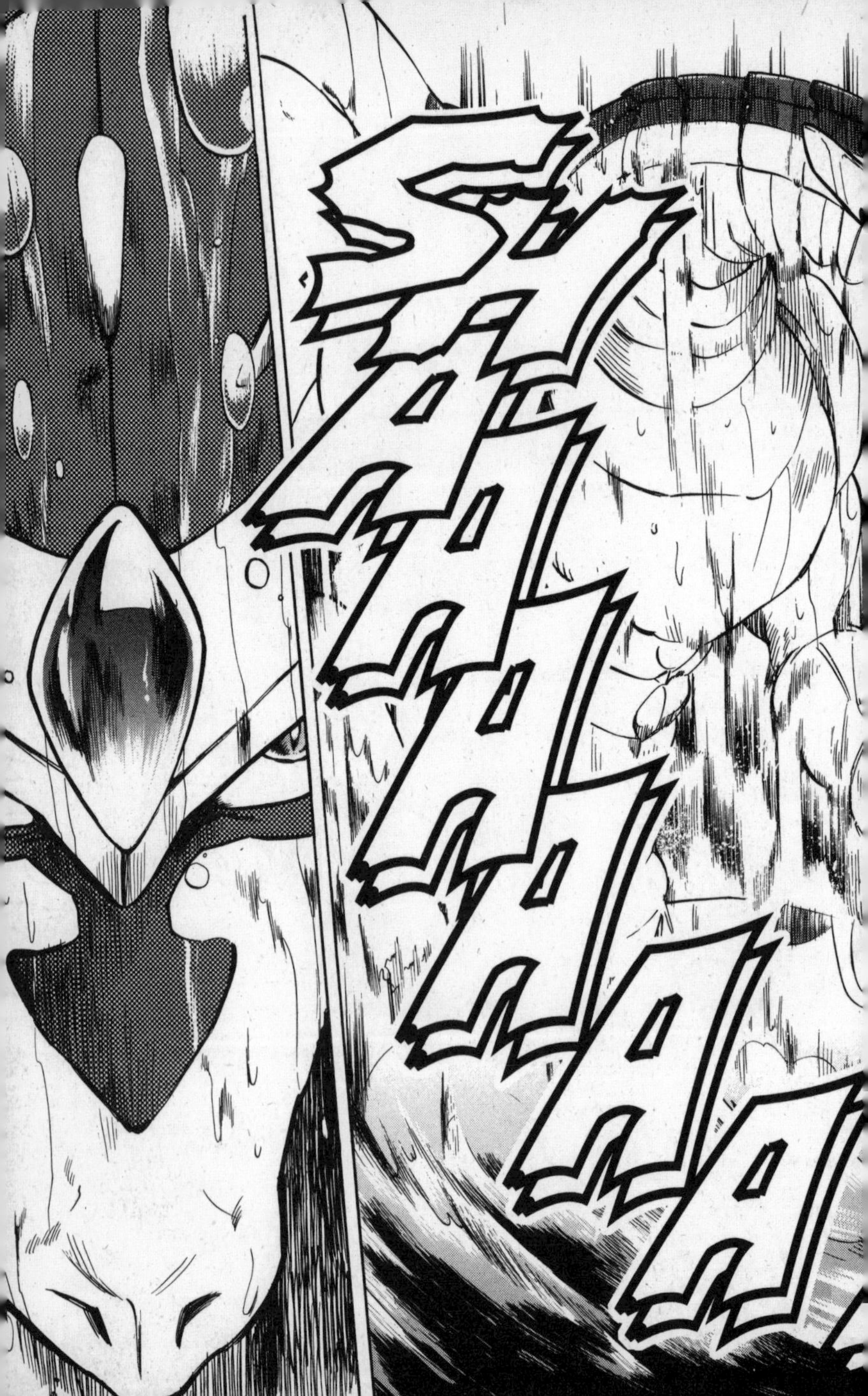

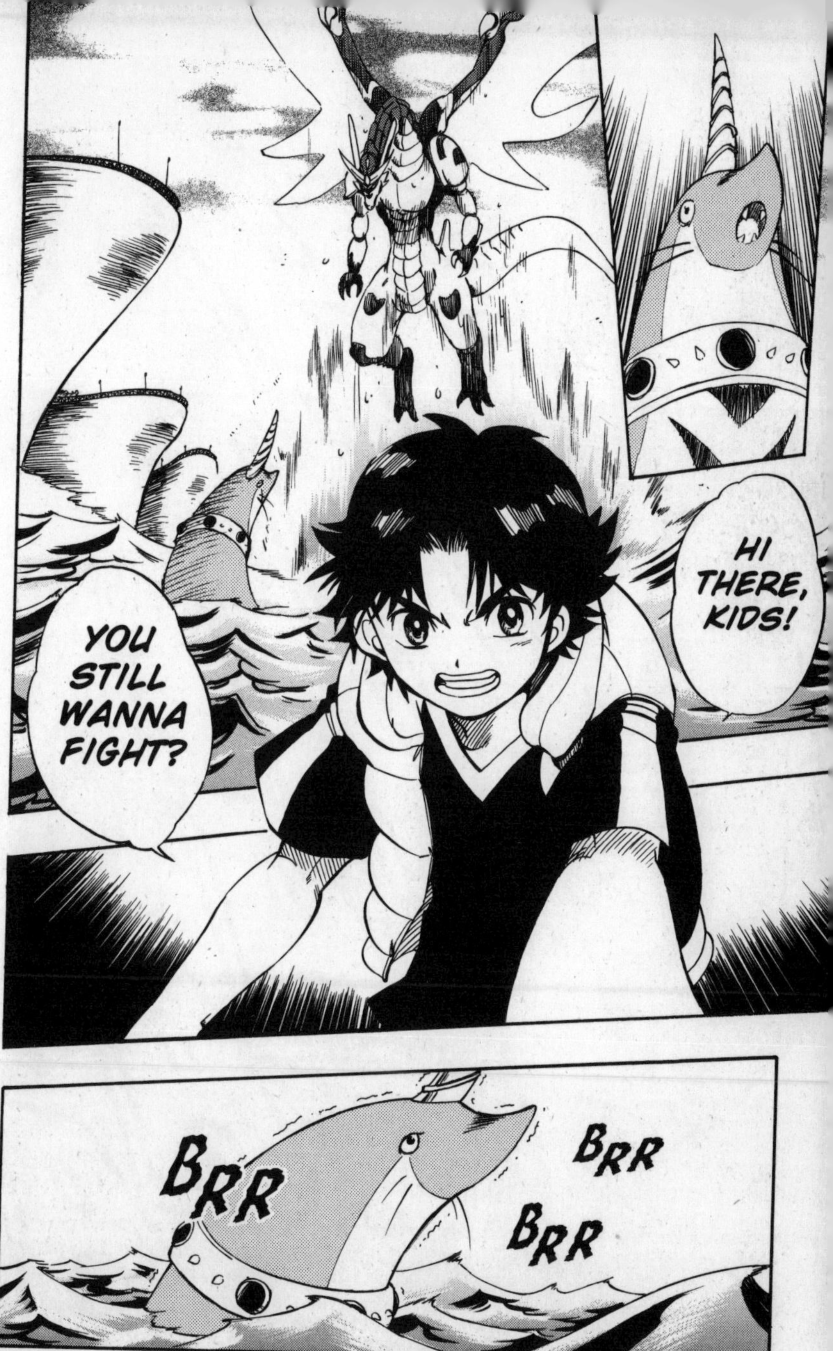
HI THERE, KIDS!
YOU STILL WANNA FIGHT?
BRR
BRR
BRR

READ THIS WAY

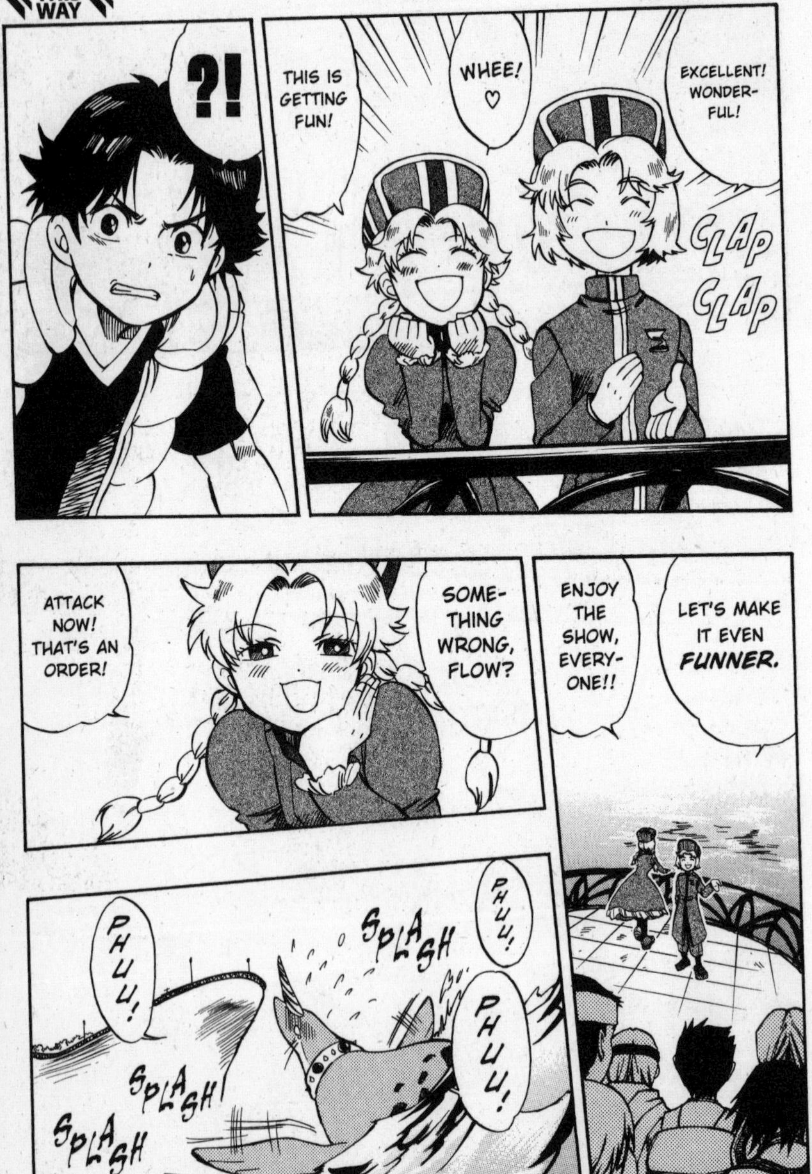
EXCELLENT! WONDERFUL!
WHEE! ♡
THIS IS GETTING FUN!
CLAP CLAP
?!
LET'S MAKE IT EVEN **FUNNER.**
ENJOY THE SHOW, EVERYONE!!
SOMETHING WRONG, FLOW?
ATTACK NOW! THAT'S AN ORDER!
PHUU!
PHUU!
SPLASH
PHUU!
SPLASH
SPLASH

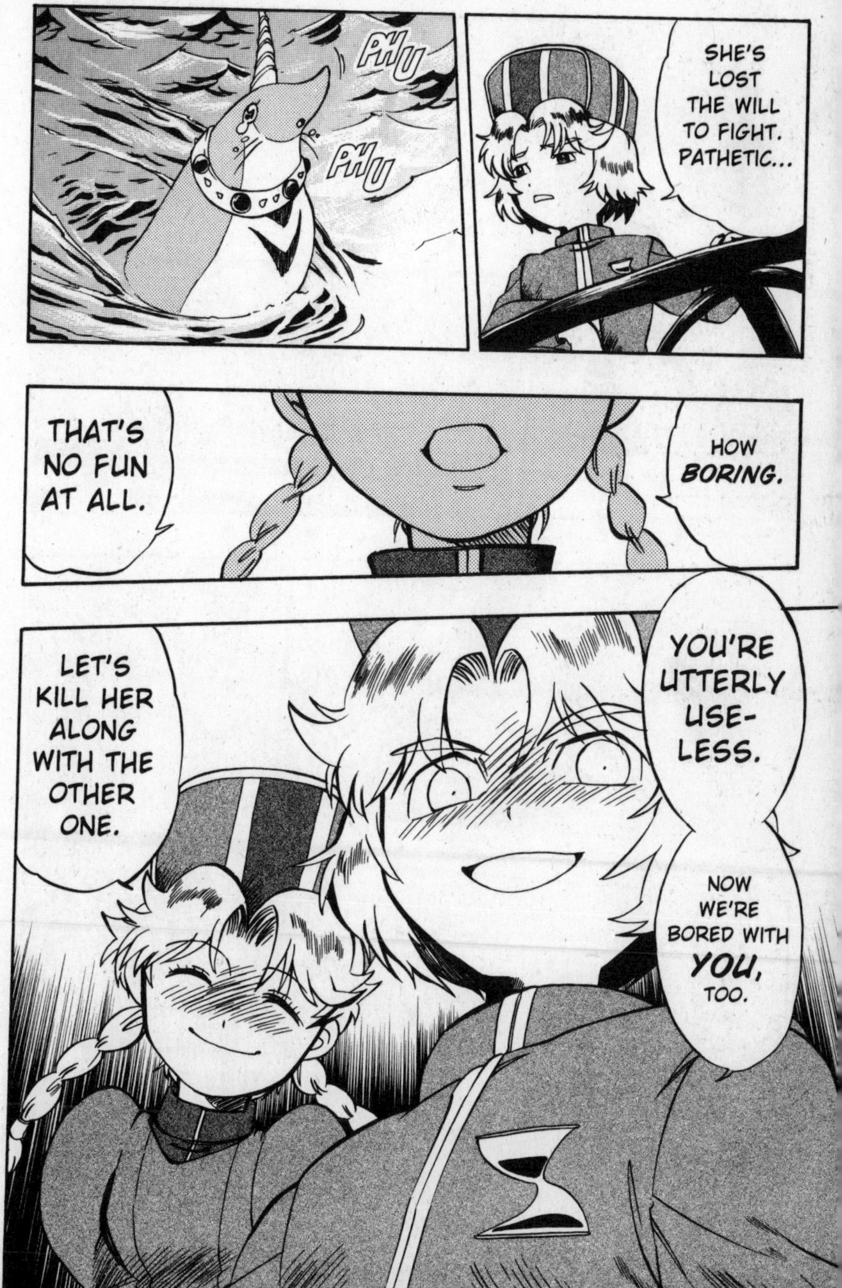
SHE'S LOST THE WILL TO FIGHT. PATHETIC...
PHU
PHU
HOW *BORING*.
THAT'S NO FUN AT ALL.
YOU'RE UTTERLY USE-LESS.
NOW WE'RE BORED WITH *YOU*, TOO.
LET'S KILL HER ALONG WITH THE OTHER ONE.

READ THIS WAY

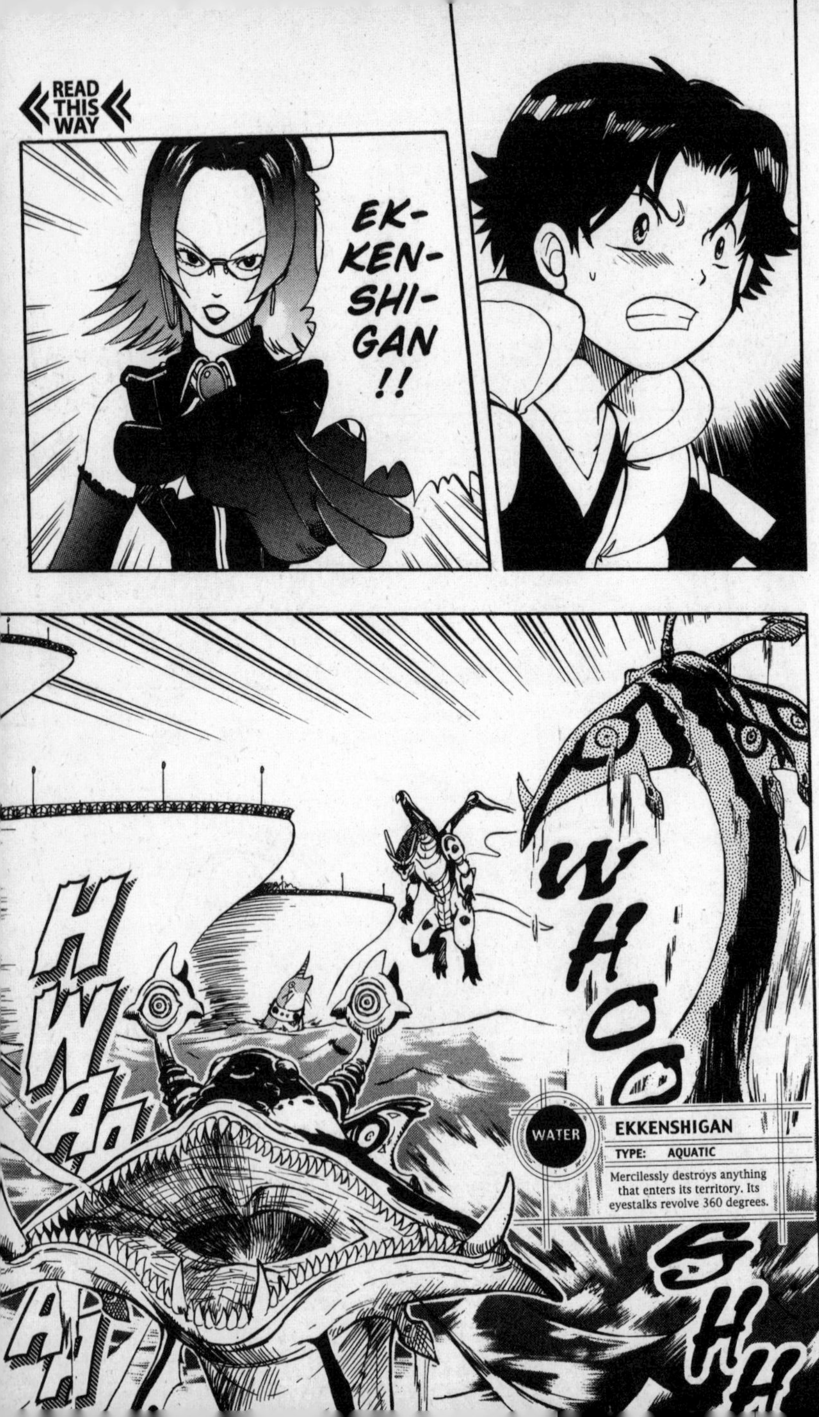
EK-KEN-SHI-GAN!!
WHOOSHH
WATER
EKKENSHIGAN
TYPE: AQUATIC
Mercilessly destroys anything that enters its territory. Its eyestalks revolve 360 degrees.
HWAAAH!

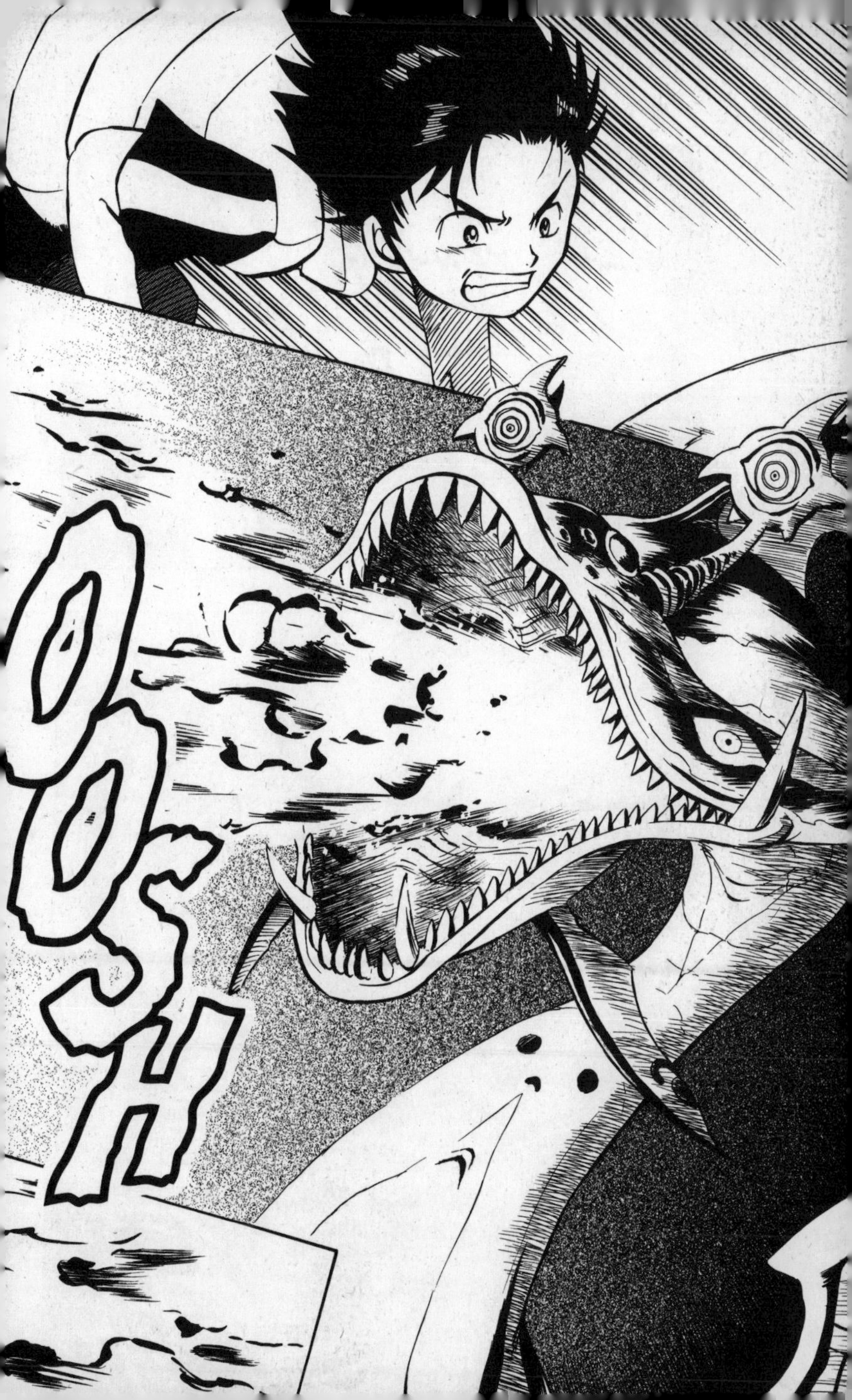
OOSH

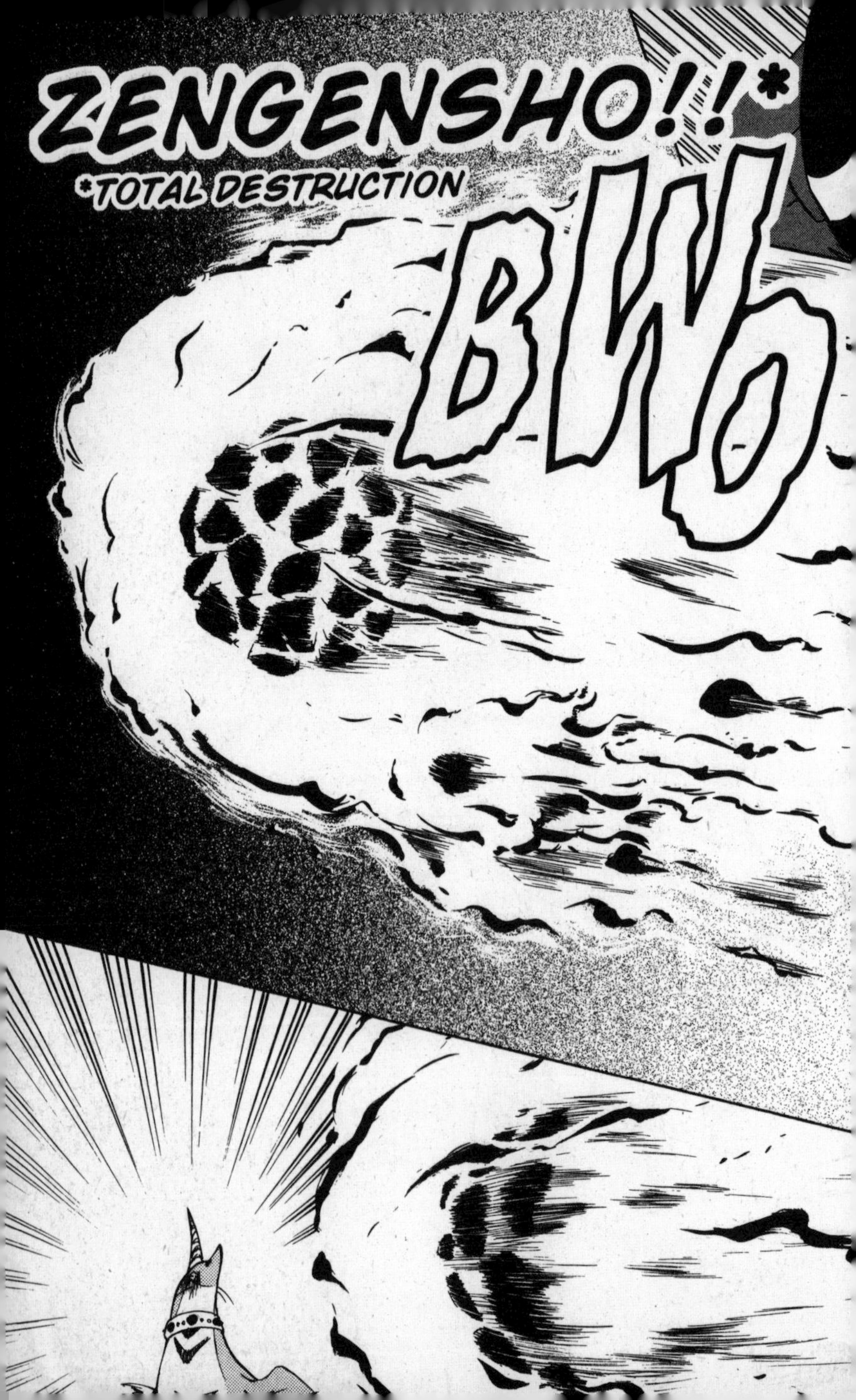
ZENGENSHO!!*
*TOTAL DESTRUCTION
BWO

THWWACK

HE CAUGHT IT!

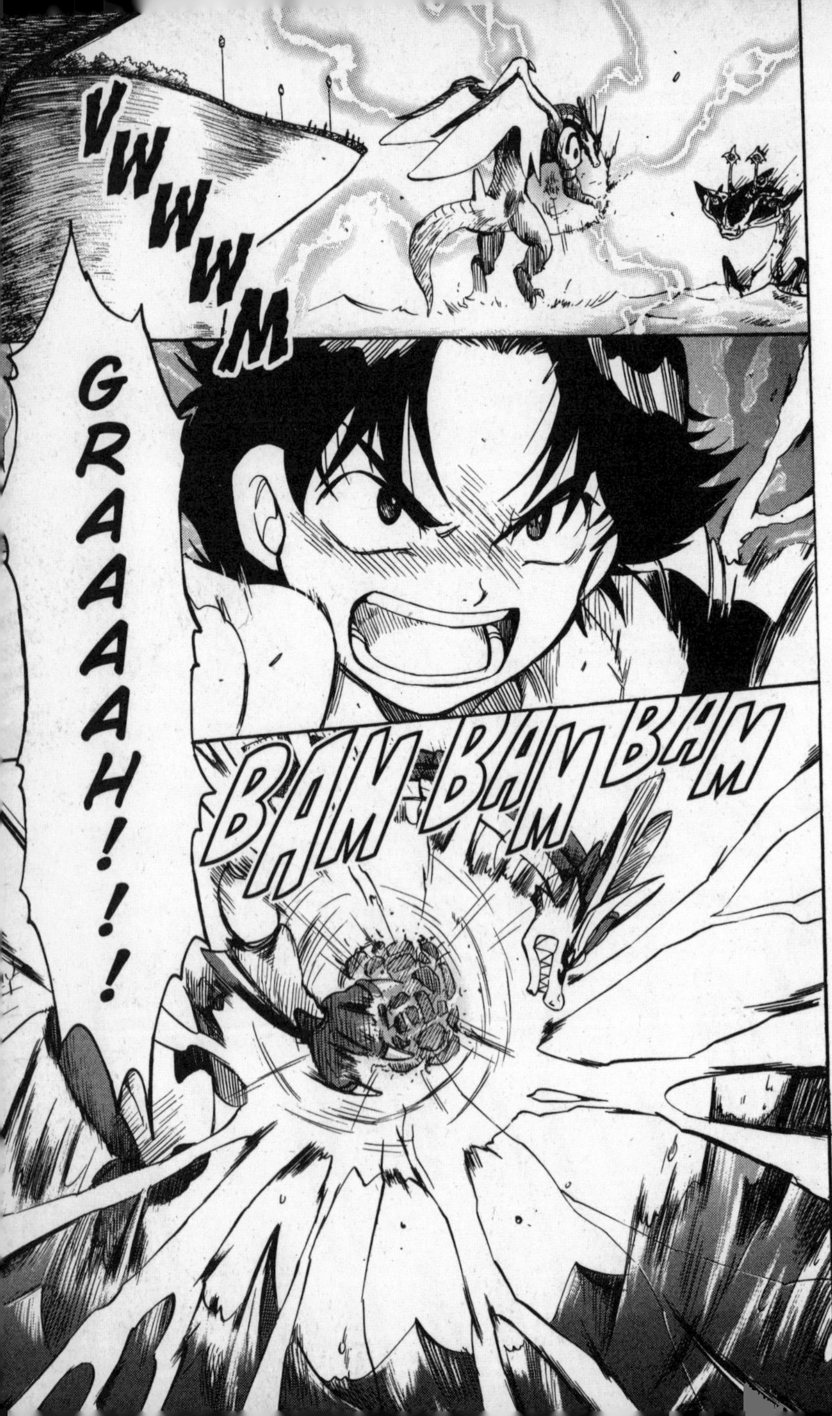
VWWWWM
GRAAAAH!!!
BAM BAM BAM

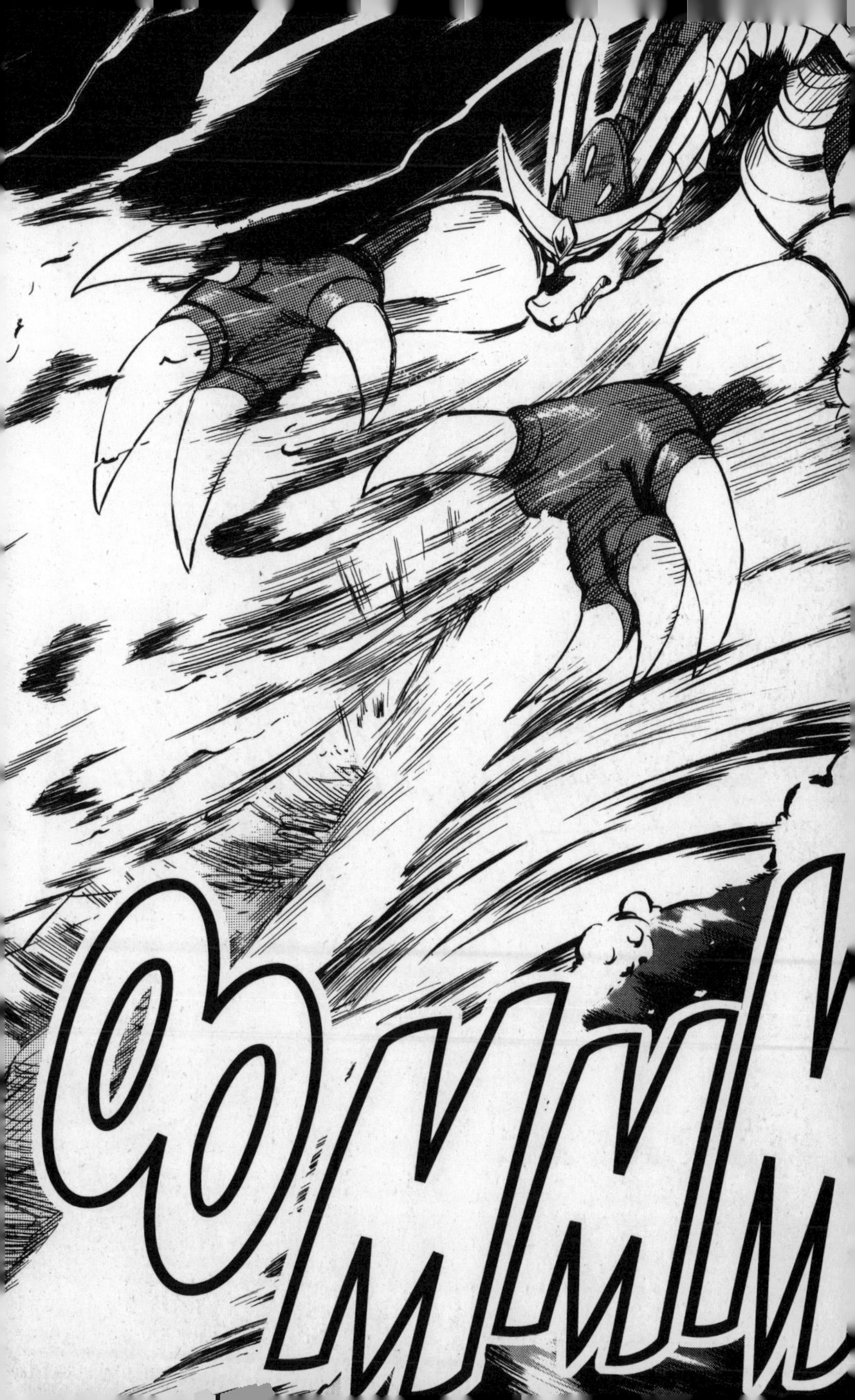

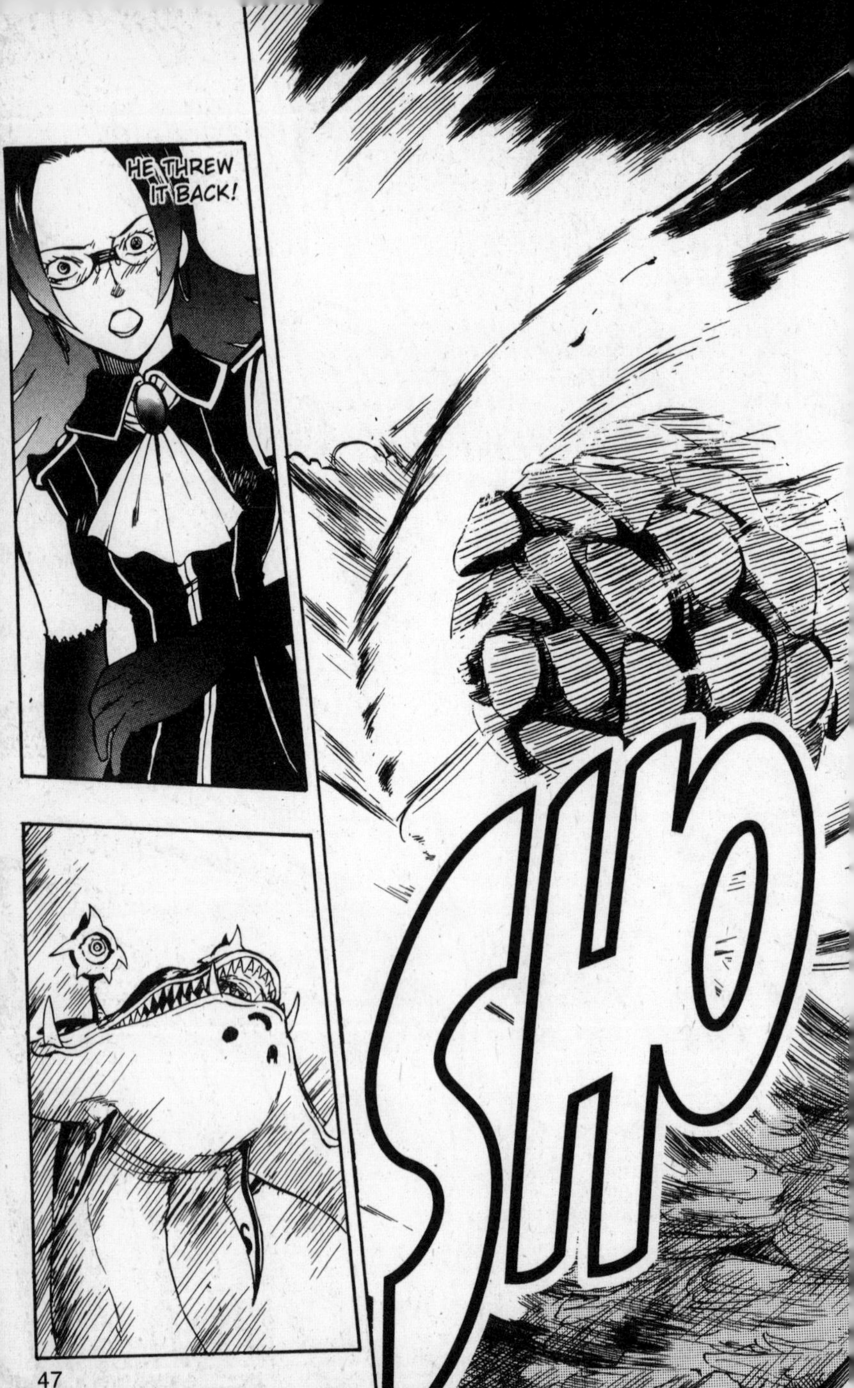
SHP
HE THREW IT BACK!

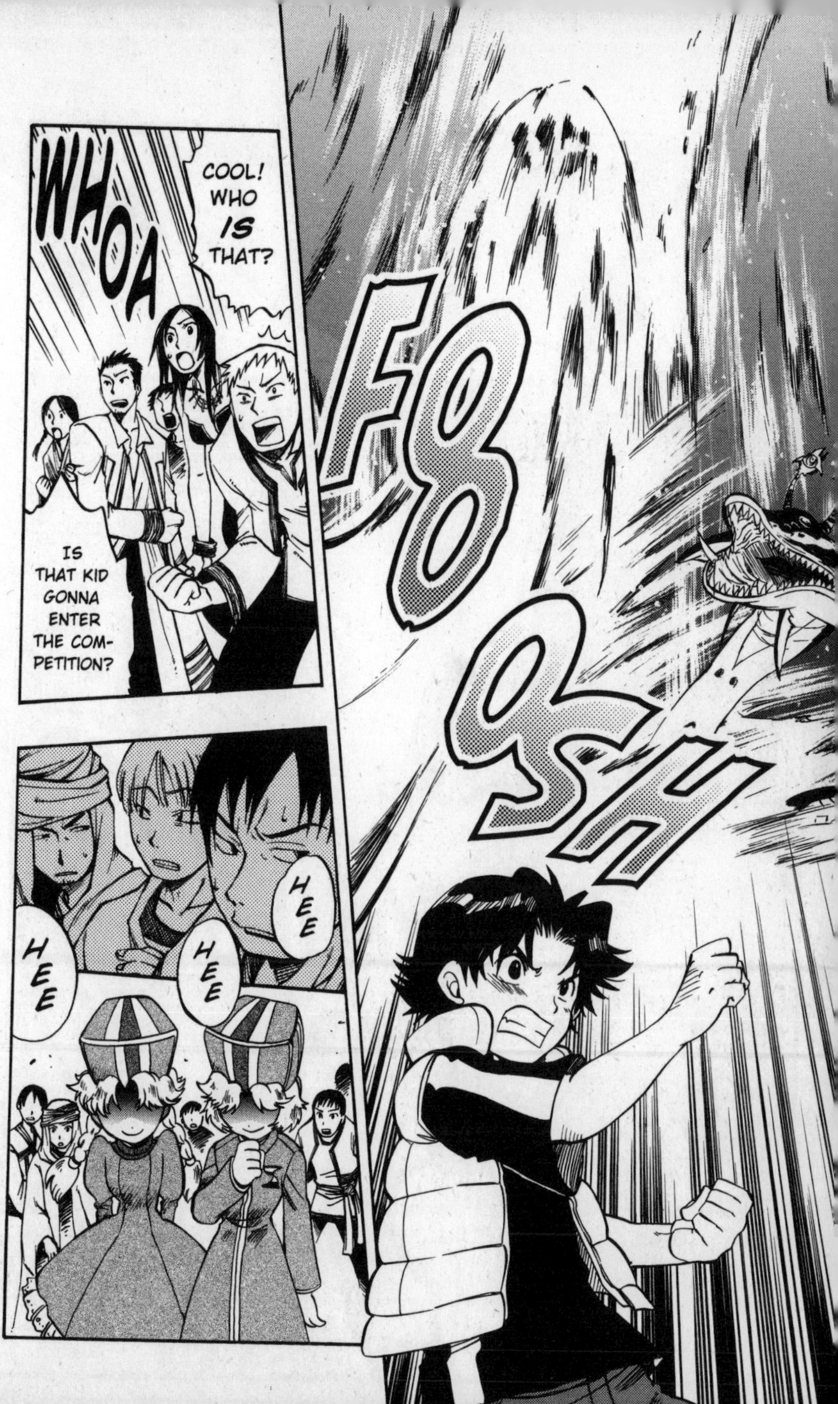
FOOSH
WHOA
COOL! WHO IS THAT?
IS THAT KID GONNA ENTER THE COMPETITION?
HEE
HEE
HEE

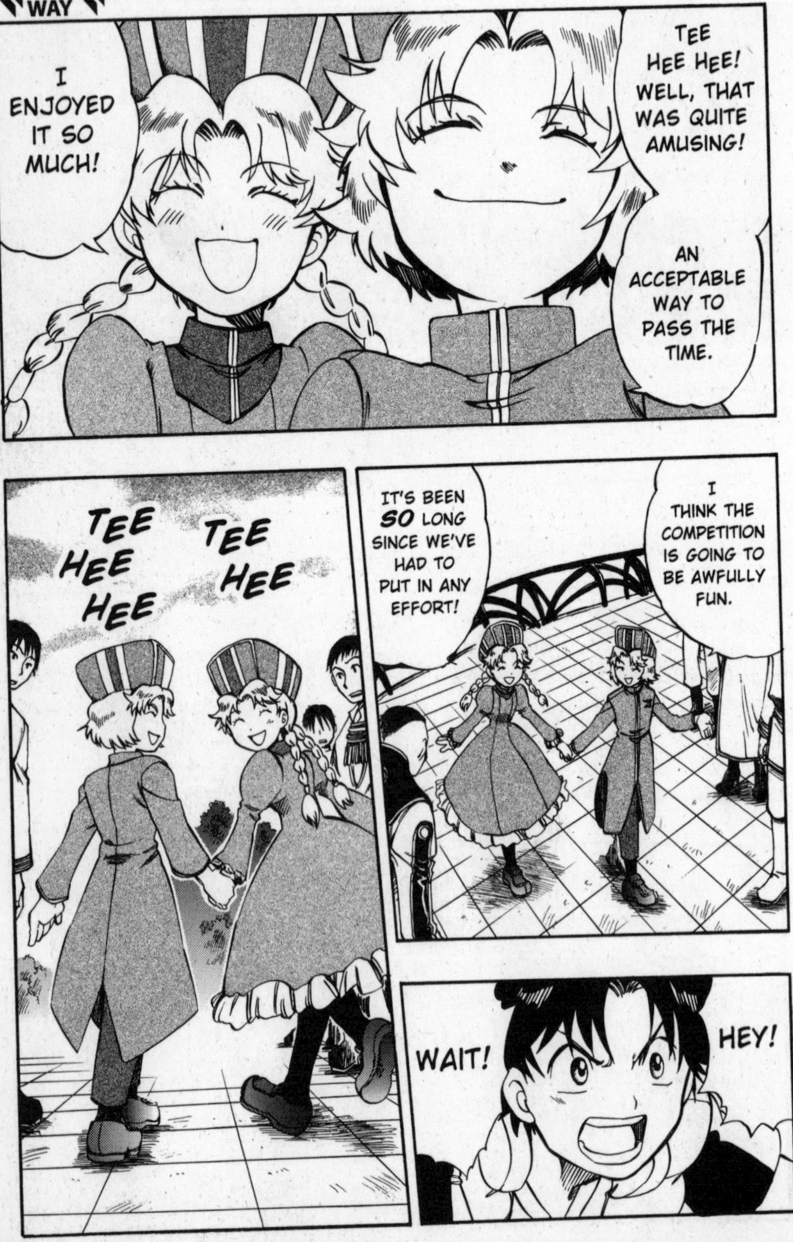
TEE HEE HEE! WELL, THAT WAS QUITE AMUSING!
AN ACCEPTABLE WAY TO PASS THE TIME.
I ENJOYED IT SO MUCH!
I THINK THE COMPETITION IS GOING TO BE AWFULLY FUN.
IT'S BEEN SO LONG SINCE WE'VE HAD TO PUT IN ANY EFFORT!
HEY!
WAIT!
TEE HEE
TEE HEE HEE

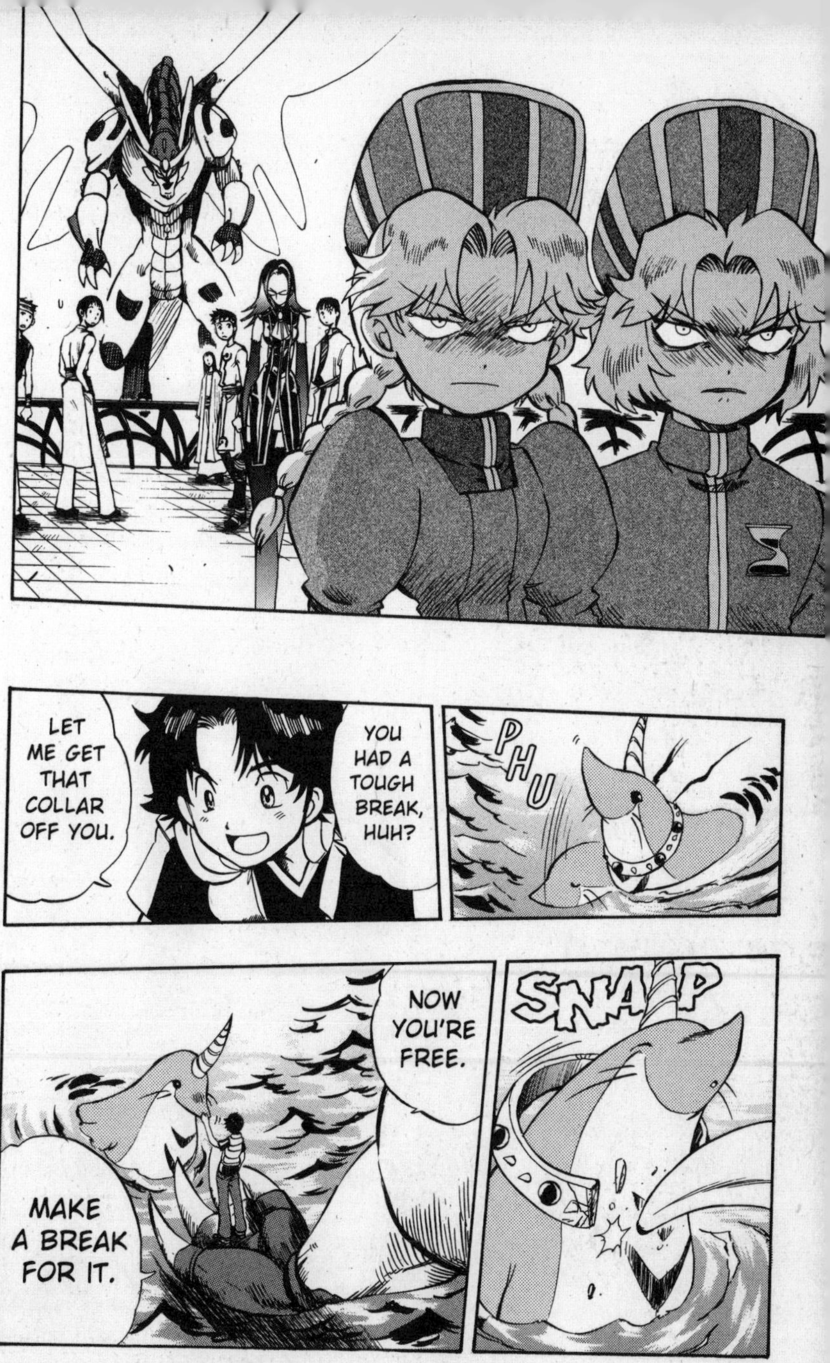
PHU
YOU HAD A TOUGH BREAK, HUH?
LET ME GET THAT COLLAR OFF YOU.
SNAP
NOW YOU'RE FREE.
MAKE A BREAK FOR IT.

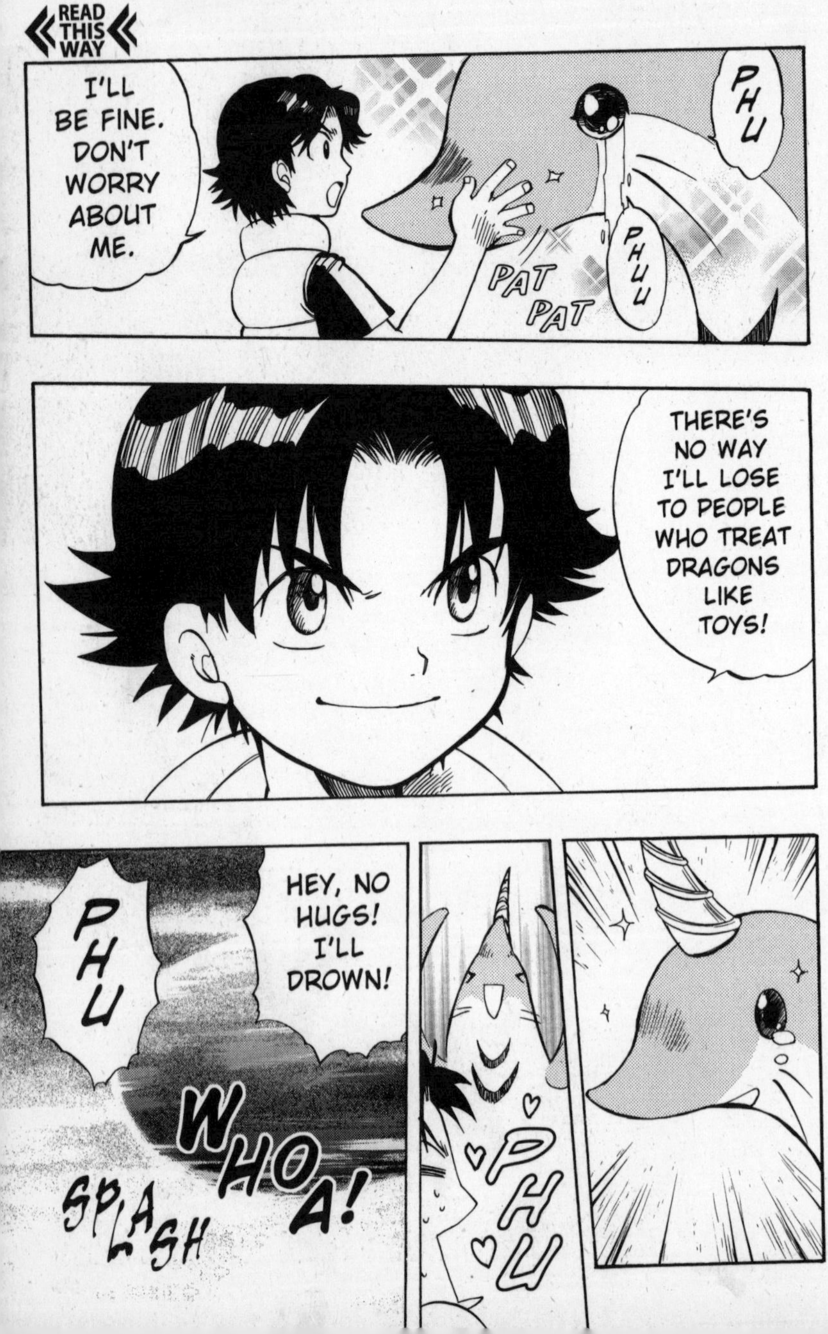
READ THIS WAY
PHU
I'LL BE FINE. DON'T WORRY ABOUT ME.
PHUU
PAT PAT
THERE'S NO WAY I'LL LOSE TO PEOPLE WHO TREAT DRAGONS LIKE TOYS!
PHU PHU
HEY, NO HUGS! I'LL DROWN!
PHU
WHOA!
SPLASH

FILLER SKETCHES.

ACTUALLY, THESE ARE REJECTED DESIGN SKETCHES FOR THE D.D. FIRST ANNIVERSARY BADGES.

IF YOU HAVE ONE, COMPARE THESE WITH THE REAL THING.

STAGE10 PRIDE

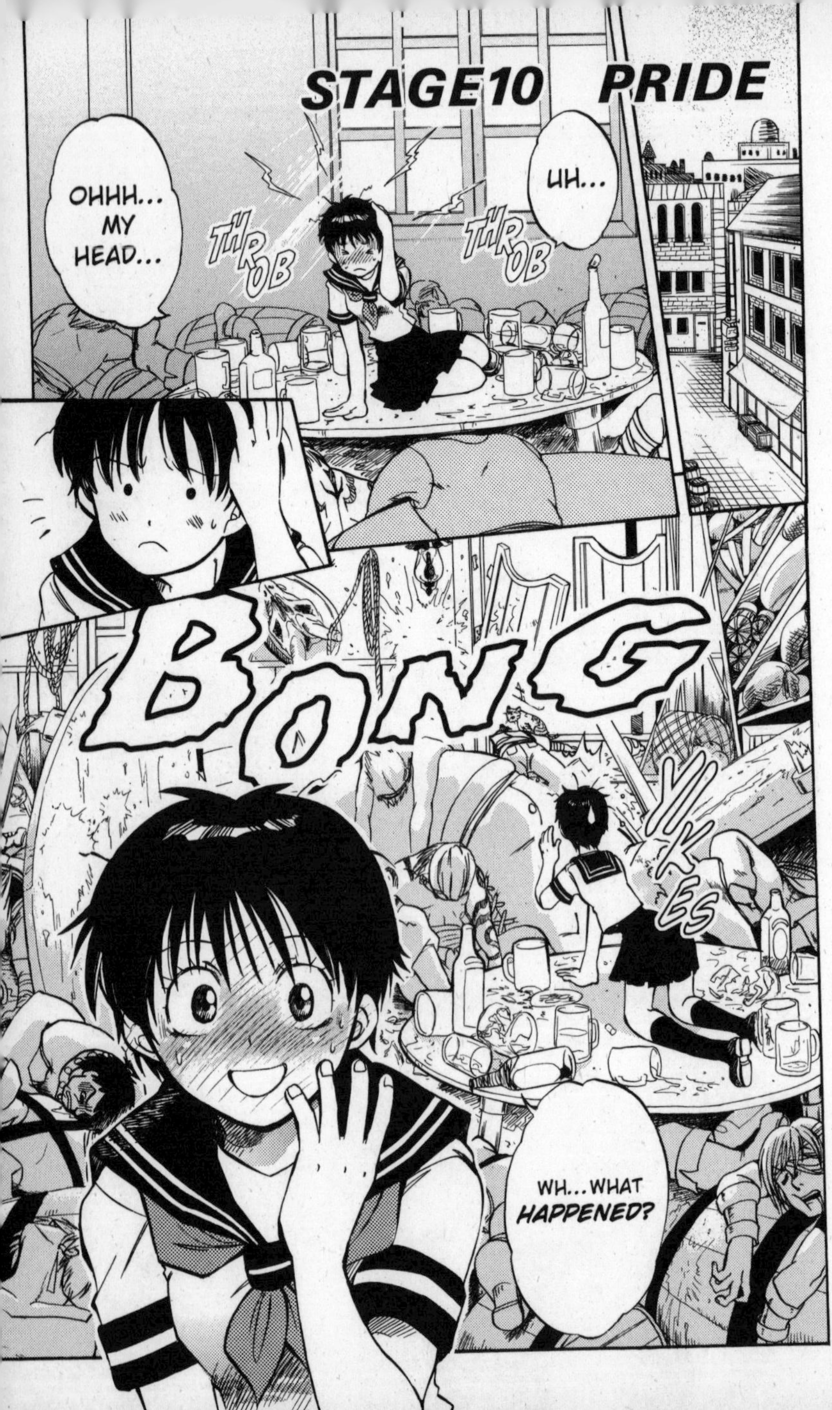
UH...
THROB
THROB
OHHH... MY HEAD...
BONG
YIKES
WH...WHAT HAPPENED?

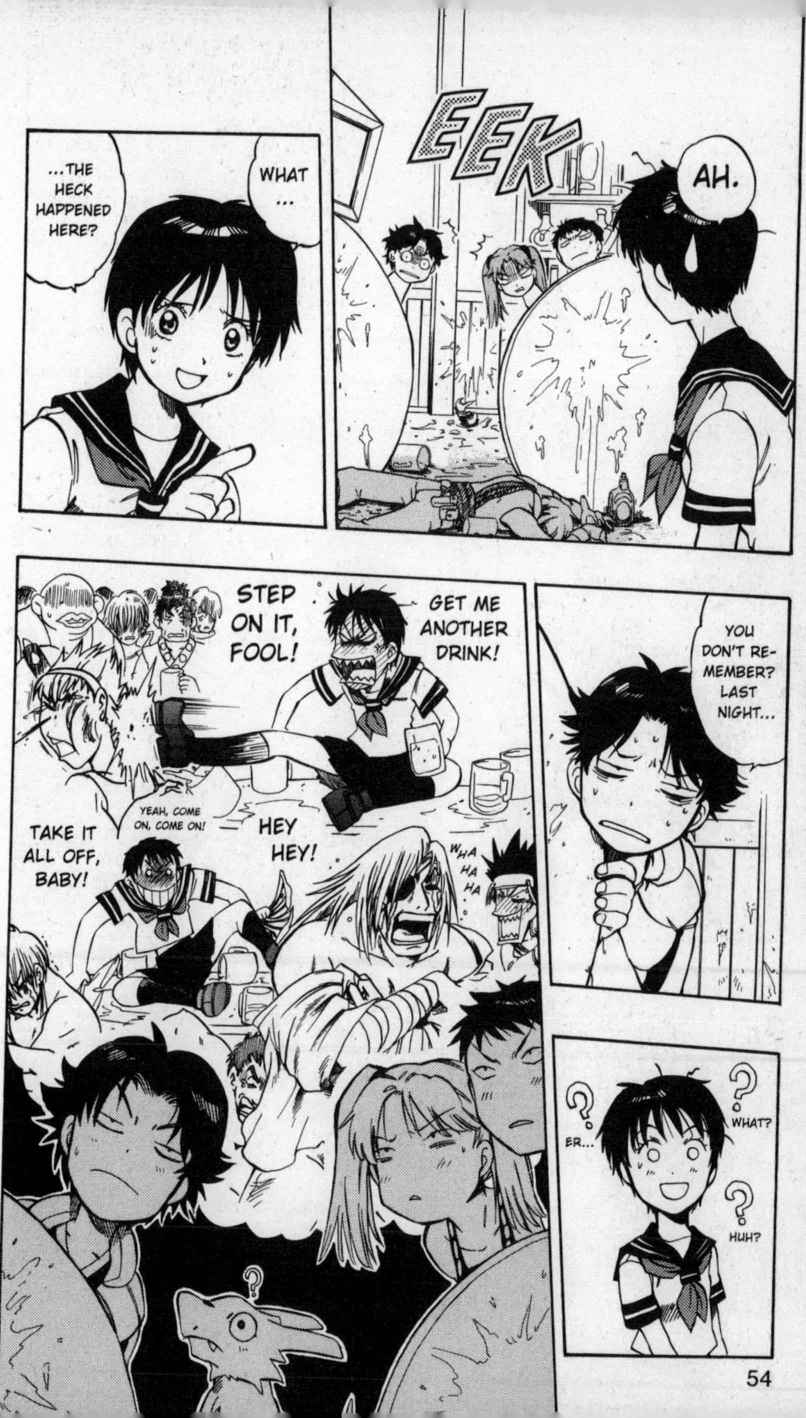
EEK
AH.
WHAT ...
...THE HECK HAPPENED HERE?
YOU DON'T RE-MEMBER? LAST NIGHT...
WHAT?
ER...
HUH?
GET ME ANOTHER DRINK!
STEP ON IT, FOOL!
HEY HEY!
YEAH, COME ON, COME ON!
WHA HA HA
TAKE IT ALL OFF, BABY!

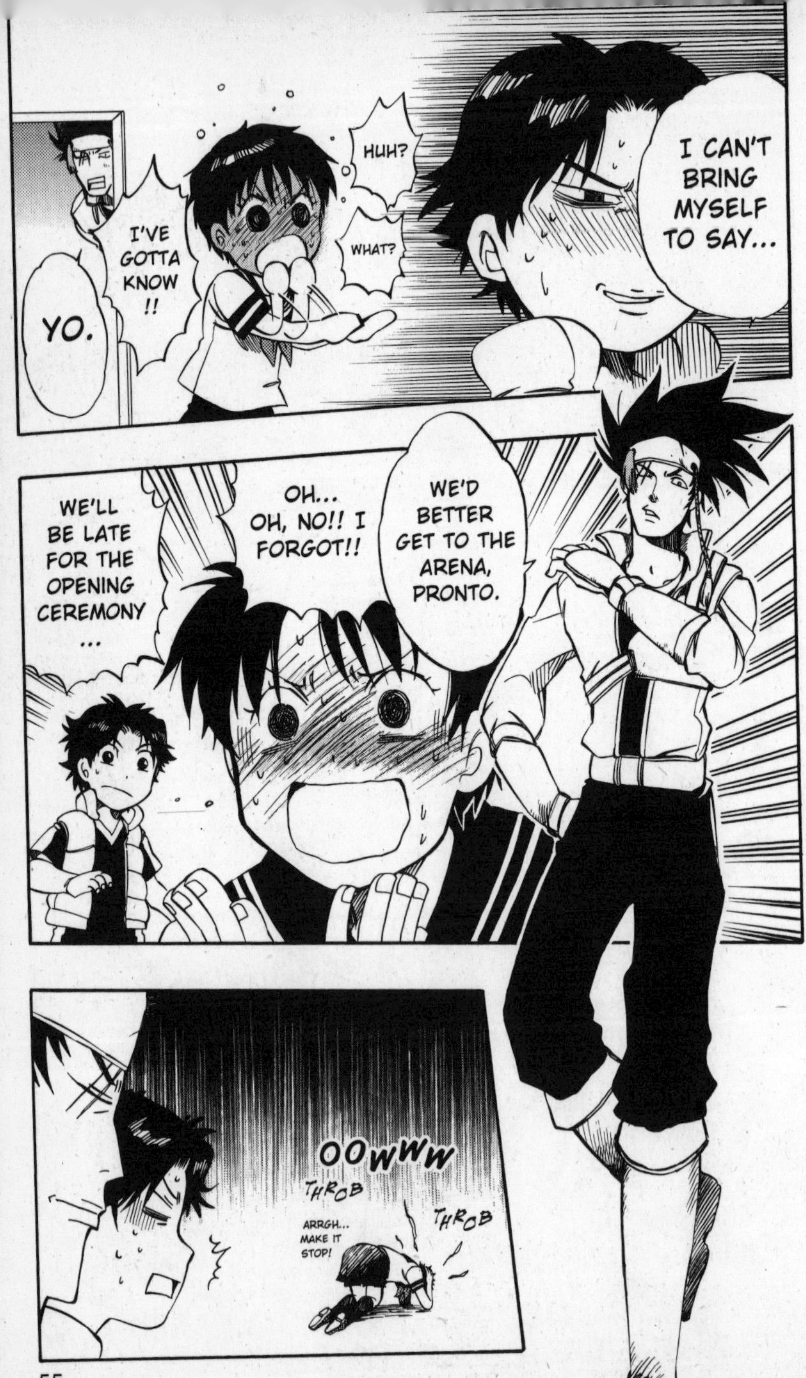
I CAN'T BRING MYSELF TO SAY...
HUH?
WHAT?
I'VE GOTTA KNOW !!
YO.
WE'D BETTER GET TO THE ARENA, PRONTO.
OH... OH, NO!! I FORGOT!!
WE'LL BE LATE FOR THE OPENING CEREMONY ...
OOWWW
THROB
THROB
ARRGH... MAKE IT STOP!

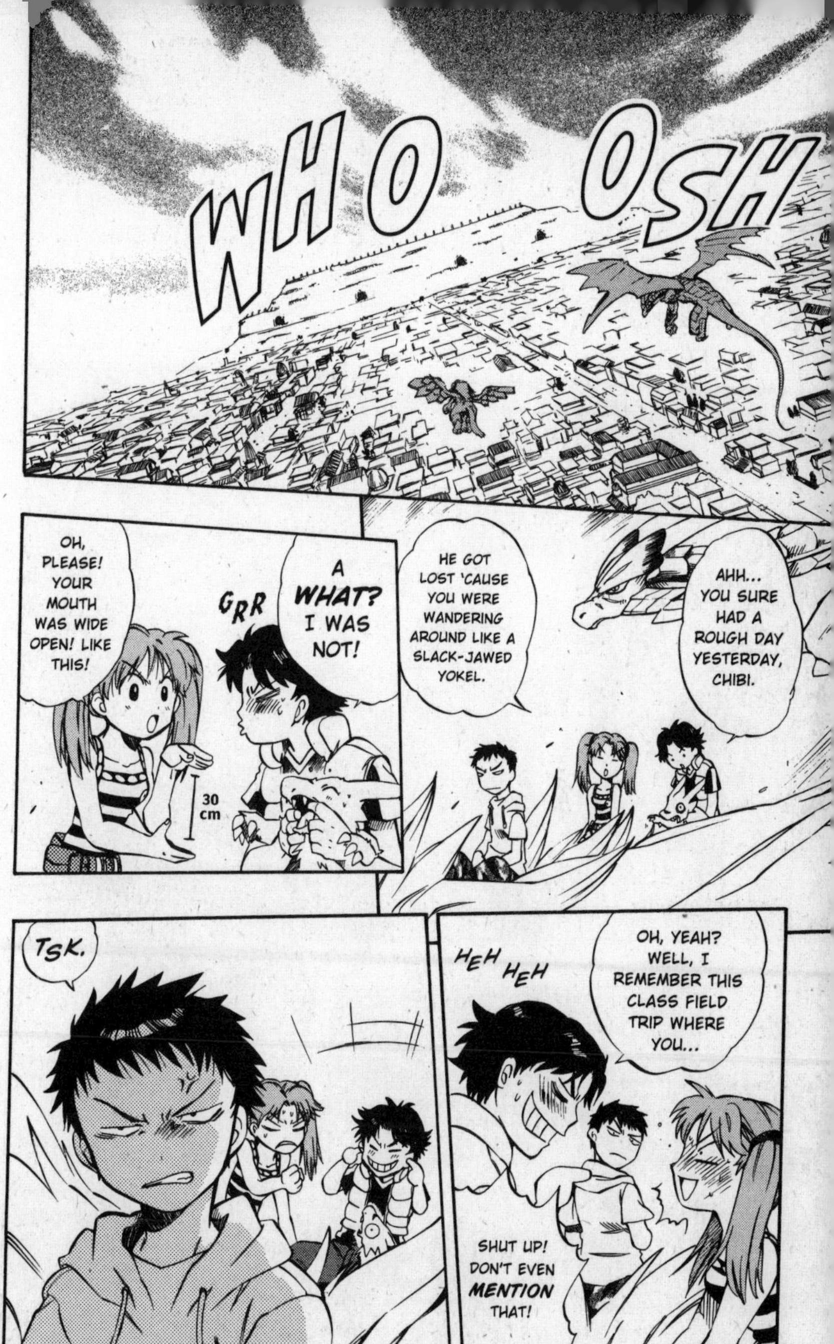
WHOOSH
AHH... YOU SURE HAD A ROUGH DAY YESTERDAY, CHIBI.
HE GOT LOST 'CAUSE YOU WERE WANDERING AROUND LIKE A SLACK-JAWED YOKEL.
A *WHAT?* I WAS NOT!
GRR
OH, PLEASE! YOUR MOUTH WAS WIDE OPEN! LIKE THIS!
30 cm
OH, YEAH? WELL, I REMEMBER THIS CLASS FIELD TRIP WHERE YOU...
HEH HEH
SHUT UP! DON'T EVEN *MENTION* THAT!
TSK.

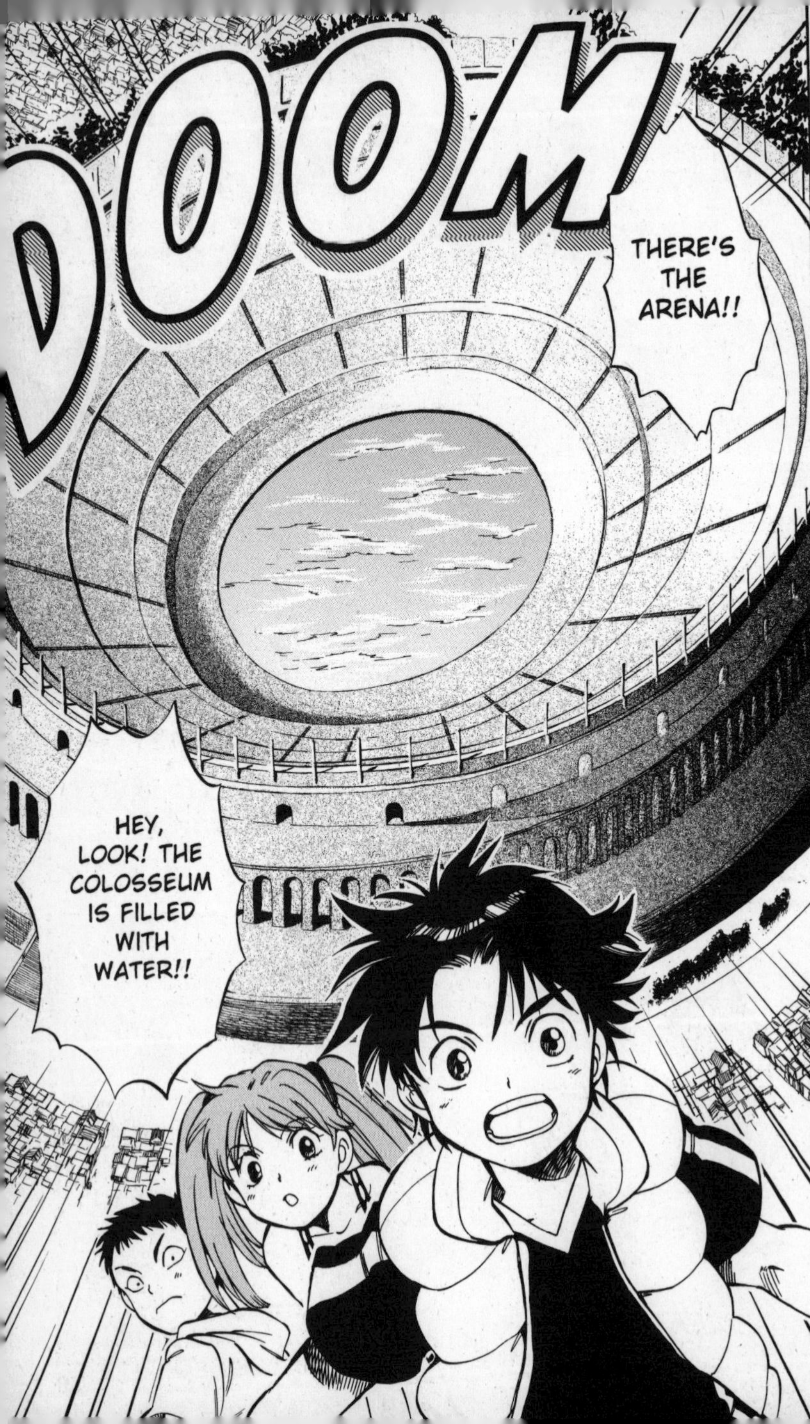
DOOM
THERE'S THE ARENA!!
HEY, LOOK! THE COLOSSEUM IS FILLED WITH WATER!!

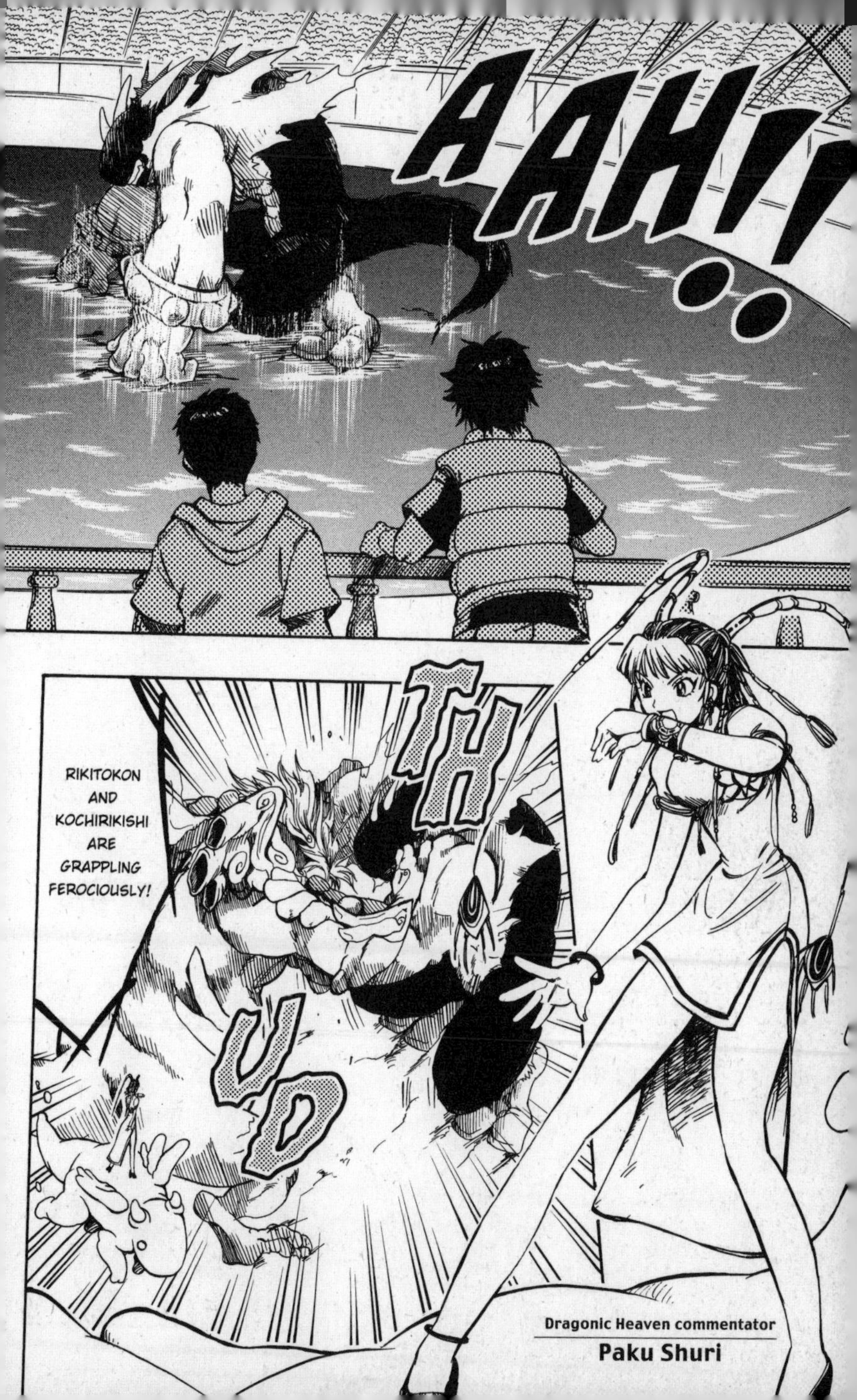
AAH!!..
THUD
RIKITOKON AND KOCHIRIKISHI ARE GRAPPLING FEROCIOUSLY!
Dragonic Heaven commentator
Paku Shuri

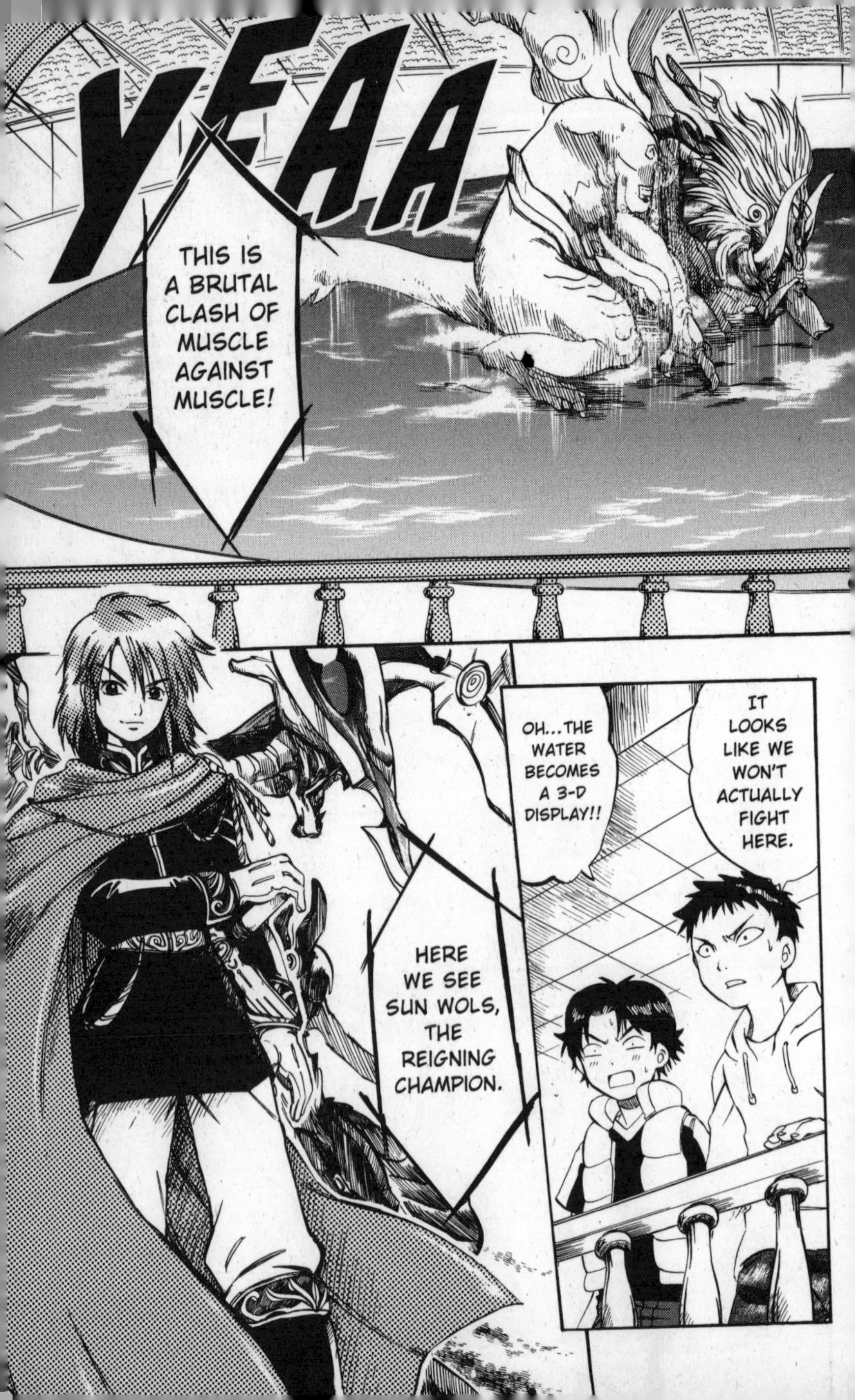
YEAA
THIS IS A BRUTAL CLASH OF MUSCLE AGAINST MUSCLE!
IT LOOKS LIKE WE WON'T ACTUALLY FIGHT HERE.
OH...THE WATER BECOMES A 3-D DISPLAY!!
HERE WE SEE SUN WOLS, THE REIGNING CHAMPION.

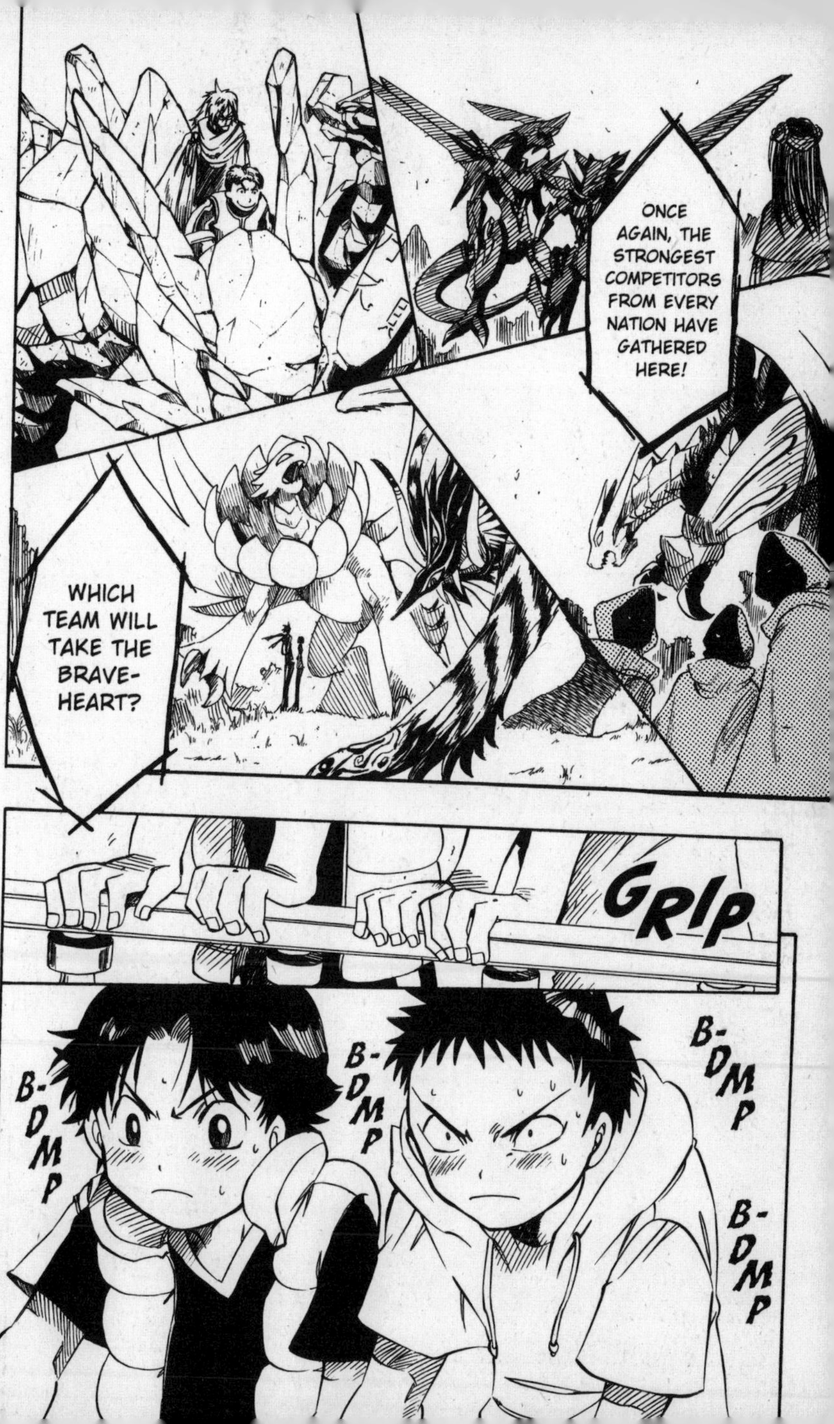
ONCE AGAIN, THE STRONGEST COMPETITORS FROM EVERY NATION HAVE GATHERED HERE!
WHICH TEAM WILL TAKE THE BRAVE-HEART?
GRIP
B-DMP
B-DMP
B-DMP
B-DMP

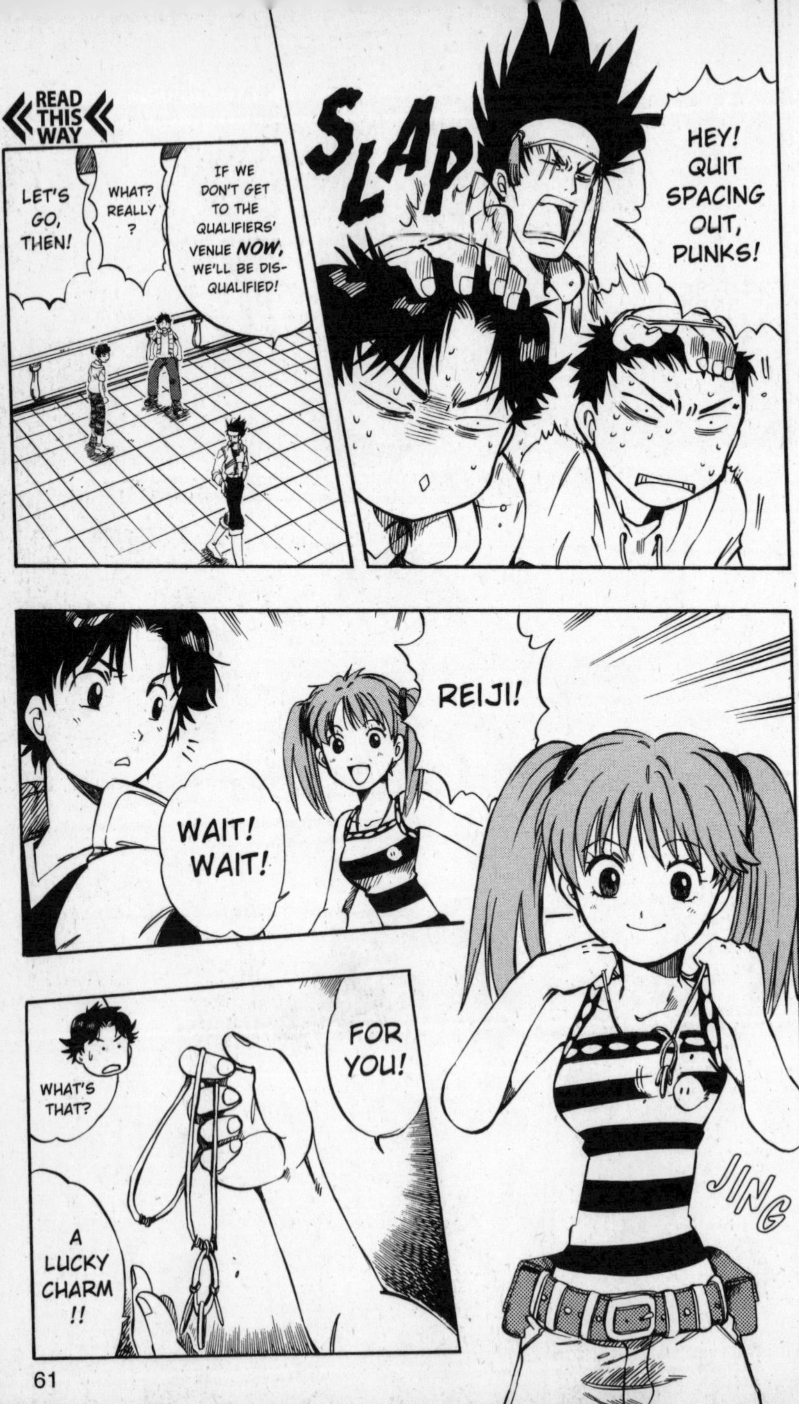
READ THIS WAY
SLAP
HEY! QUIT SPACING OUT, PUNKS!
IF WE DON'T GET TO THE QUALIFIERS' VENUE NOW, WE'LL BE DIS-QUALIFIED!
WHAT? REALLY?
LET'S GO, THEN!
REIJI!
WAIT! WAIT!
JING
FOR YOU!
WHAT'S THAT?
A LUCKY CHARM!!

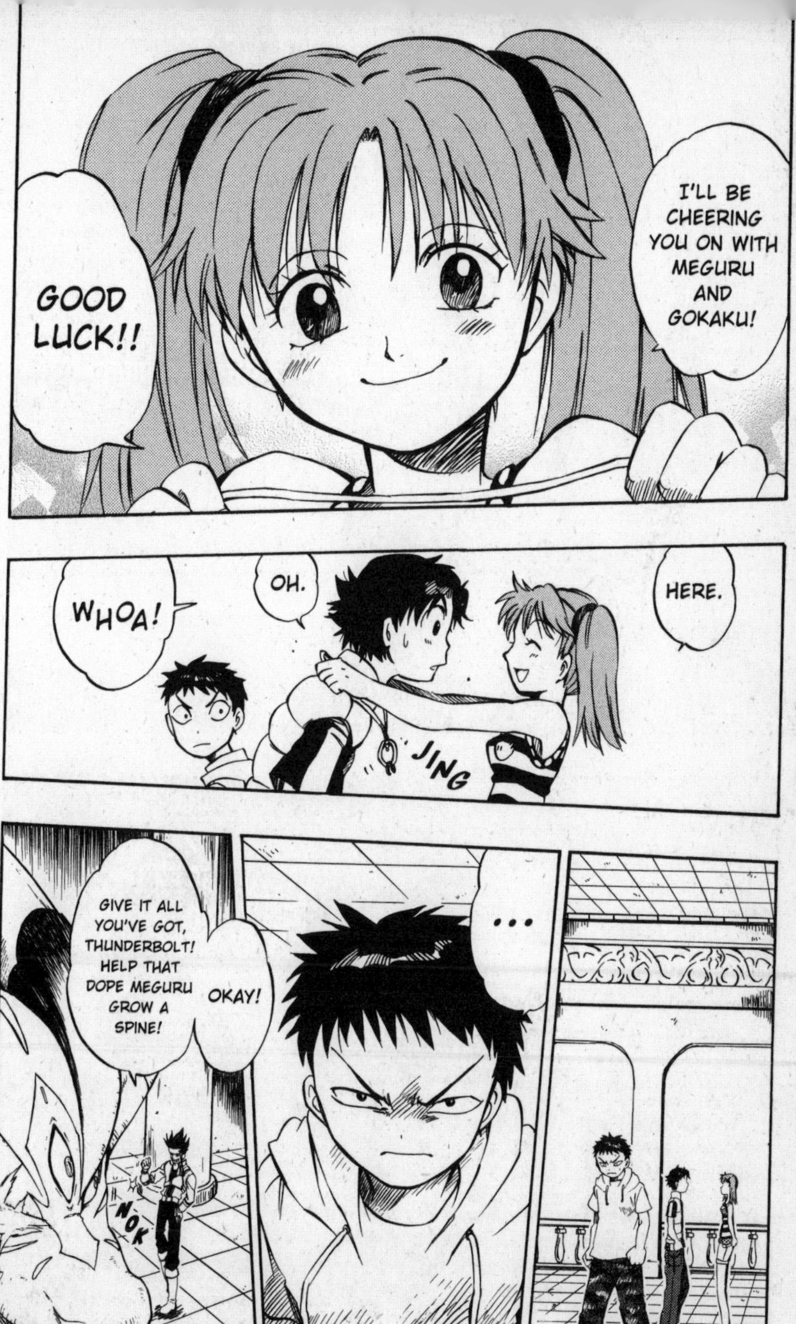
I'LL BE CHEERING YOU ON WITH MEGURU AND GOKAKU!
GOOD LUCK!!
HERE.
OH.
WHOA!
JING
...
GIVE IT ALL YOU'VE GOT, THUNDERBOLT! HELP THAT DOPE MEGURU GROW A SPINE!
OKAY!
NOK

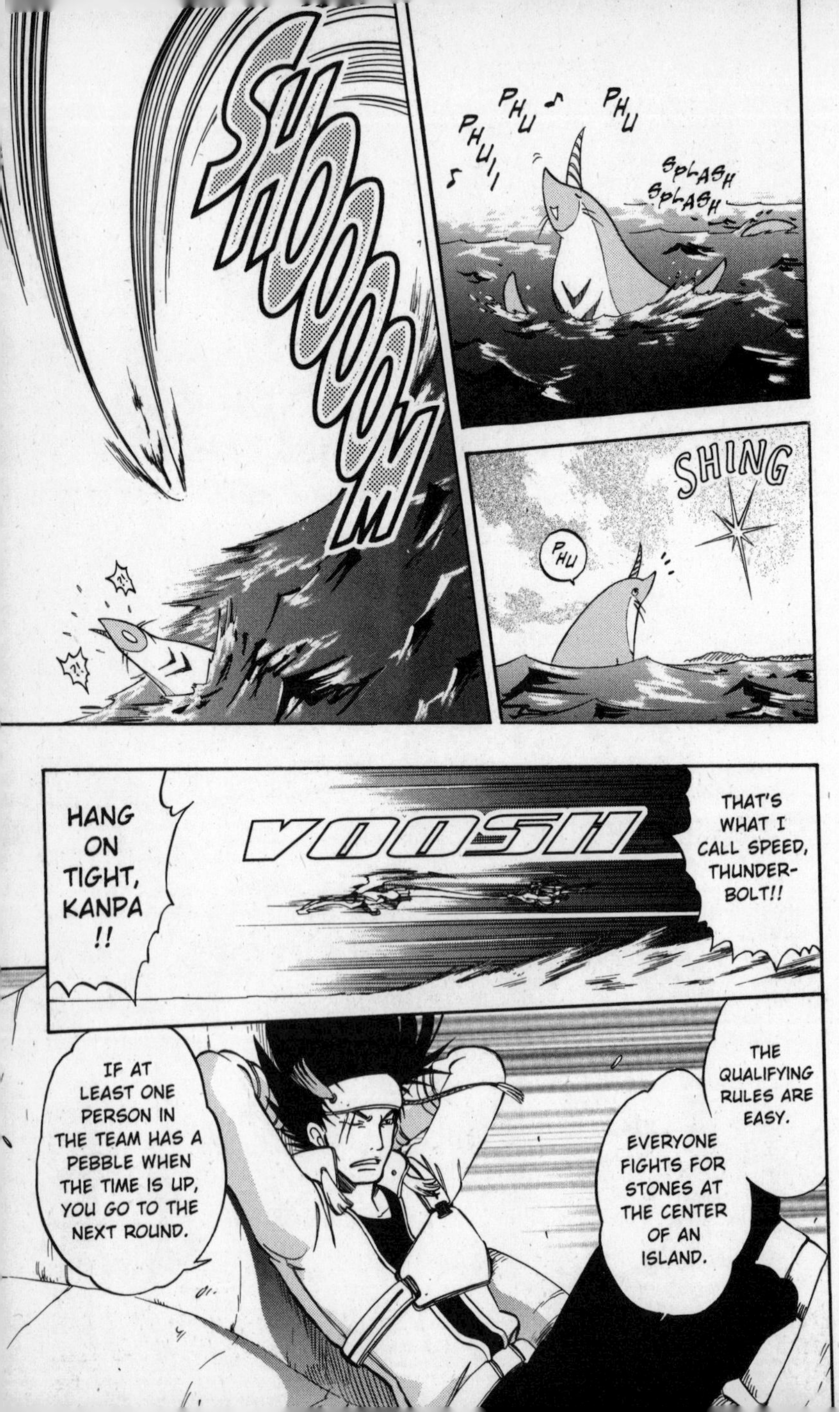
PHU
PHU
PHUII
SPLASH SPLASH
SHING
PHU
SHOOOOOM
?!
?!
THAT'S WHAT I CALL SPEED, THUNDER-BOLT!!
VOOSH
HANG ON TIGHT, KANPA!!
THE QUALIFYING RULES ARE EASY.
EVERYONE FIGHTS FOR STONES AT THE CENTER OF AN ISLAND.
IF AT LEAST ONE PERSON IN THE TEAM HAS A PEBBLE WHEN THE TIME IS UP, YOU GO TO THE NEXT ROUND.

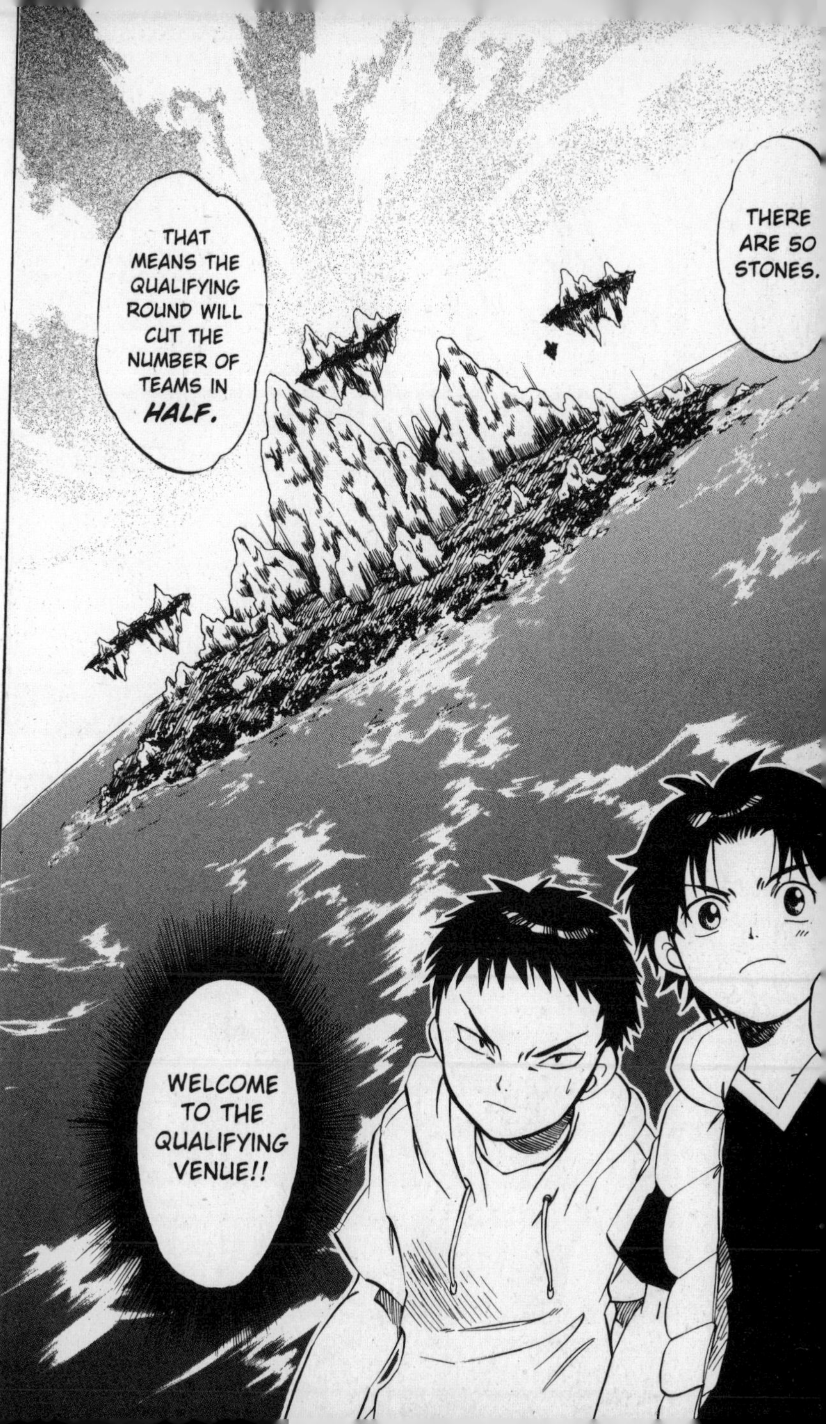
THERE ARE 50 STONES.
THAT MEANS THE QUALIFYING ROUND WILL CUT THE NUMBER OF TEAMS IN HALF.
WELCOME TO THE QUALIFYING VENUE!!

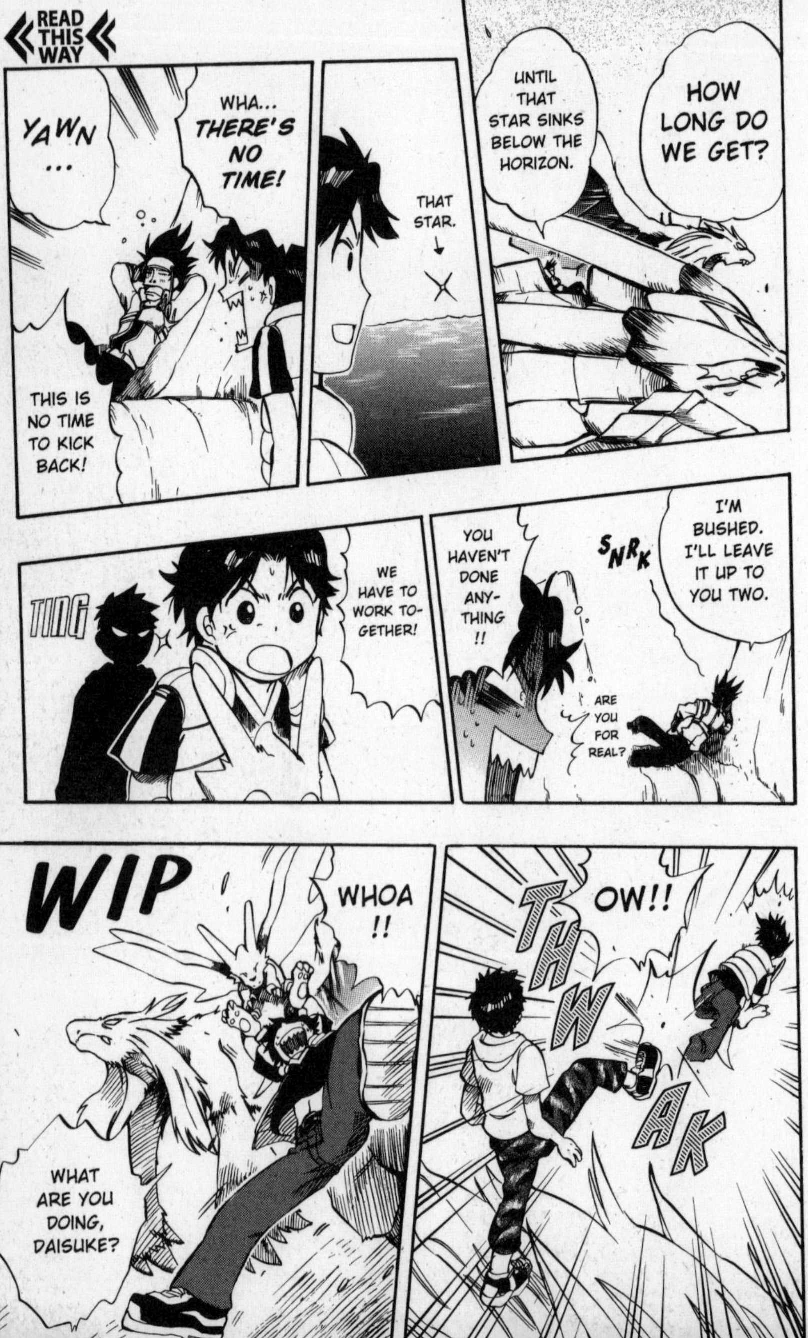
READ THIS WAY
HOW LONG DO WE GET?
UNTIL THAT STAR SINKS BELOW THE HORIZON.
THAT STAR.
WHA... THERE'S NO TIME!
YAWN ...
THIS IS NO TIME TO KICK BACK!
I'M BUSHED. I'LL LEAVE IT UP TO YOU TWO.
SNRK
YOU HAVEN'T DONE ANYTHING!!
ARE YOU FOR REAL?
WE HAVE TO WORK TOGETHER!
TING
OW!!
THWAK
WHOA!!
WIP
WHAT ARE YOU DOING, DAISUKE?

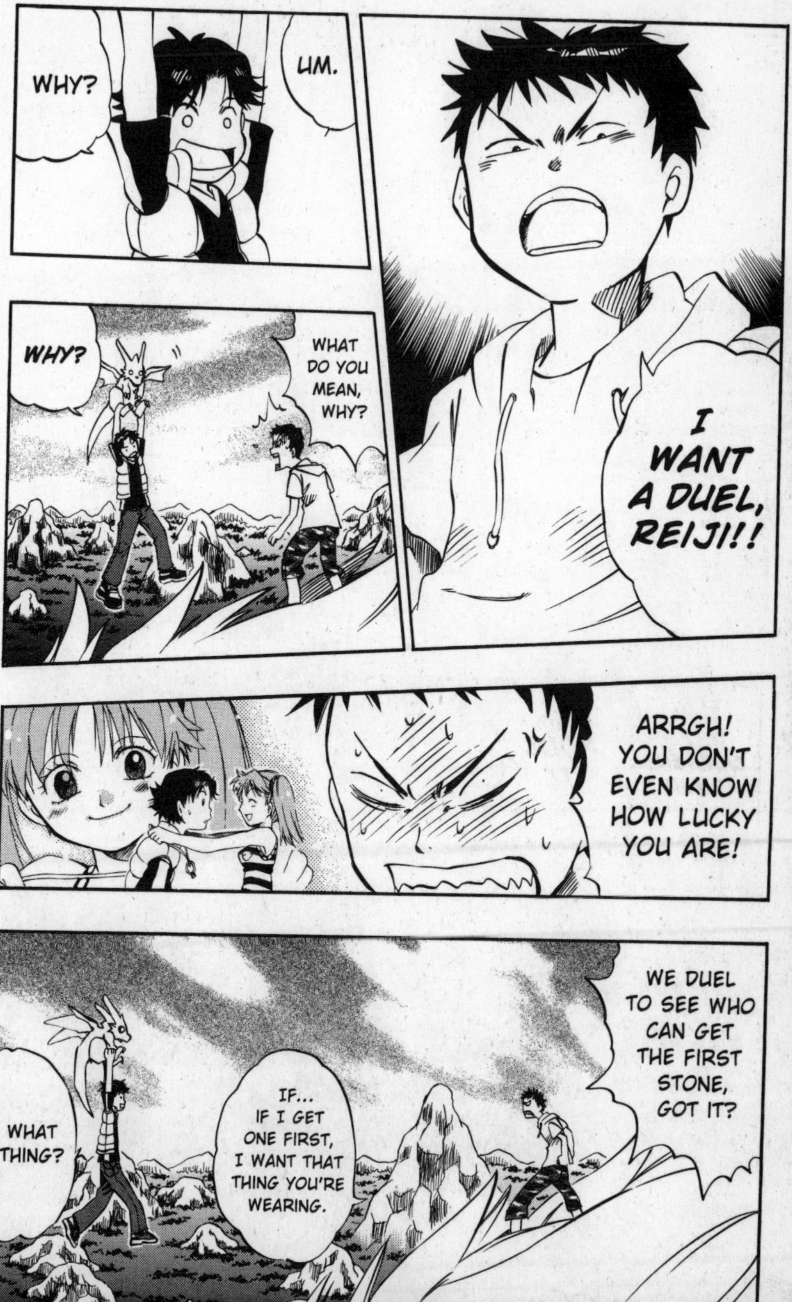
I WANT A DUEL, REIJI!!
UM.
WHY?
WHAT DO YOU MEAN, WHY?
WHY?
ARRGH! YOU DON'T EVEN KNOW HOW LUCKY YOU ARE!
WE DUEL TO SEE WHO CAN GET THE FIRST STONE, GOT IT?
IF... IF I GET ONE FIRST, I WANT THAT THING YOU'RE WEARING.
WHAT THING?

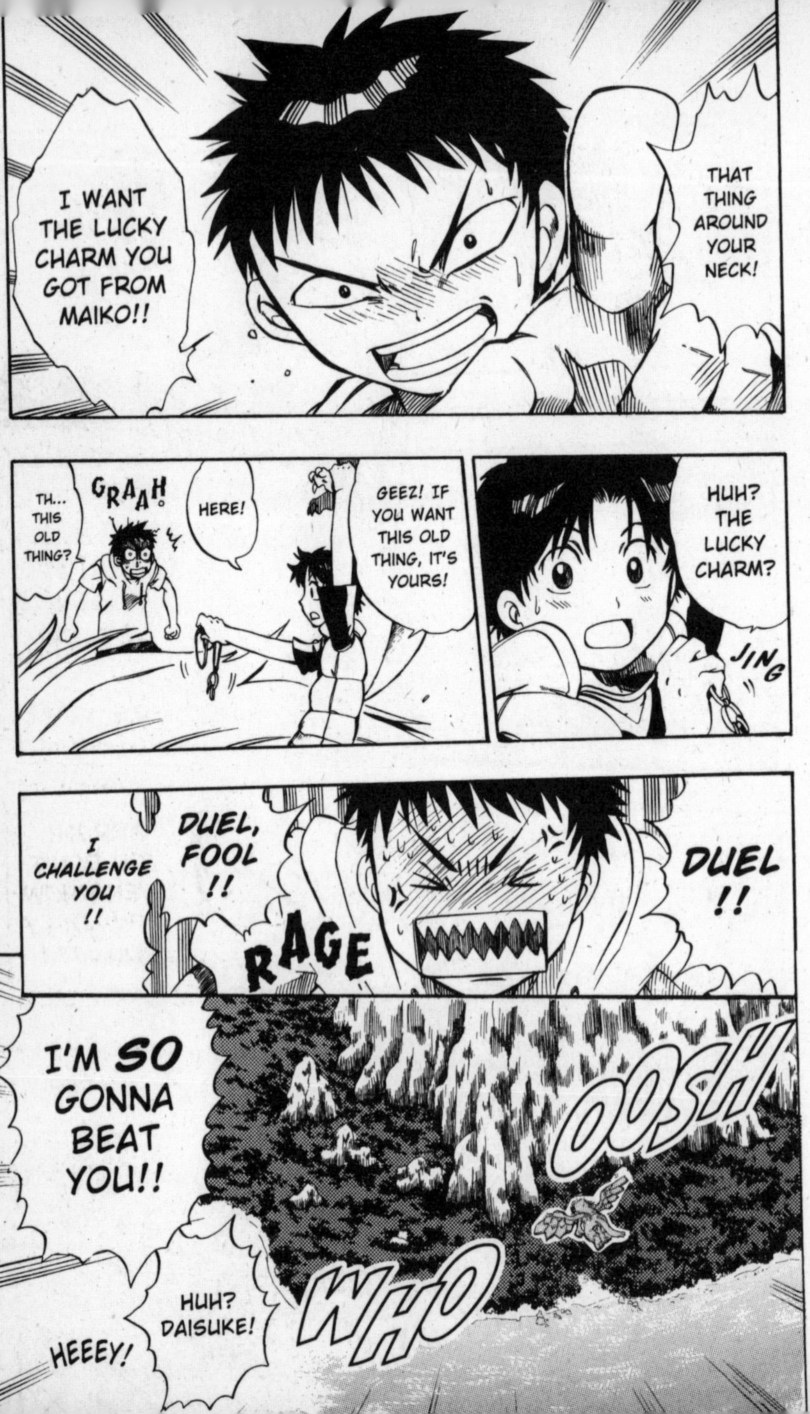
THAT THING AROUND YOUR NECK!
I WANT THE LUCKY CHARM YOU GOT FROM MAIKO!!
HUH? THE LUCKY CHARM?
JING
GEEZ! IF YOU WANT THIS OLD THING, IT'S YOURS!
HERE!
GRAAH!
TH... THIS OLD THING?
DUEL!!
DUEL, FOOL!!
I CHALLENGE YOU!!
RAGE
OOSH
I'M SO GONNA BEAT YOU!!
WHO
HUH? DAISUKE!
HEEEY!

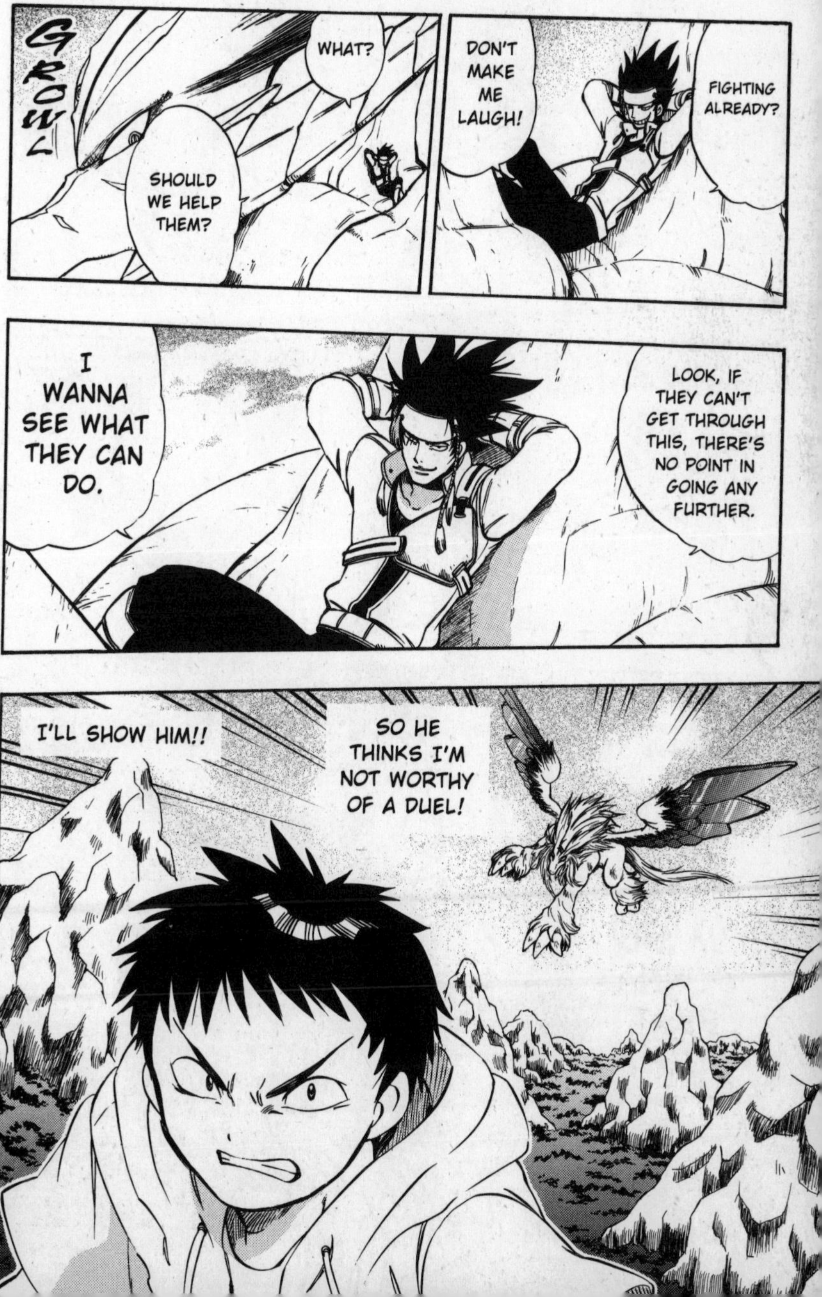
FIGHTING ALREADY?
DON'T MAKE ME LAUGH!
WHAT?
GROWL
SHOULD WE HELP THEM?
LOOK, IF THEY CAN'T GET THROUGH THIS, THERE'S NO POINT IN GOING ANY FURTHER.
I WANNA SEE WHAT THEY CAN DO.
SO HE THINKS I'M NOT WORTHY OF A DUEL!
I'LL SHOW HIM!!

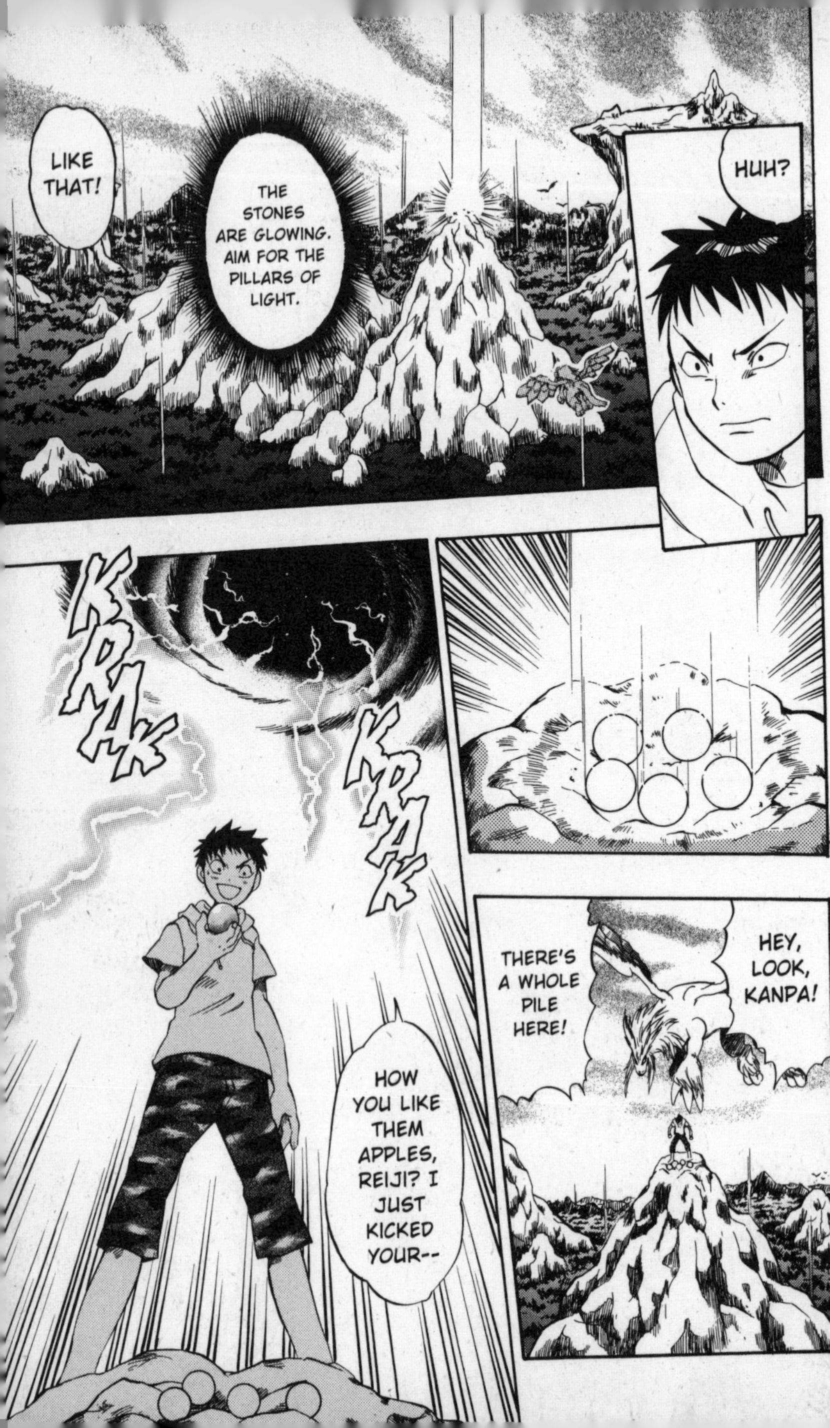
HUH?
THE STONES ARE GLOWING. AIM FOR THE PILLARS OF LIGHT.
LIKE THAT!
HEY, LOOK, KANPA!
THERE'S A WHOLE PILE HERE!
KRAK
KRAK
HOW YOU LIKE THEM APPLES, REIJI? I JUST KICKED YOUR--

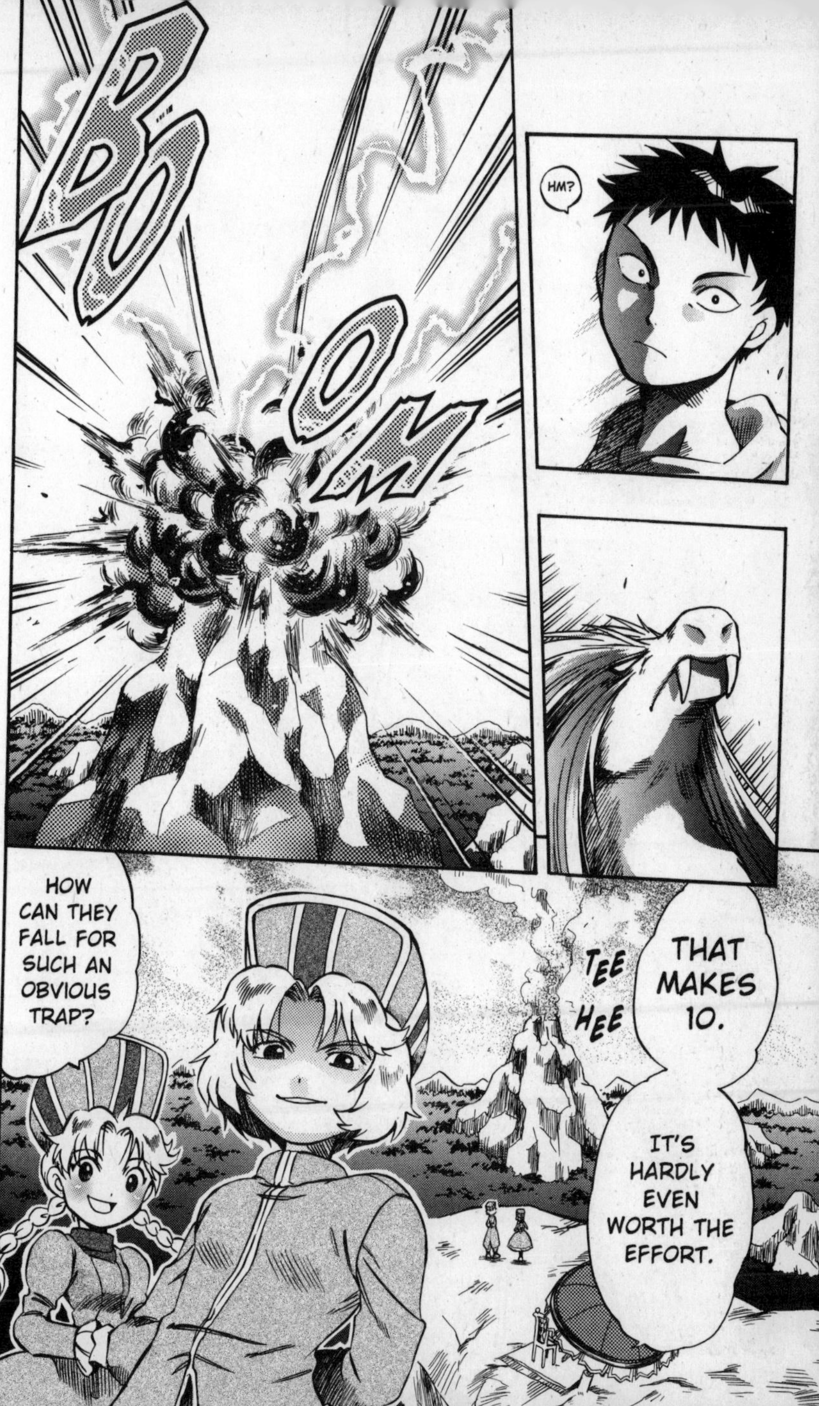
HM?
BOOM
TEE HEE
THAT MAKES 10.
HOW CAN THEY FALL FOR SUCH AN OBVIOUS TRAP?
IT'S HARDLY EVEN WORTH THE EFFORT.

READ THIS WAY

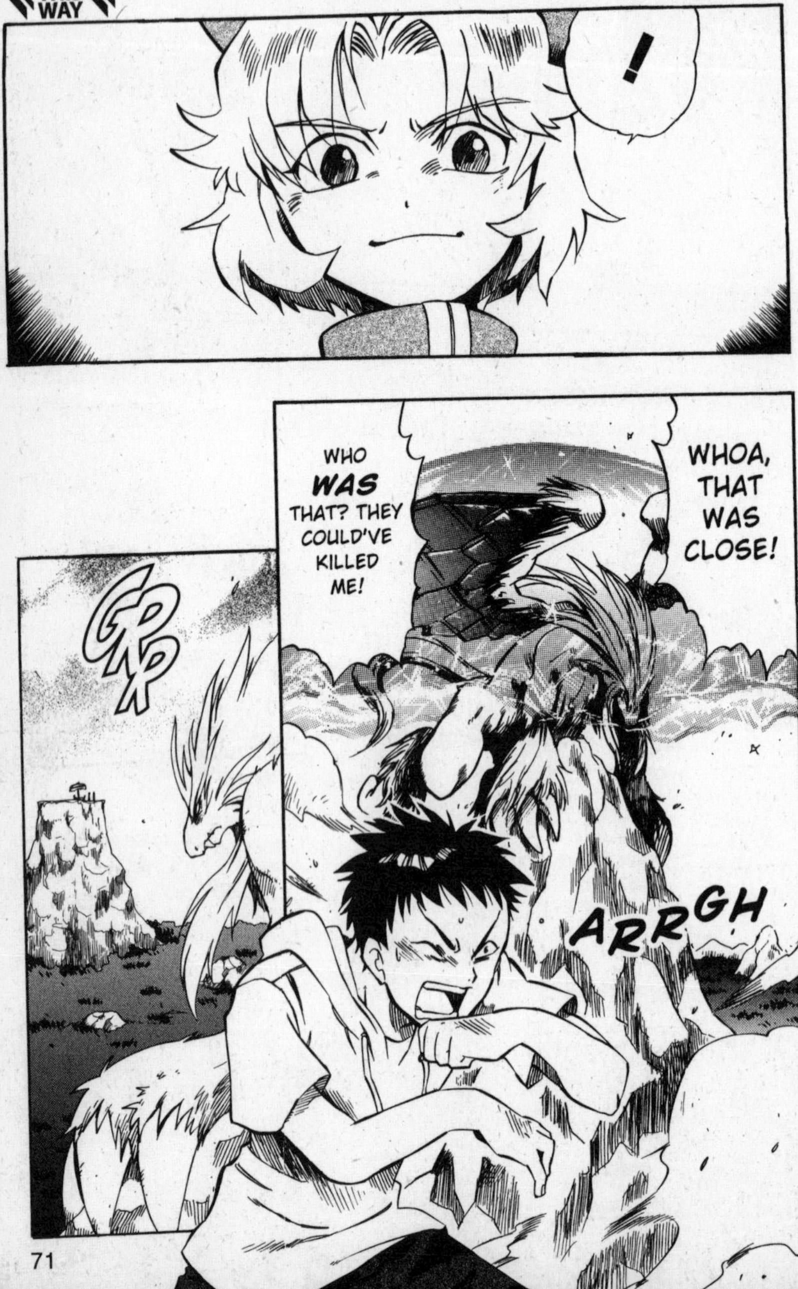
!
WHOA, THAT WAS CLOSE!
WHO WAS THAT? THEY COULD'VE KILLED ME!
ARRGH
GRR

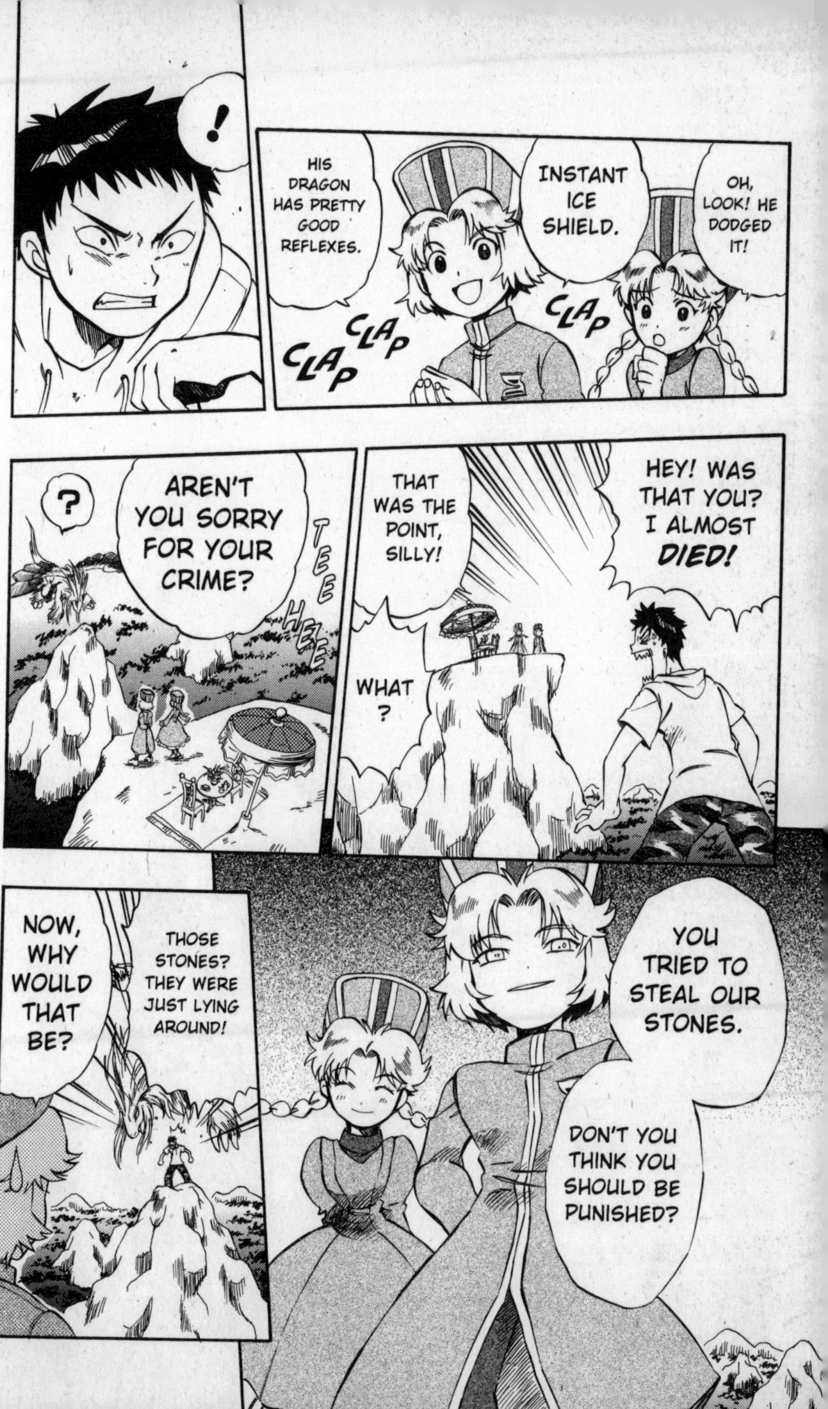
OH, LOOK! HE DODGED IT!
INSTANT ICE SHIELD.
HIS DRAGON HAS PRETTY GOOD REFLEXES.
CLAP
CLAP
CLAP
!
HEY! WAS THAT YOU? I ALMOST DIED!
THAT WAS THE POINT, SILLY!
WHAT?
AREN'T YOU SORRY FOR YOUR CRIME?
TEE HEE
?
YOU TRIED TO STEAL OUR STONES.
DON'T YOU THINK YOU SHOULD BE PUNISHED?
THOSE STONES? THEY WERE JUST LYING AROUND!
NOW, WHY WOULD THAT BE?

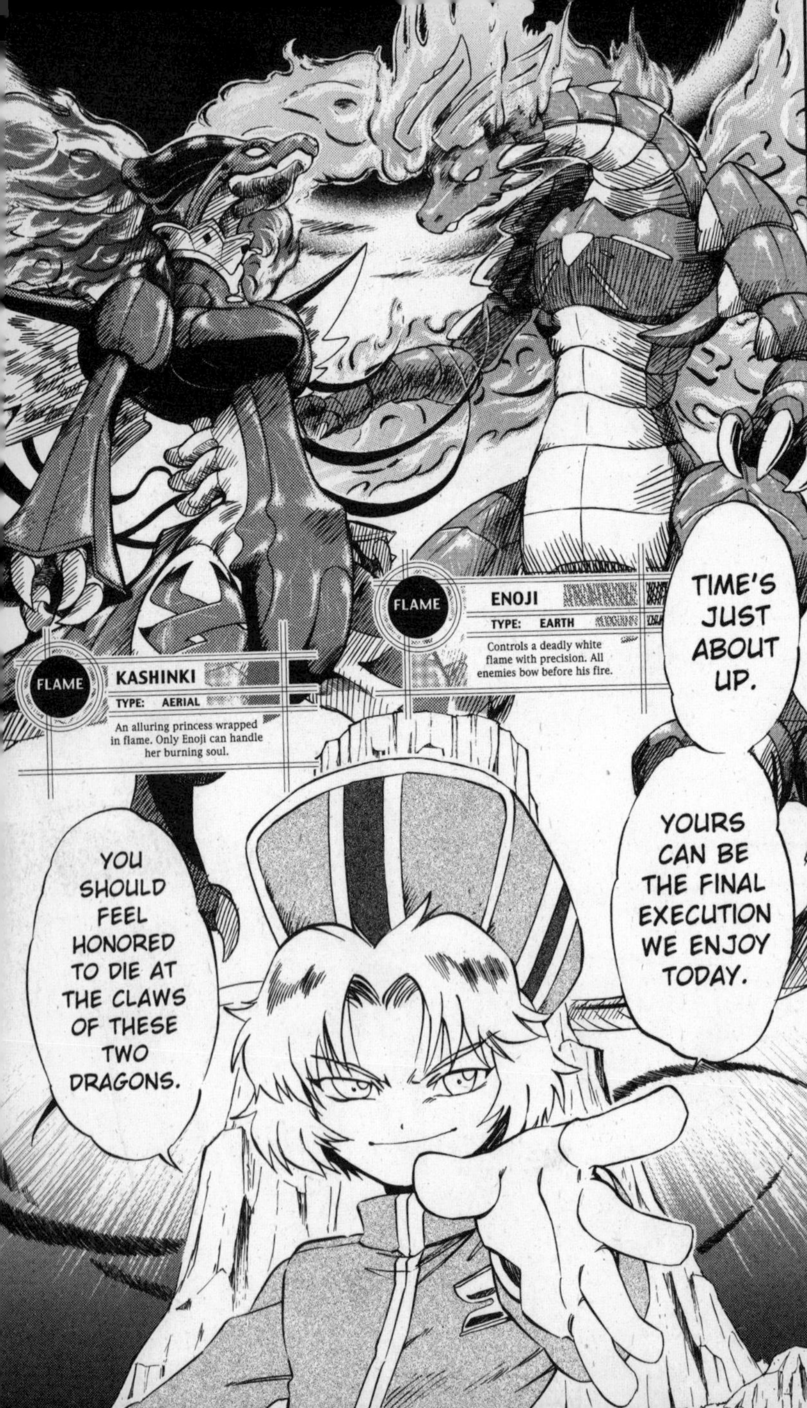
TIME'S JUST ABOUT UP.
FLAME
ENOJI
TYPE: EARTH
Controls a deadly white flame with precision. All enemies bow before his fire.
FLAME
KASHINKI
TYPE: AERIAL
An alluring princess wrapped in flame. Only Enoji can handle her burning soul.
YOURS CAN BE THE FINAL EXECUTION WE ENJOY TODAY.
YOU SHOULD FEEL HONORED TO DIE AT THE CLAWS OF THESE TWO DRAGONS.

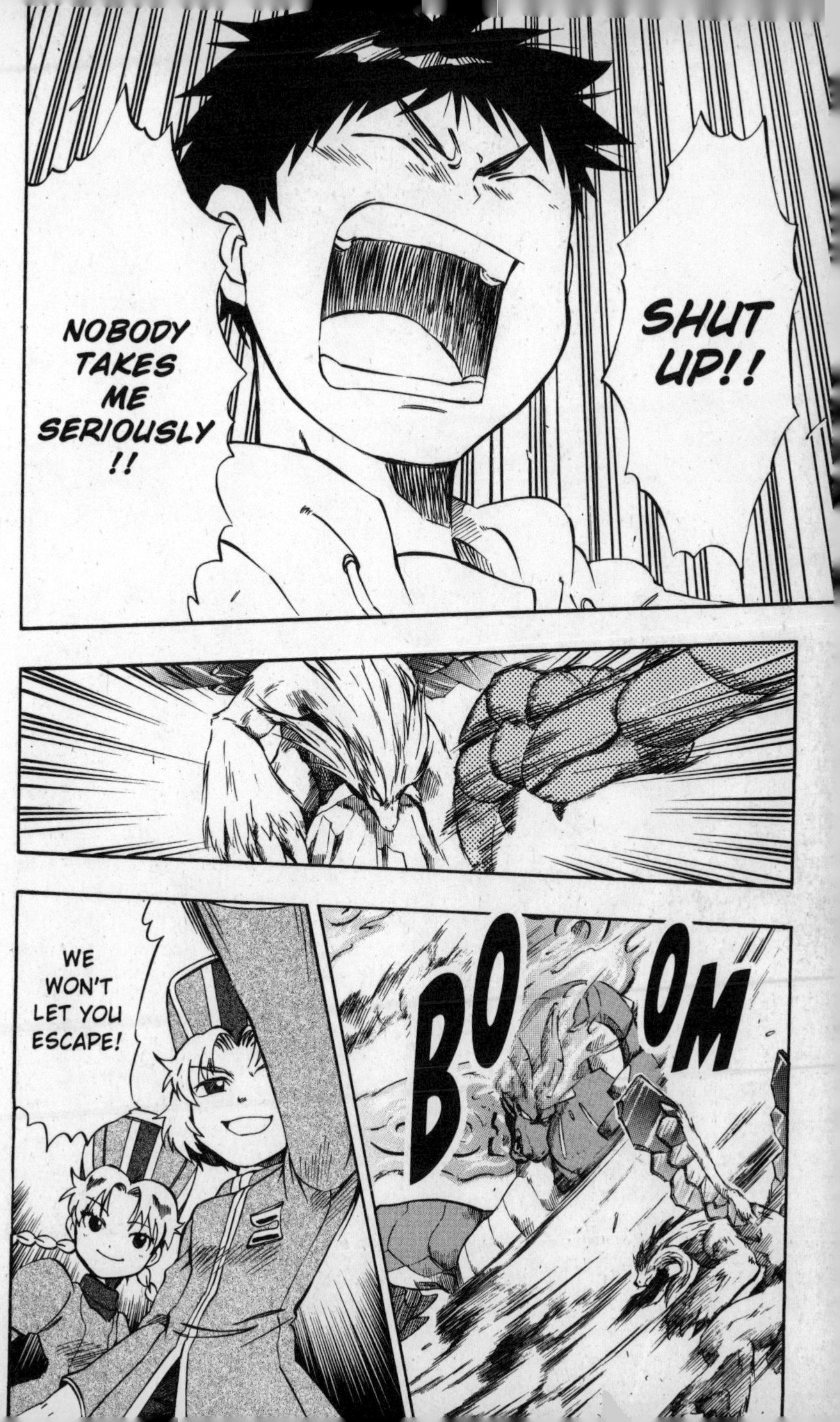
SHUT UP!!
NOBODY TAKES ME SERIOUSLY!!
BOOM
WE WON'T LET YOU ESCAPE!

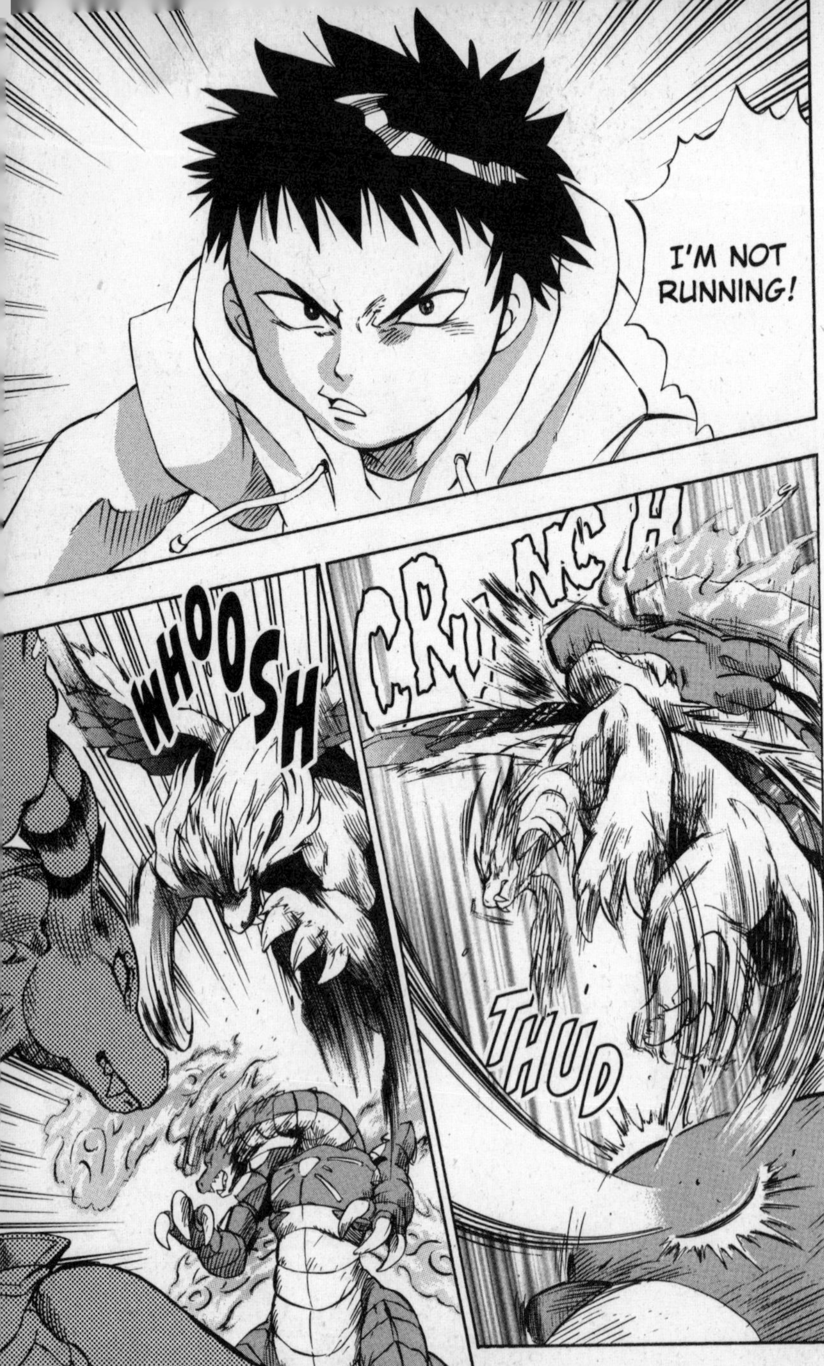
I'M NOT RUNNING!
CRUNCH
THUD
WHOOSH

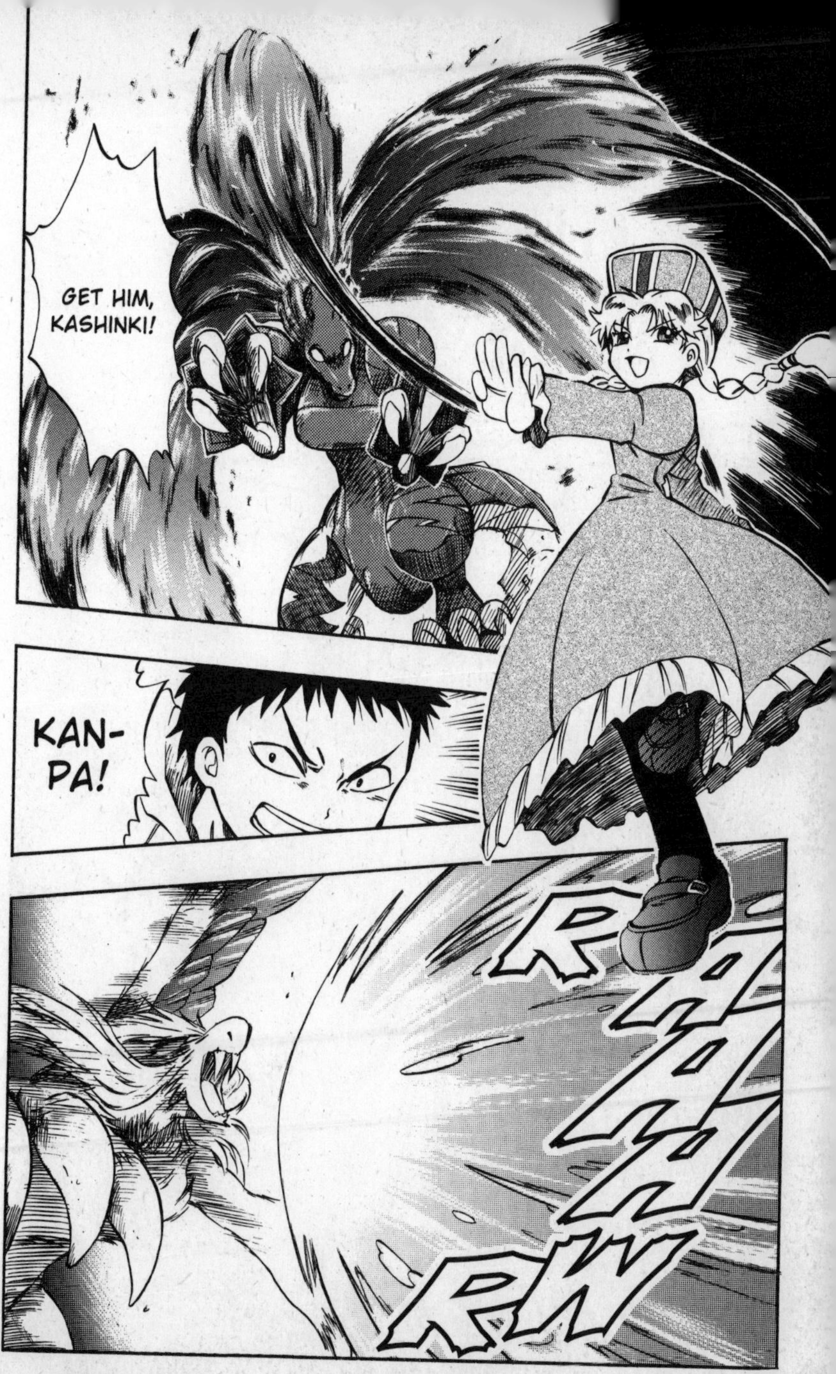
GET HIM, KASHINKI!
KAN-PA!
RRRRAAAWW

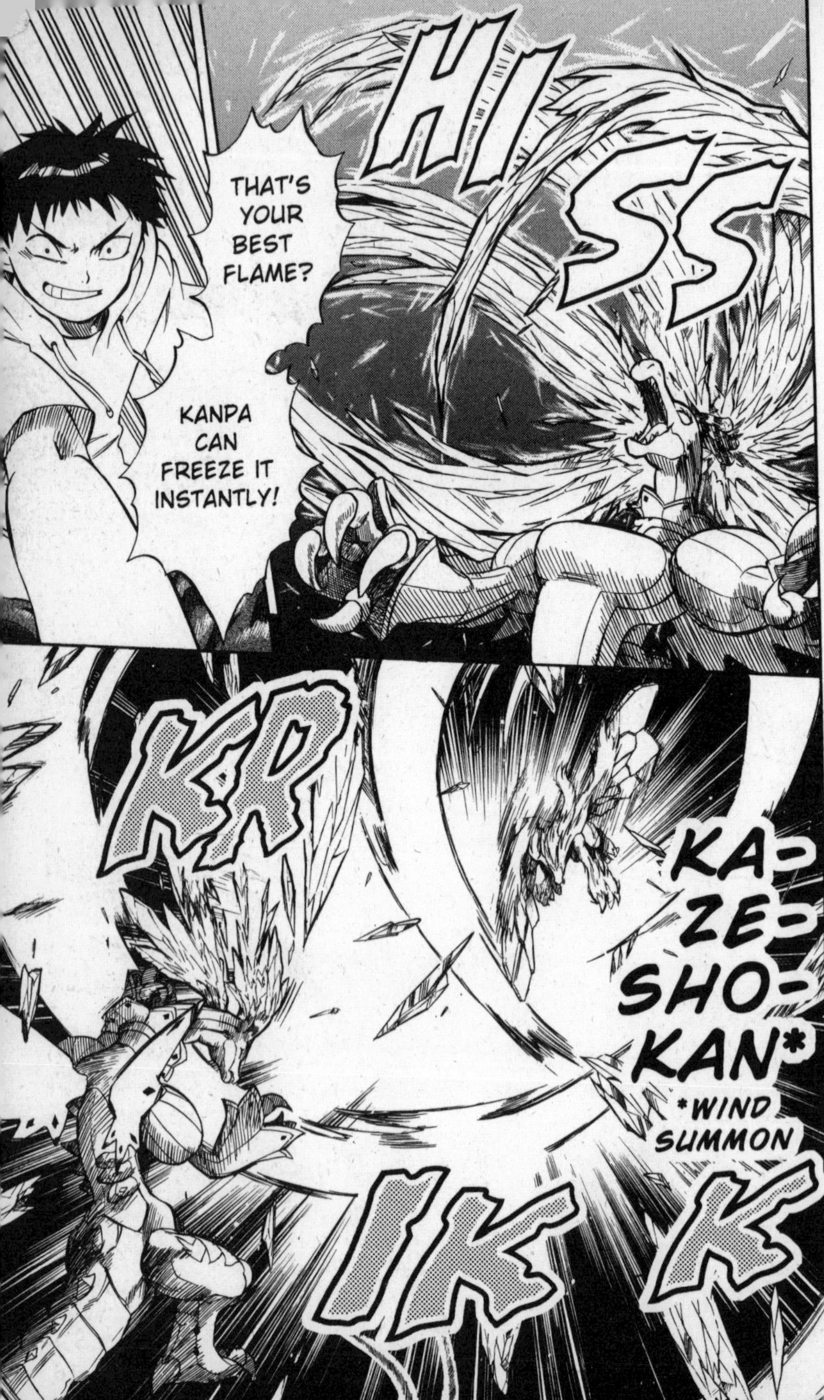
HISS
THAT'S YOUR BEST FLAME?
KANPA CAN FREEZE IT INSTANTLY!
KA-ZE-SHO-KAN*
*WIND SUMMON
KRIKK

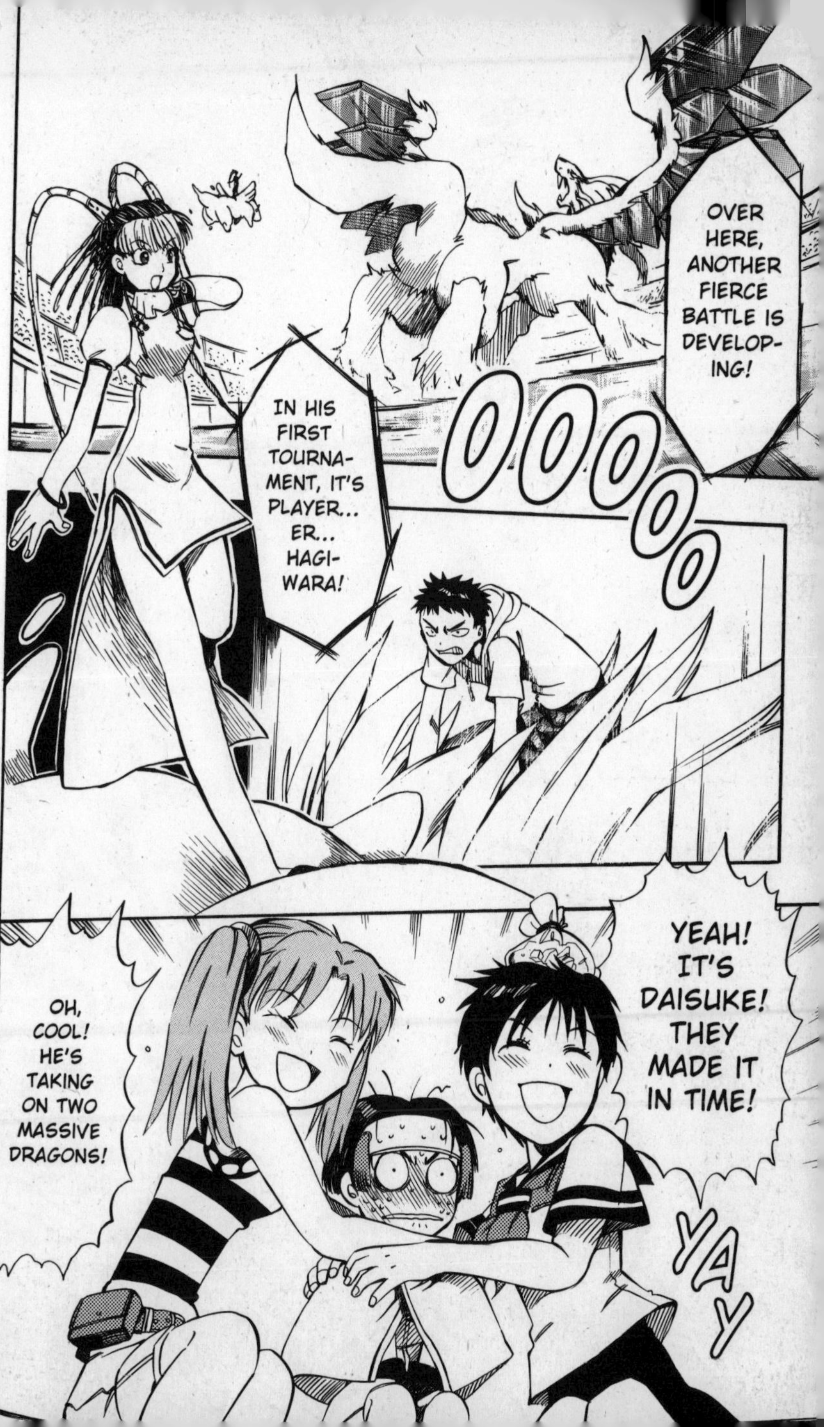
OVER HERE, ANOTHER FIERCE BATTLE IS DEVELOP-ING!
OOOOOO
IN HIS FIRST TOURNA-MENT, IT'S PLAYER... ER... HAGI-WARA!
YEAH! IT'S DAISUKE! THEY MADE IT IN TIME!
YAY
OH, COOL! HE'S TAKING ON TWO MASSIVE DRAGONS!

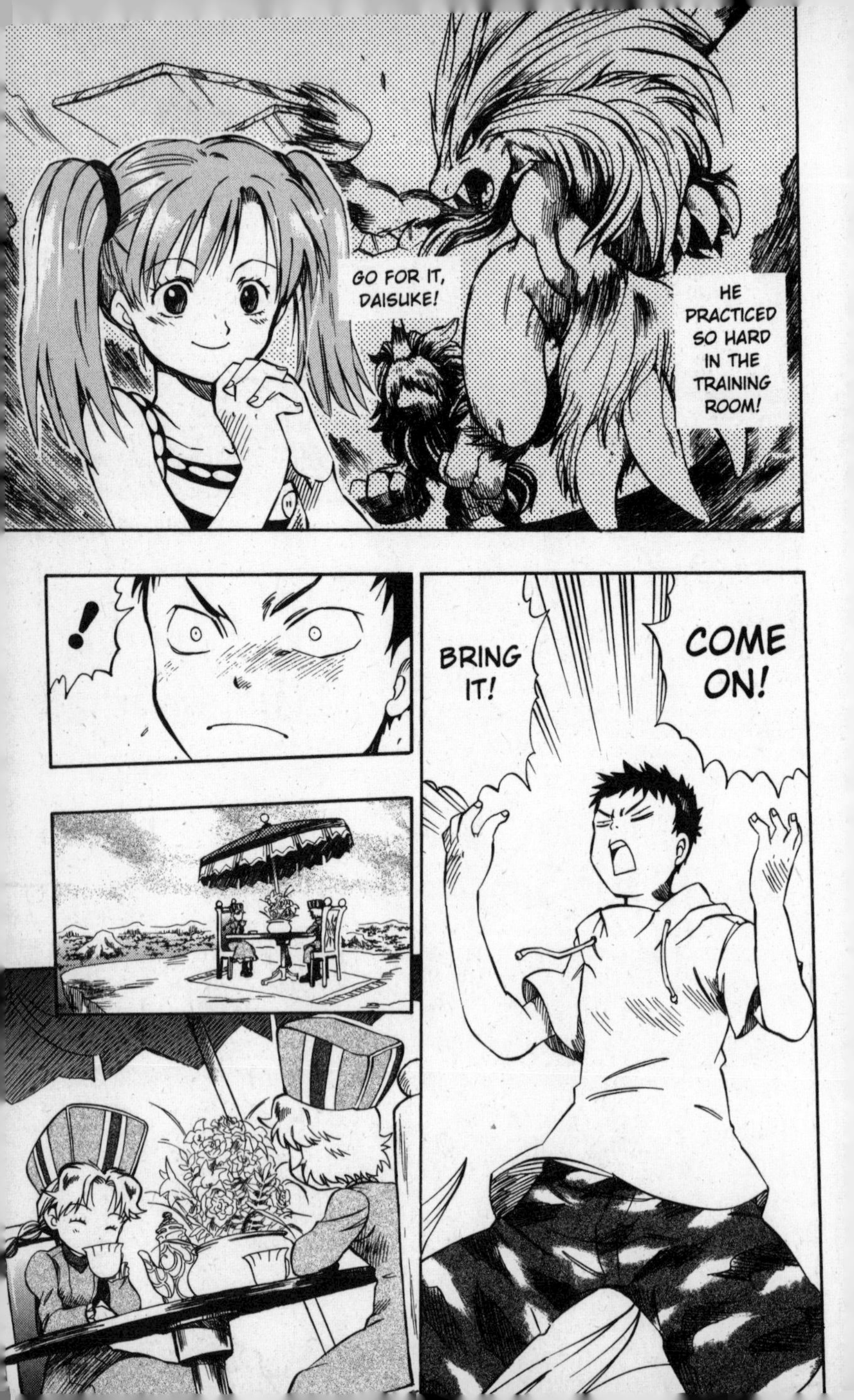
HE PRACTICED SO HARD IN THE TRAINING ROOM!
GO FOR IT, DAISUKE!
COME ON!
BRING IT!
!

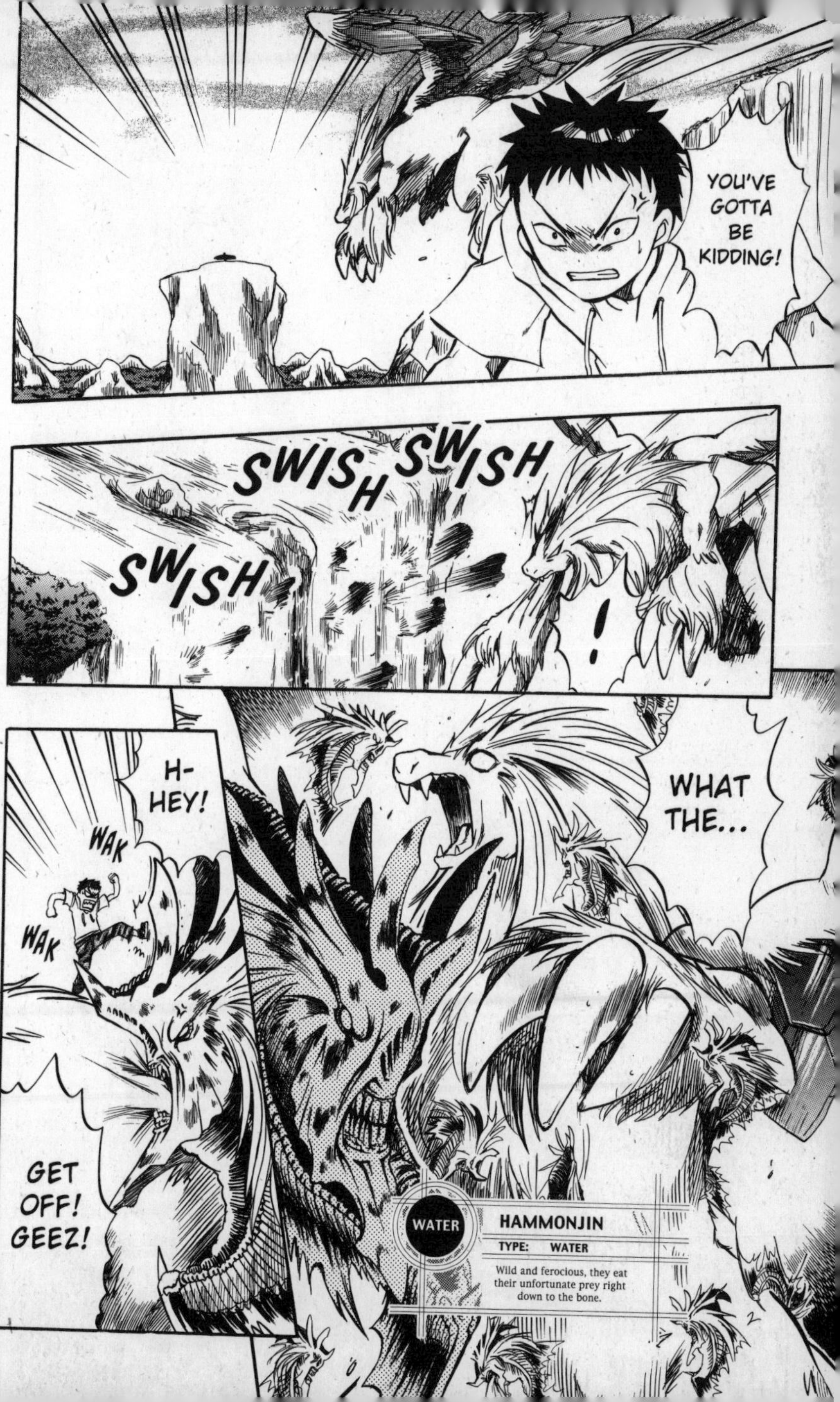
YOU'VE GOTTA BE KIDDING!
SWISH
SWISH
SWISH
!
WHAT THE...
WATER
HAMMONJIN
TYPE: WATER
Wild and ferocious, they eat their unfortunate prey right down to the bone.
H- HEY!
WAK
WAK
GET OFF! GEEZ!

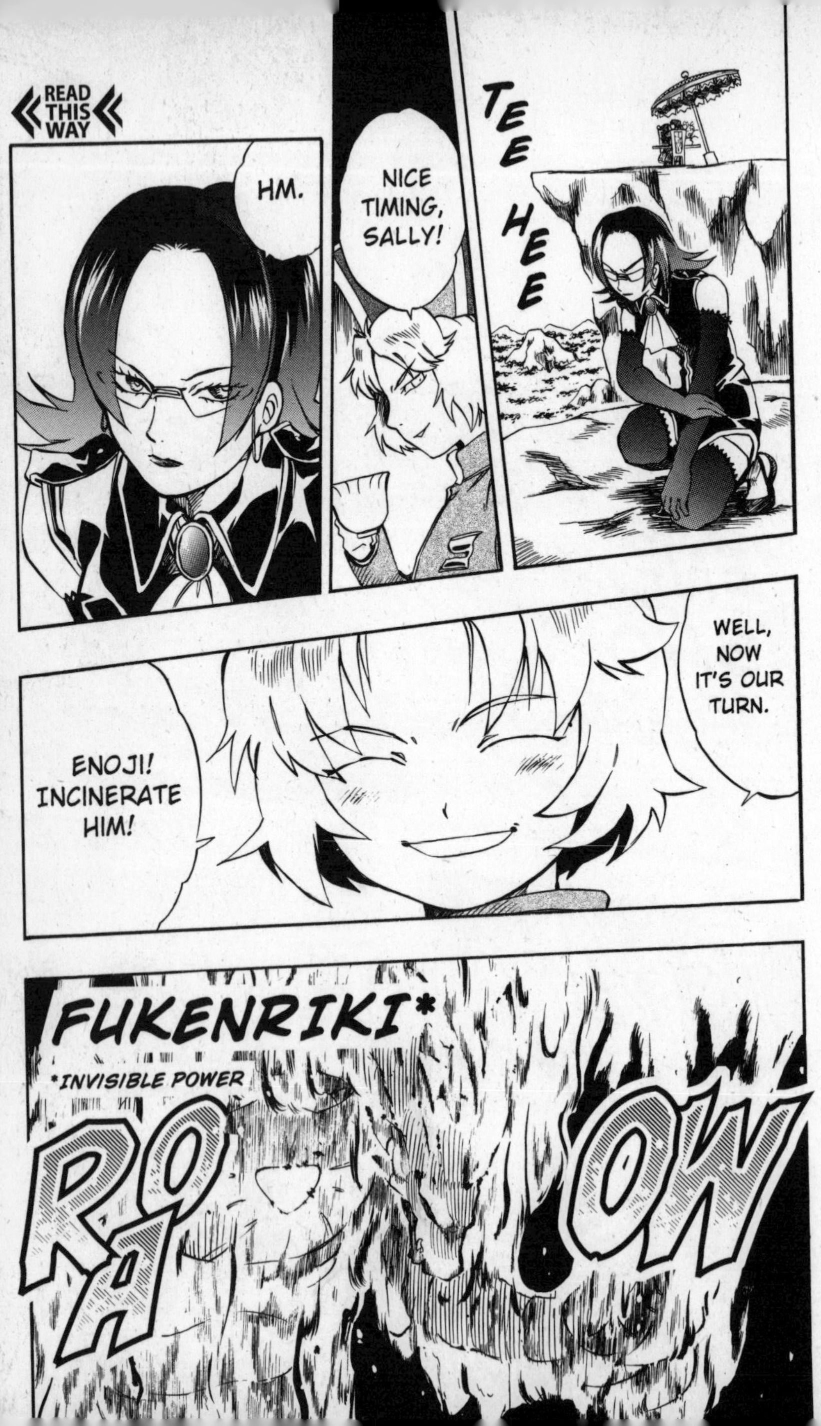
READ THIS WAY
TEE HEE
NICE TIMING, SALLY!
HM.
WELL, NOW IT'S OUR TURN.
ENOJI! INCINERATE HIM!
FUKENRIKI*
*INVISIBLE POWER
ROAOW

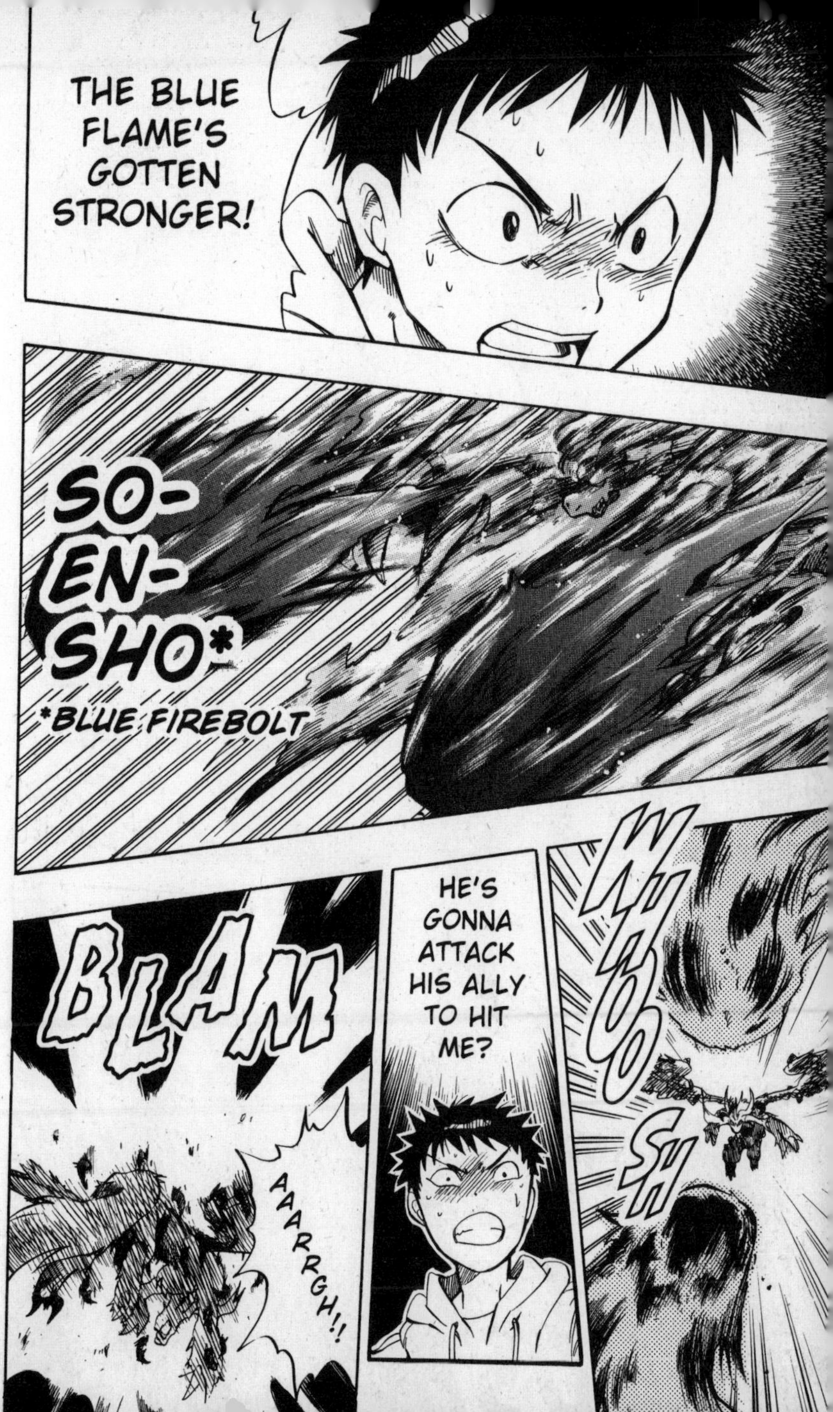
THE BLUE FLAME'S GOTTEN STRONGER!
SO-EN-SHO*
*BLUE FIREBOLT
WHOOSH
HE'S GONNA ATTACK HIS ALLY TO HIT ME?
BLAM
AAARRGH!!

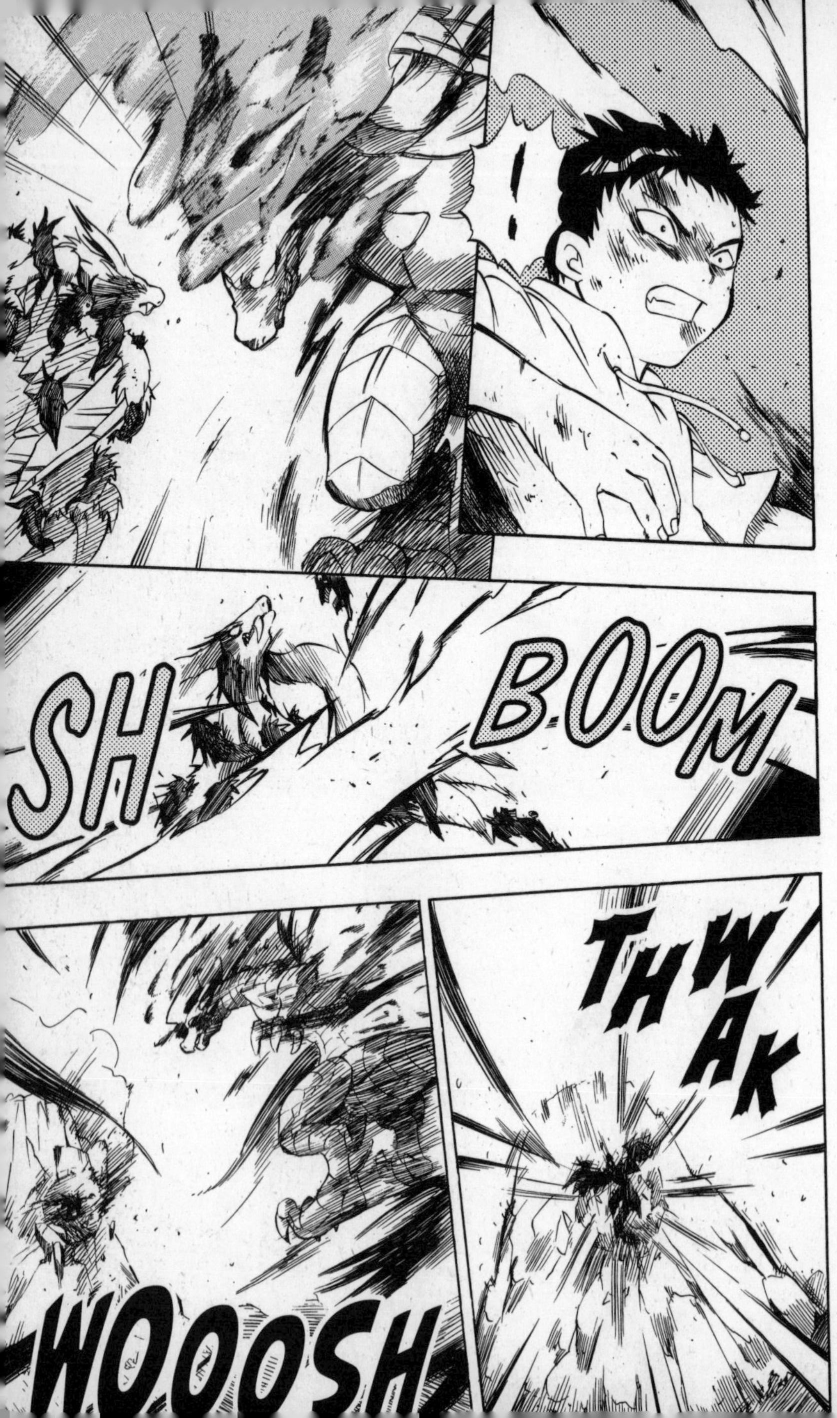
!
SH BOOM
THWAK
WHOOSH

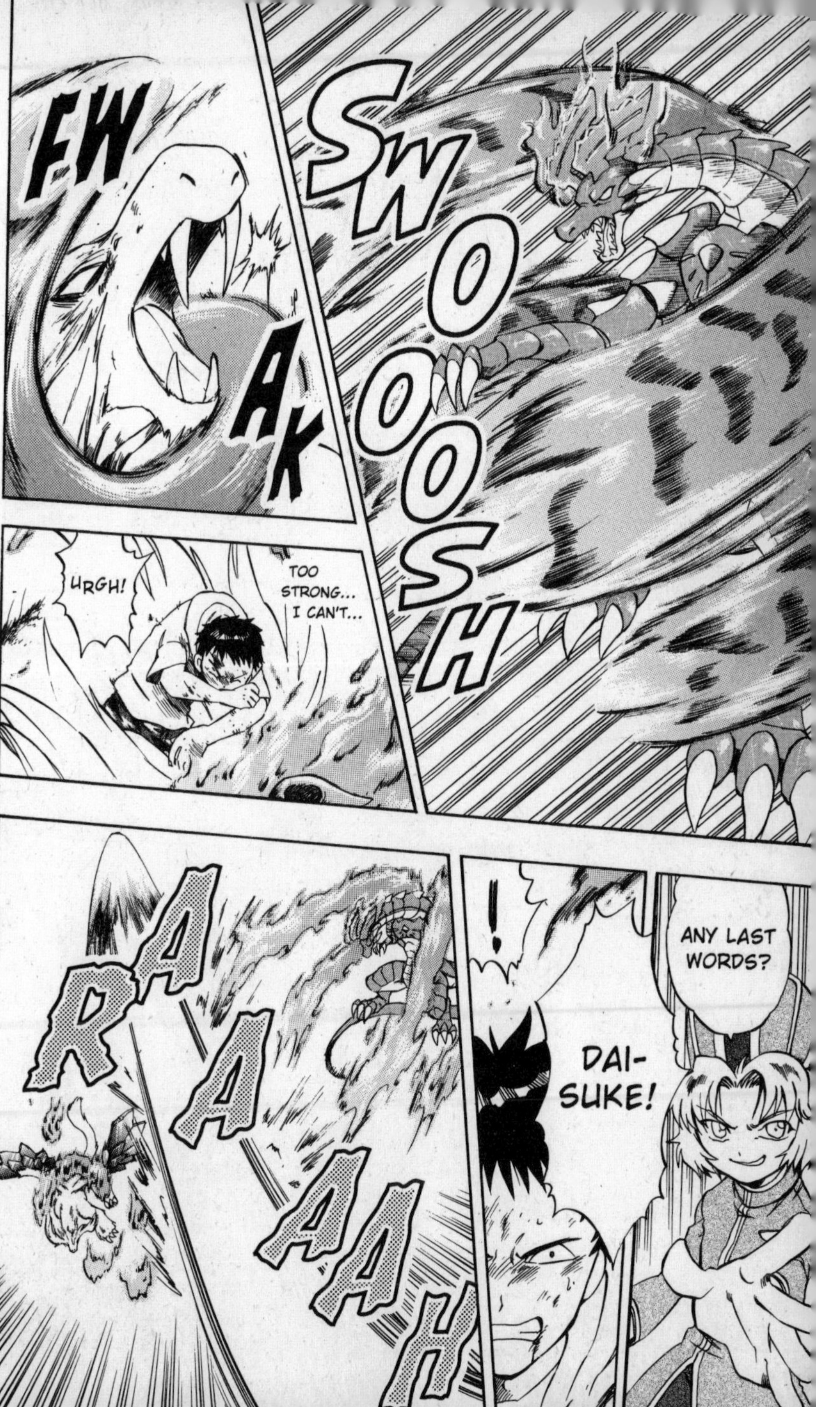
SWOOOOSH
FWAK
TOO STRONG... I CAN'T...
URGH!
ANY LAST WORDS?
!
DAI-SUKE!
RAAAAAH

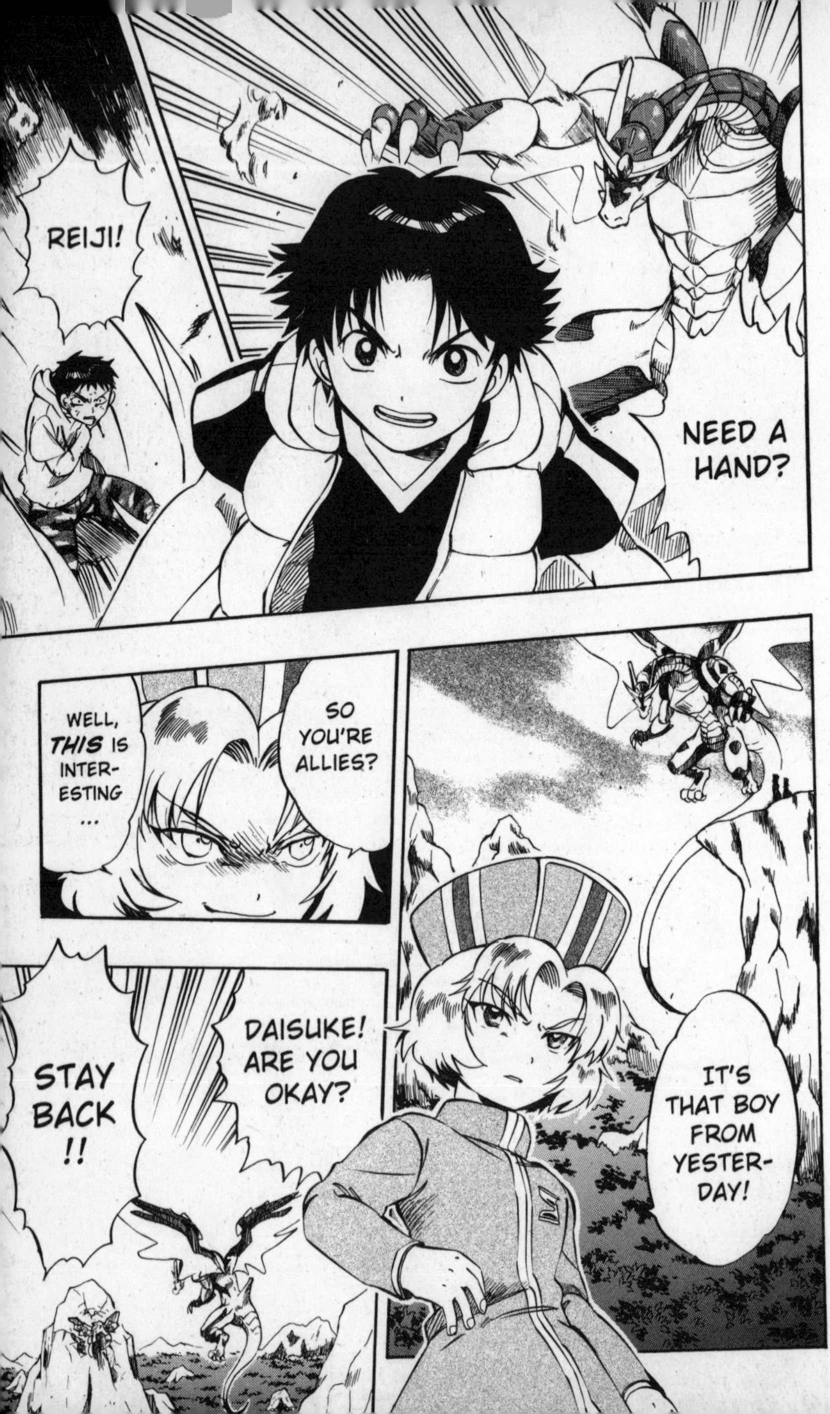
NEED A HAND?
REIJI!
IT'S THAT BOY FROM YESTER-DAY!
SO YOU'RE ALLIES?
WELL, *THIS* IS INTER-ESTING ...
DAISUKE! ARE YOU OKAY?
STAY BACK !!

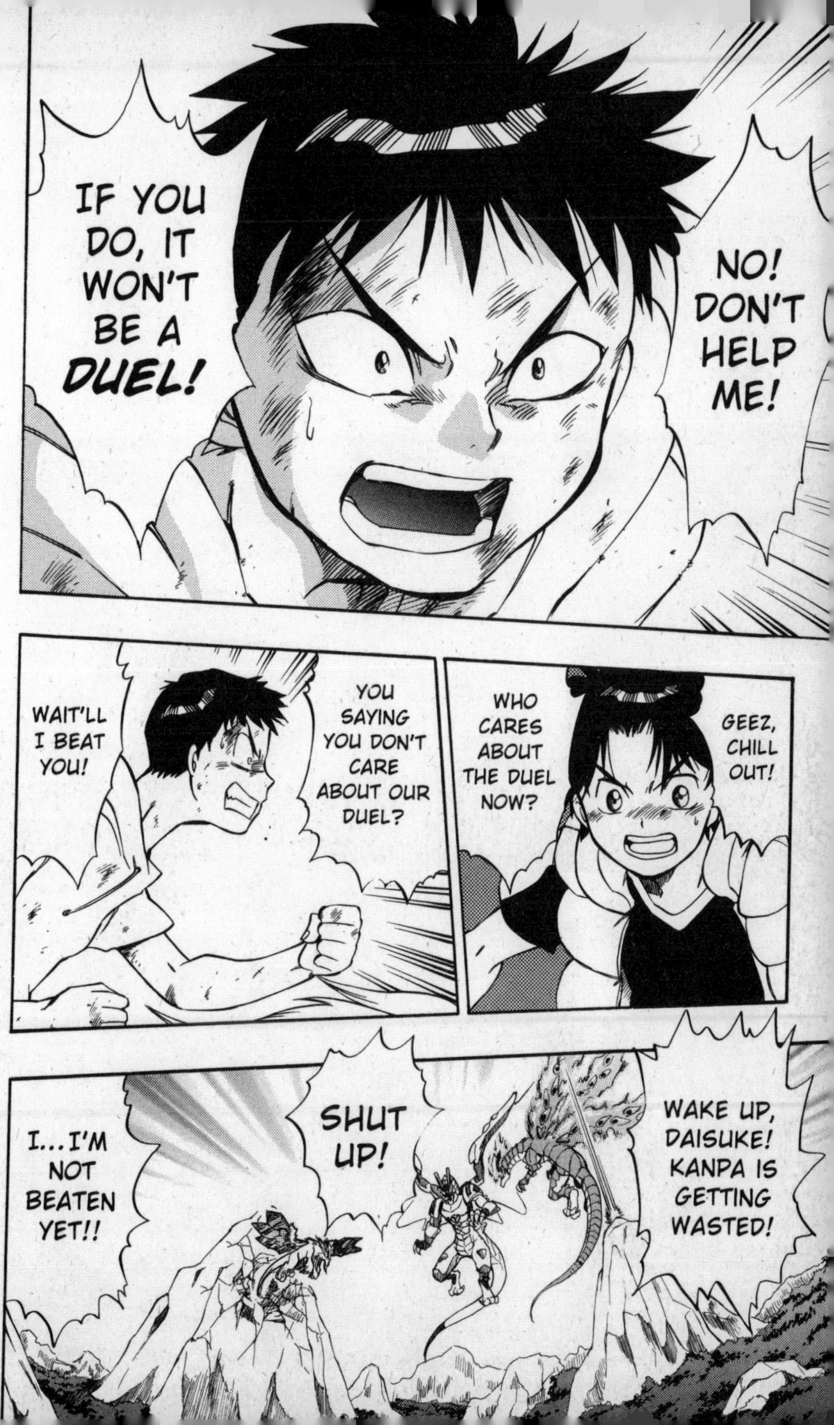
NO! DON'T HELP ME!
IF YOU DO, IT WON'T BE A DUEL!
GEEZ, CHILL OUT!
WHO CARES ABOUT THE DUEL NOW?
YOU SAYING YOU DON'T CARE ABOUT OUR DUEL?
WAIT'LL I BEAT YOU!
WAKE UP, DAISUKE! KANPA IS GETTING WASTED!
SHUT UP!
I...I'M NOT BEATEN YET!!

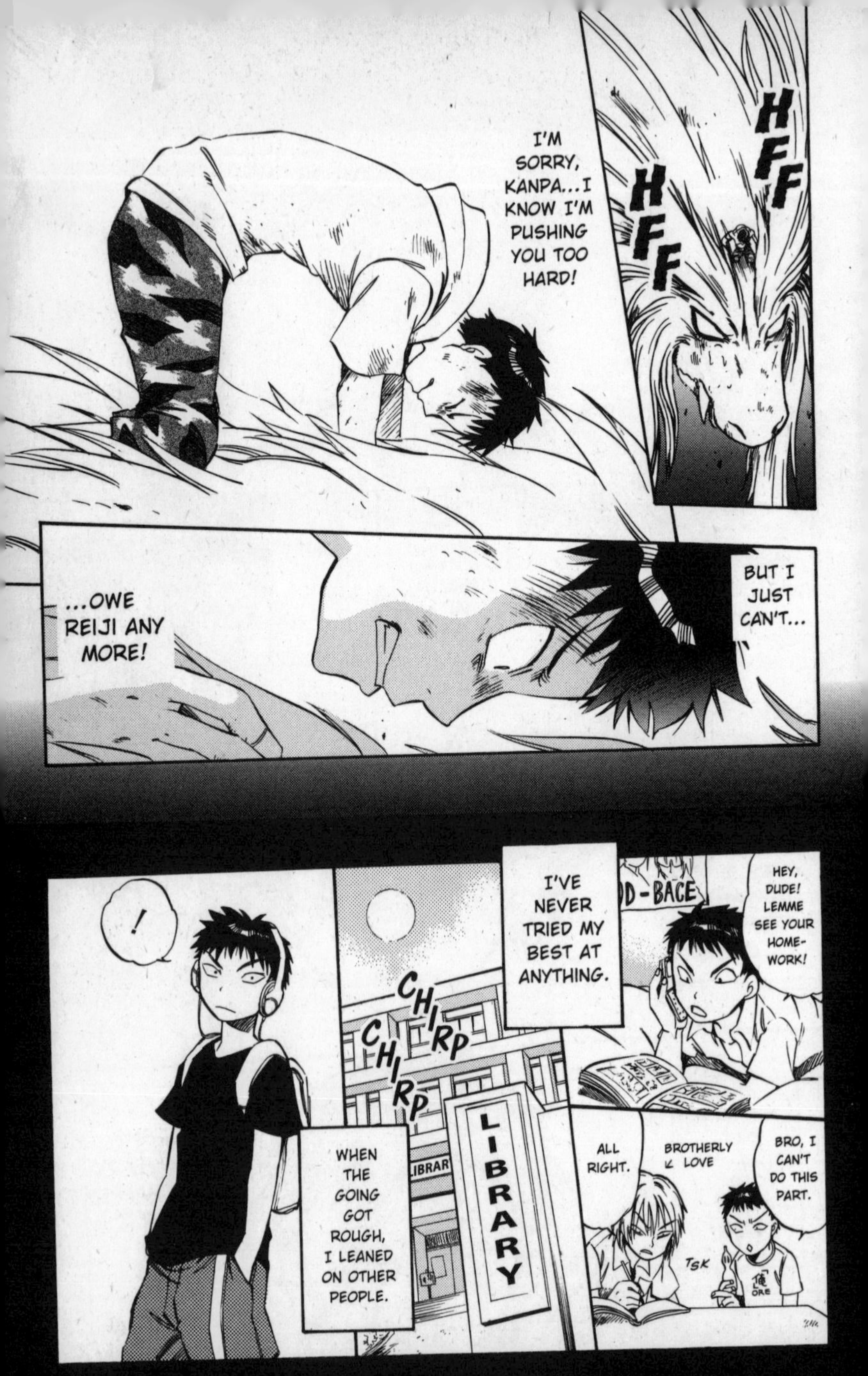
HFF HFF
I'M SORRY, KANPA...I KNOW I'M PUSHING YOU TOO HARD!
BUT I JUST CAN'T...
...OWE REIJI ANY MORE!
I'VE NEVER TRIED MY BEST AT ANYTHING.
HEY, DUDE! LEMME SEE YOUR HOME-WORK!
BRO, I CAN'T DO THIS PART.
BROTHERLY LOVE
ALL RIGHT.
TSK
CHIRP CHIRP
LIBRARY
WHEN THE GOING GOT ROUGH, I LEANED ON OTHER PEOPLE.
!

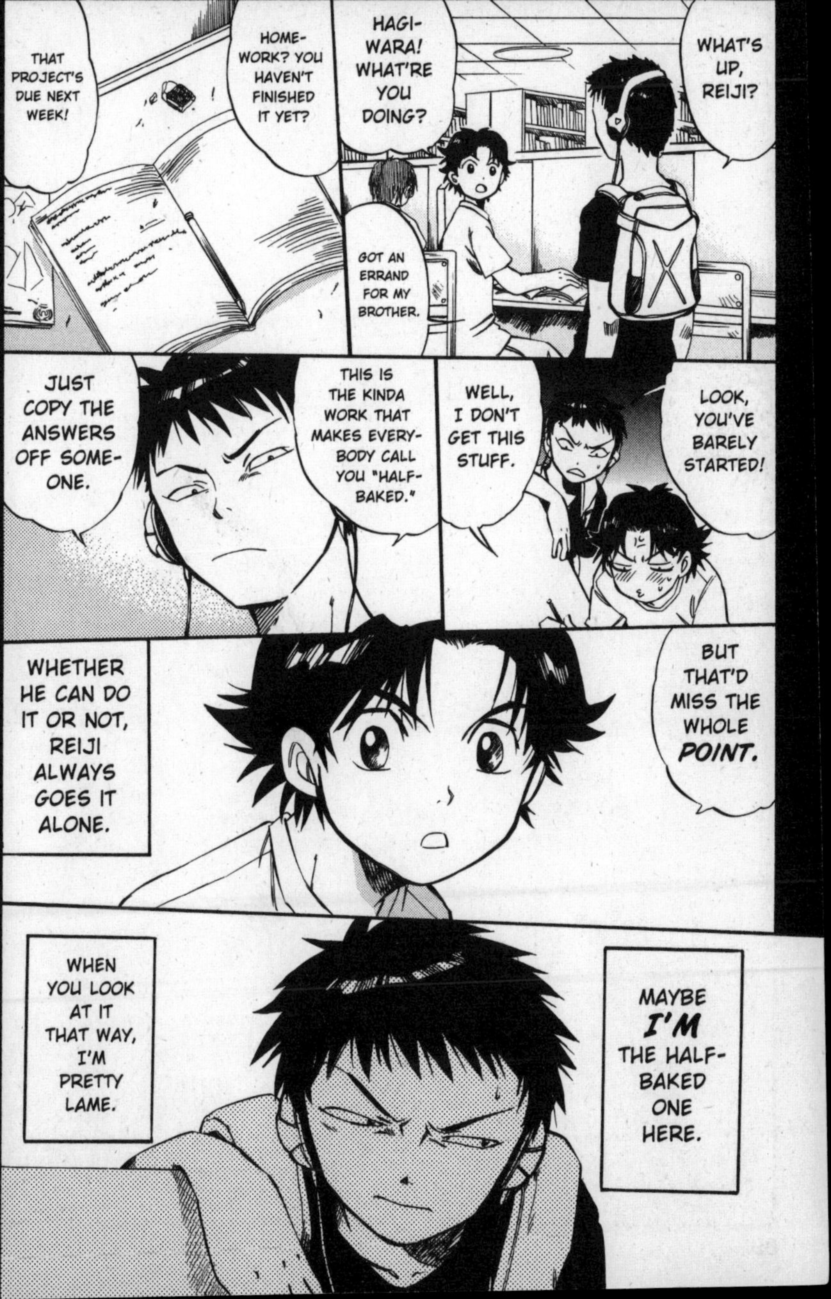
WHAT'S UP, REIJI?
HAGI-WARA! WHAT'RE YOU DOING?
GOT AN ERRAND FOR MY BROTHER.
HOME-WORK? YOU HAVEN'T FINISHED IT YET?
THAT PROJECT'S DUE NEXT WEEK!
LOOK, YOU'VE BARELY STARTED!
WELL, I DON'T GET THIS STUFF.
THIS IS THE KINDA WORK THAT MAKES EVERY-BODY CALL YOU "HALF-BAKED."
JUST COPY THE ANSWERS OFF SOME-ONE.
BUT THAT'D MISS THE WHOLE *POINT*.
WHETHER HE CAN DO IT OR NOT, REIJI ALWAYS GOES IT ALONE.
MAYBE ***I'M*** THE HALF-BAKED ONE HERE.
WHEN YOU LOOK AT IT THAT WAY, I'M PRETTY LAME.

READ THIS WAY

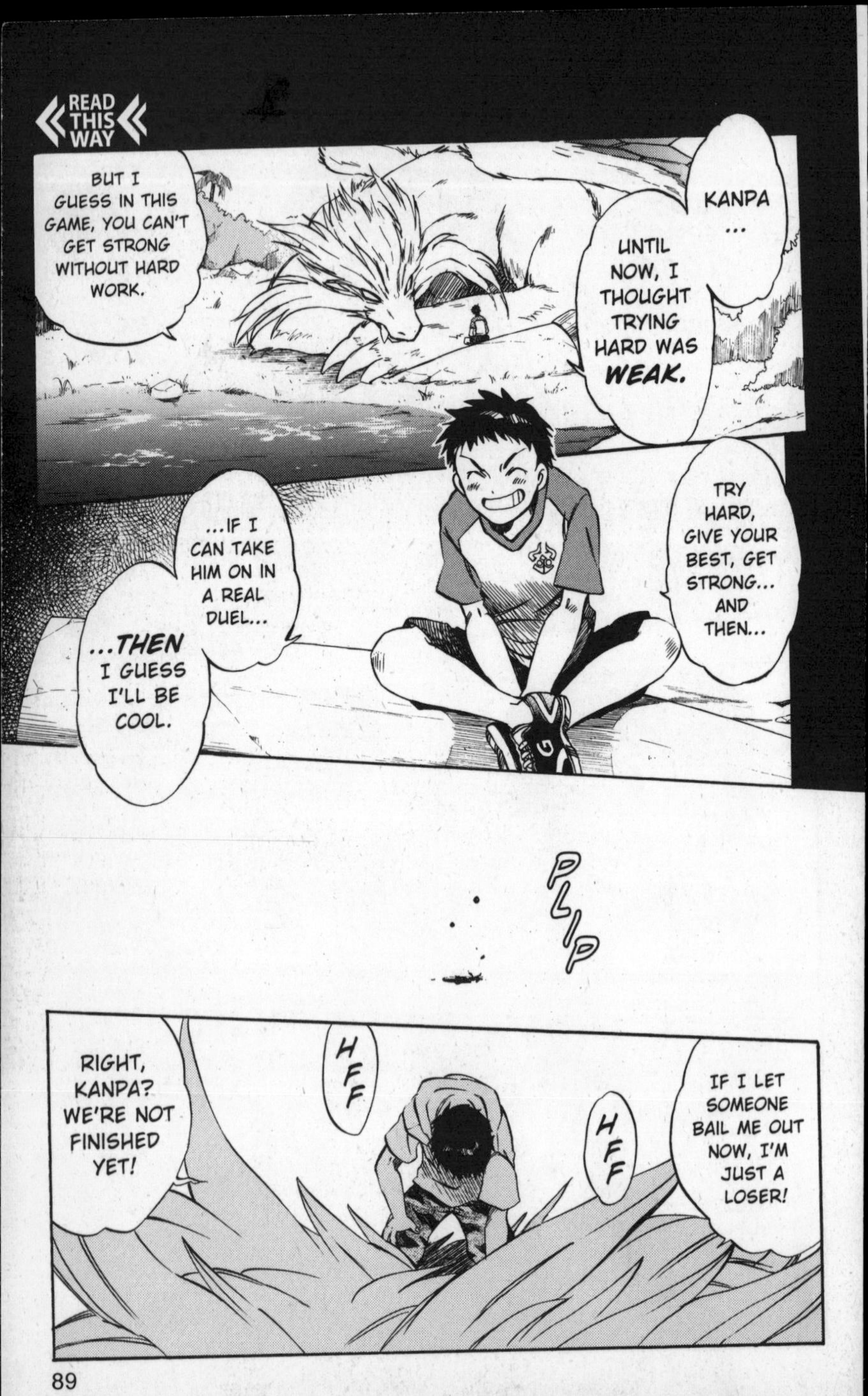
KANPA ...
UNTIL NOW, I THOUGHT TRYING HARD WAS WEAK.
BUT I GUESS IN THIS GAME, YOU CAN'T GET STRONG WITHOUT HARD WORK.
TRY HARD, GIVE YOUR BEST, GET STRONG... AND THEN...
...IF I CAN TAKE HIM ON IN A REAL DUEL...
...THEN I GUESS I'LL BE COOL.
PLIP
IF I LET SOMEONE BAIL ME OUT NOW, I'M JUST A LOSER!
HFF
HFF
RIGHT, KANPA? WE'RE NOT FINISHED YET!

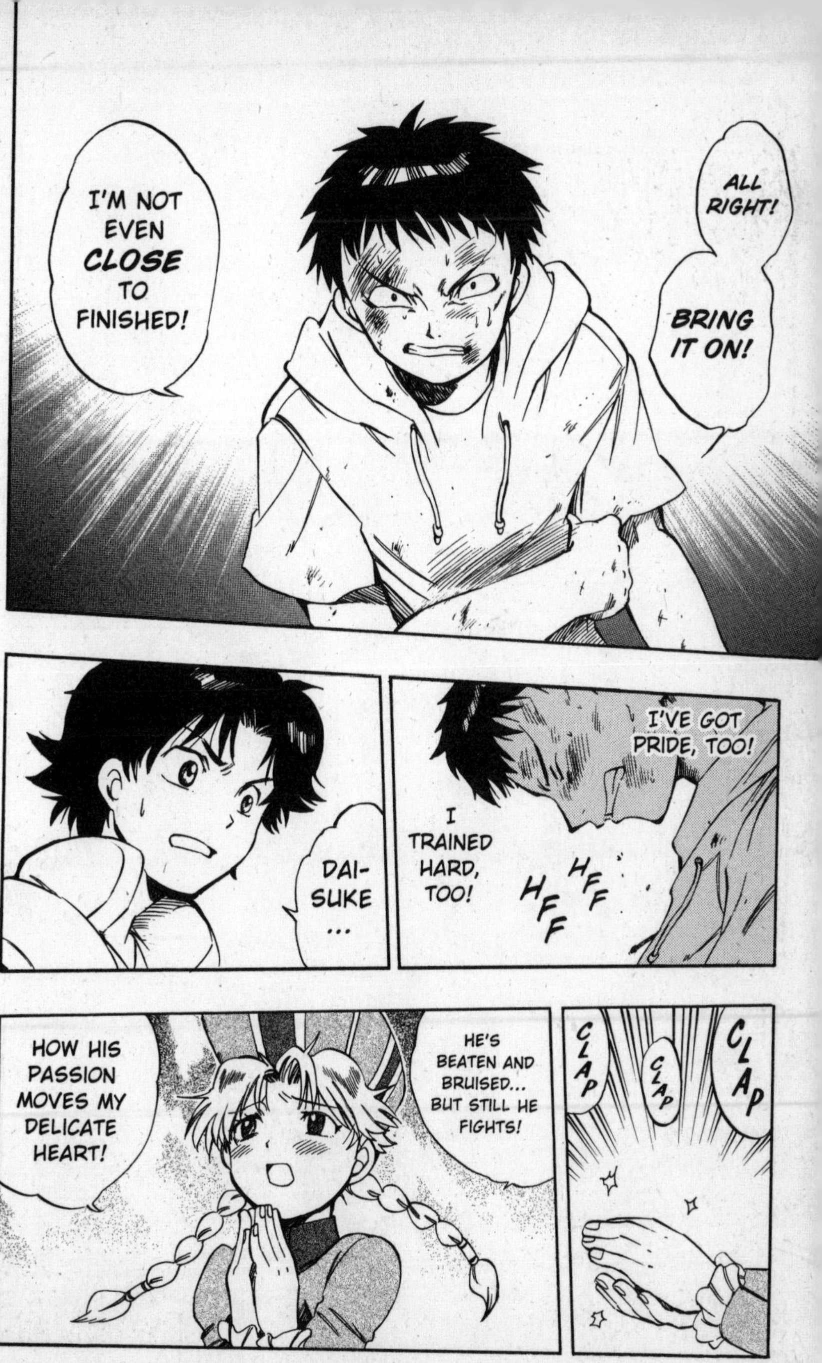
ALL RIGHT!
BRING IT ON!
I'M NOT EVEN CLOSE TO FINISHED!
I'VE GOT PRIDE, TOO!
HFF HFF
I TRAINED HARD, TOO!
DAI-SUKE...
CLAP CLAP CLAP
HE'S BEATEN AND BRUISED... BUT STILL HE FIGHTS!
HOW HIS PASSION MOVES MY DELICATE HEART!

READ THIS WAY

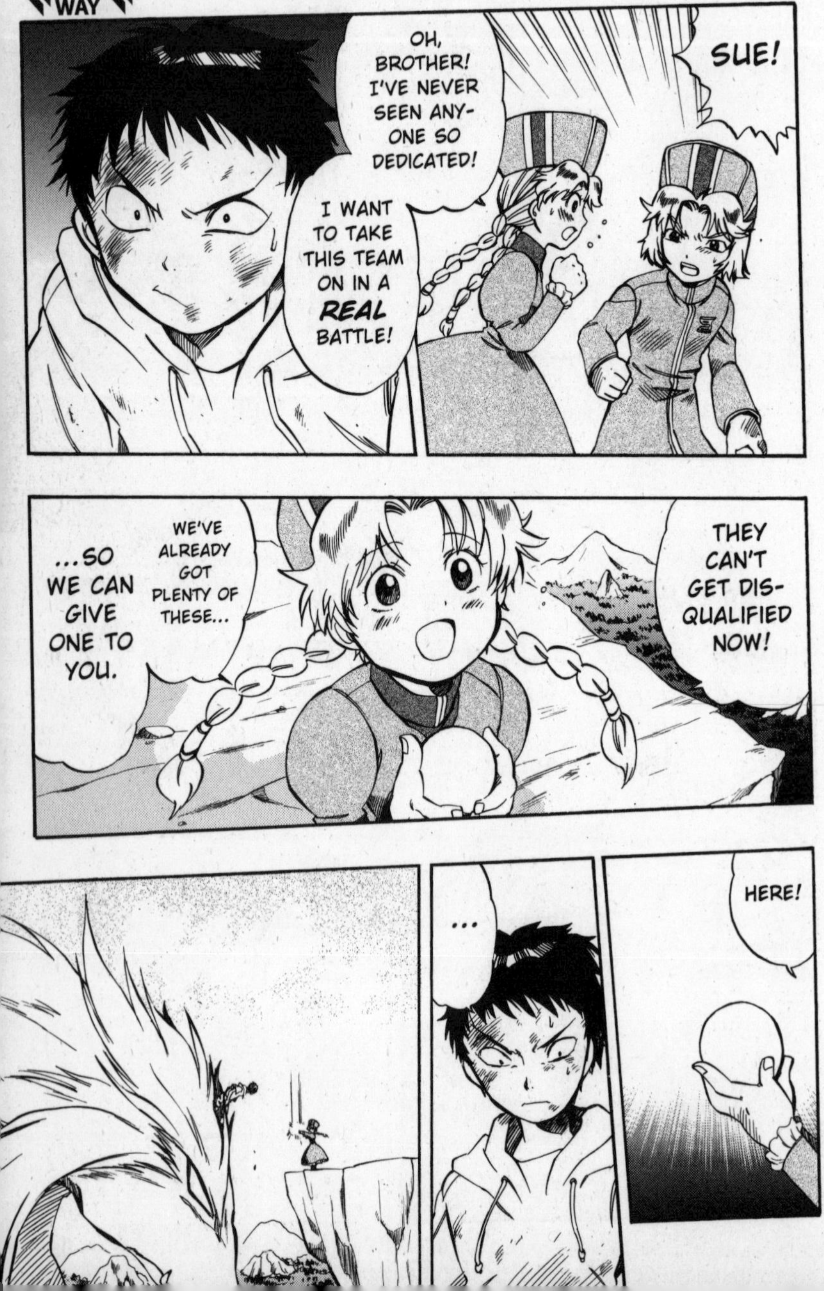

SUE!
OH, BROTHER! I'VE NEVER SEEN ANY-ONE SO DEDICATED!
I WANT TO TAKE THIS TEAM ON IN A REAL BATTLE!
THEY CAN'T GET DIS-QUALIFIED NOW!
WE'VE ALREADY GOT PLENTY OF THESE...
...SO WE CAN GIVE ONE TO YOU.
HERE!
...

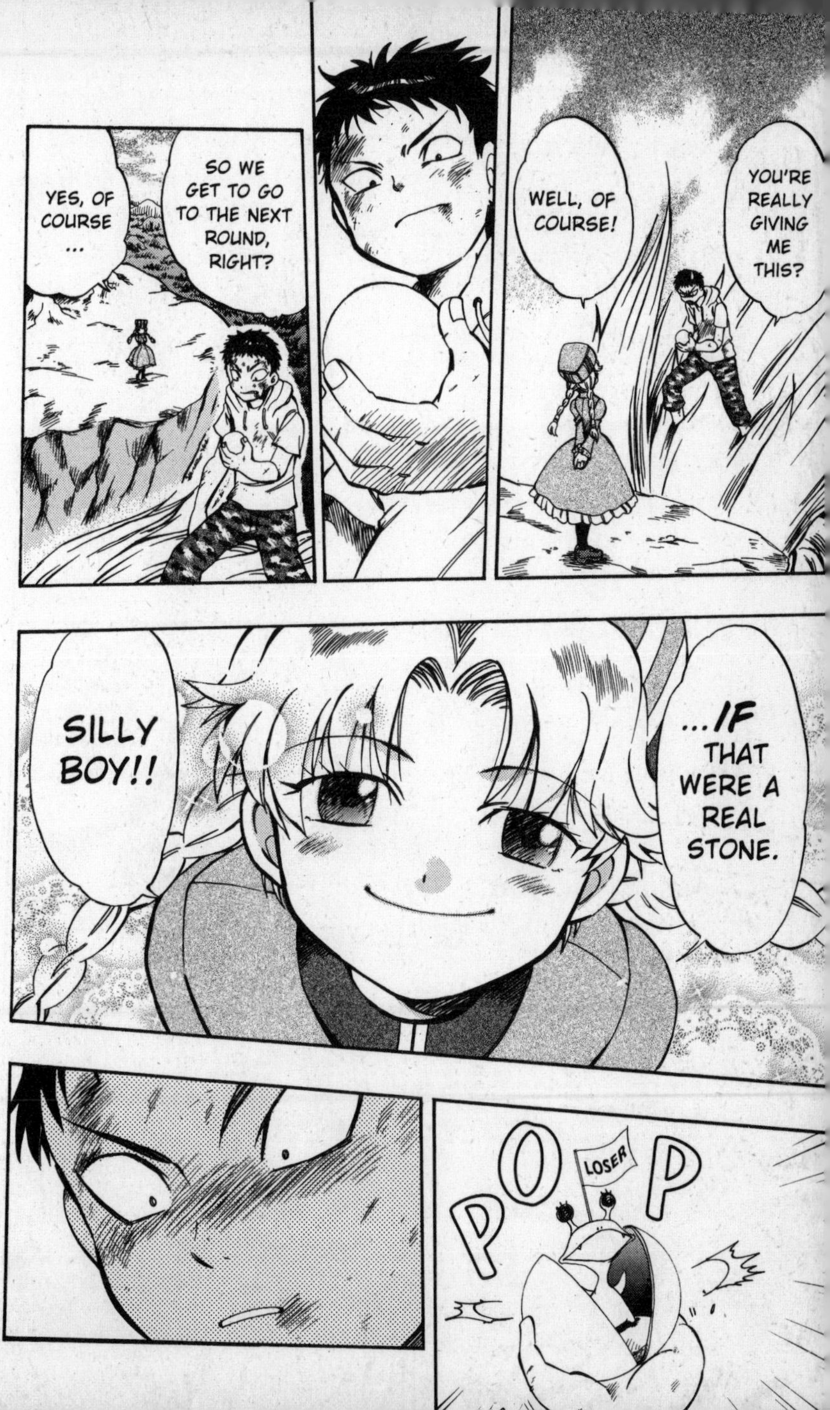
YOU'RE REALLY GIVING ME THIS?
WELL, OF COURSE!
SO WE GET TO GO TO THE NEXT ROUND, RIGHT?
YES, OF COURSE ...
...IF THAT WERE A REAL STONE.
SILLY BOY!!
POP
LOSER

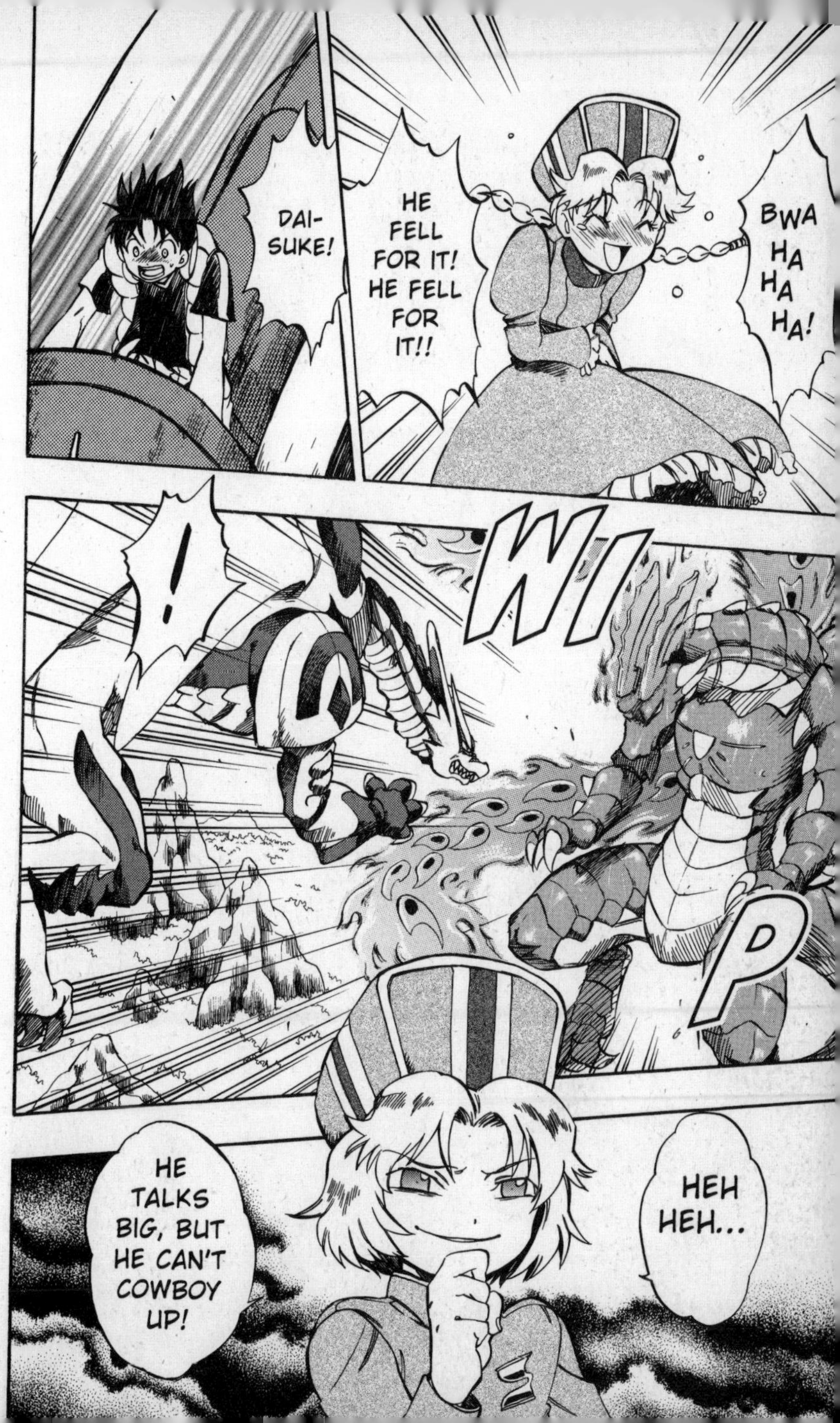
BWA HA HA HA!
HE FELL FOR IT! HE FELL FOR IT!!
DAI-SUKE!
WI
P
!
HEH HEH...
HE TALKS BIG, BUT HE CAN'T COWBOY UP!

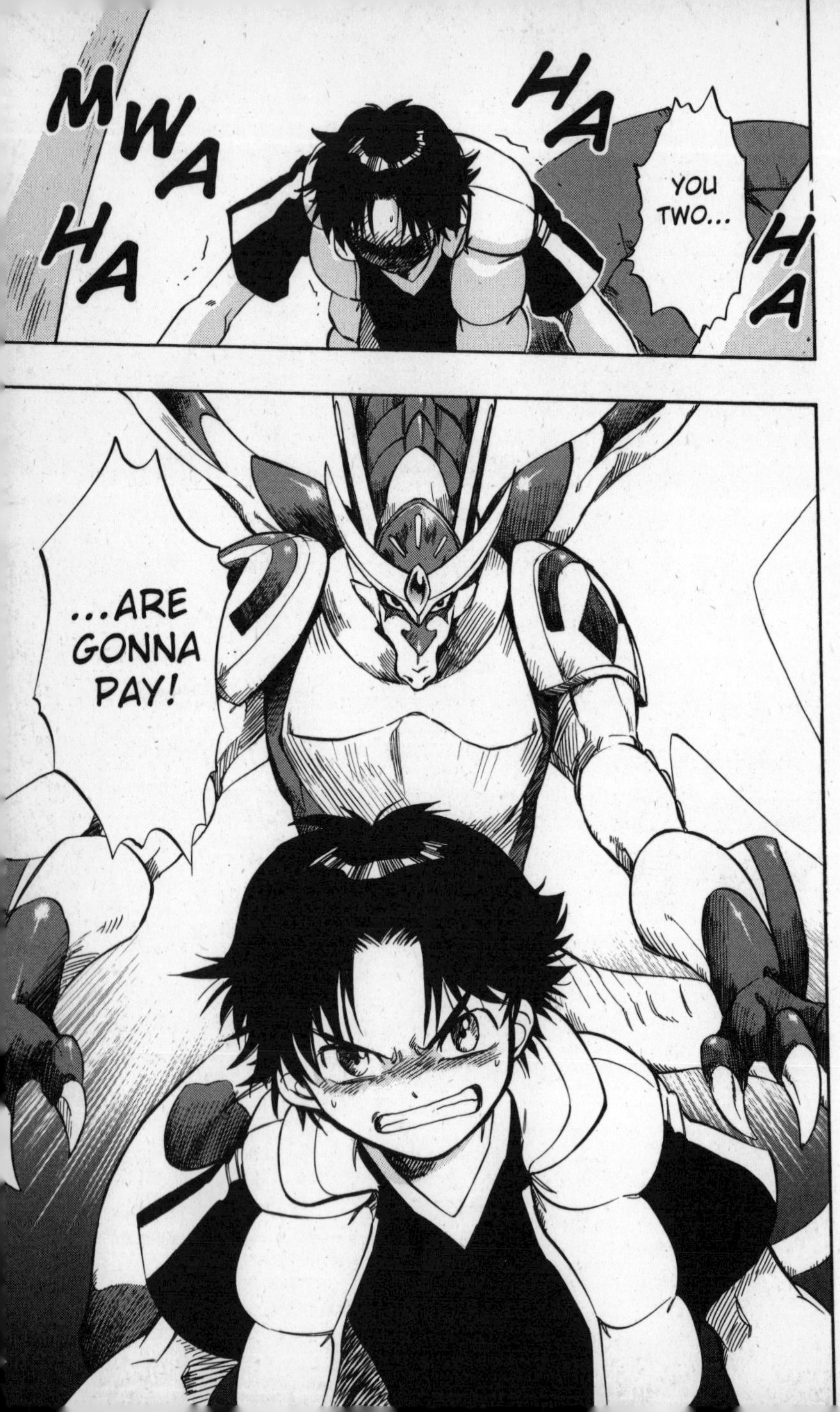
HA
YOU TWO...
HA HA
MWA HA HA
...ARE GONNA PAY!

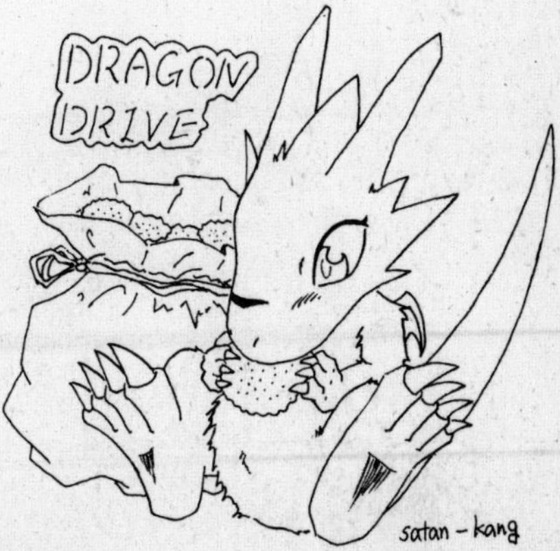
DRAGON DRIVE
satan - kang

AMAZING!
I GOT A LETTER
FROM A FAN IN KOREA!
THANK YOU!
THANK YOU!!!
I GOT YOUR LETTER!!!

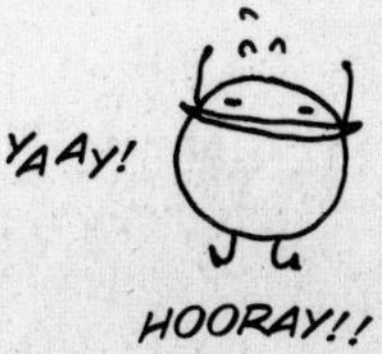
YAAY!
HOORAY!!

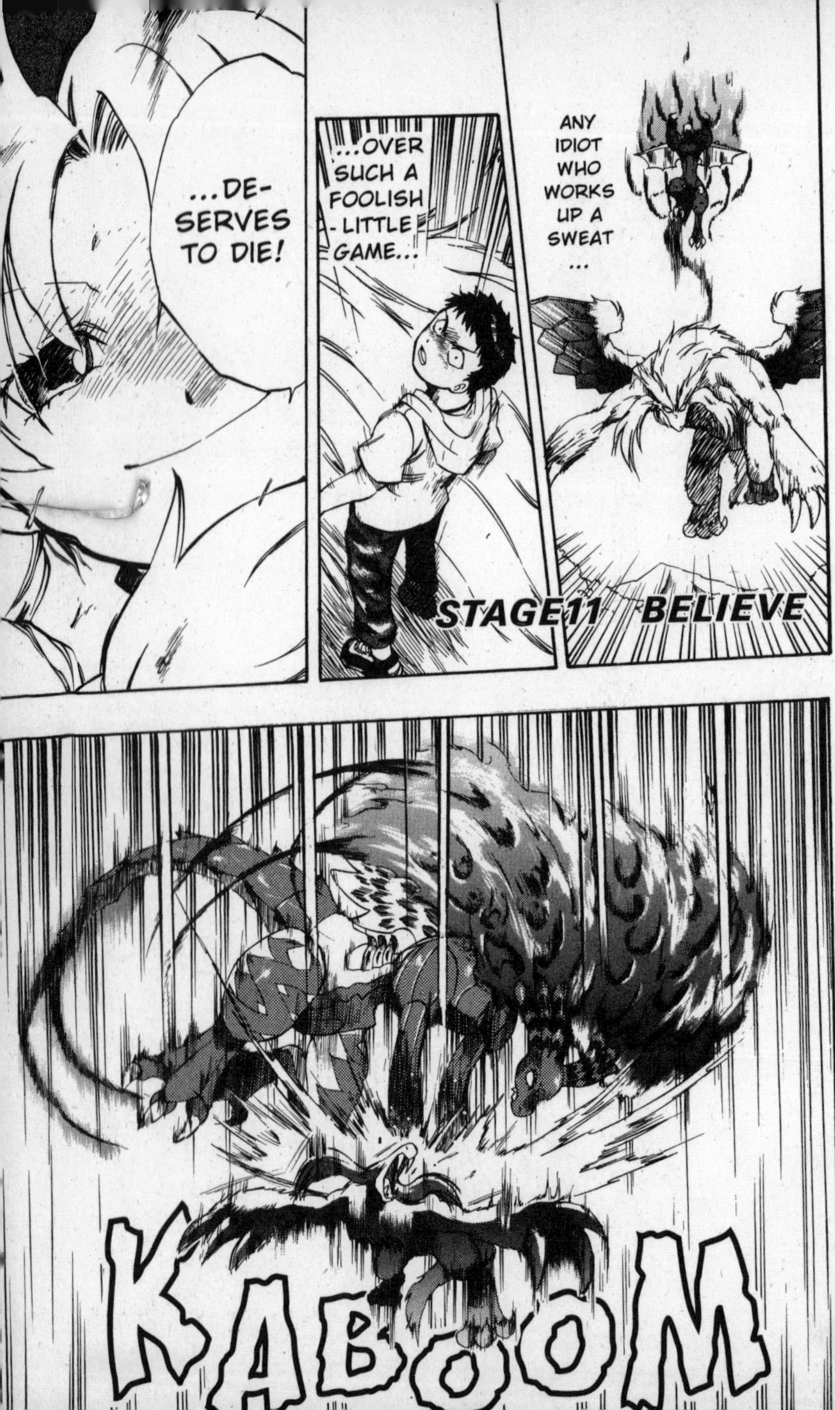
ANY IDIOT WHO WORKS UP A SWEAT ...
STAGE11 BELIEVE
...OVER SUCH A FOOLISH LITTLE GAME...
...DE-SERVES TO DIE!
KABOOM

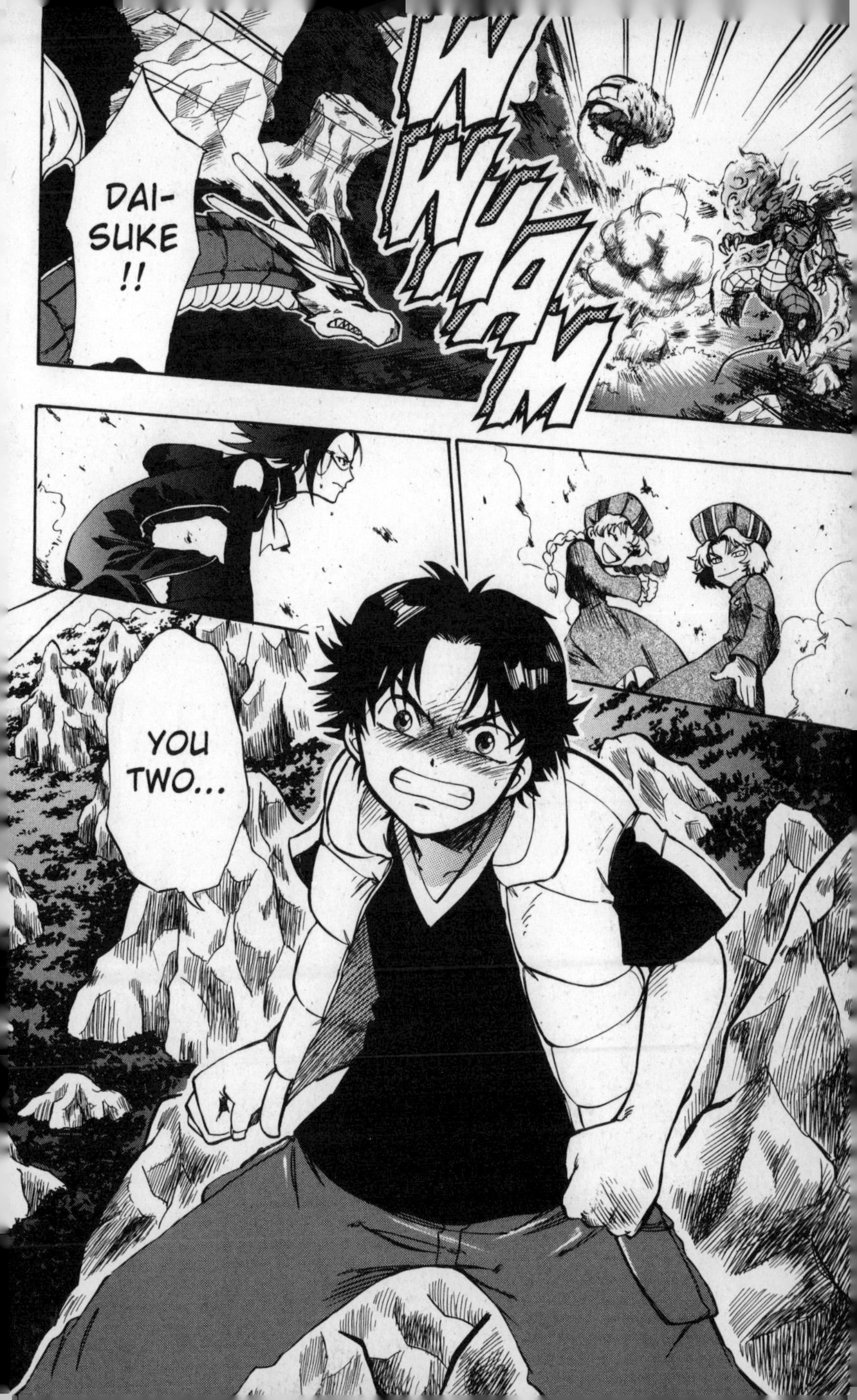
DAI-
SUKE
!!
YOU
TWO...

STAGE11 BELIEVE

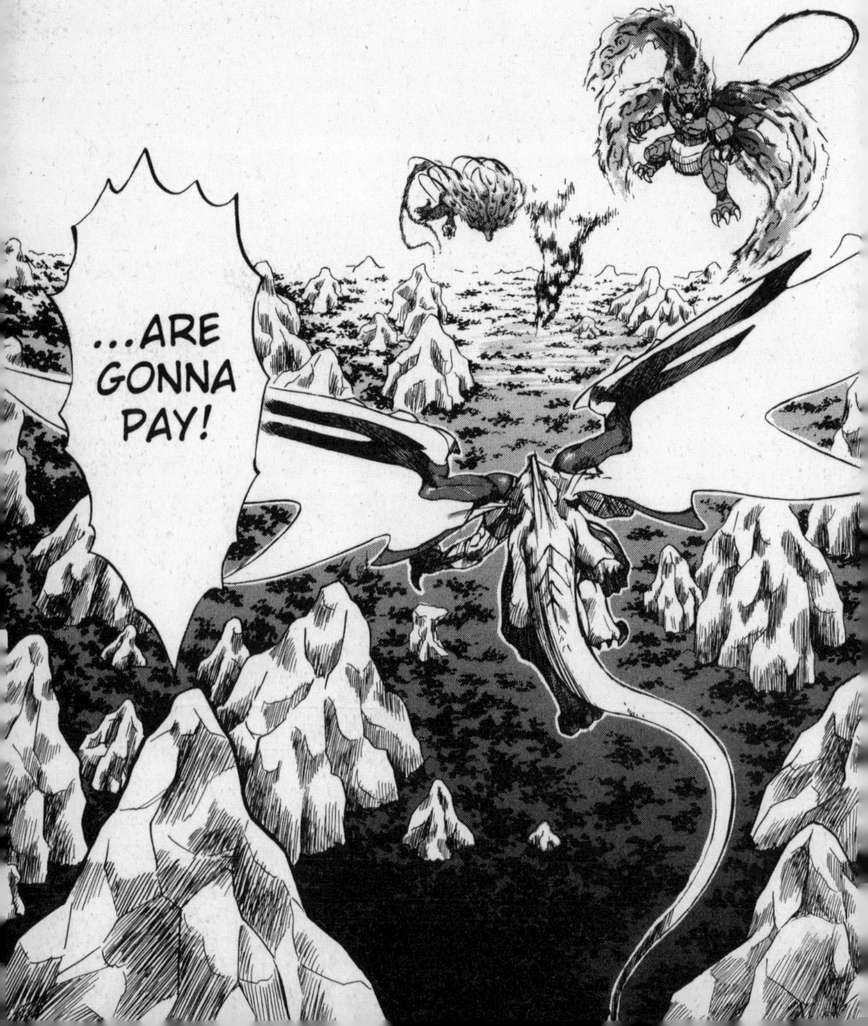
...ARE GONNA PAY!

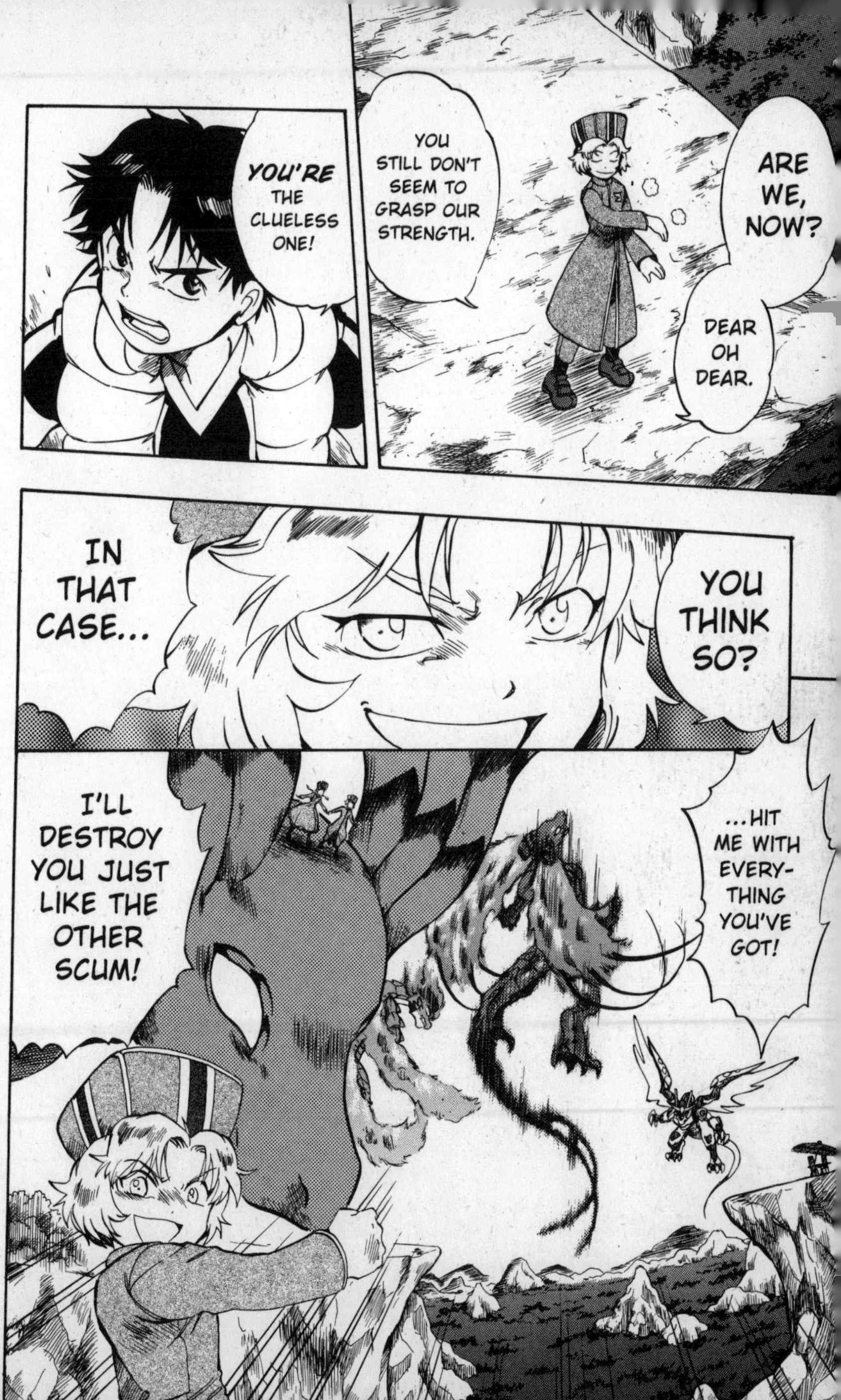
ARE WE, NOW?
DEAR OH DEAR.
YOU STILL DON'T SEEM TO GRASP OUR STRENGTH.
YOU'RE THE CLUELESS ONE!
YOU THINK SO?
IN THAT CASE...
...HIT ME WITH EVERY-THING YOU'VE GOT!
I'LL DESTROY YOU JUST LIKE THE OTHER SCUM!

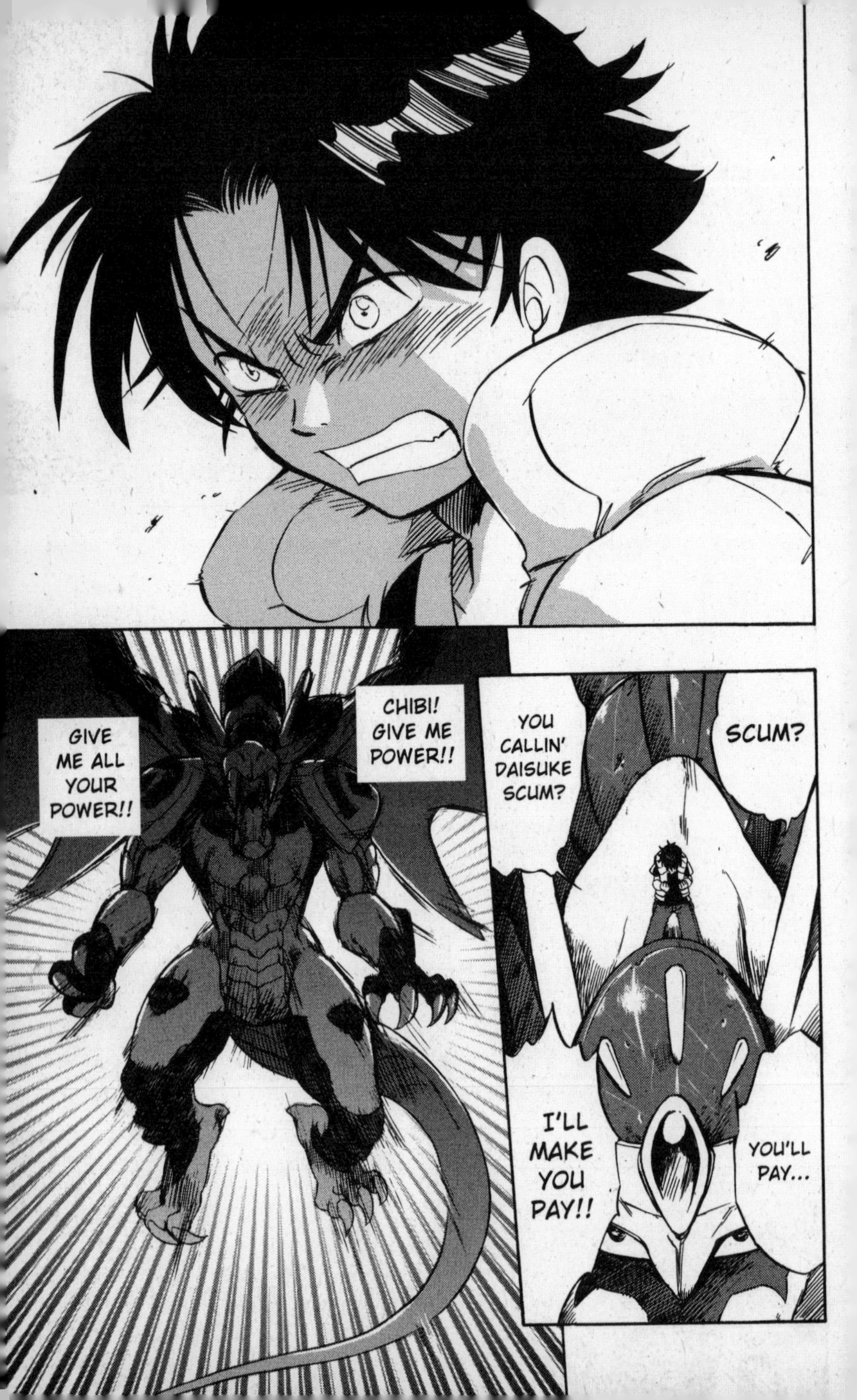
SCUM?
YOU CALLIN' DAISUKE SCUM?
YOU'LL PAY...
I'LL MAKE YOU PAY!!
CHIBI! GIVE ME POWER!!
GIVE ME ALL YOUR POWER!!

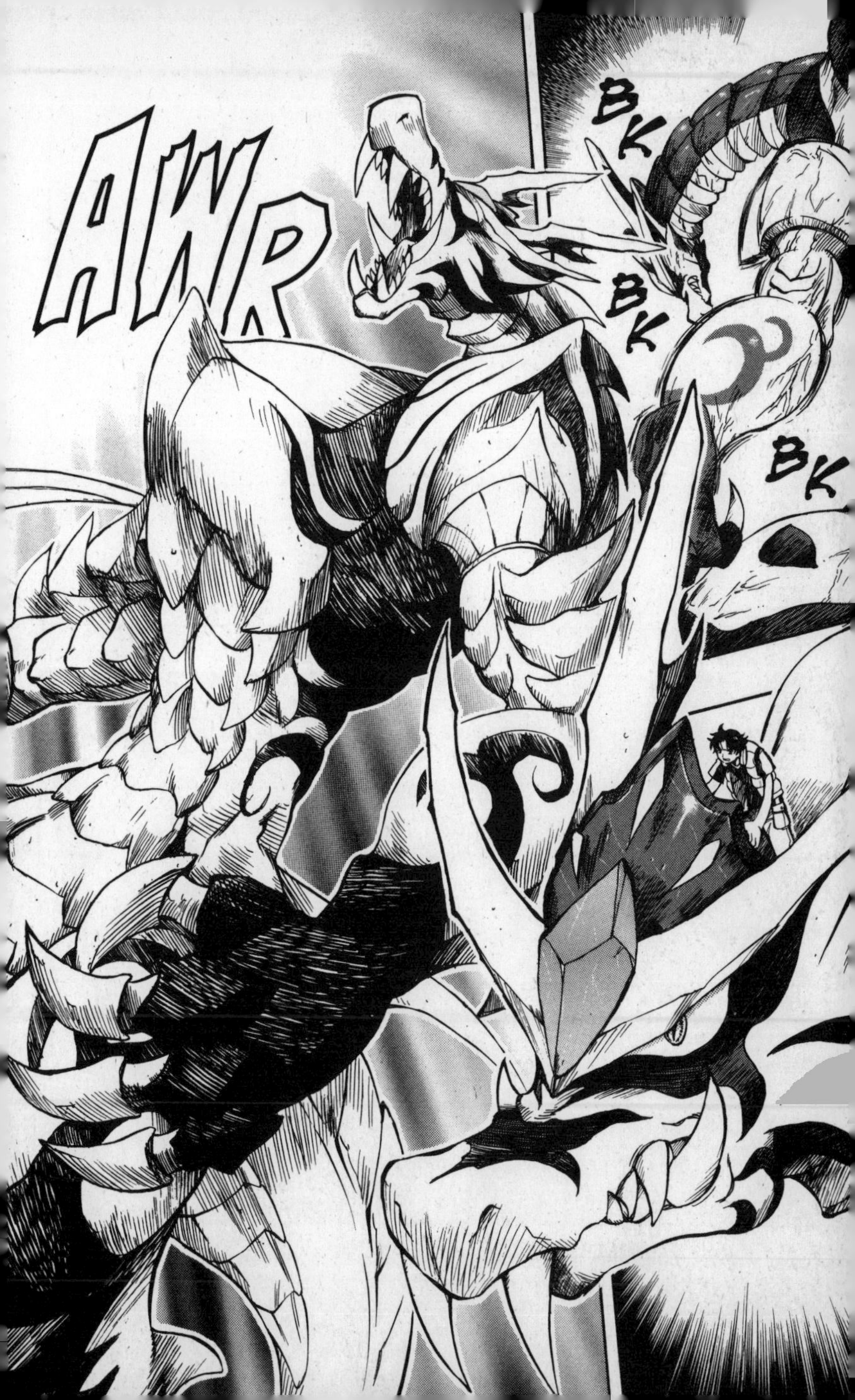
BK
BK
BK
AWR

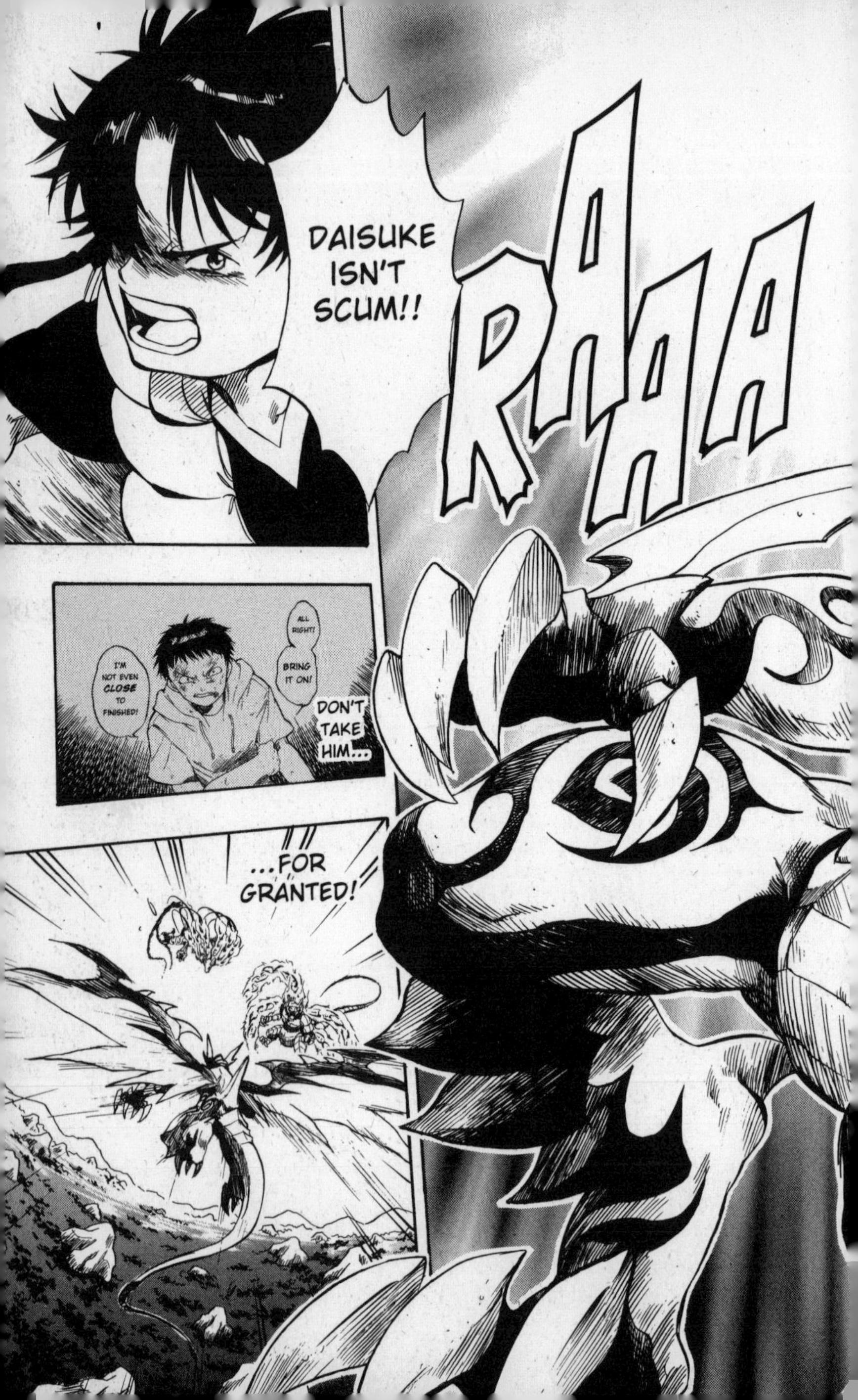
RAAA
DAISUKE ISN'T SCUM!!
ALL RIGHT!
BRING IT ON!
DON'T TAKE HIM...
I'M NOT EVEN CLOSE TO FINISHED!
...FOR GRANTED!

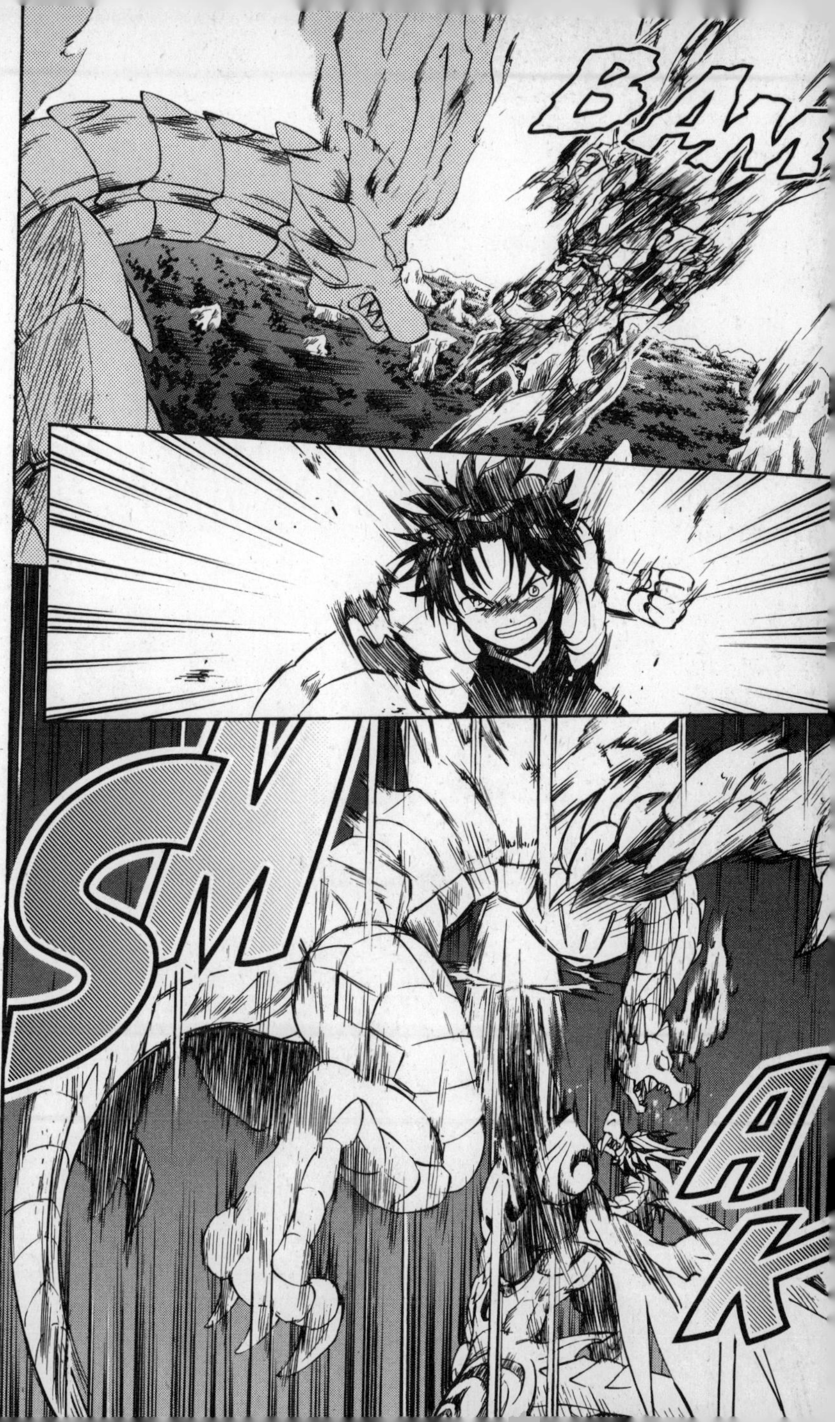
BAM
SMAK

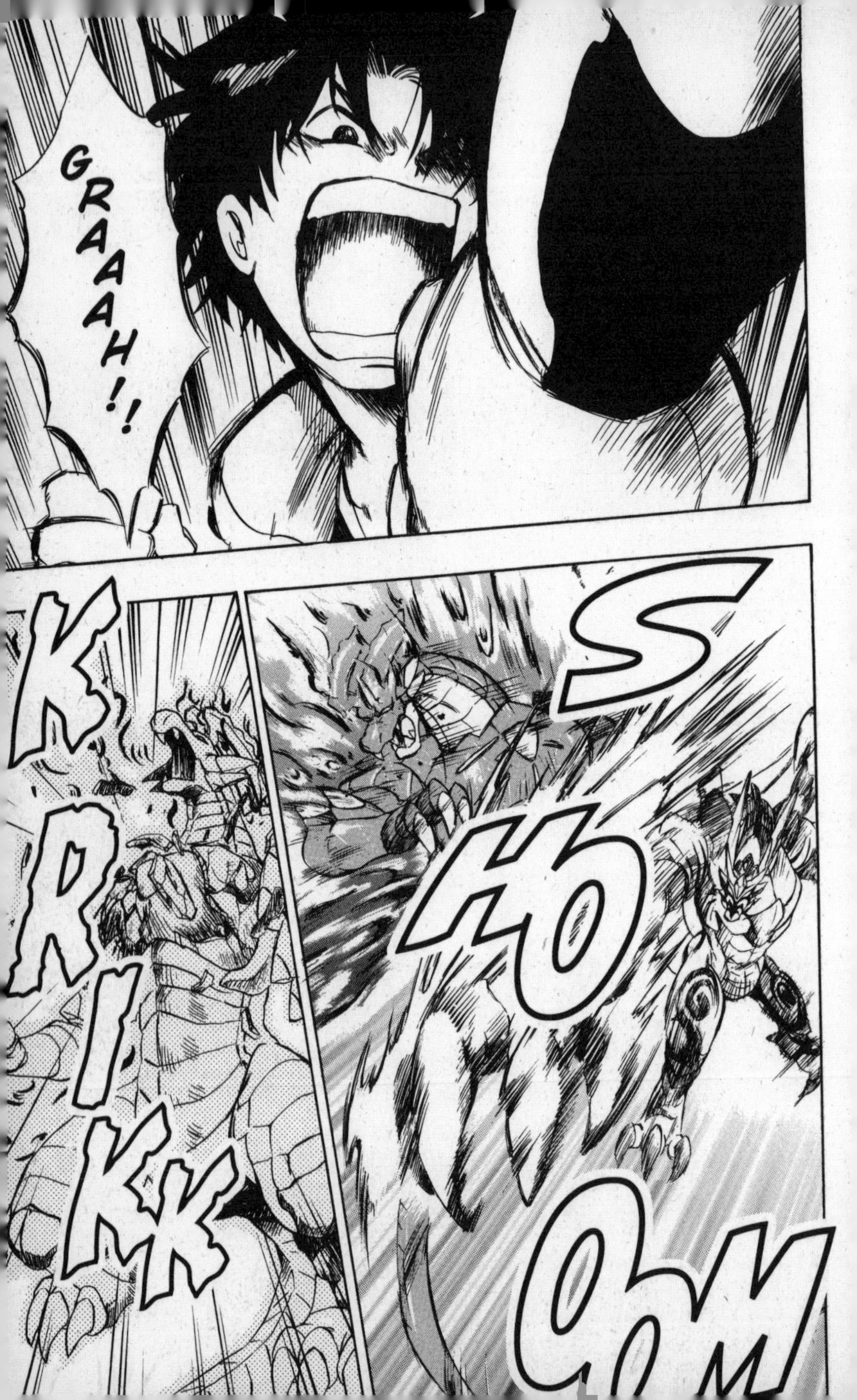
GRAAAH!!
SHOOM
KRIKK

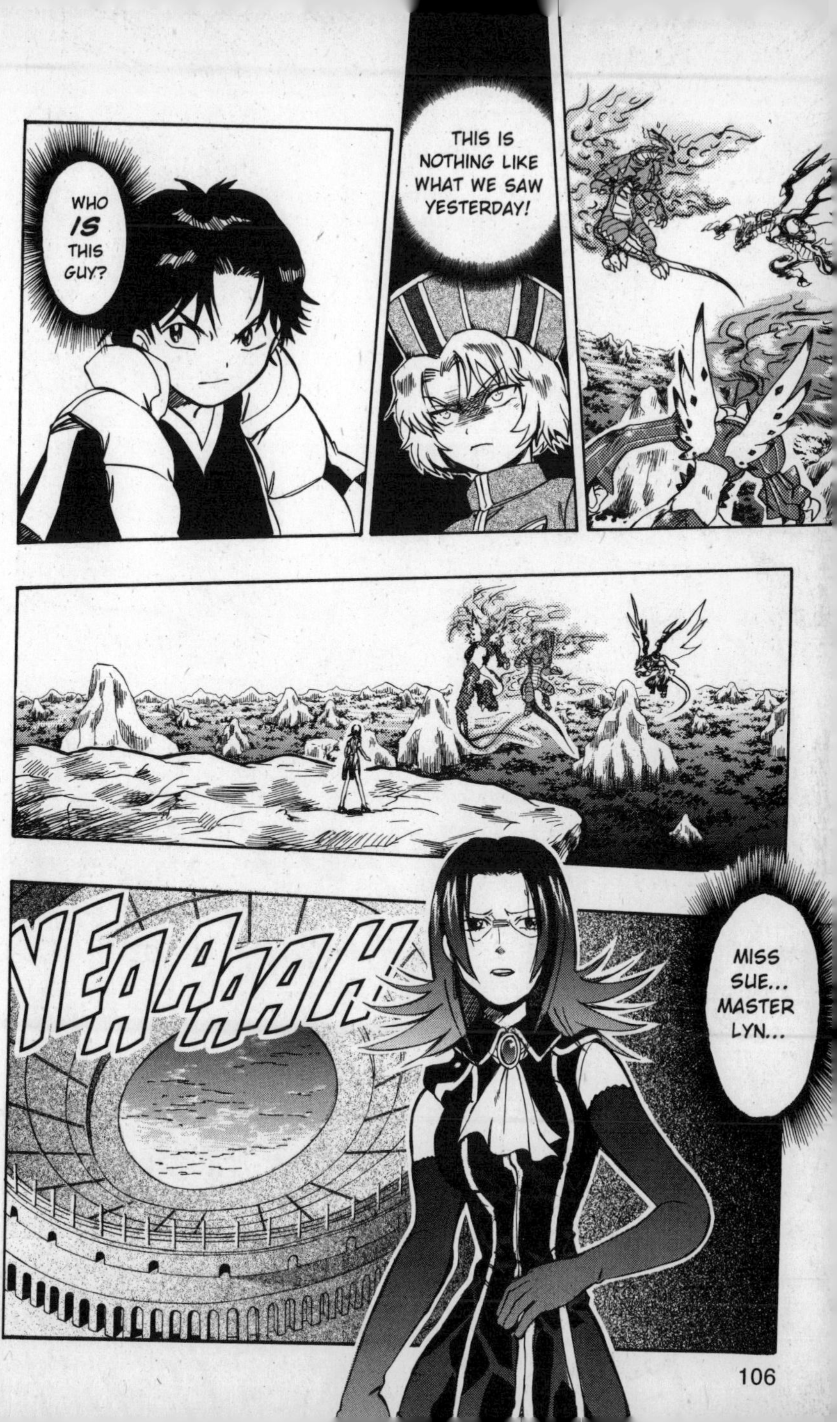
THIS IS NOTHING LIKE WHAT WE SAW YESTERDAY!
WHO IS THIS GUY?
MISS SUE... MASTER LYN...
YEAAAAH!

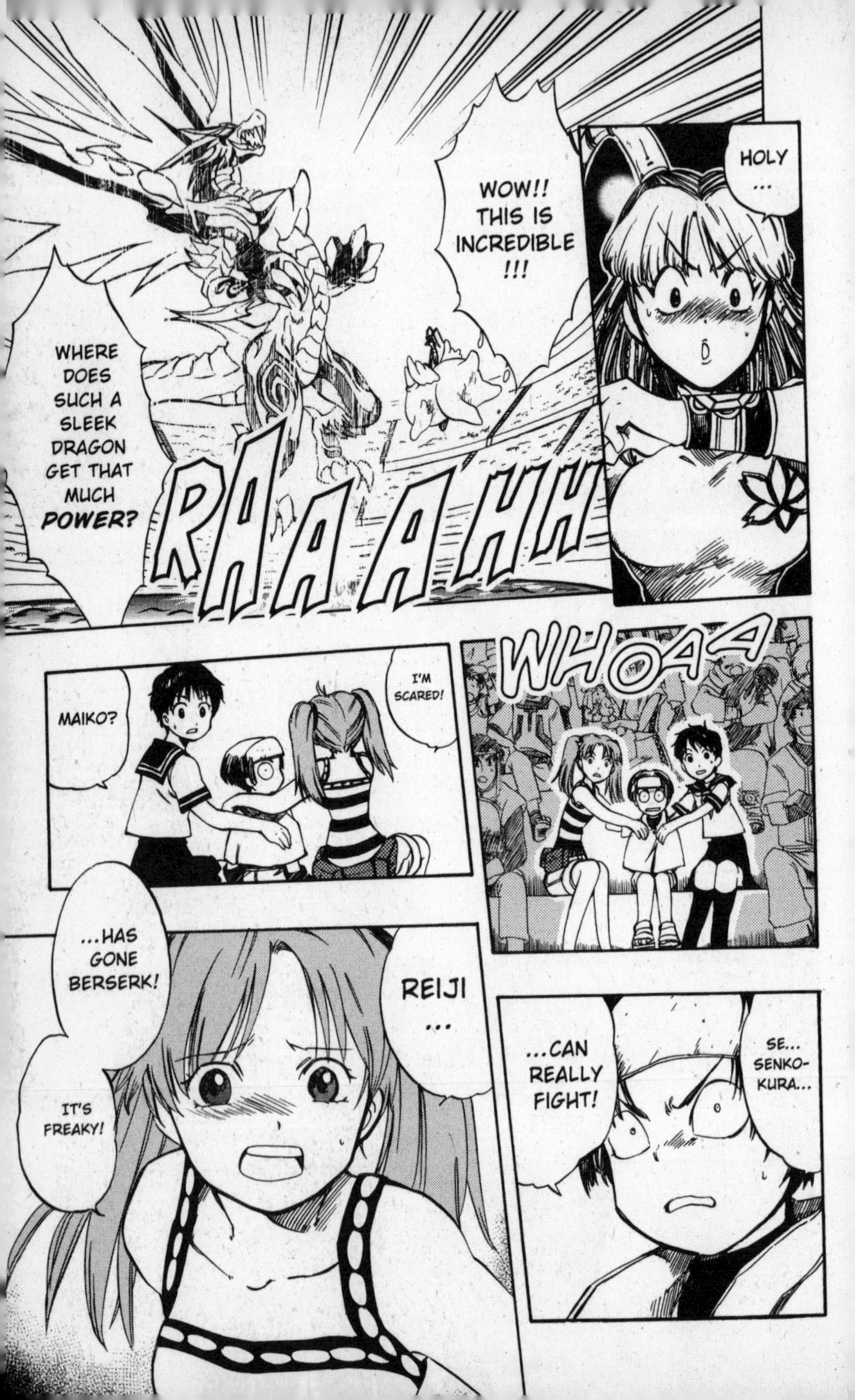
HOLY ...
WOW!! THIS IS INCREDIBLE !!!
RAAAHH
WHERE DOES SUCH A SLEEK DRAGON GET THAT MUCH POWER?
WHOAA
I'M SCARED!
MAIKO?
SE... SENKO-KURA...
...CAN REALLY FIGHT!
REIJI ...
...HAS GONE BERSERK!
IT'S FREAKY!

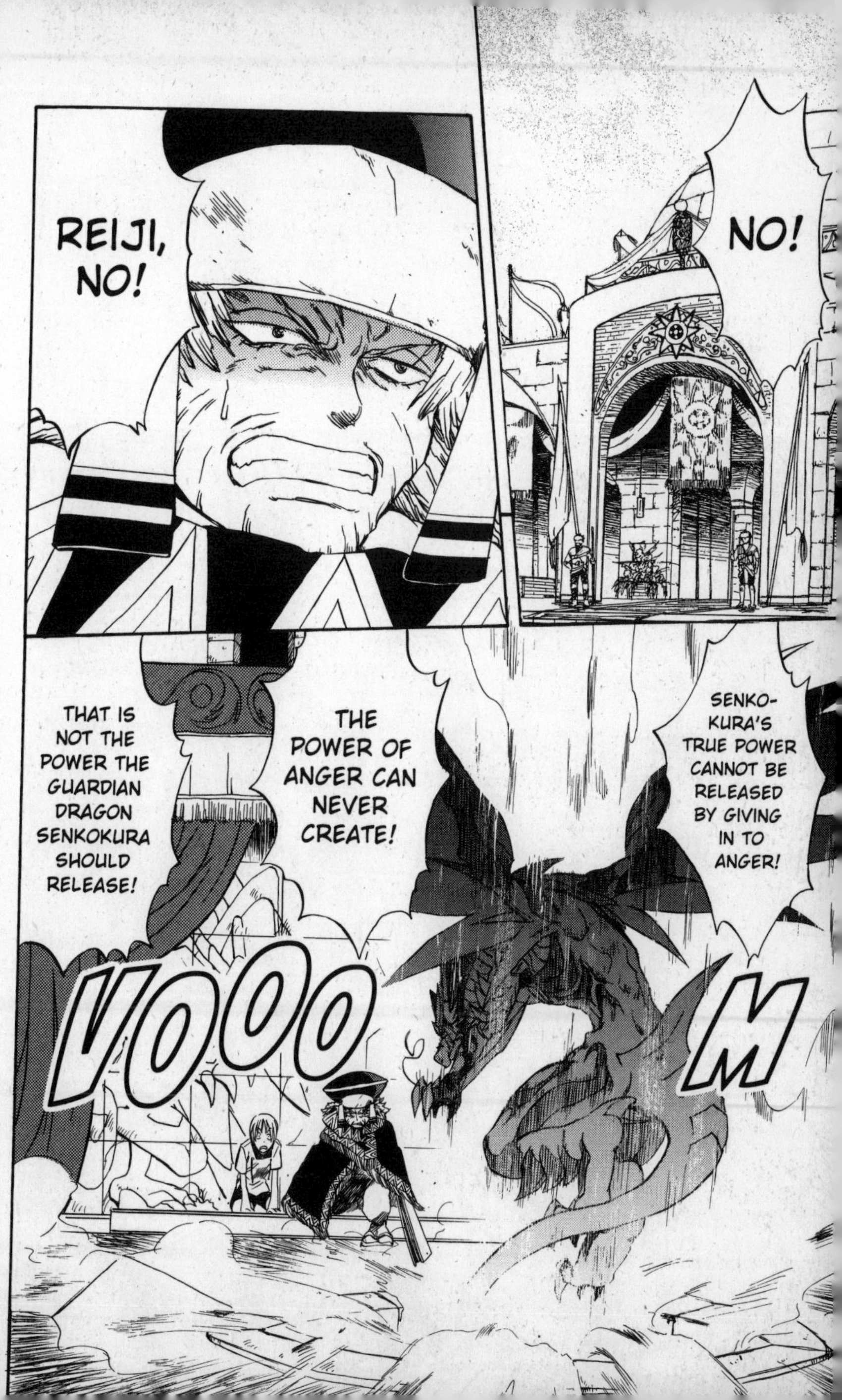
NO!
REIJI, NO!
SENKO-KURA'S TRUE POWER CANNOT BE RELEASED BY GIVING IN TO ANGER!
THE POWER OF ANGER CAN NEVER CREATE!
THAT IS NOT THE POWER THE GUARDIAN DRAGON SENKOKURA SHOULD RELEASE!
VOOOM

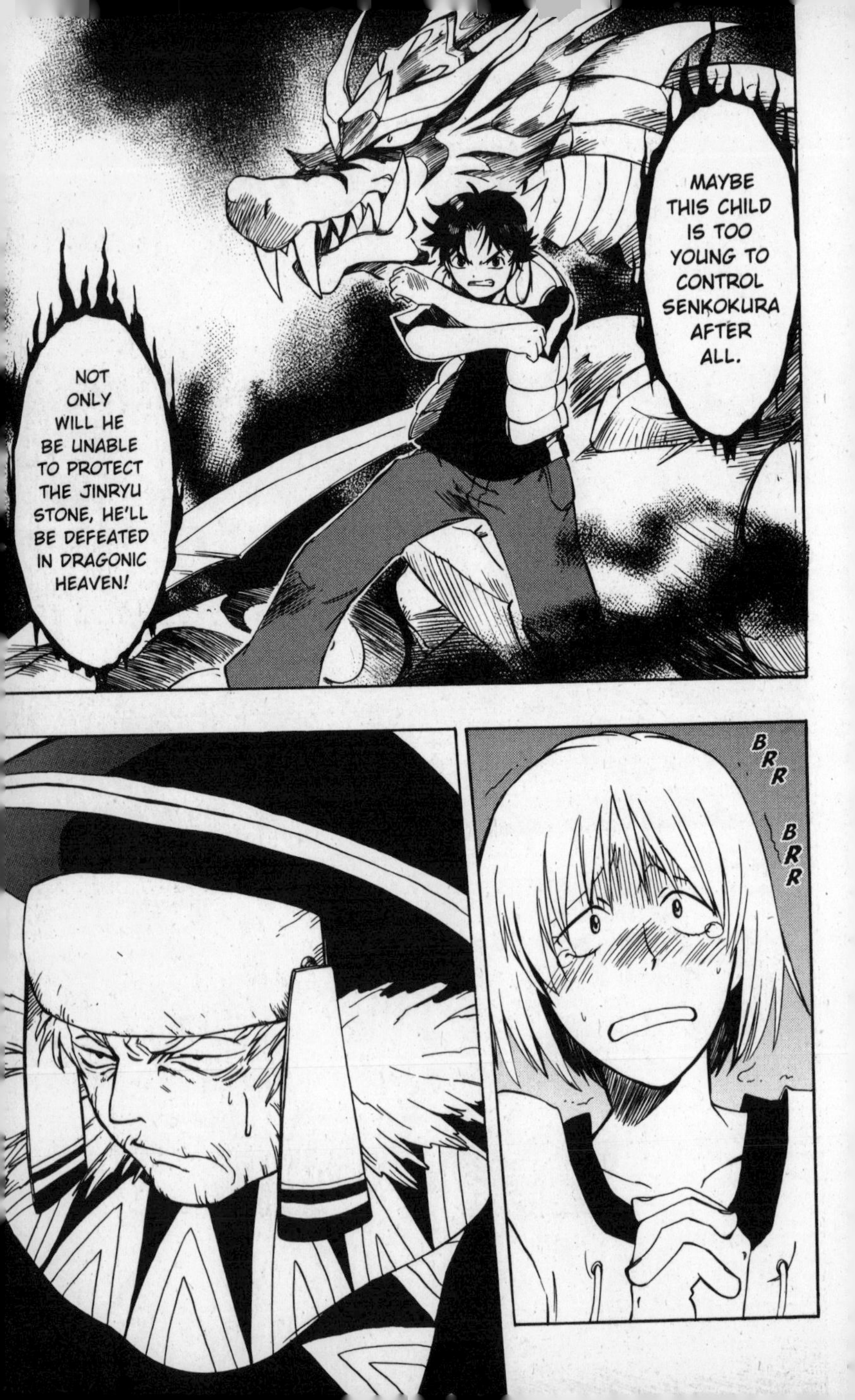
MAYBE THIS CHILD IS TOO YOUNG TO CONTROL SENKOKURA AFTER ALL.
NOT ONLY WILL HE BE UNABLE TO PROTECT THE JINRYU STONE, HE'LL BE DEFEATED IN DRAGONIC HEAVEN!
BRR BRR

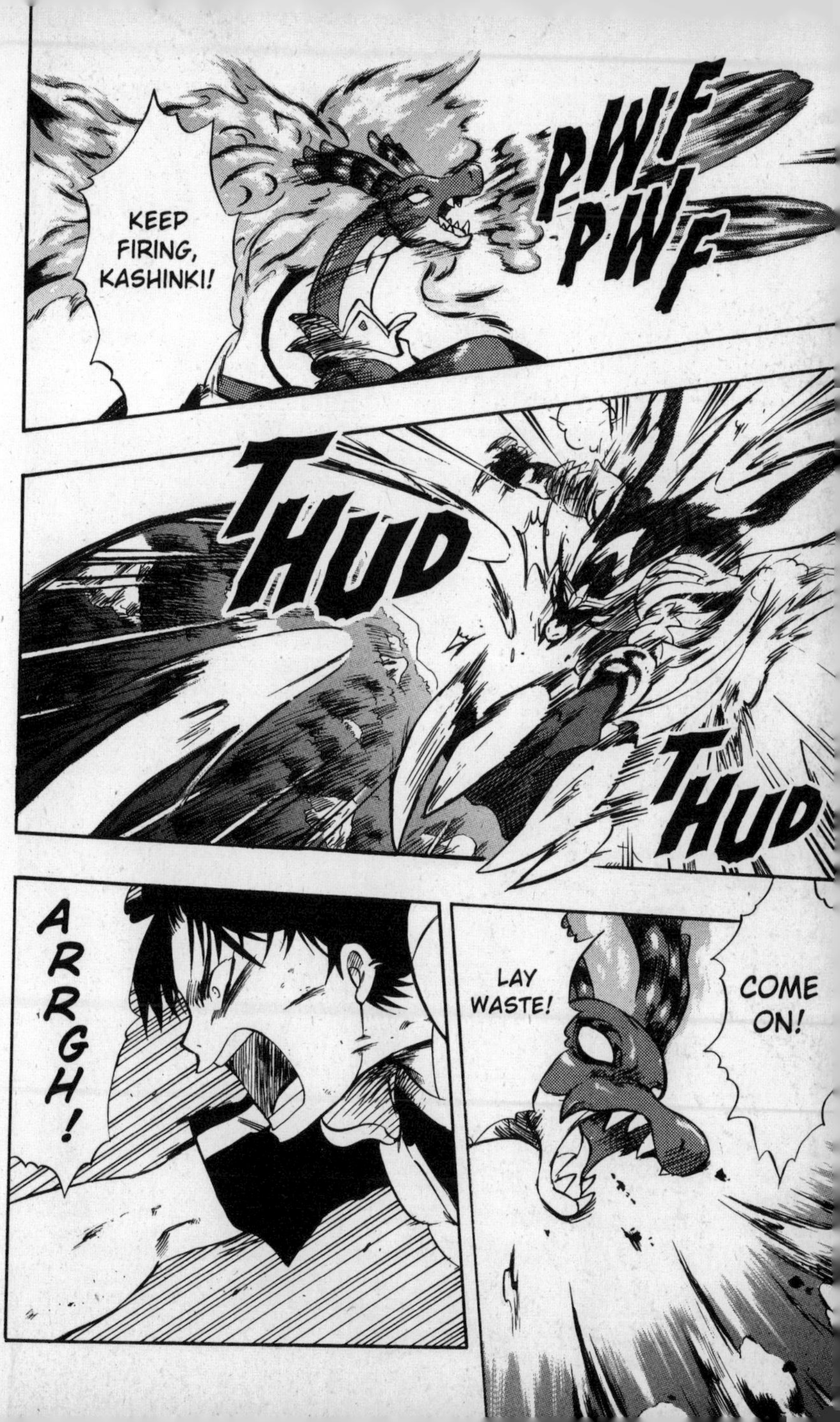
PWF
PWF
KEEP FIRING, KASHINKI!
THUD
THUD
COME ON!
LAY WASTE!
ARRGH!

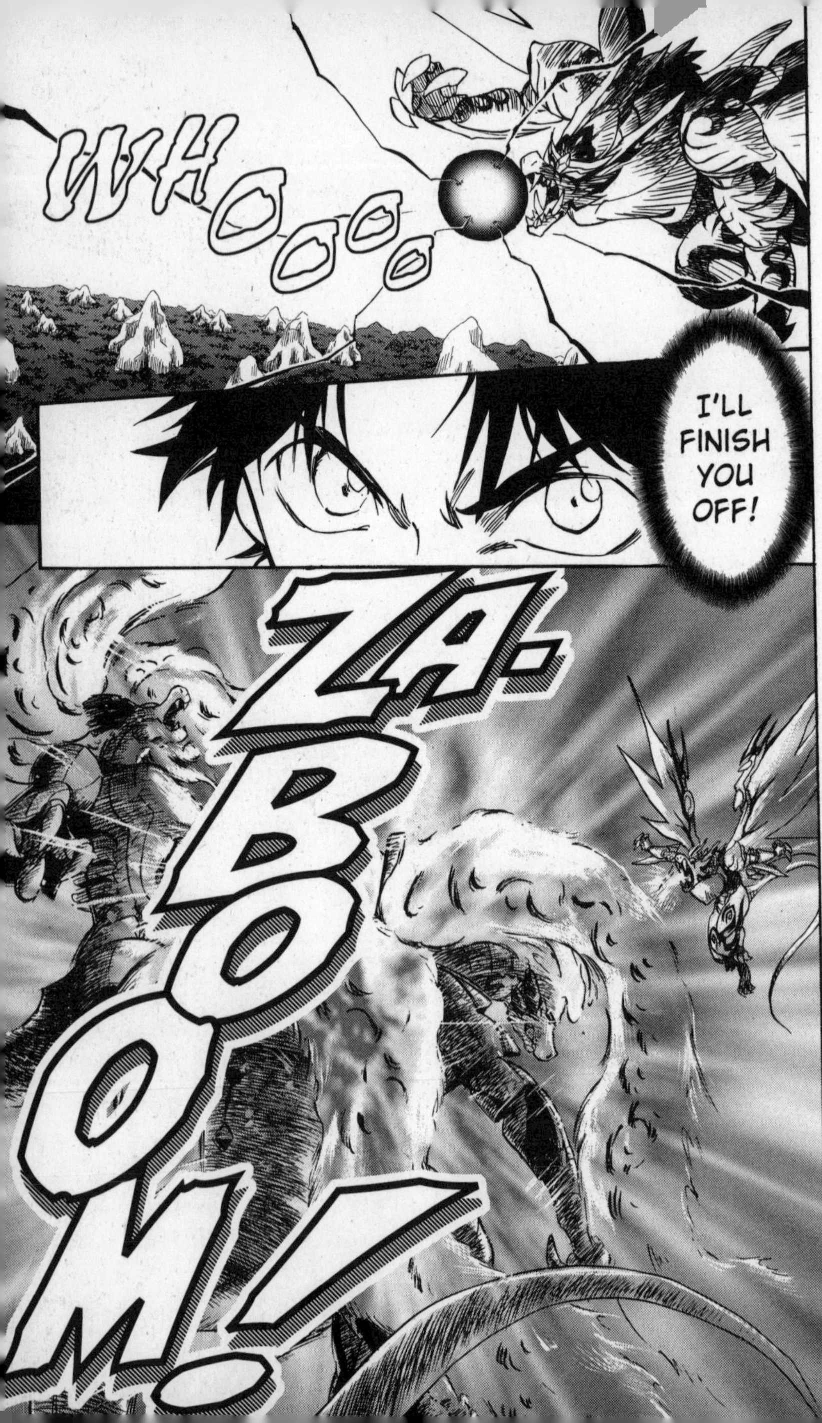
WHOOOOO
I'LL FINISH YOU OFF!
ZA-BOOM!

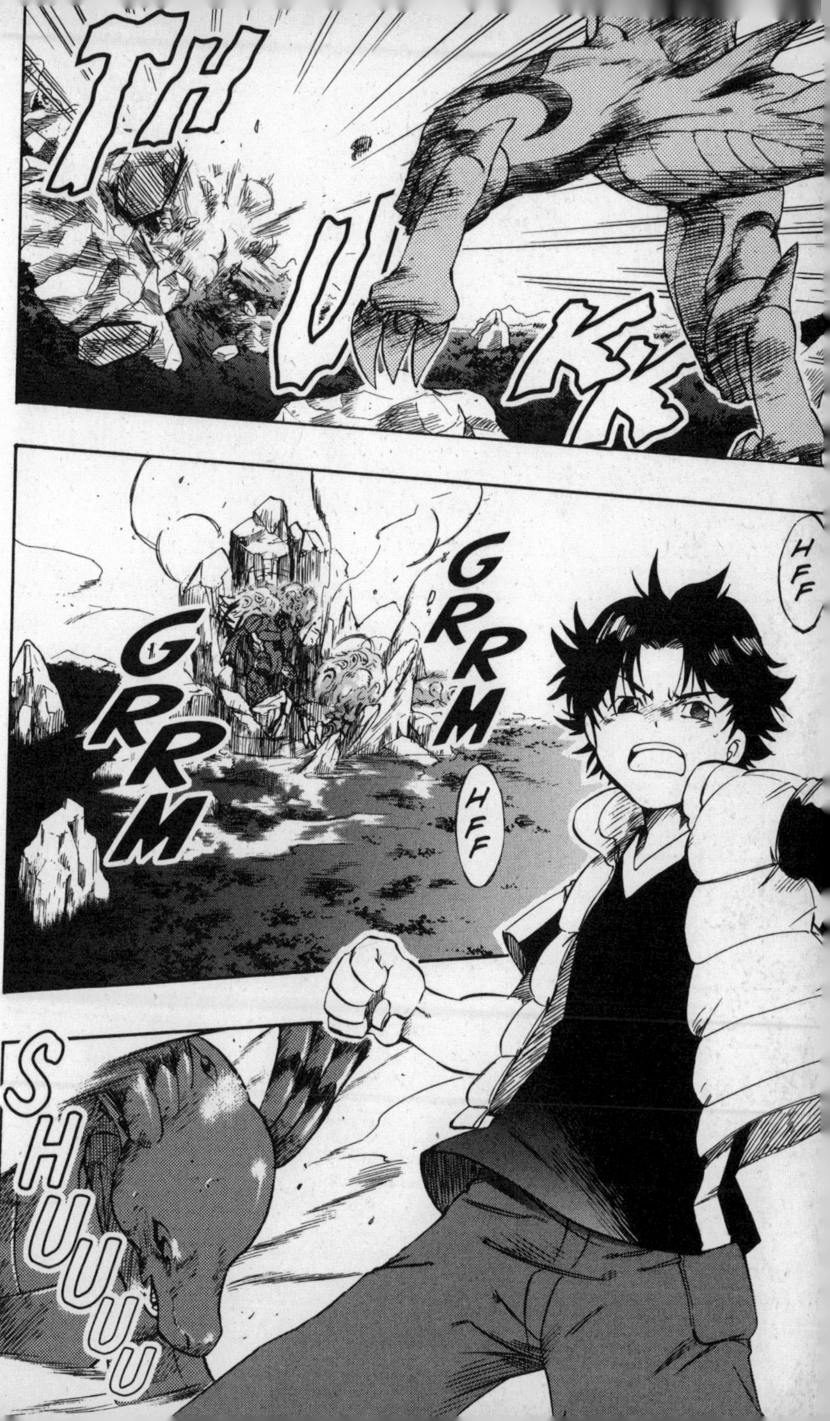
THUKK
HFF
GRRM
HFF
GRRM
SHUUUU

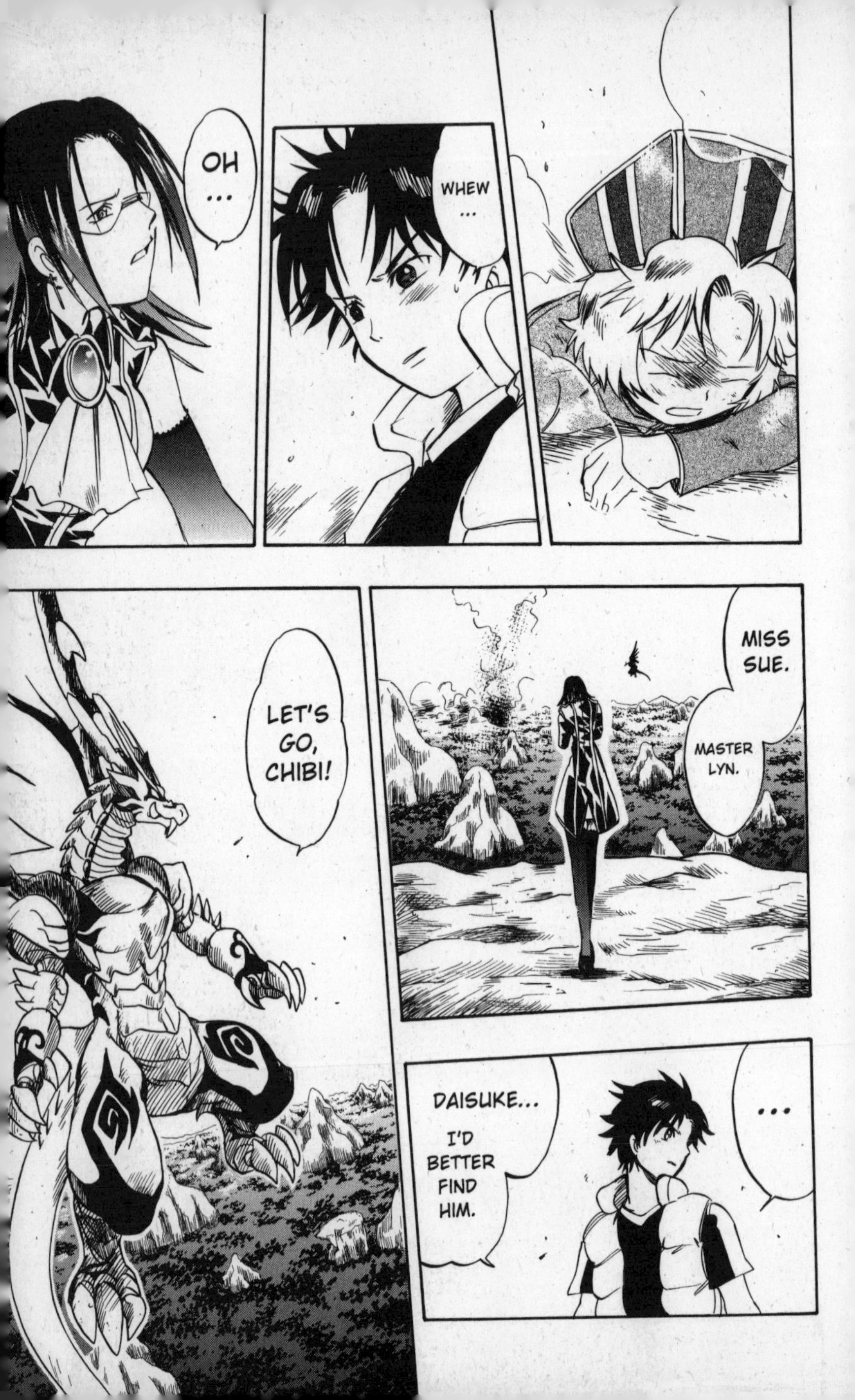
WHEW ...
OH ...
MISS SUE.
MASTER LYN.
...
DAISUKE... I'D BETTER FIND HIM.
LET'S GO, CHIBI!

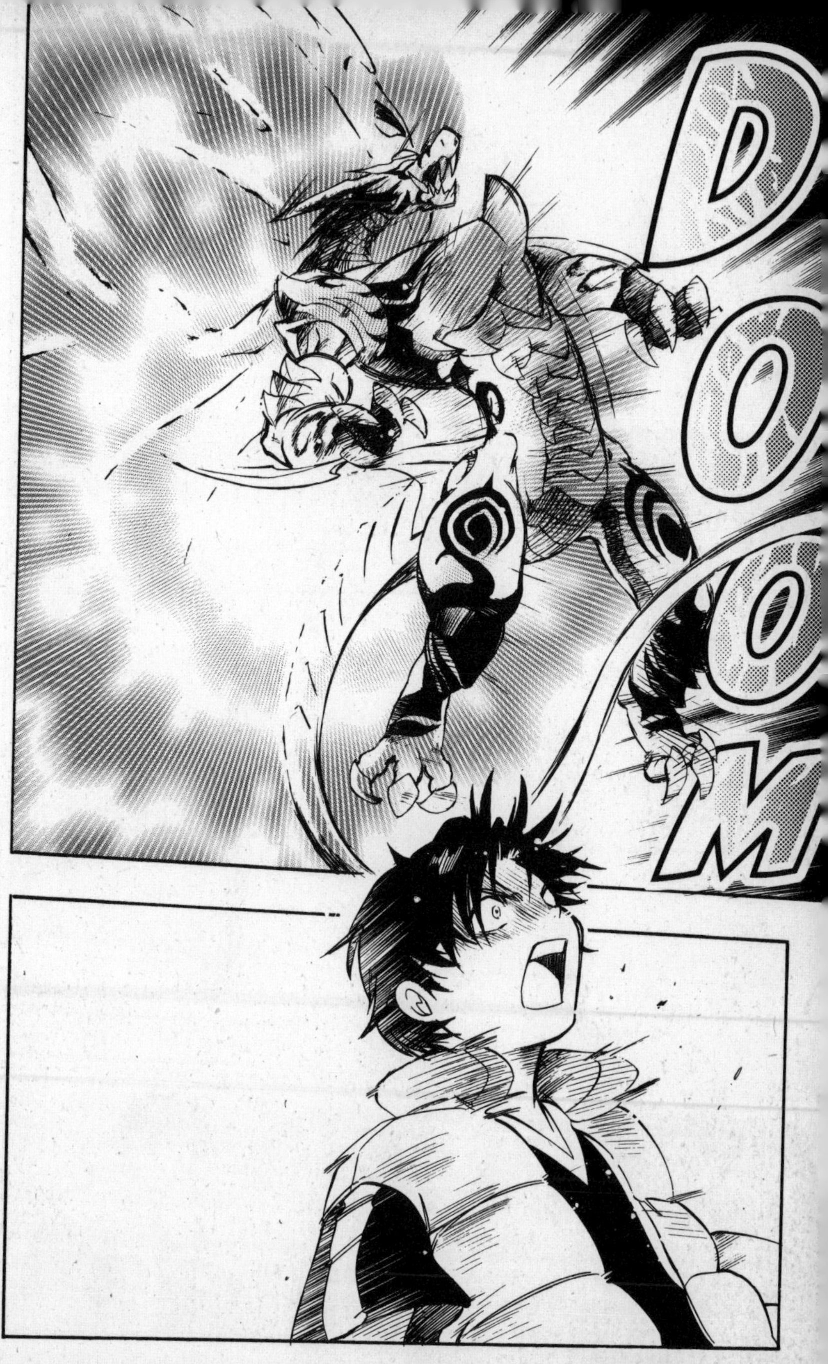
DOOM

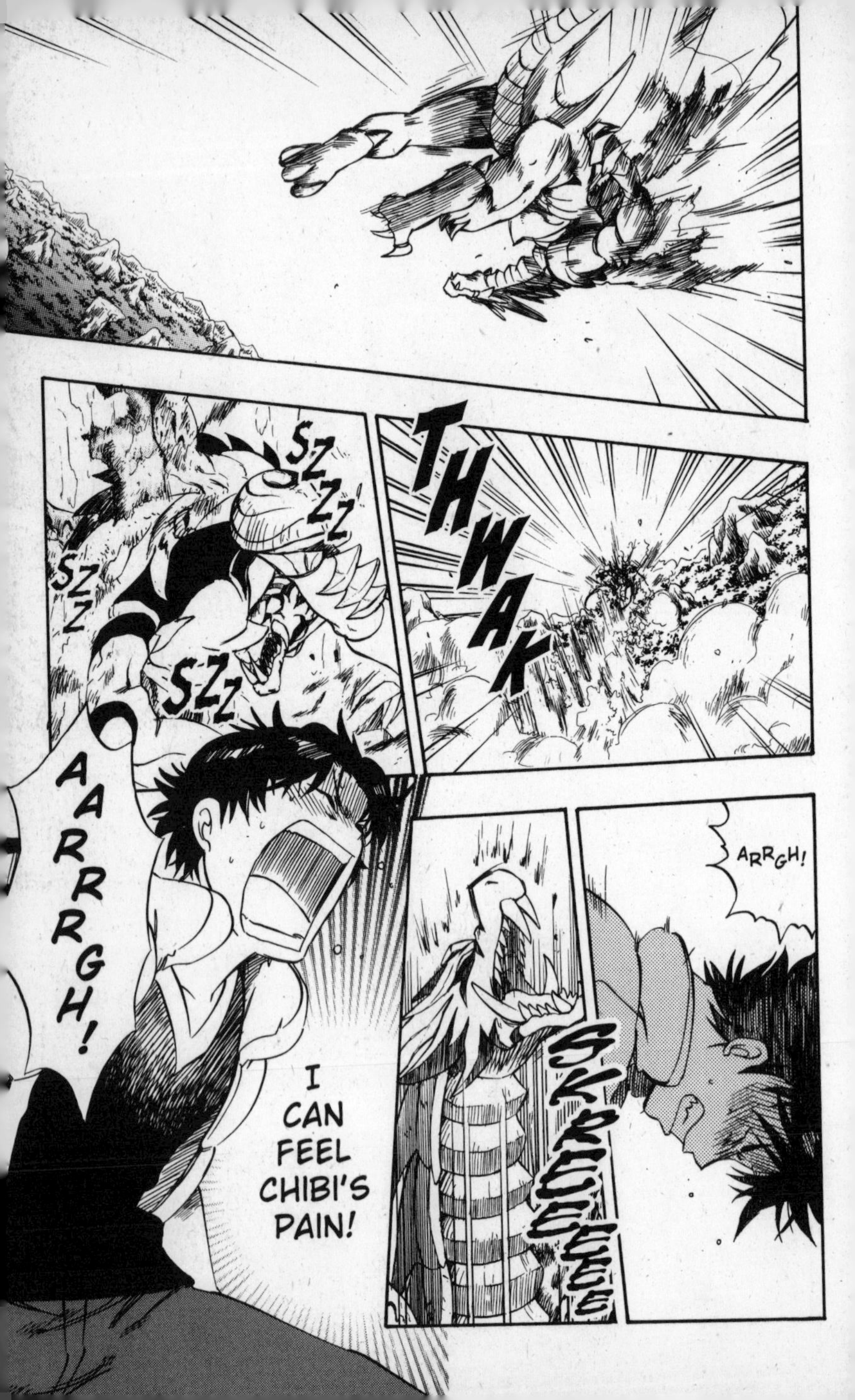
THWAK
SZZZ
SZZ
SZZ
ARRGH!
SKREEEEEE
AARRRRGH!
I CAN FEEL CHIBI'S PAIN!

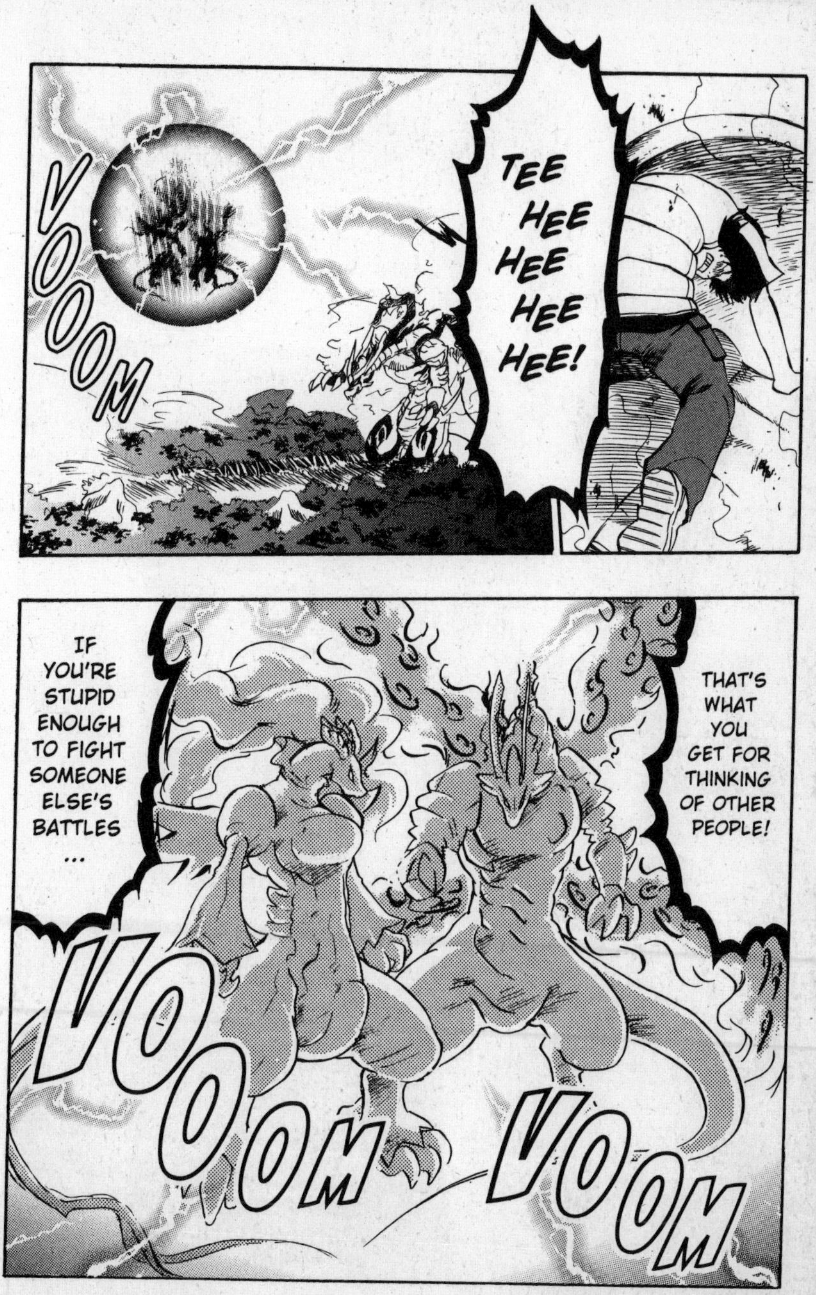
TEE HEE HEE HEE HEE!
VOOOM
IF YOU'RE STUPID ENOUGH TO FIGHT SOMEONE ELSE'S BATTLES...
THAT'S WHAT YOU GET FOR THINKING OF OTHER PEOPLE!
VOOOM
VOOOM

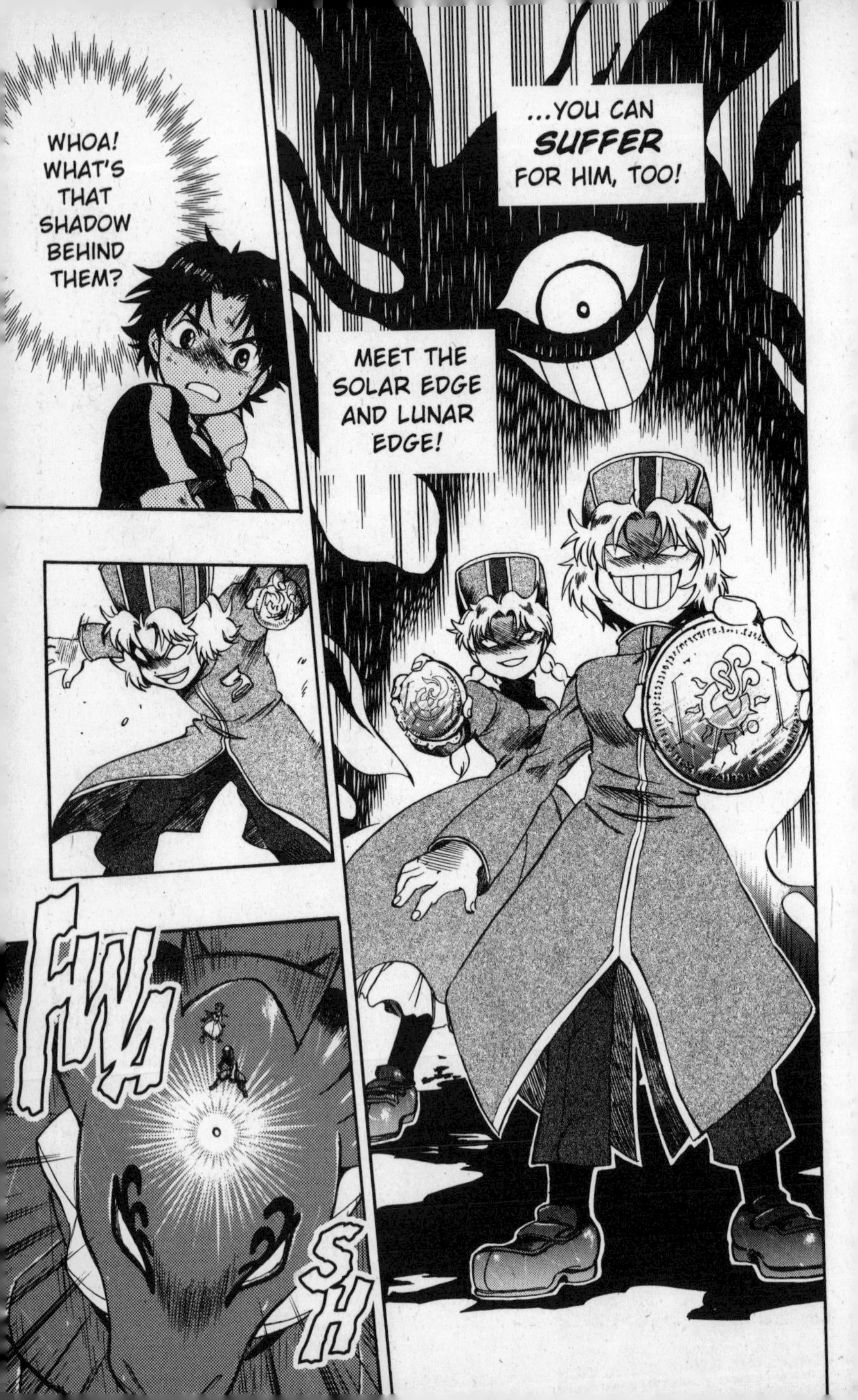
...YOU CAN SUFFER FOR HIM, TOO!
MEET THE SOLAR EDGE AND LUNAR EDGE!
WHOA! WHAT'S THAT SHADOW BEHIND THEM?
FWA
SH

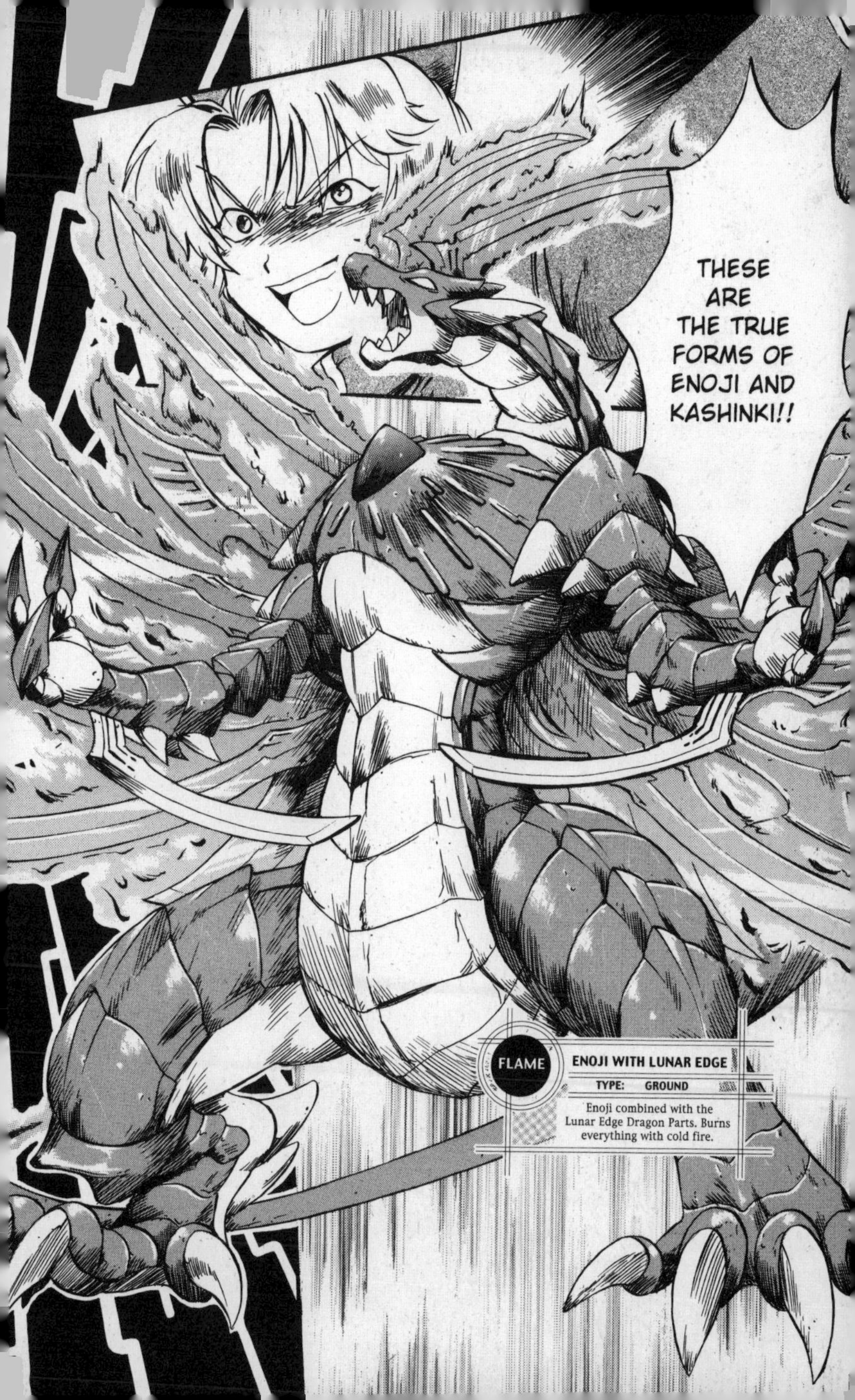
THESE ARE THE TRUE FORMS OF ENOJI AND KASHINKI!!
FLAME
ENOJI WITH LUNAR EDGE
TYPE: GROUND
Enoji combined with the Lunar Edge Dragon Parts. Burns everything with cold fire.

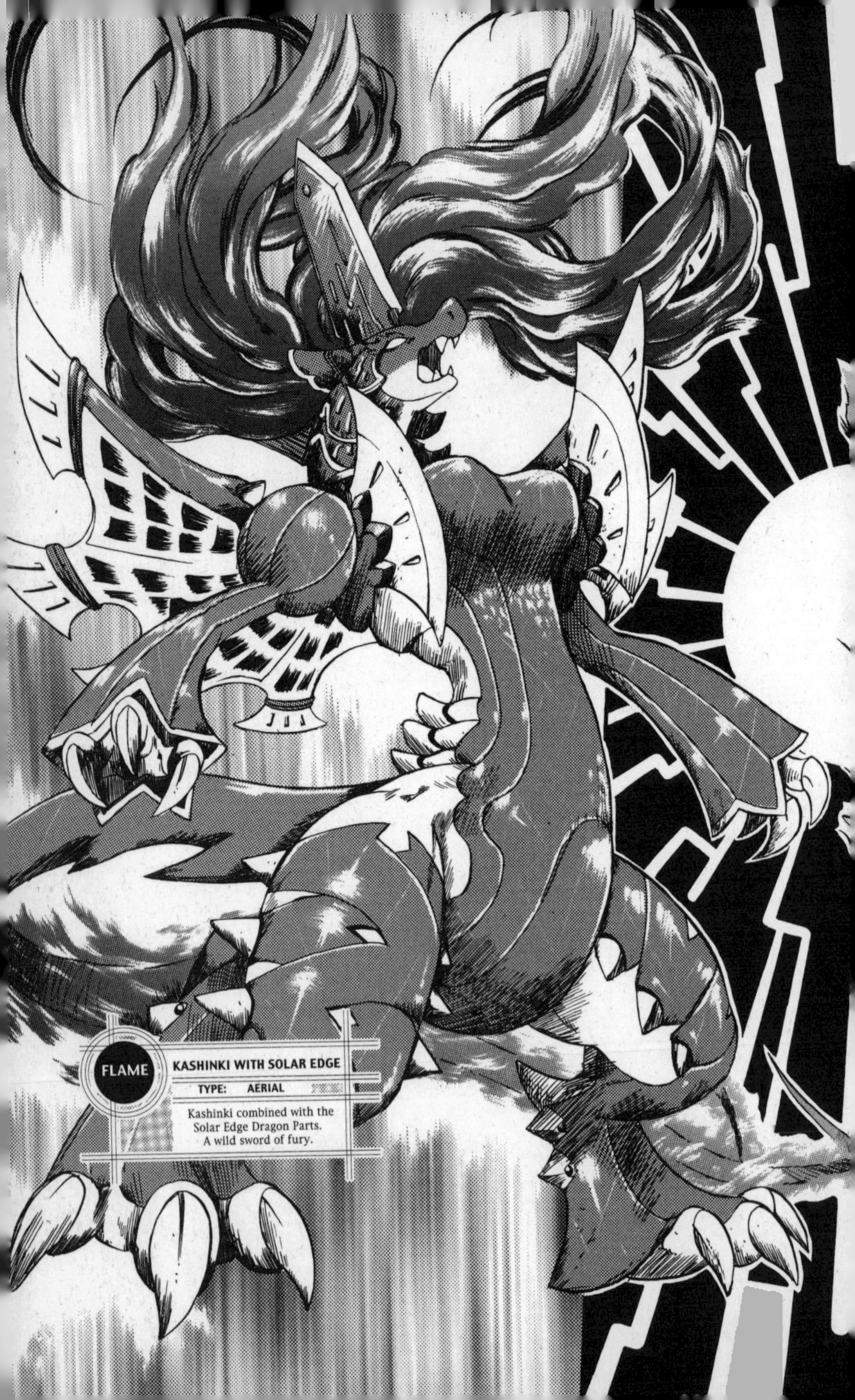
FLAME
KASHINKI WITH SOLAR EDGE
TYPE: AERIAL
Kashinki combined with the Solar Edge Dragon Parts. A wild sword of fury.

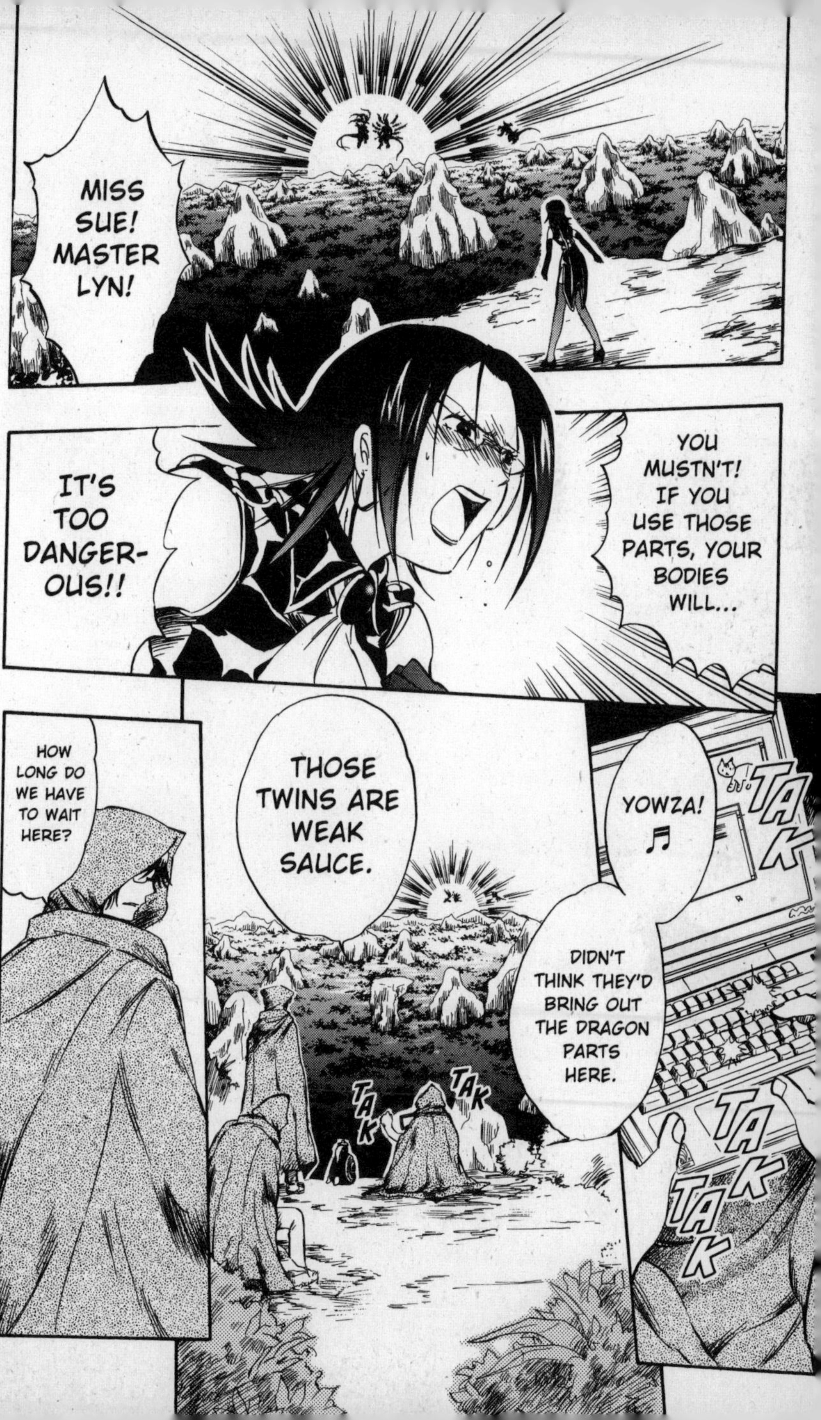
MISS SUE! MASTER LYN!
YOU MUSTN'T! IF YOU USE THOSE PARTS, YOUR BODIES WILL...
IT'S TOO DANGER-OUS!!
TAK
YOWZA! ♪
DIDN'T THINK THEY'D BRING OUT THE DRAGON PARTS HERE.
TAK
TAK
TAK
THOSE TWINS ARE WEAK SAUCE.
TAK
TAK
HOW LONG DO WE HAVE TO WAIT HERE?

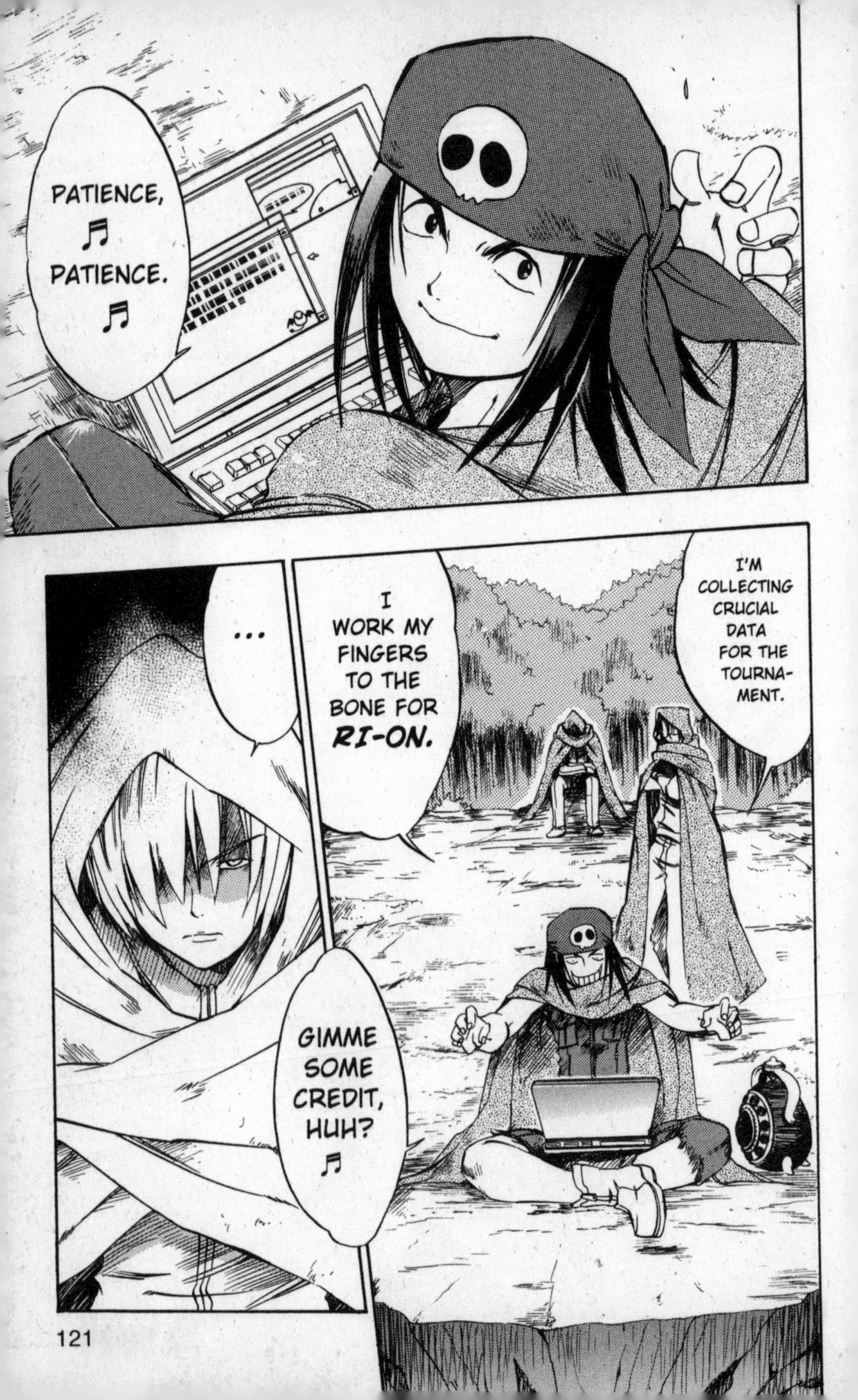
PATIENCE, ♬ PATIENCE. ♬
I'M COLLECTING CRUCIAL DATA FOR THE TOURNA-MENT.
I WORK MY FINGERS TO THE BONE FOR RI-ON.
GIMME SOME CREDIT, HUH? ♬
...

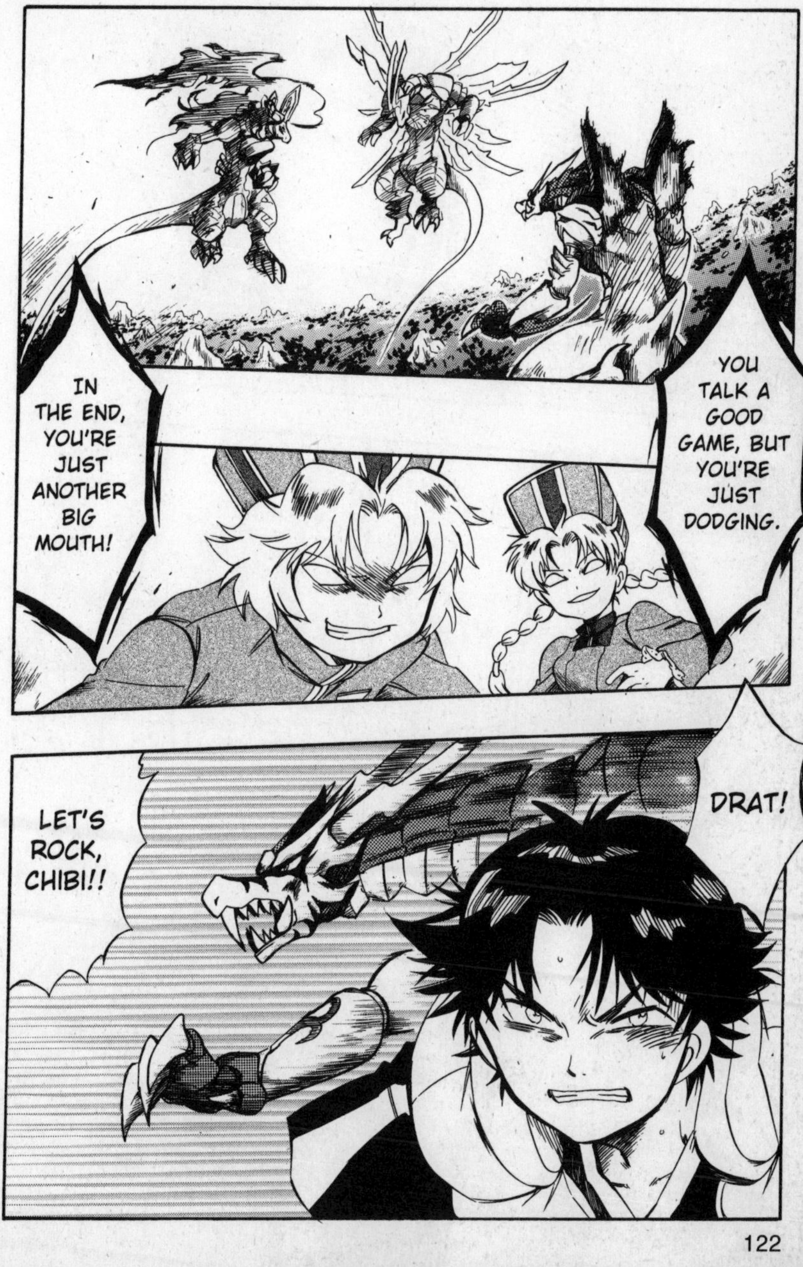
YOU TALK A GOOD GAME, BUT YOU'RE JUST DODGING.
IN THE END, YOU'RE JUST ANOTHER BIG MOUTH!
DRAT!
LET'S ROCK, CHIBI!!

READ THIS WAY

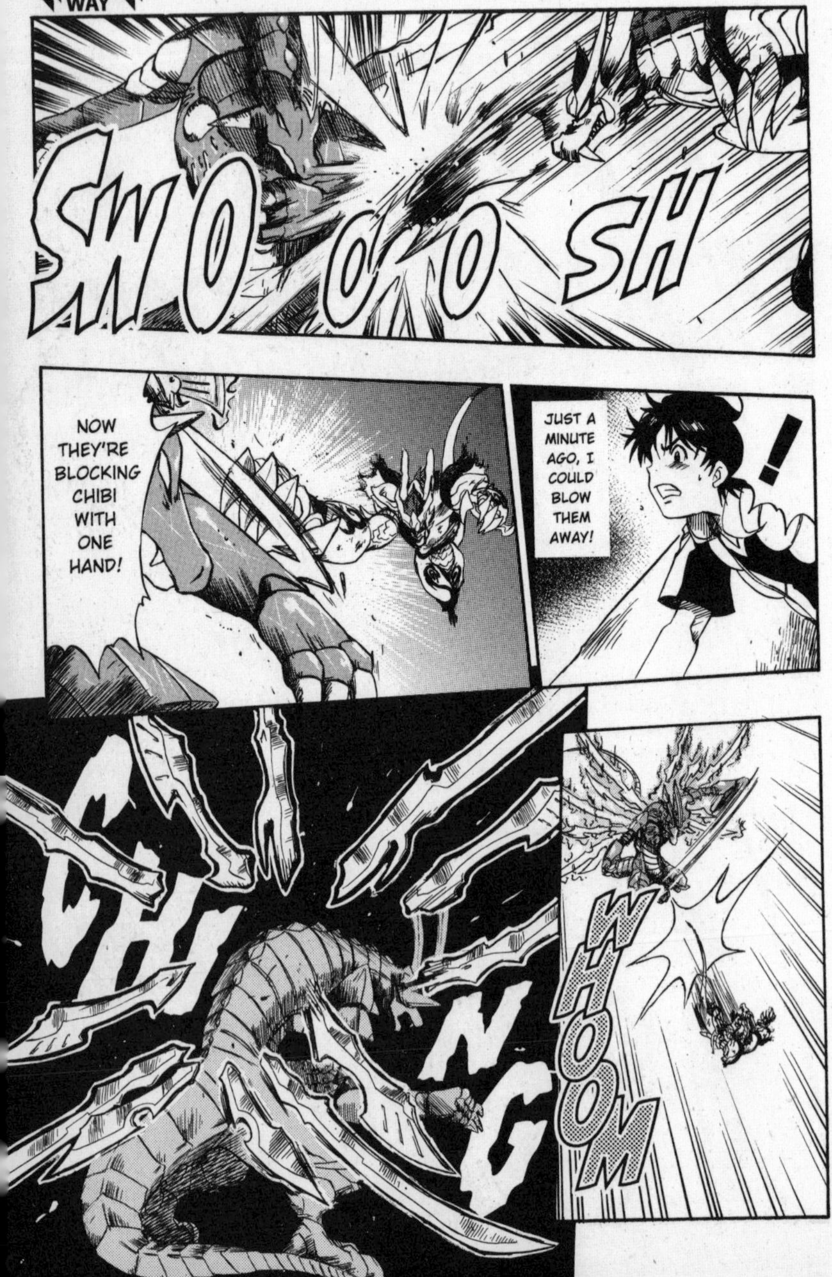
SHWOOOSH
JUST A MINUTE AGO, I COULD BLOW THEM AWAY!
!
NOW THEY'RE BLOCKING CHIBI WITH ONE HAND!
WHOOM
CHING

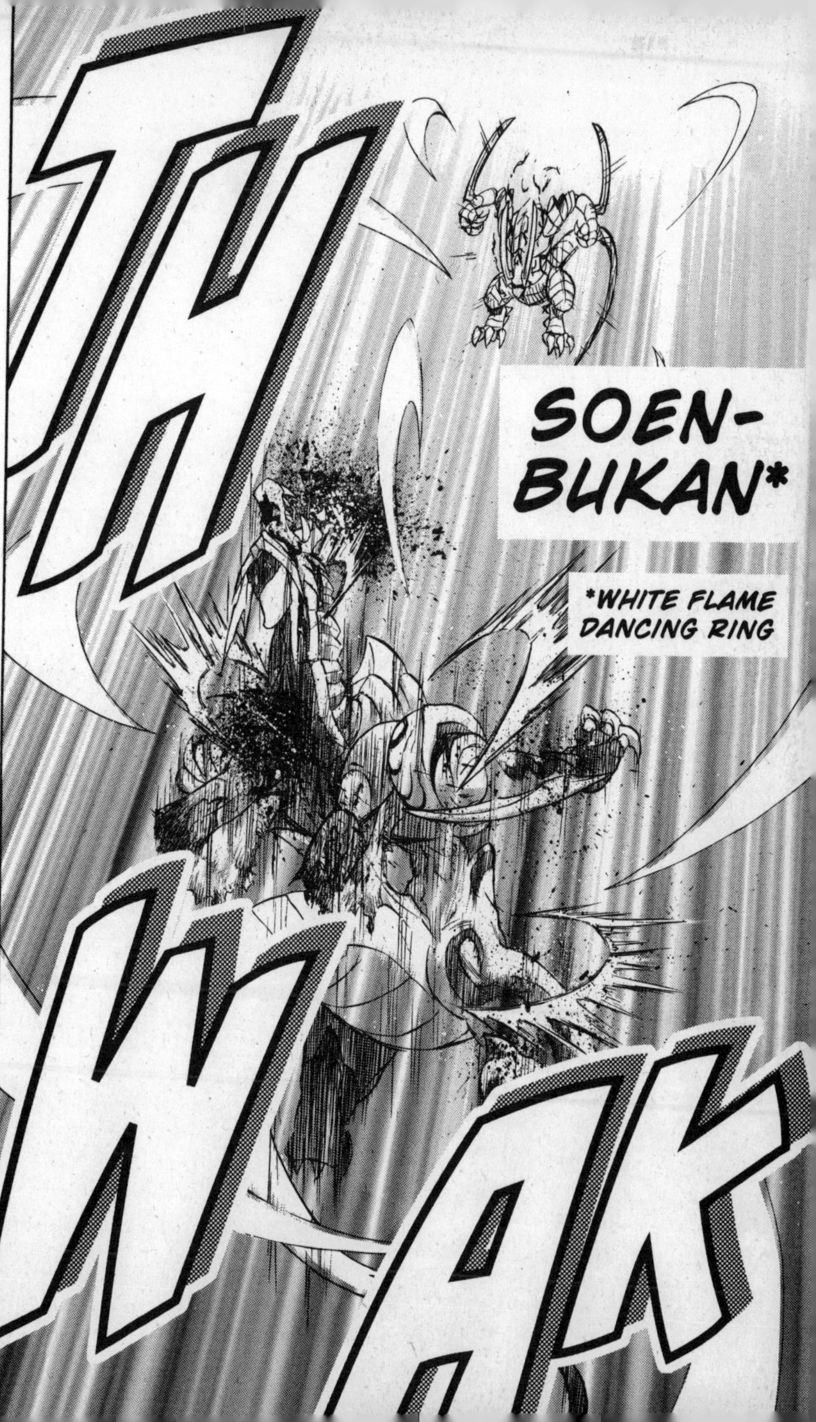
THWAK
SOEN-
BUKAN*
*WHITE FLAME
DANCING RING

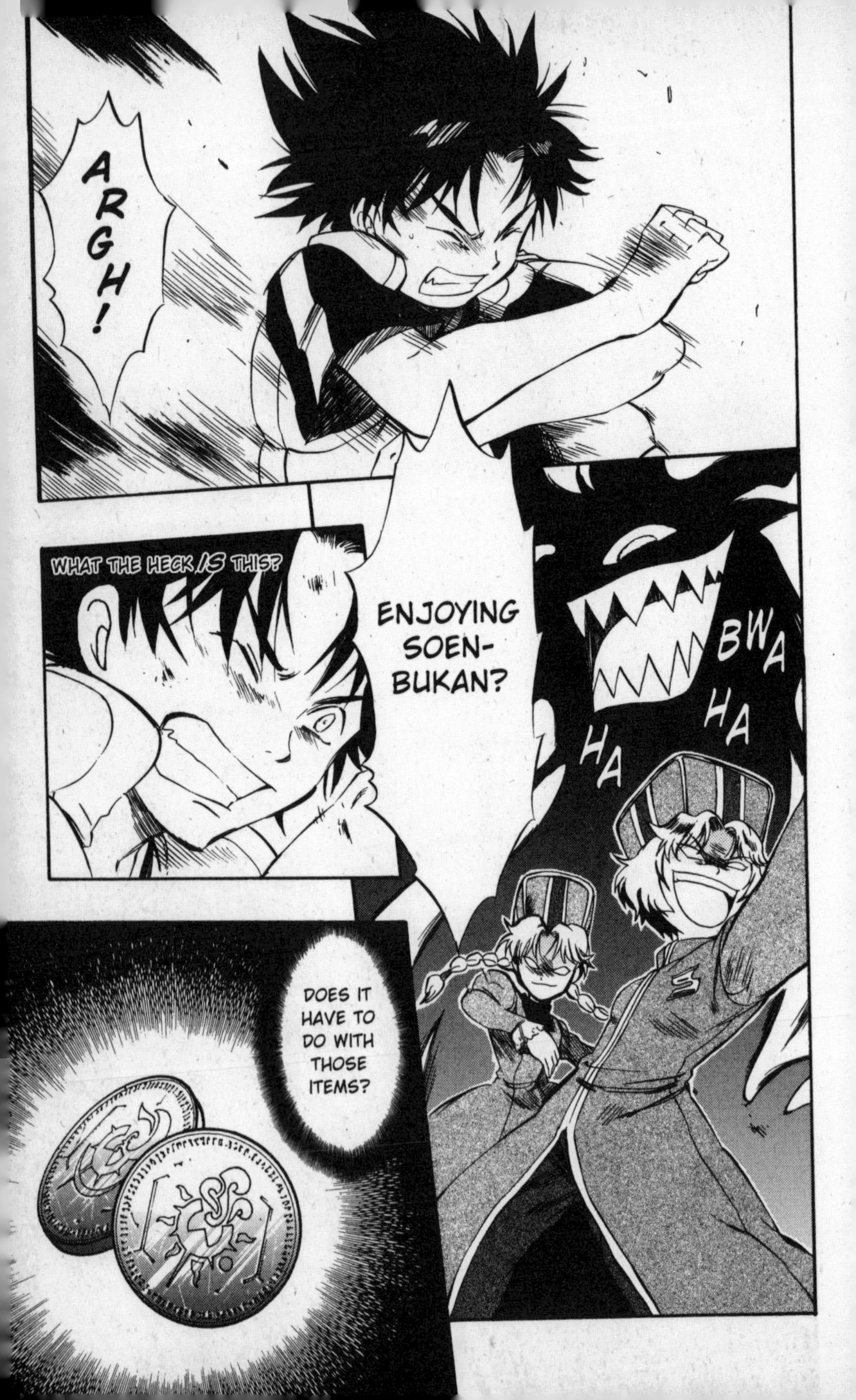
ARGH!
ENJOYING SOEN-BUKAN?
BWA HA HA HA
WHAT THE HECK *IS* THIS?
DOES IT HAVE TO DO WITH THOSE ITEMS?

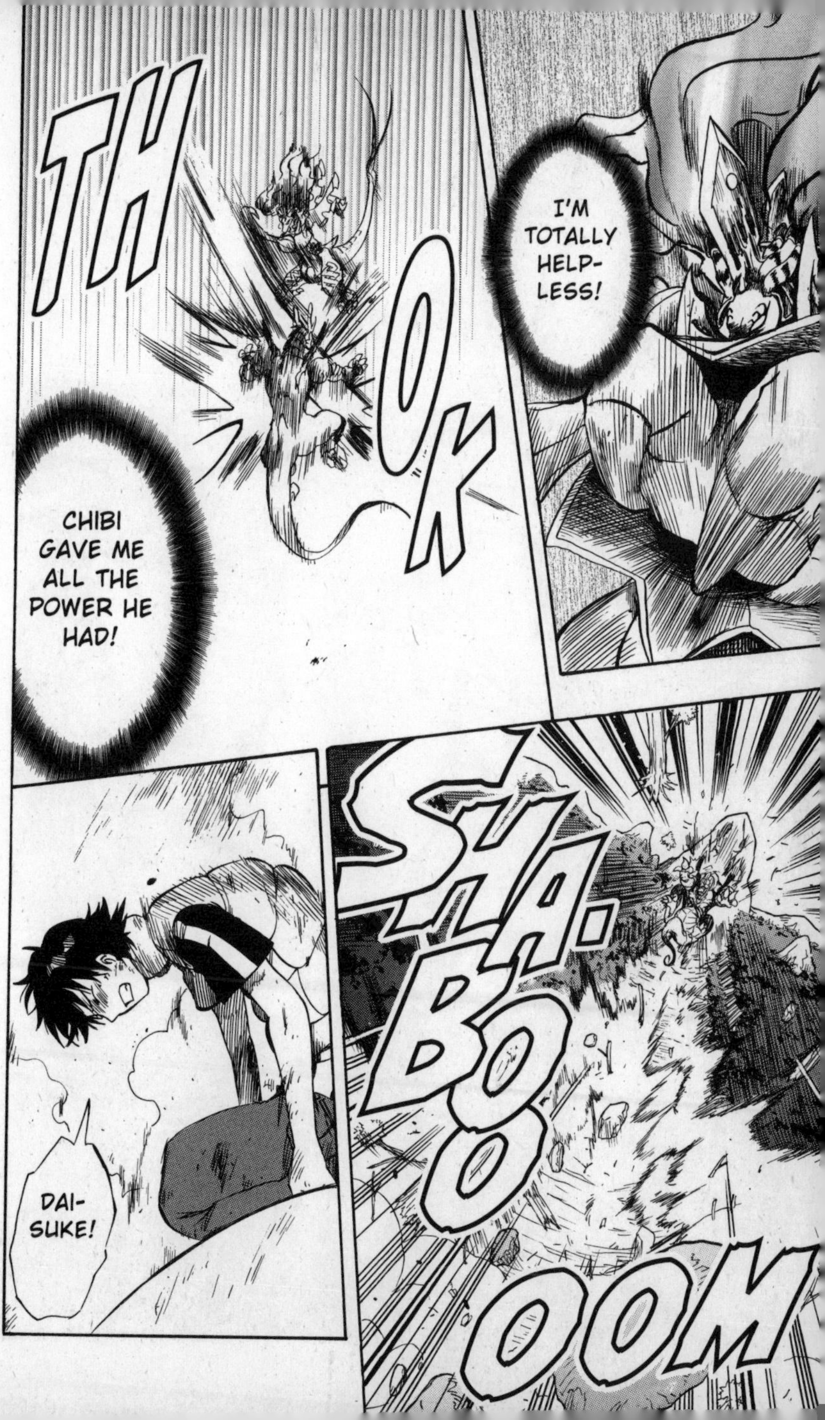
I'M TOTALLY HELP-LESS!
THOOK
CHIBI GAVE ME ALL THE POWER HE HAD!
SHA-BOOOOM
DAI-SUKE!

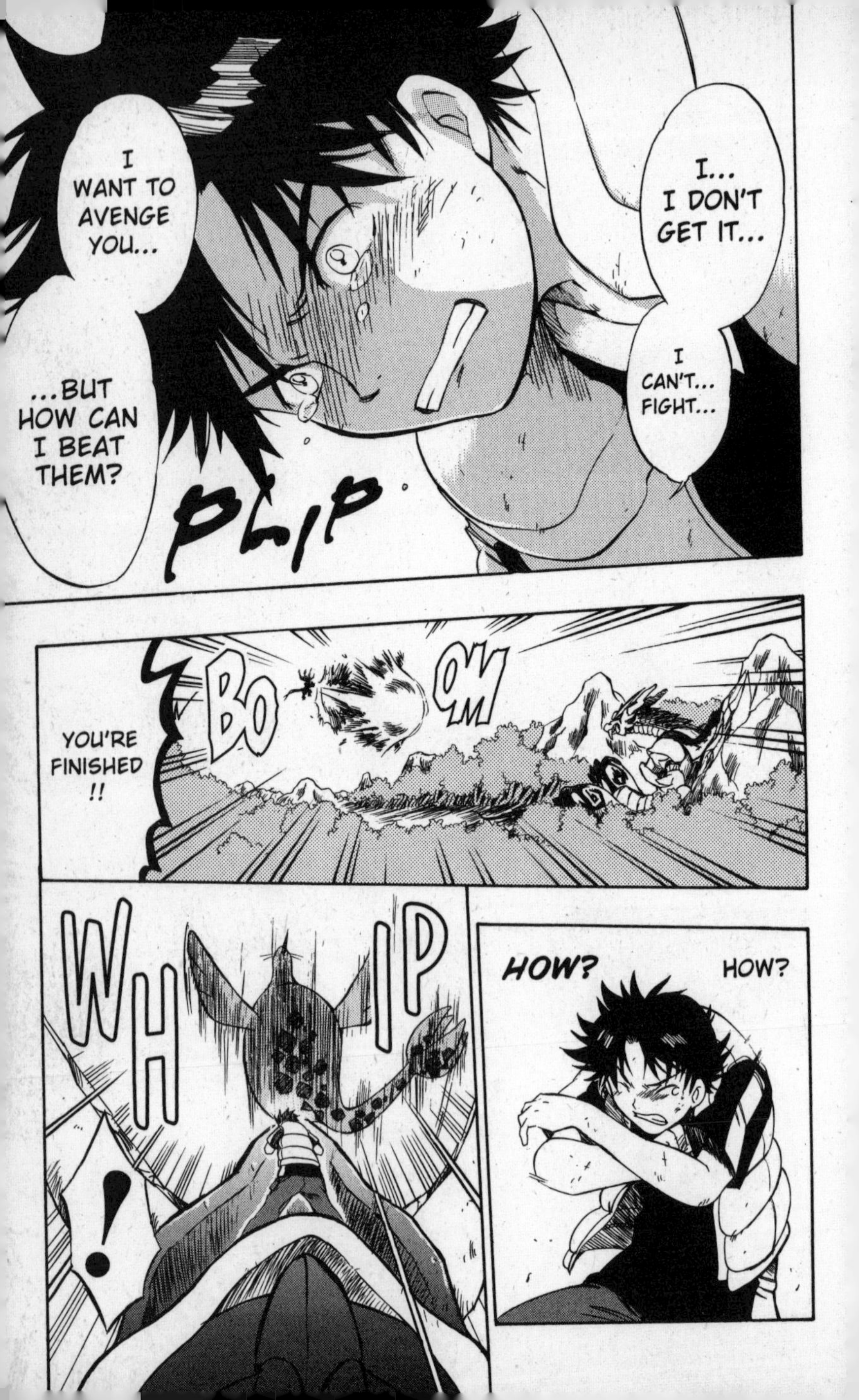
I... I DON'T GET IT...
I CAN'T... FIGHT...
I WANT TO AVENGE YOU...
...BUT HOW CAN I BEAT THEM?
PLIP
BOOM
YOU'RE FINISHED !!
HOW?
HOW?
WHIP
!

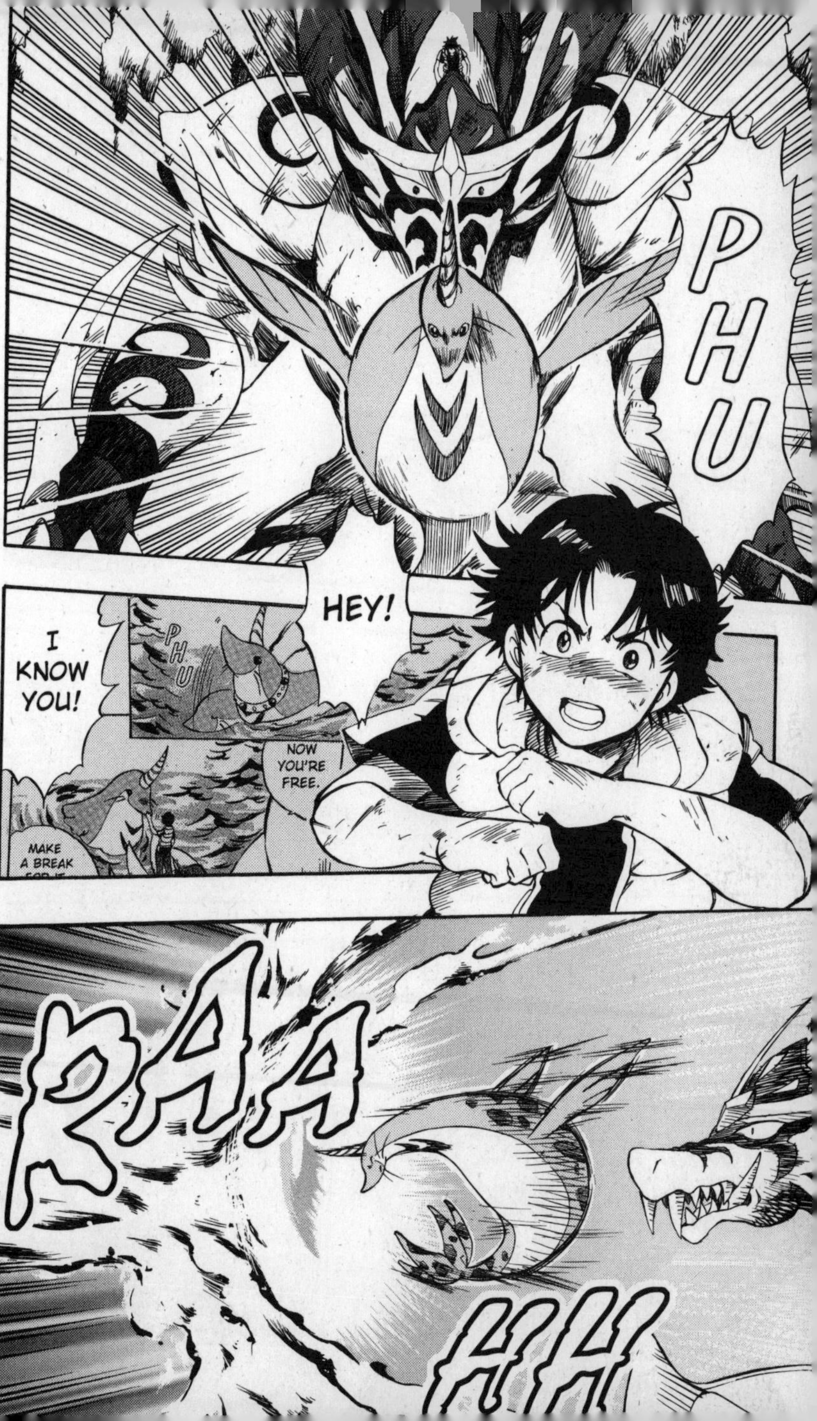
PHU
HEY!
I KNOW YOU!
PHU
NOW YOU'RE FREE.
MAKE A BREAK
RAAAHH

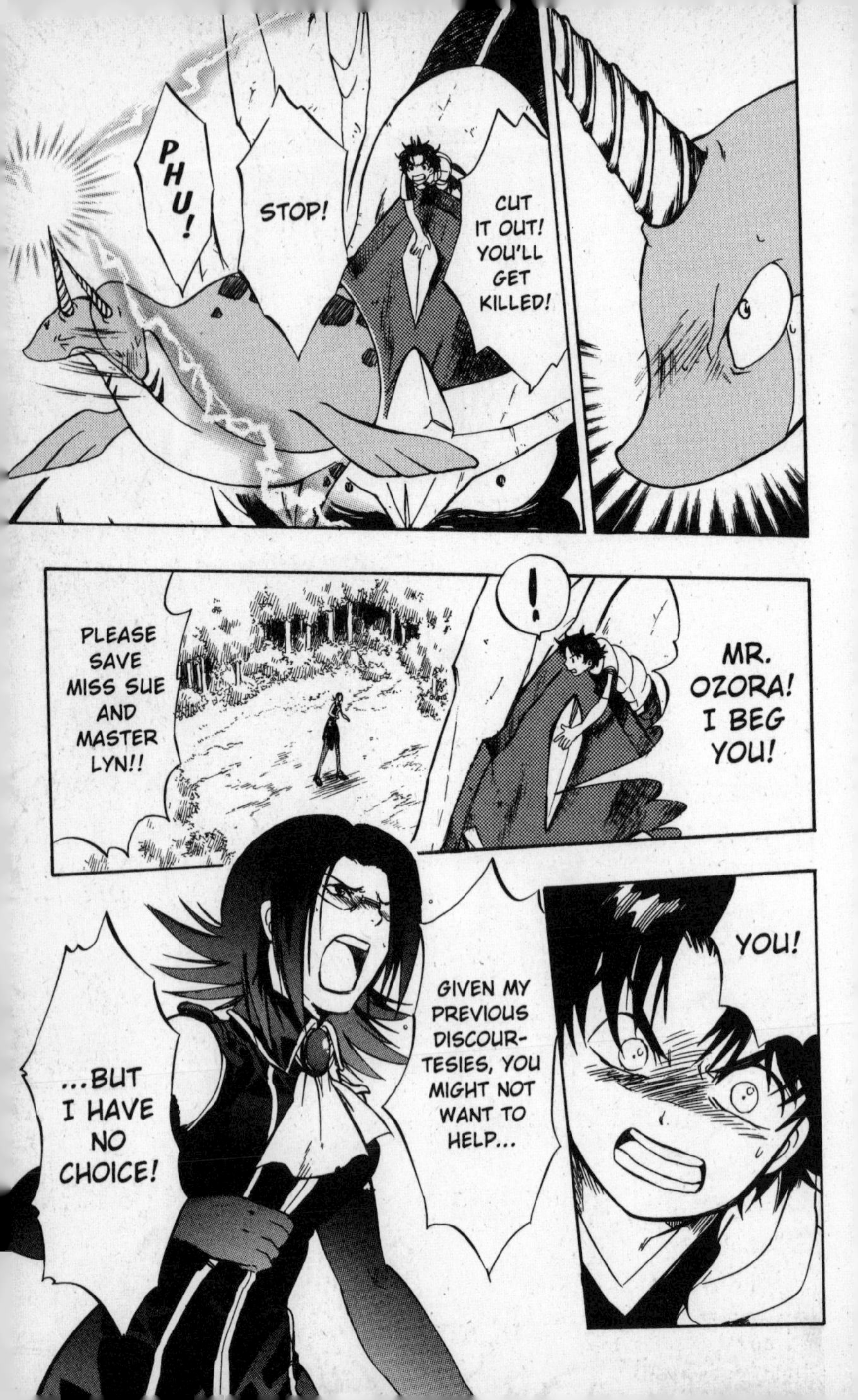
CUT IT OUT! YOU'LL GET KILLED!
STOP!
PHU!
!
MR. OZORA! I BEG YOU!
PLEASE SAVE MISS SUE AND MASTER LYN!!
YOU!
GIVEN MY PREVIOUS DISCOUR-TESIES, YOU MIGHT NOT WANT TO HELP...
...BUT I HAVE NO CHOICE!

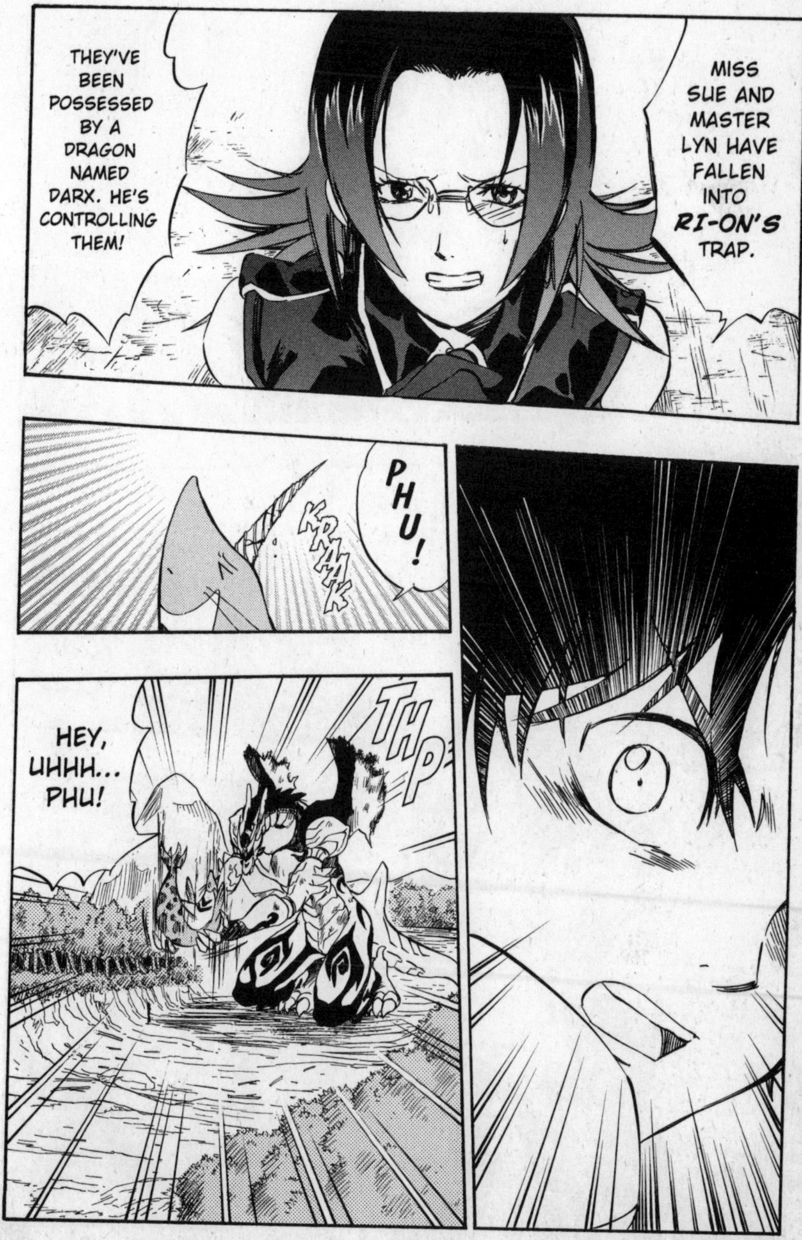
MISS SUE AND MASTER LYN HAVE FALLEN INTO RI-ON'S TRAP.
THEY'VE BEEN POSSESSED BY A DRAGON NAMED DARX. HE'S CONTROLLING THEM!
PHU!
KRAMK
THP
HEY, UHHH... PHU!

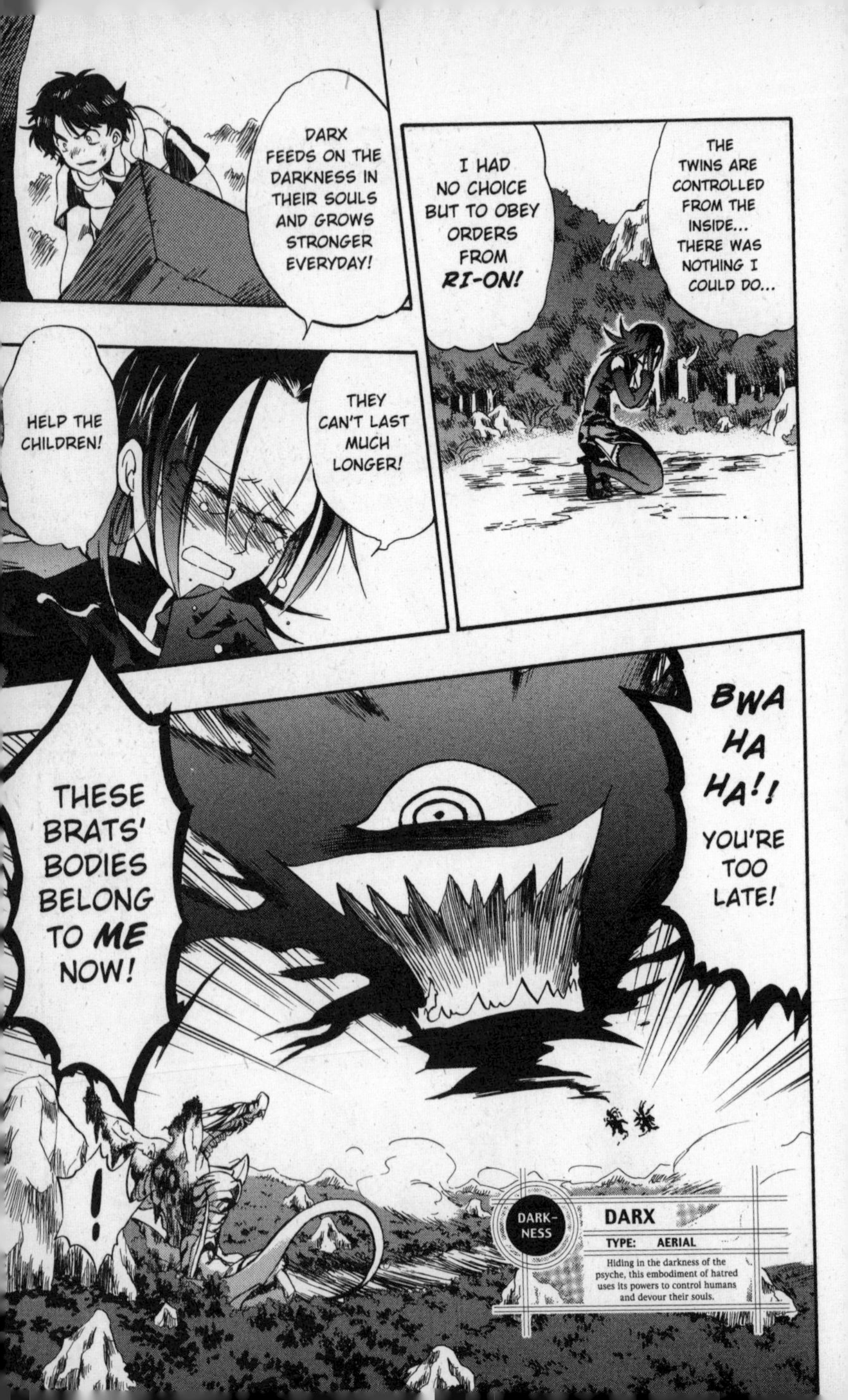
THE TWINS ARE CONTROLLED FROM THE INSIDE... THERE WAS NOTHING I COULD DO...
I HAD NO CHOICE BUT TO OBEY ORDERS FROM RI-ON!
DARX FEEDS ON THE DARKNESS IN THEIR SOULS AND GROWS STRONGER EVERYDAY!
THEY CAN'T LAST MUCH LONGER!
HELP THE CHILDREN!
BWA HA HA!!
YOU'RE TOO LATE!
THESE BRATS' BODIES BELONG TO ME NOW!
!
DARK-NESS
DARX
TYPE: AERIAL
Hiding in the darkness of the psyche, this embodiment of hatred uses its powers to control humans and devour their souls.

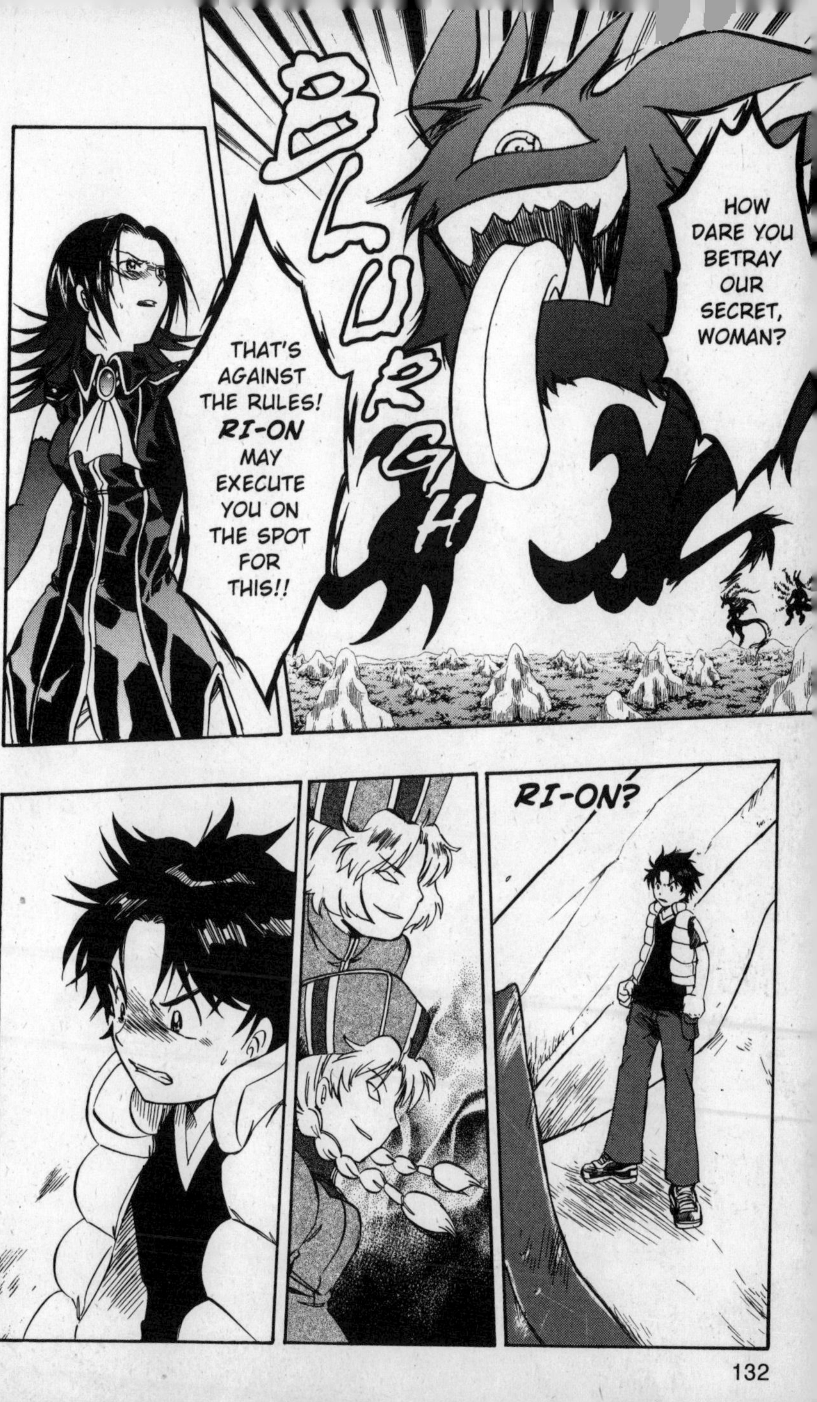
HOW DARE YOU BETRAY OUR SECRET, WOMAN?
SLURGH
THAT'S AGAINST THE RULES! RI-ON MAY EXECUTE YOU ON THE SPOT FOR THIS!!
RI-ON?

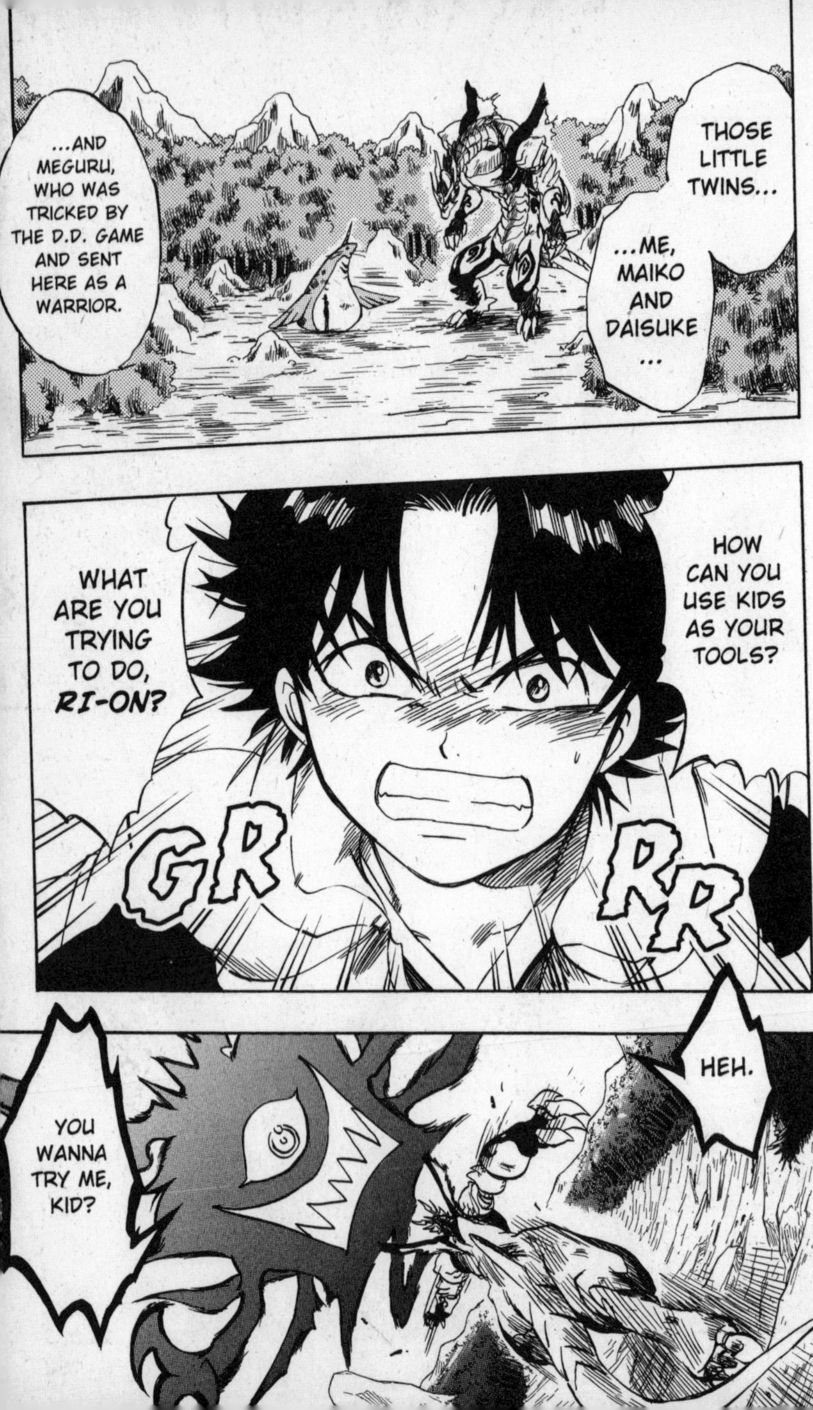
THOSE LITTLE TWINS...
...ME, MAIKO AND DAISUKE...
...AND MEGURU, WHO WAS TRICKED BY THE D.D. GAME AND SENT HERE AS A WARRIOR.
HOW CAN YOU USE KIDS AS YOUR TOOLS?
WHAT ARE YOU TRYING TO DO, *RI-ON*?
GRRR
HEH.
YOU WANNA TRY ME, KID?

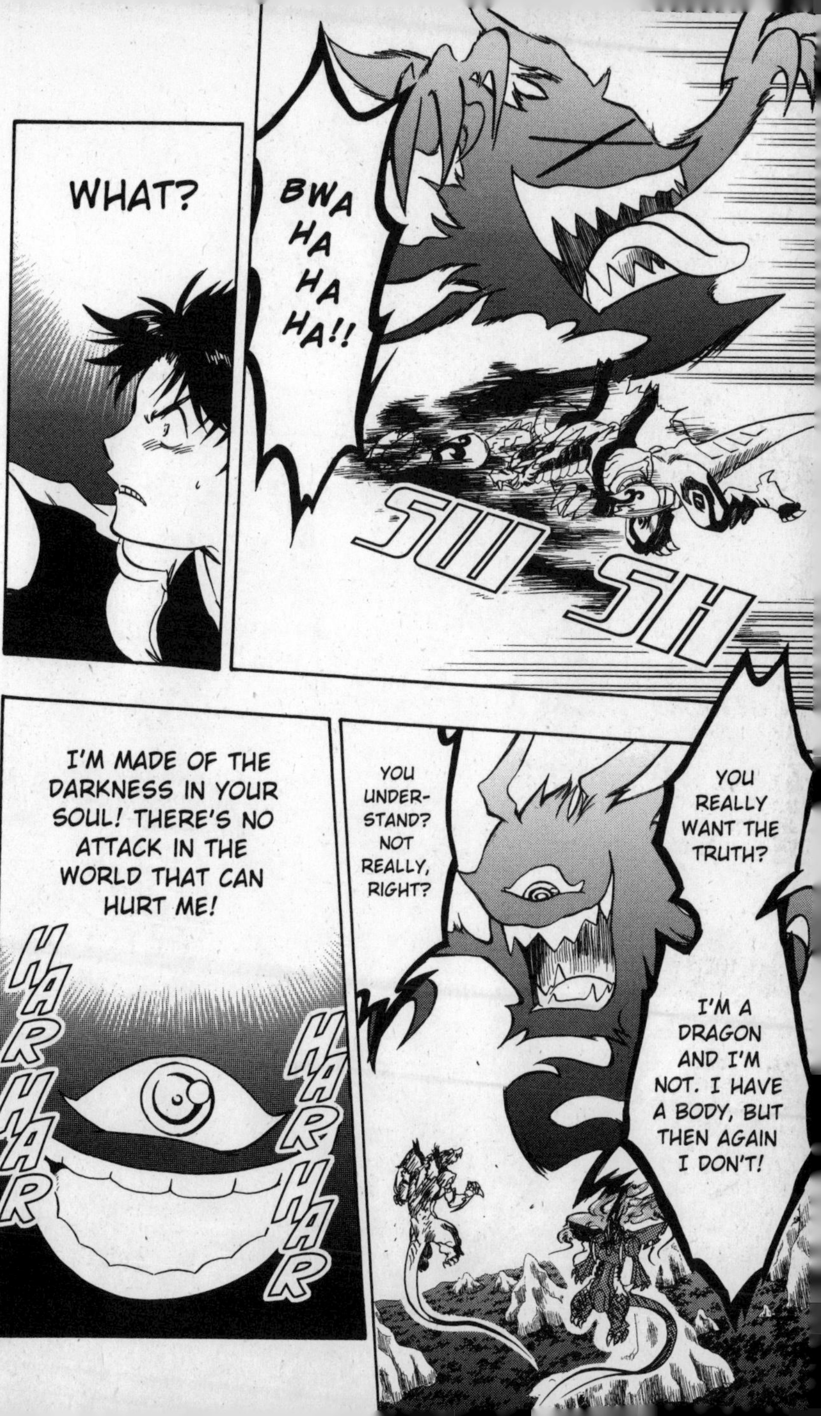
BWA HA HA HA HA!!
SWISH
WHAT?
YOU REALLY WANT THE TRUTH?
I'M A DRAGON AND I'M NOT. I HAVE A BODY, BUT THEN AGAIN I DON'T!
YOU UNDERSTAND? NOT REALLY, RIGHT?
I'M MADE OF THE DARKNESS IN YOUR SOUL! THERE'S NO ATTACK IN THE WORLD THAT CAN HURT ME!
HAR HAR HAR
HAR HAR HAR

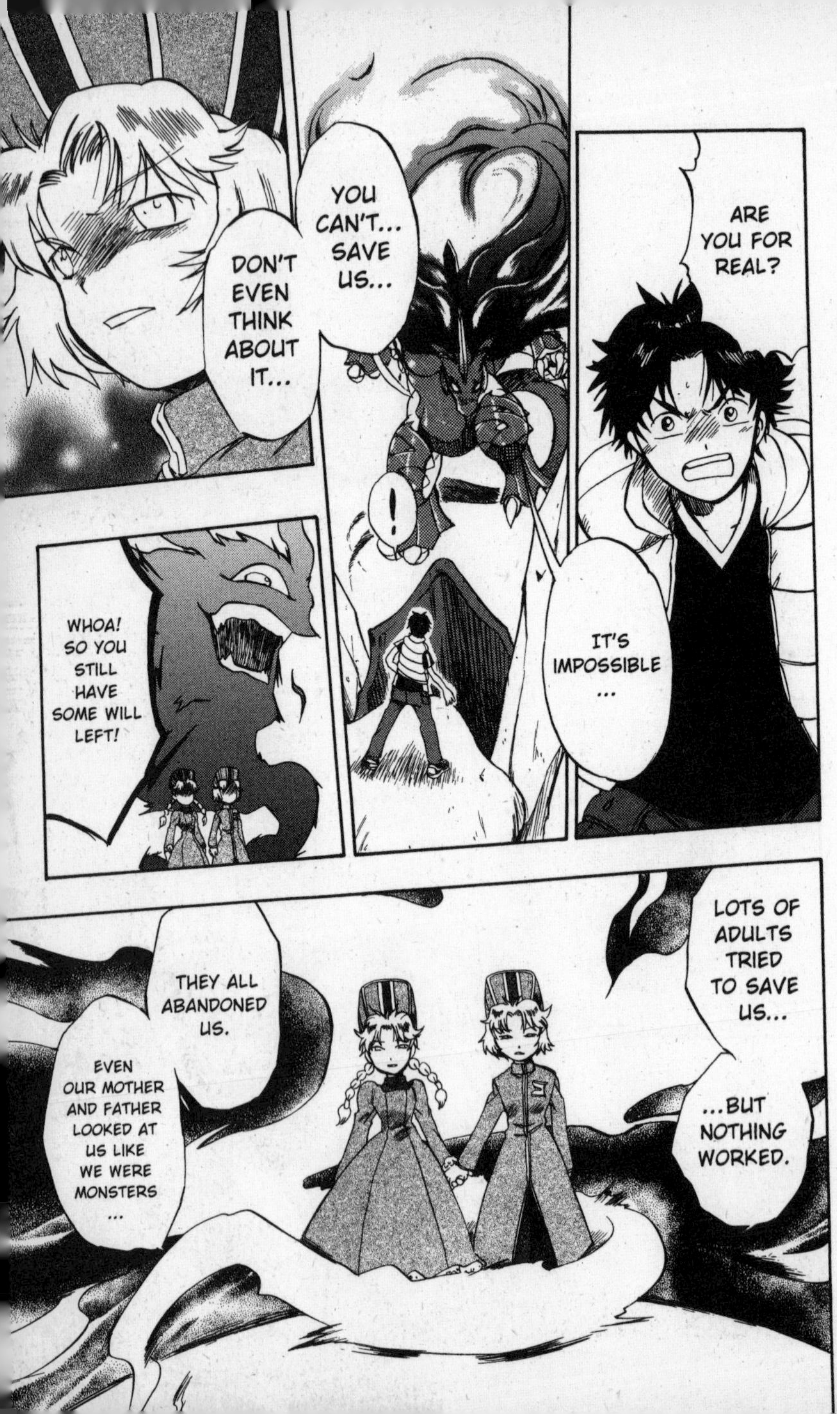
ARE YOU FOR REAL?
IT'S IMPOSSIBLE ...
YOU CAN'T... SAVE US...
!
DON'T EVEN THINK ABOUT IT...
WHOA! SO YOU STILL HAVE SOME WILL LEFT!
LOTS OF ADULTS TRIED TO SAVE US...
...BUT NOTHING WORKED.
THEY ALL ABANDONED US.
EVEN OUR MOTHER AND FATHER LOOKED AT US LIKE WE WERE MONSTERS ...

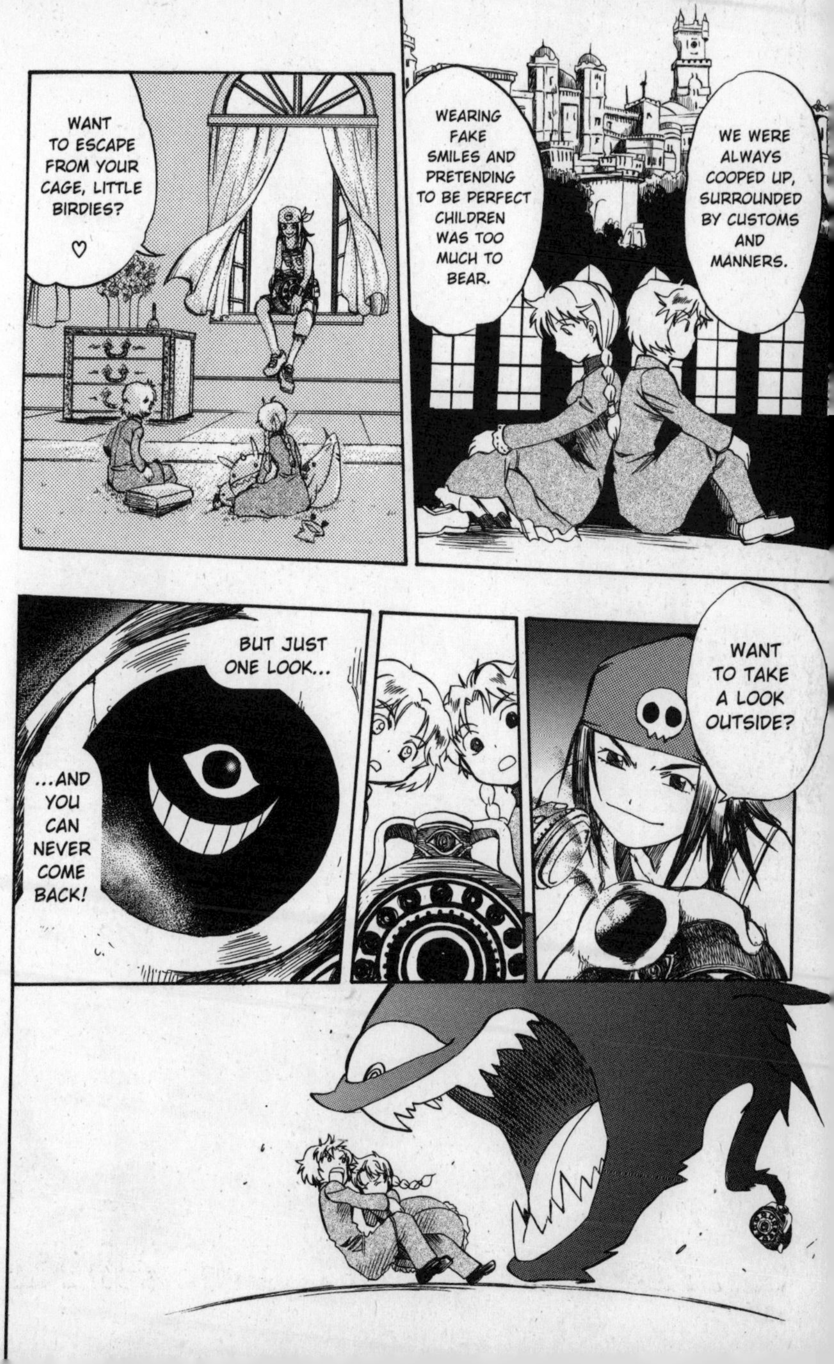
WE WERE ALWAYS COOPED UP, SURROUNDED BY CUSTOMS AND MANNERS.
WEARING FAKE SMILES AND PRETENDING TO BE PERFECT CHILDREN WAS TOO MUCH TO BEAR.
WANT TO ESCAPE FROM YOUR CAGE, LITTLE BIRDIES? ♡
WANT TO TAKE A LOOK OUTSIDE?
BUT JUST ONE LOOK...
...AND YOU CAN NEVER COME BACK!

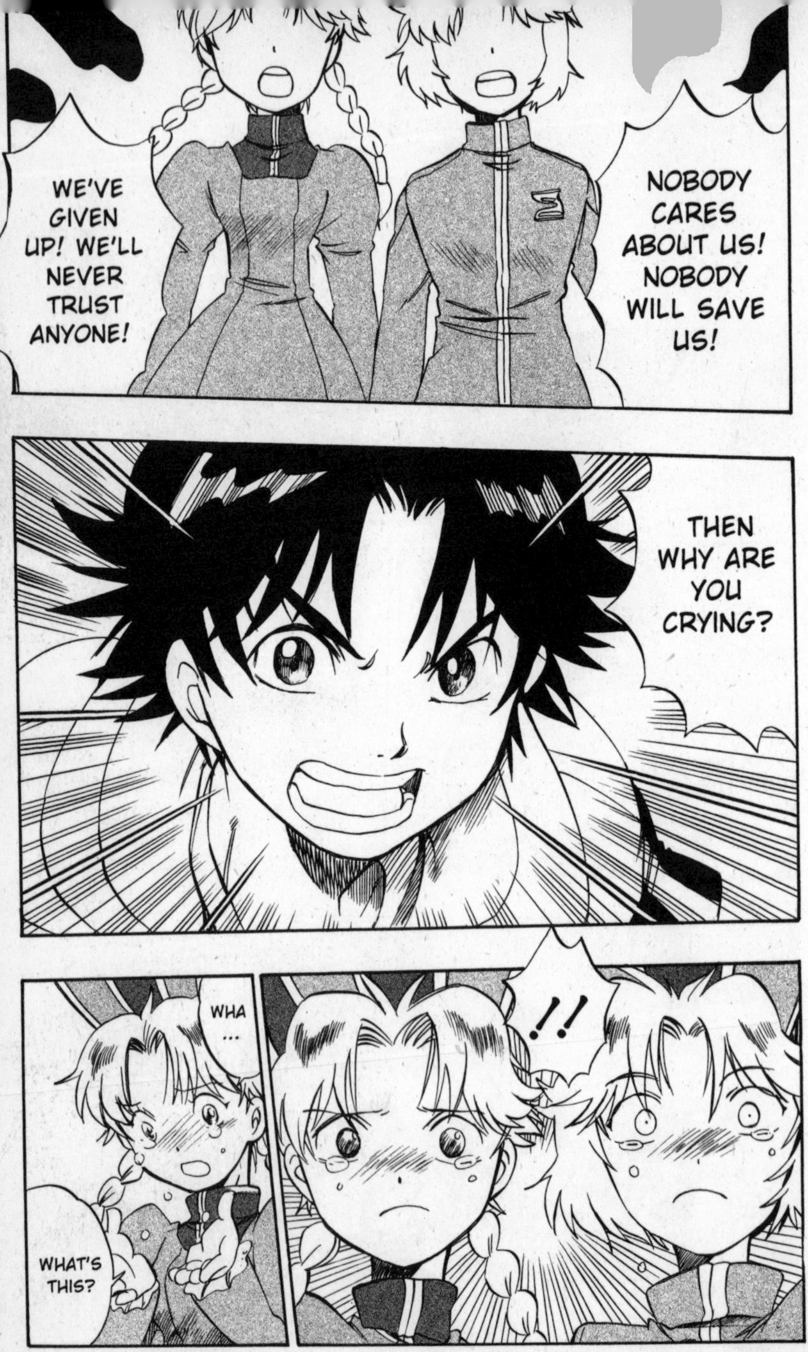
NOBODY CARES ABOUT US! NOBODY WILL SAVE US!
WE'VE GIVEN UP! WE'LL NEVER TRUST ANYONE!
THEN WHY ARE YOU CRYING?
!!
WHA...
WHAT'S THIS?

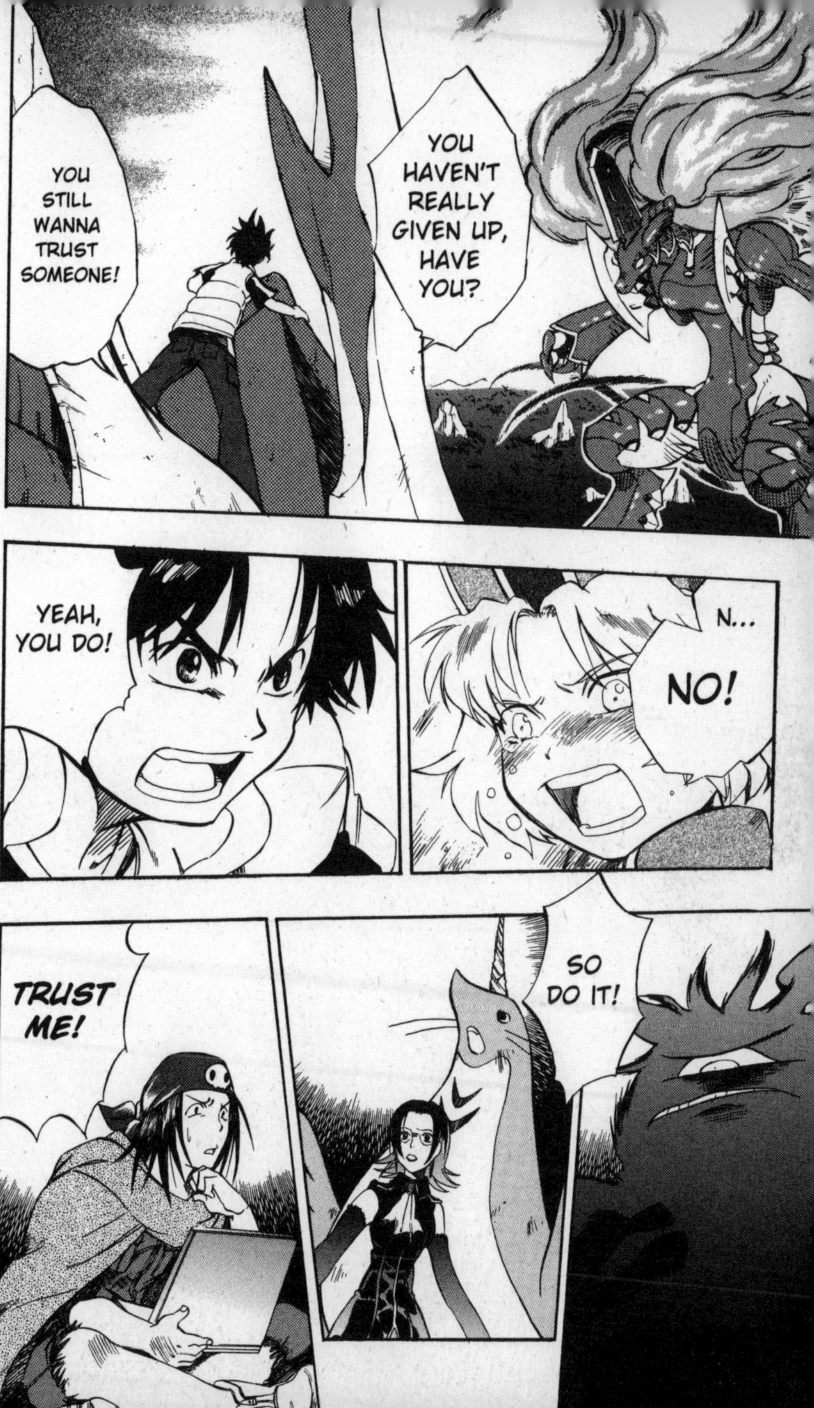
YOU HAVEN'T REALLY GIVEN UP, HAVE YOU?
YOU STILL WANNA TRUST SOMEONE!
N...
NO!
YEAH, YOU DO!
SO DO IT!
TRUST ME!

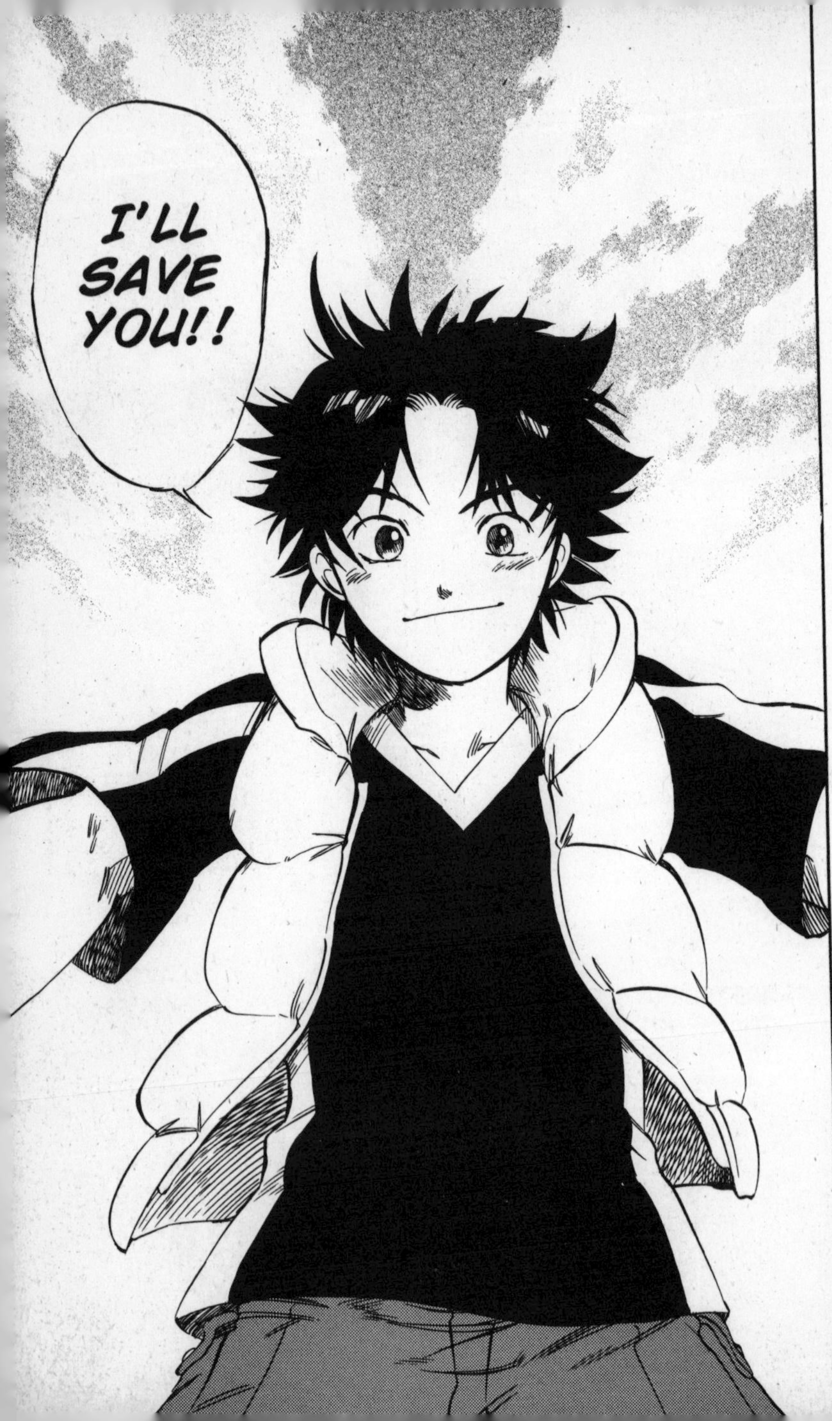
I'LL SAVE YOU!!

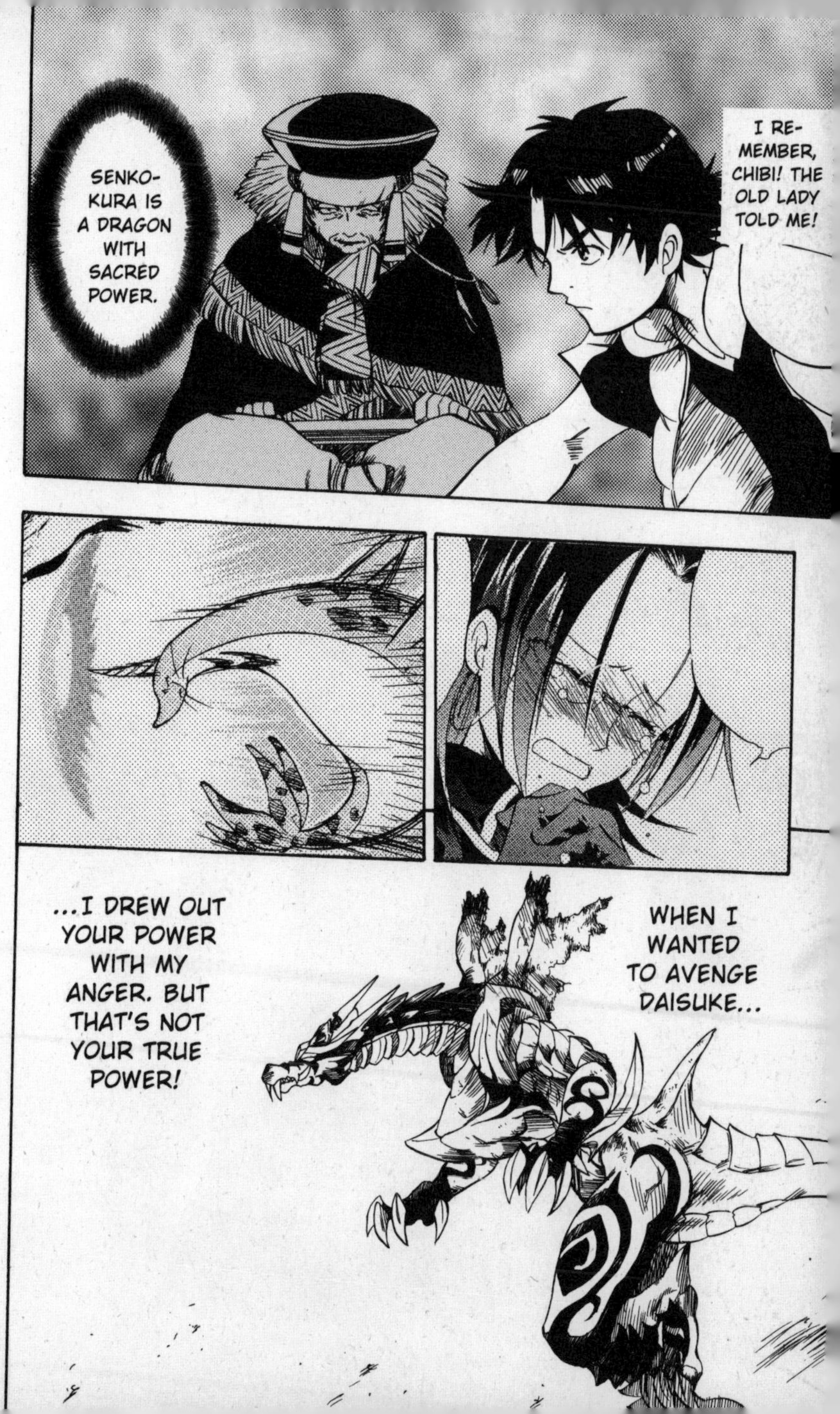
I RE-MEMBER, CHIBI! THE OLD LADY TOLD ME!
SENKO-KURA IS A DRAGON WITH SACRED POWER.
WHEN I WANTED TO AVENGE DAISUKE...
...I DREW OUT YOUR POWER WITH MY ANGER. BUT THAT'S NOT YOUR TRUE POWER!

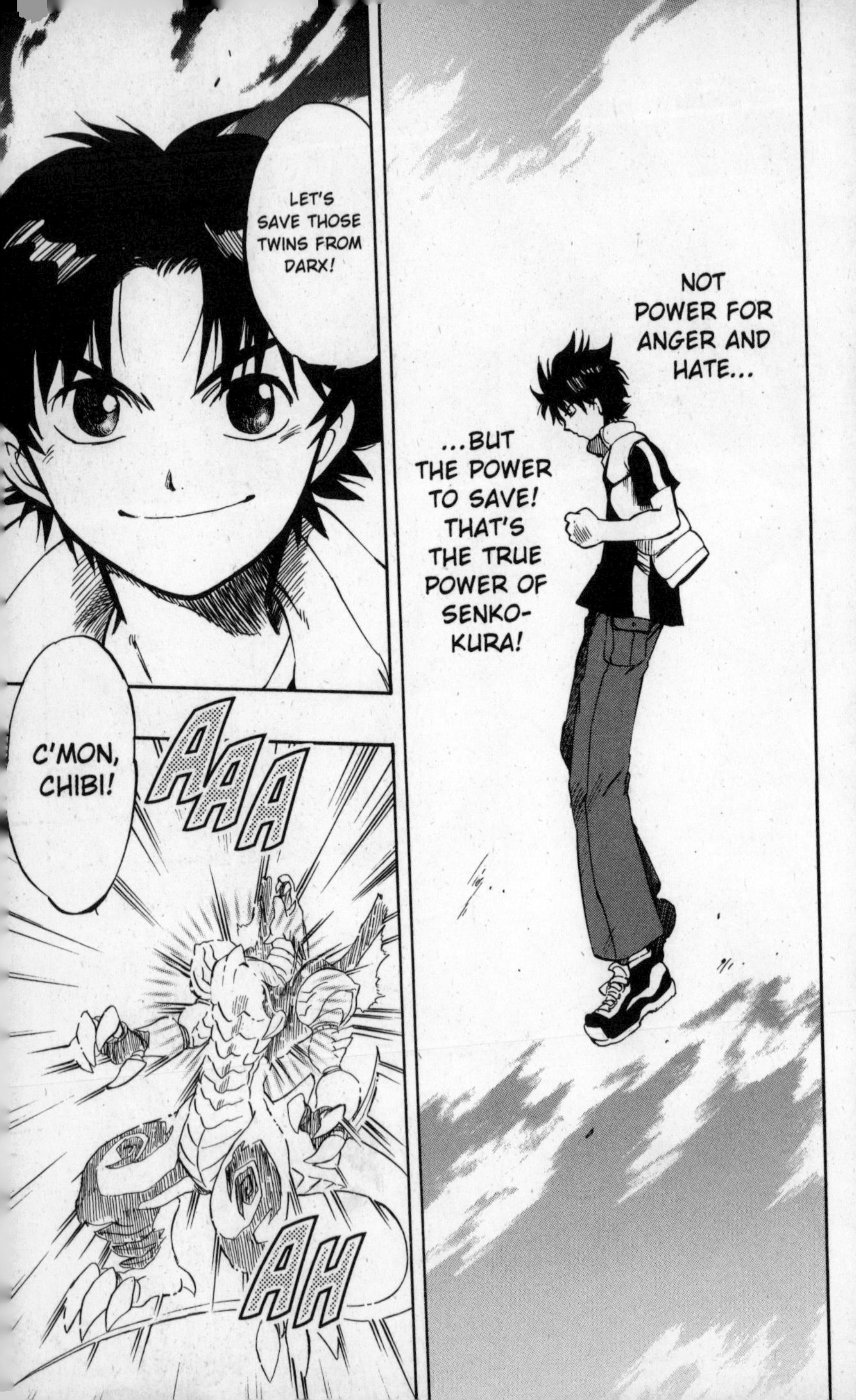
NOT POWER FOR ANGER AND HATE...
...BUT THE POWER TO SAVE! THAT'S THE TRUE POWER OF SENKO-KURA!
LET'S SAVE THOSE TWINS FROM DARX!
C'MON, CHIBI!
AAAA
AH

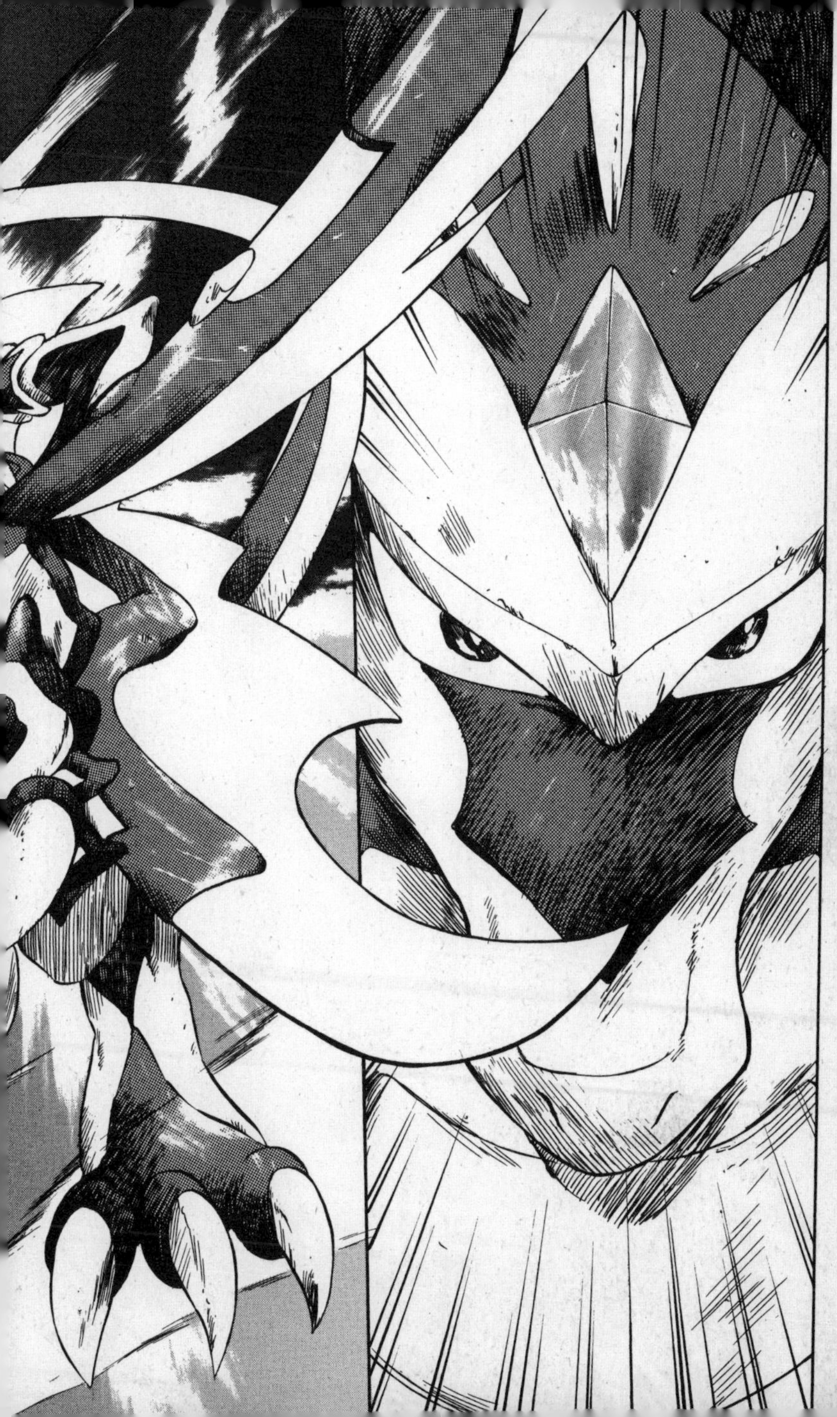

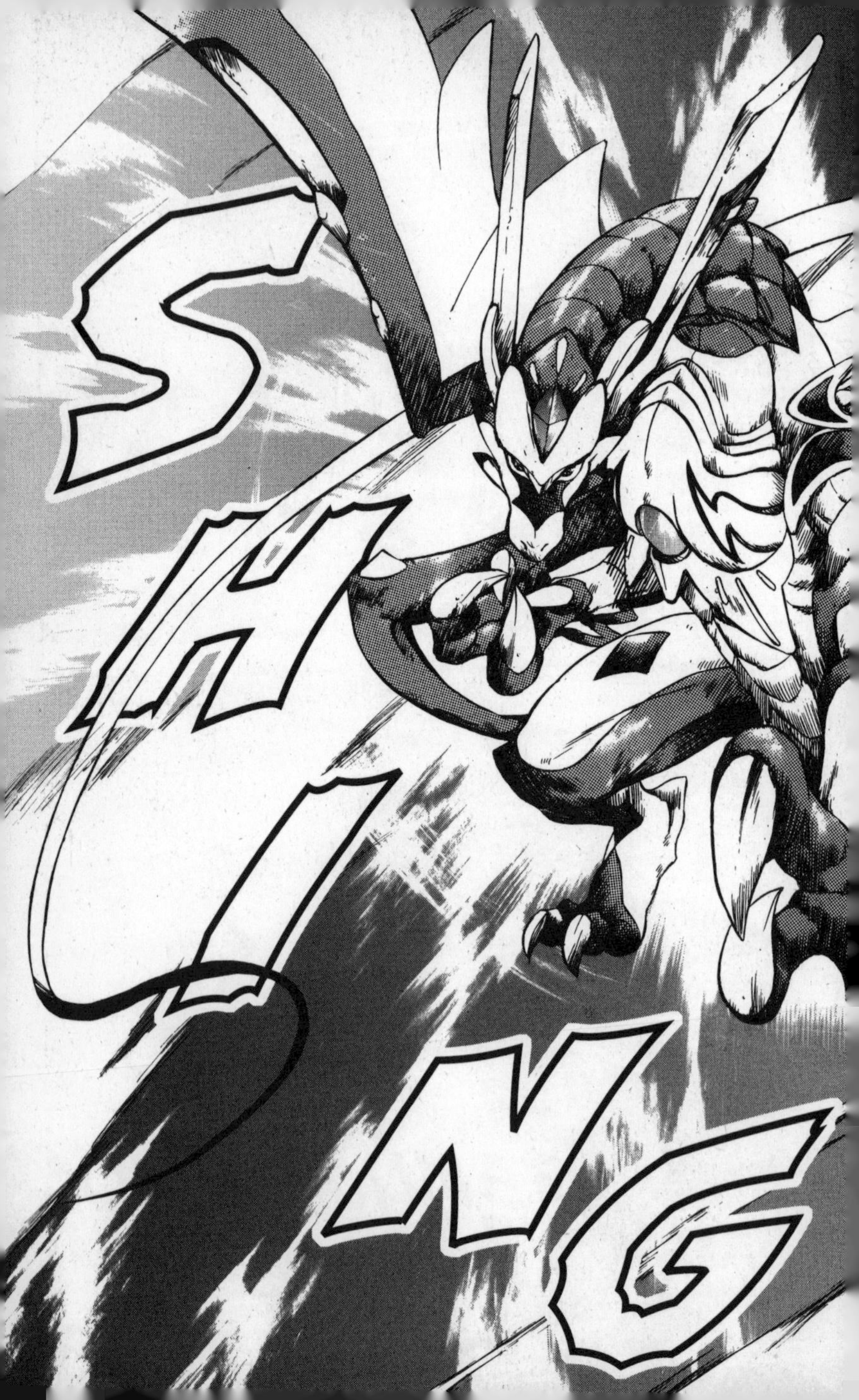
SHING

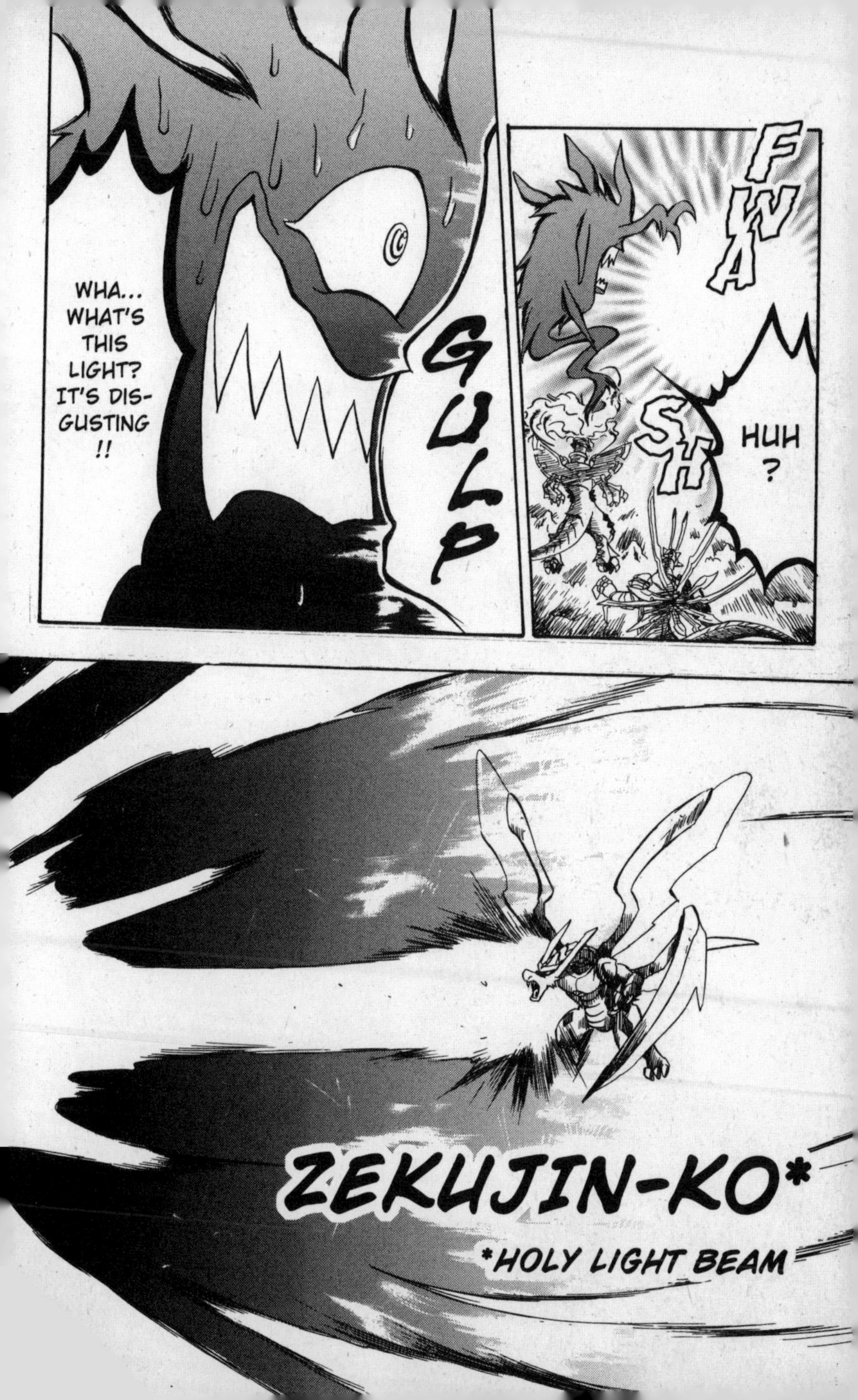
FWASH
HUH ?
WHA... WHAT'S THIS LIGHT? IT'S DISGUSTING !!
GULP
ZEKUJIN-KO*
*HOLY LIGHT BEAM

READ THIS WAY

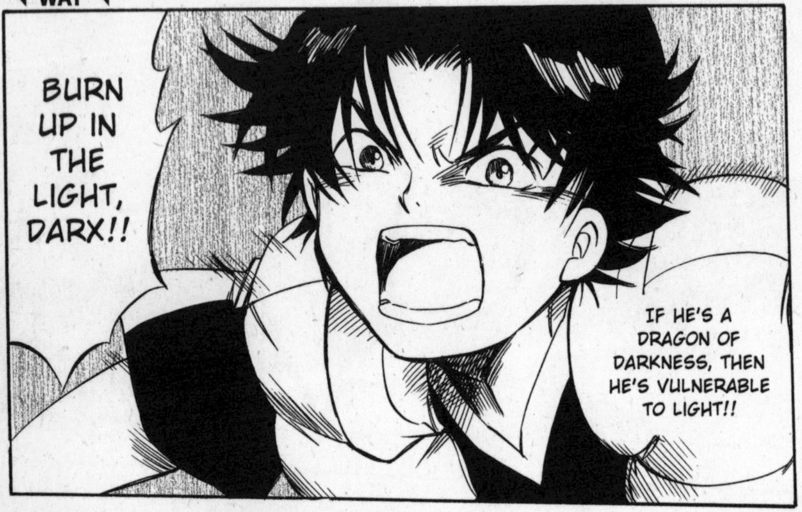
IF HE'S A DRAGON OF DARKNESS, THEN HE'S VULNERABLE TO LIGHT!!
BURN UP IN THE LIGHT, DARX!!

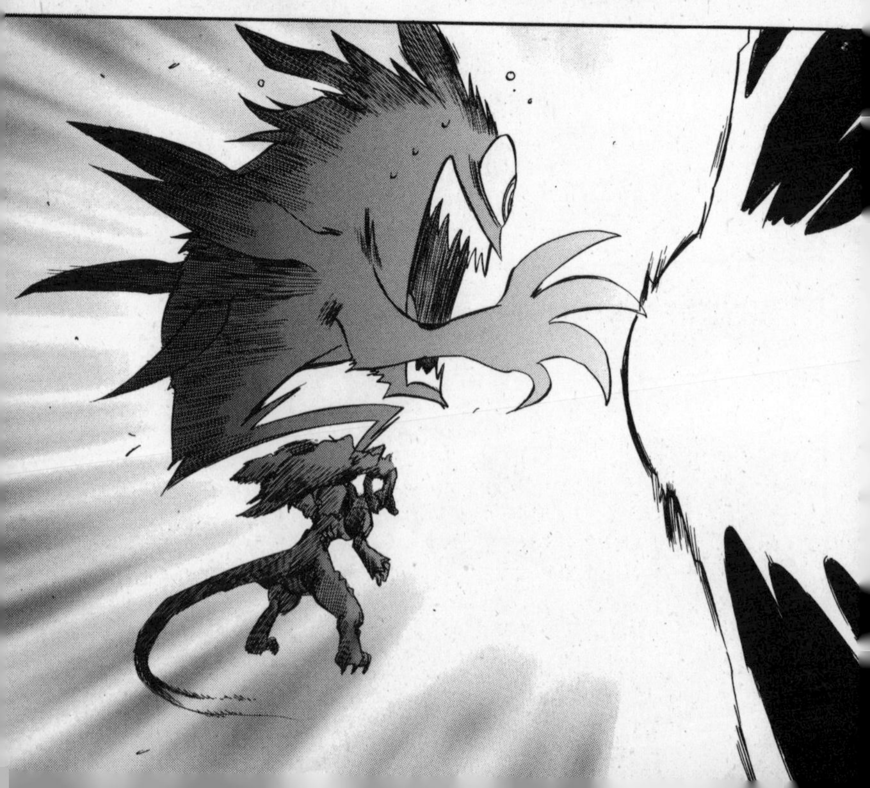

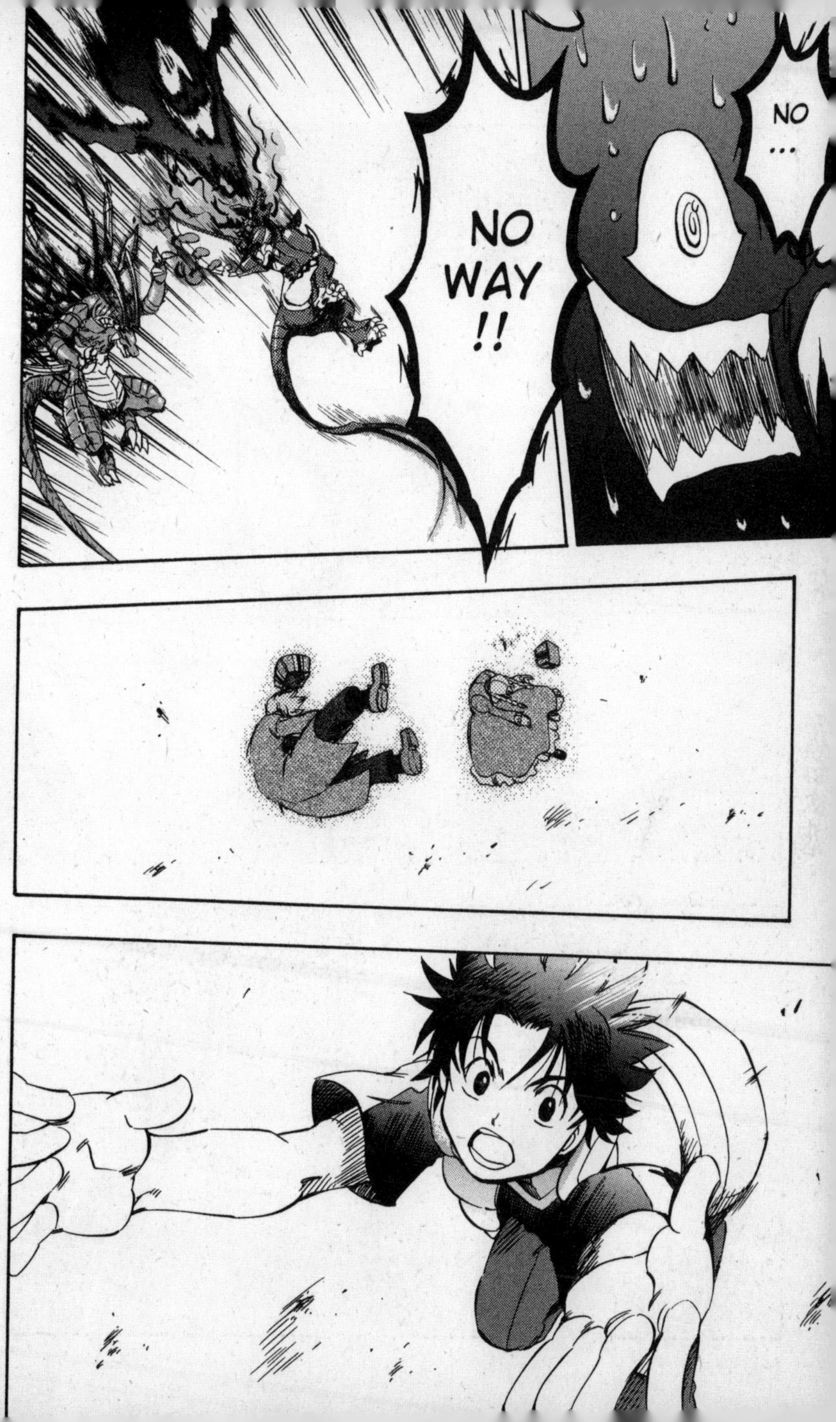
NO ...
NO WAY !!

READ THIS WAY

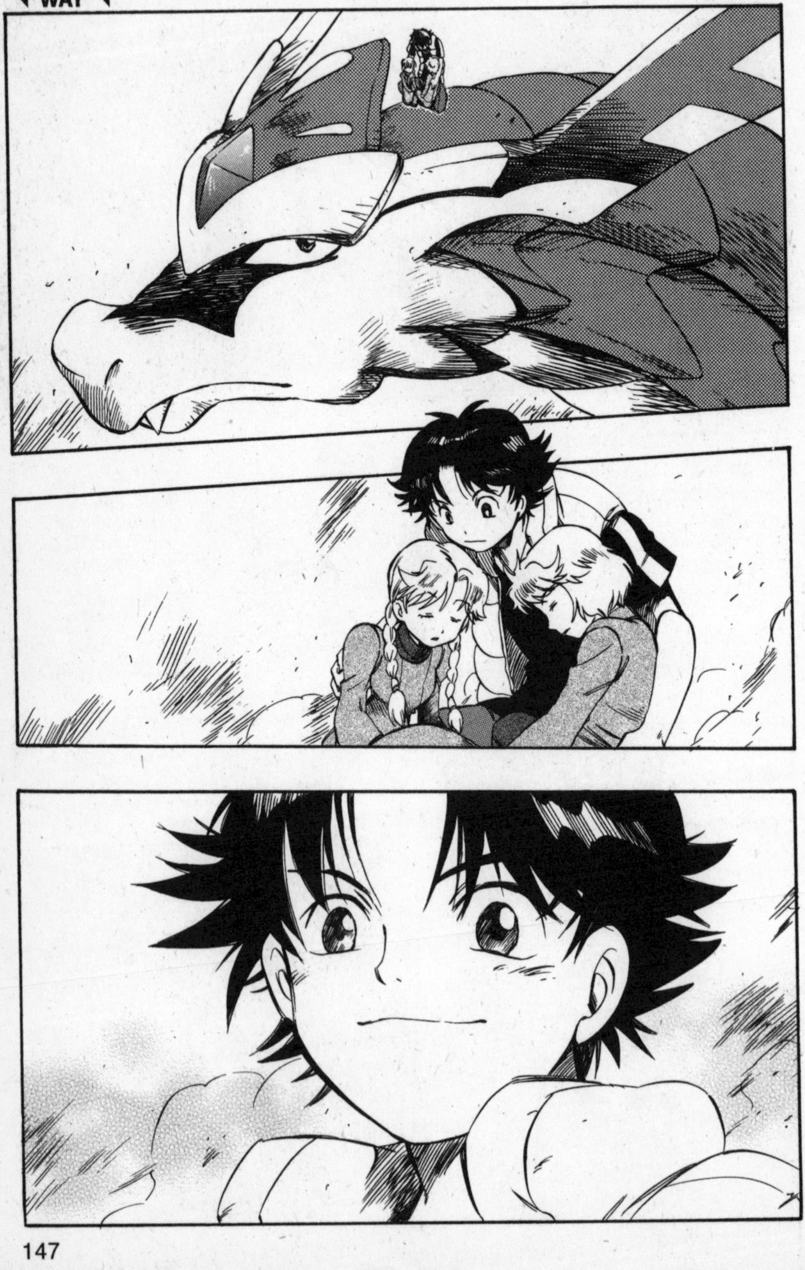

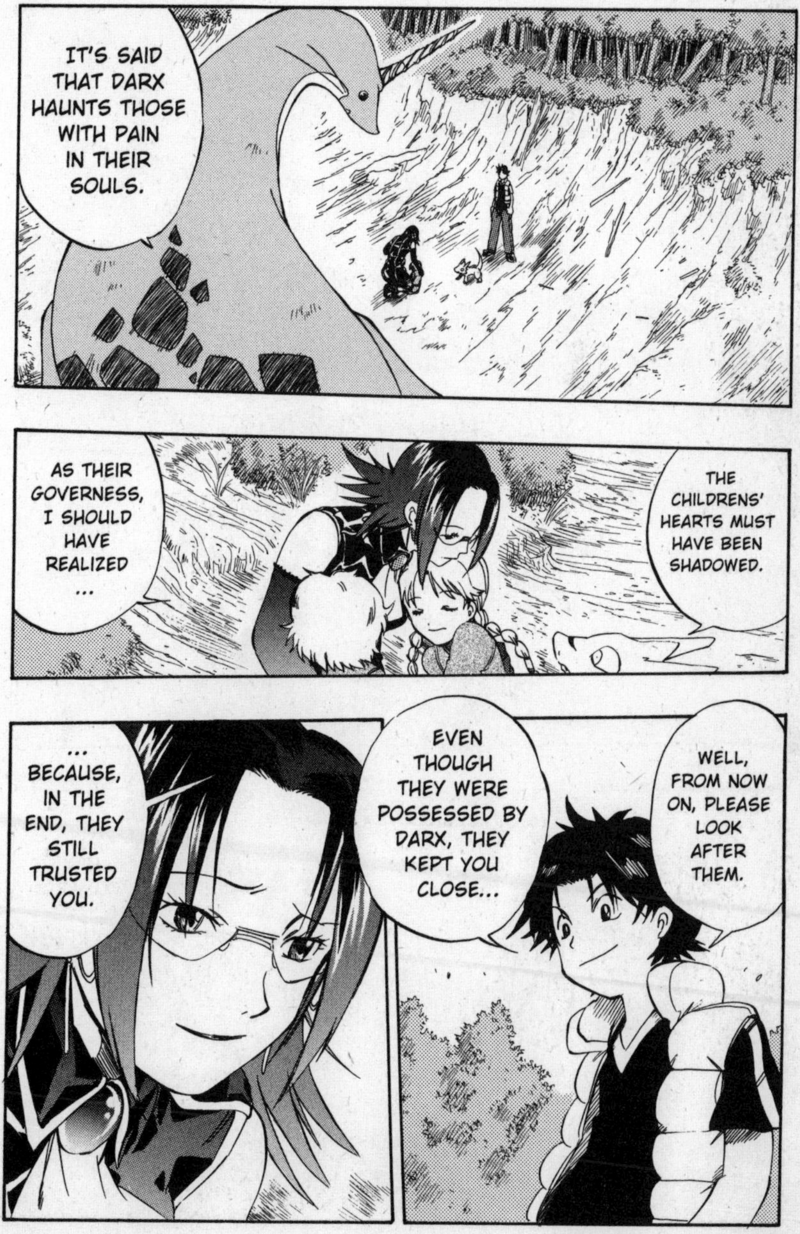
IT'S SAID THAT DARX HAUNTS THOSE WITH PAIN IN THEIR SOULS.
THE CHILDRENS' HEARTS MUST HAVE BEEN SHADOWED.
AS THEIR GOVERNESS, I SHOULD HAVE REALIZED ...
WELL, FROM NOW ON, PLEASE LOOK AFTER THEM.
EVEN THOUGH THEY WERE POSSESSED BY DARX, THEY KEPT YOU CLOSE...
... BECAUSE, IN THE END, THEY STILL TRUSTED YOU.

READ THIS WAY

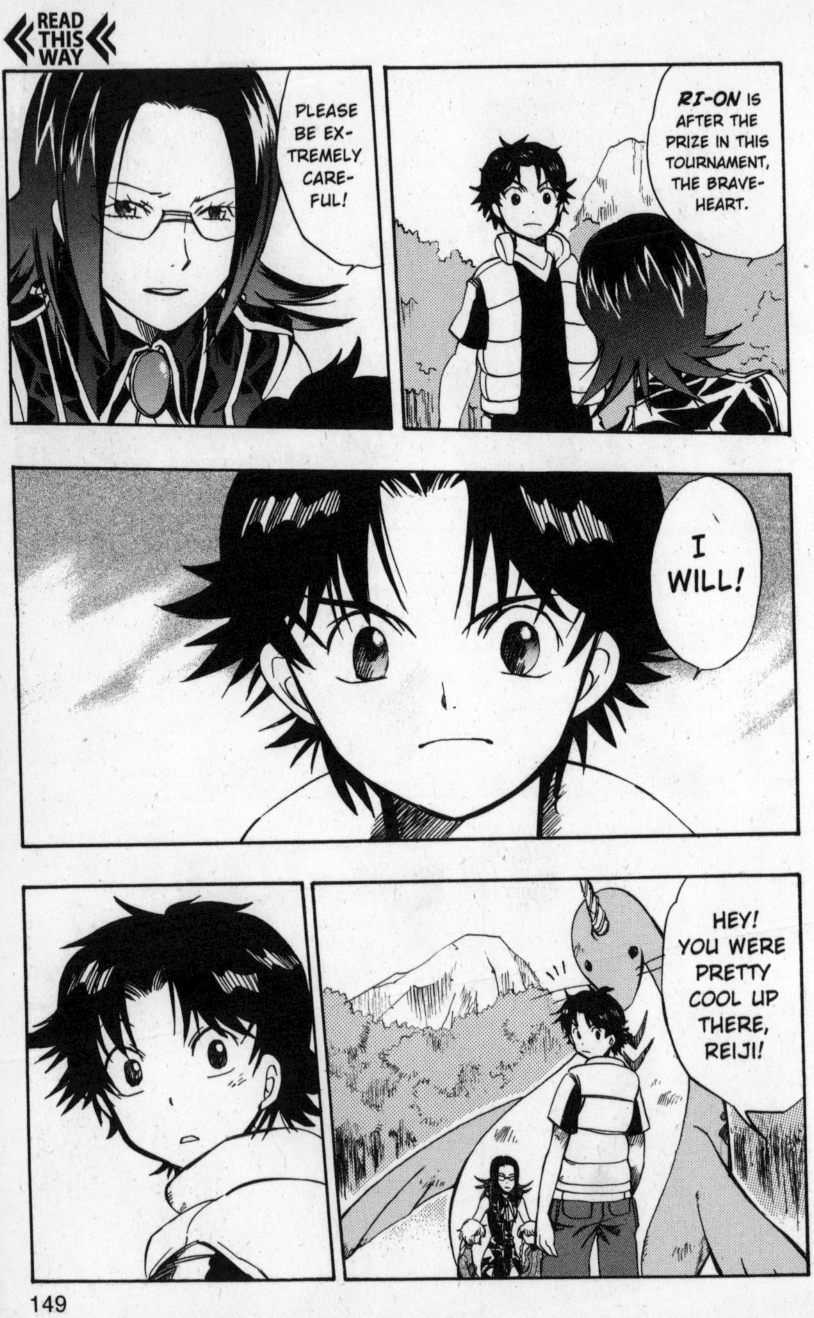
RI-ON IS AFTER THE PRIZE IN THIS TOURNAMENT, THE BRAVE-HEART.
PLEASE BE EX-TREMELY CARE-FUL!
I WILL!
HEY! YOU WERE PRETTY COOL UP THERE, REIJI!

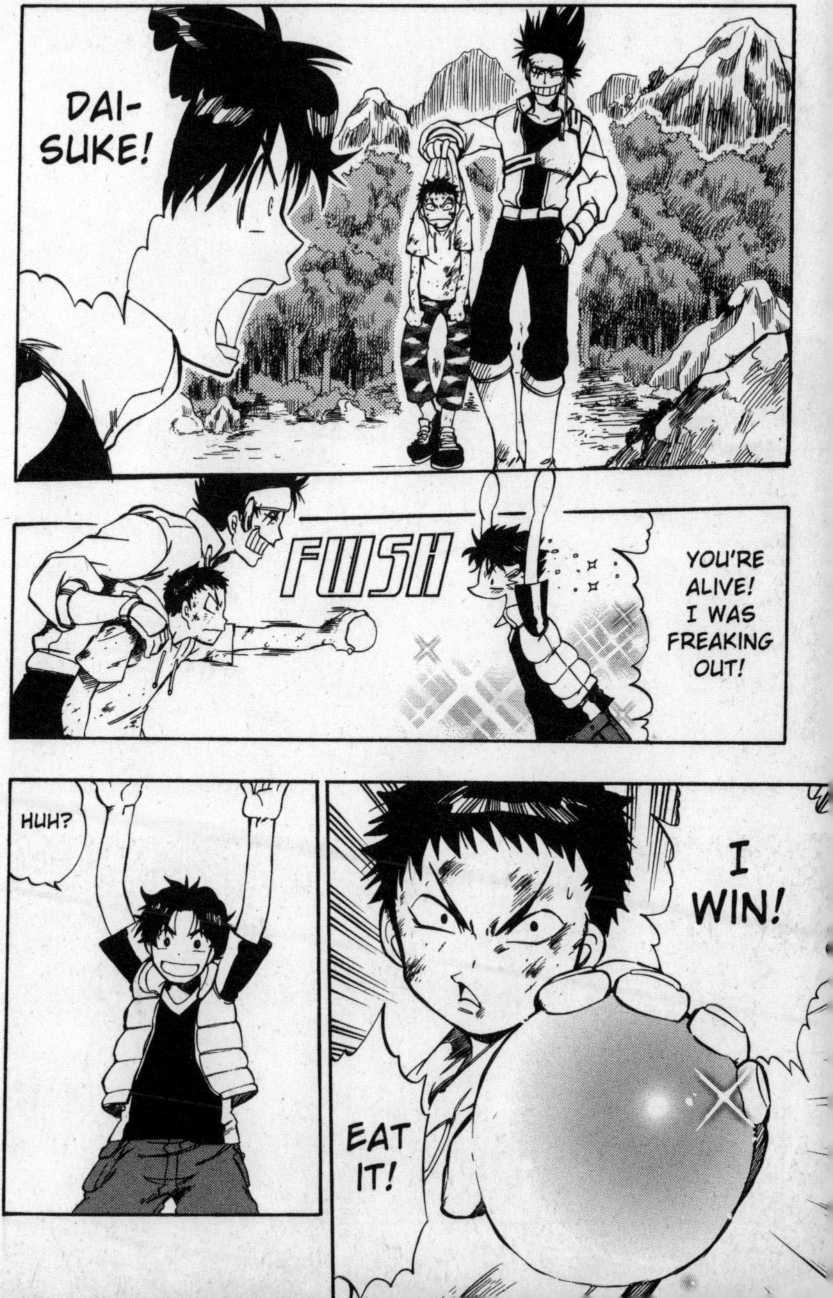
DAI-SUKE!
YOU'RE ALIVE! I WAS FREAKING OUT!
FWSH
I WIN!
EAT IT!
HUH?

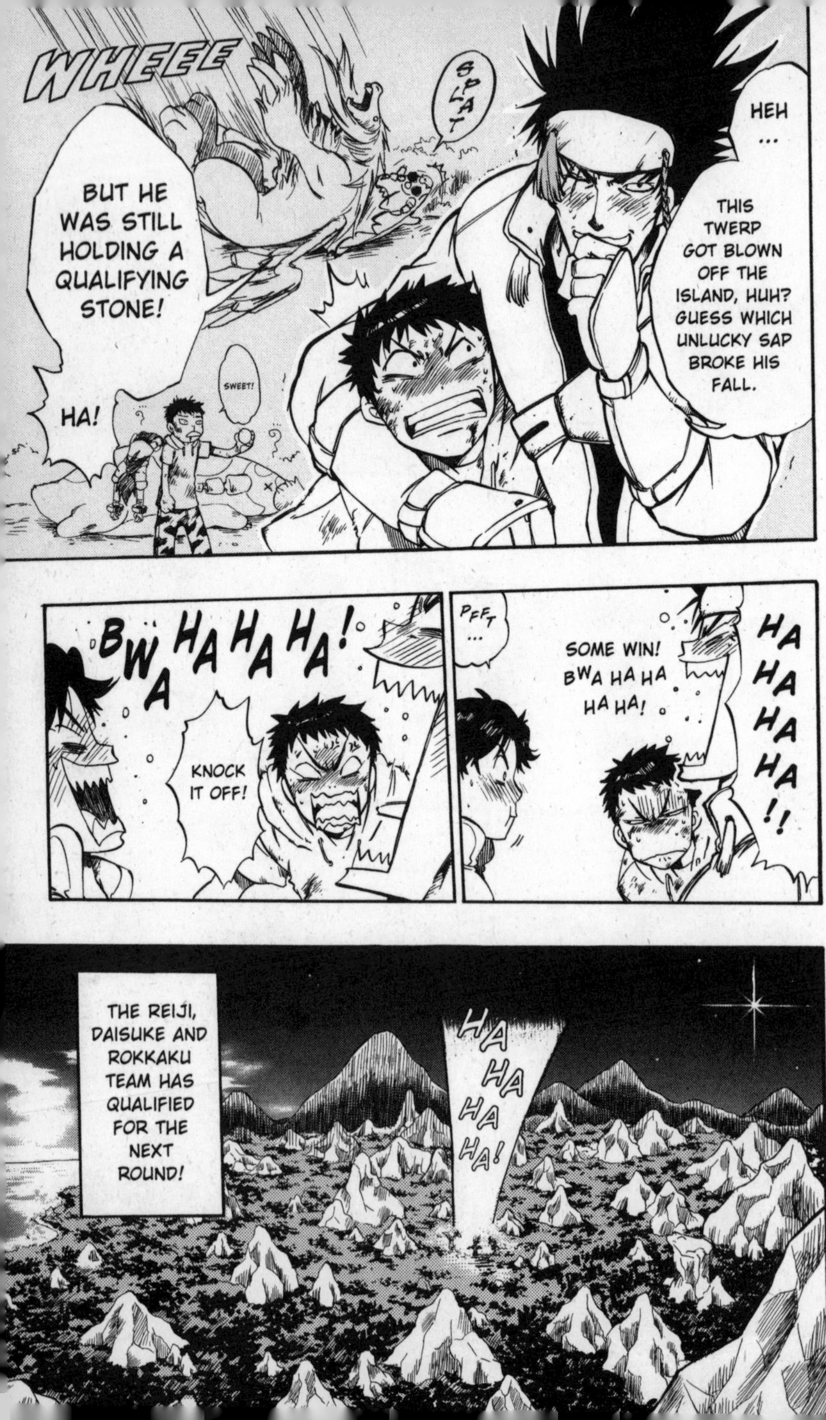
HEH ...
THIS TWERP GOT BLOWN OFF THE ISLAND, HUH? GUESS WHICH UNLUCKY SAP BROKE HIS FALL.
SPLAT
WHEEE
BUT HE WAS STILL HOLDING A QUALIFYING STONE!
SWEET!
HA!
PFFT ...
SOME WIN! BWA HA HA HA HA!
HA HA HA HA HA!!
BWA HA HA HA HA!
KNOCK IT OFF!
THE REIJI, DAISUKE AND ROKKAKU TEAM HAS QUALIFIED FOR THE NEXT ROUND!
HA HA HA HA!

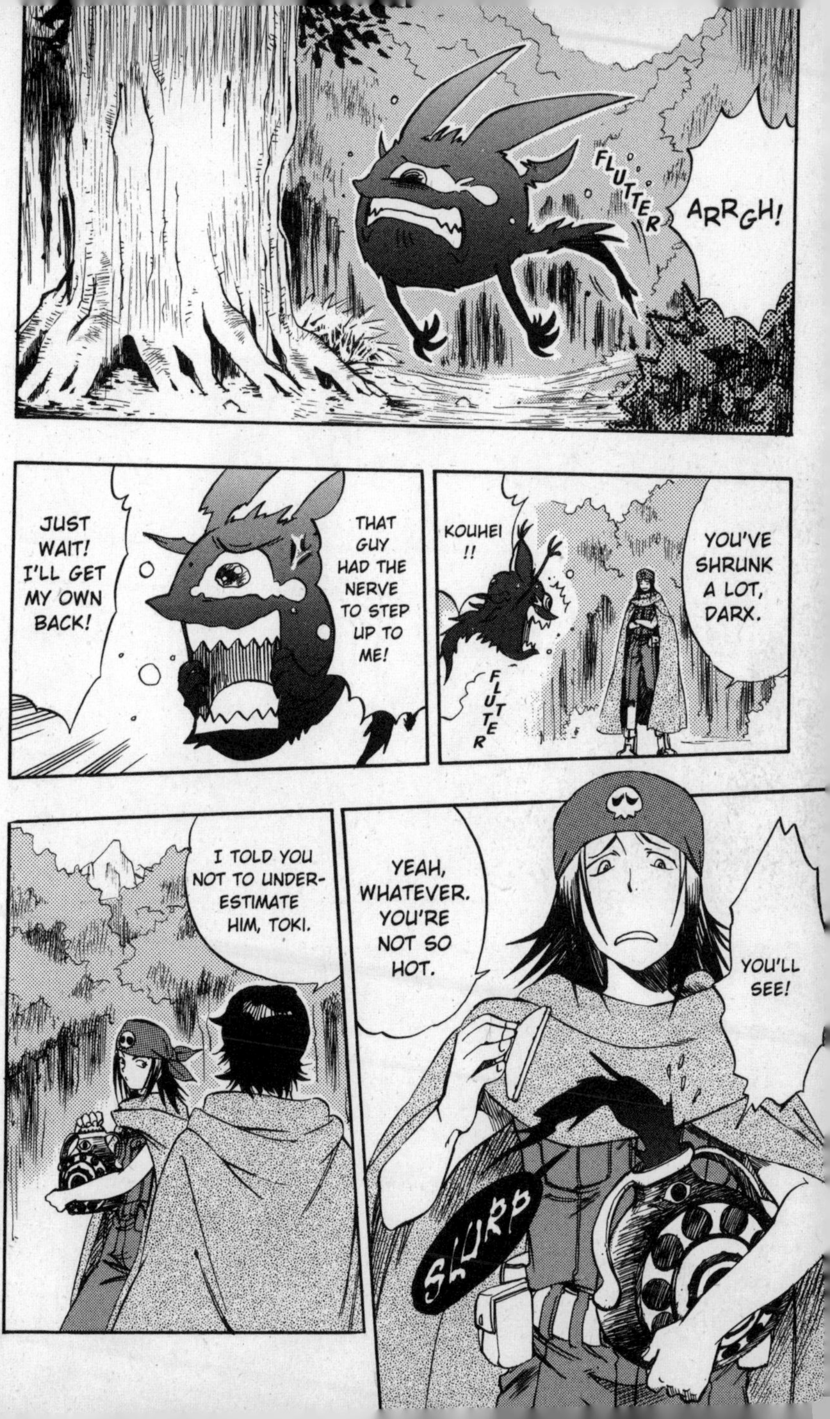
ARRGH!
FLUTTER
YOU'VE SHRUNK A LOT, DARX.
KOUHEI !!
FLUTTER
THAT GUY HAD THE NERVE TO STEP UP TO ME!
JUST WAIT! I'LL GET MY OWN BACK!
YOU'LL SEE!
YEAH, WHATEVER. YOU'RE NOT SO HOT.
SLURP
I TOLD YOU NOT TO UNDER-ESTIMATE HIM, TOKI.

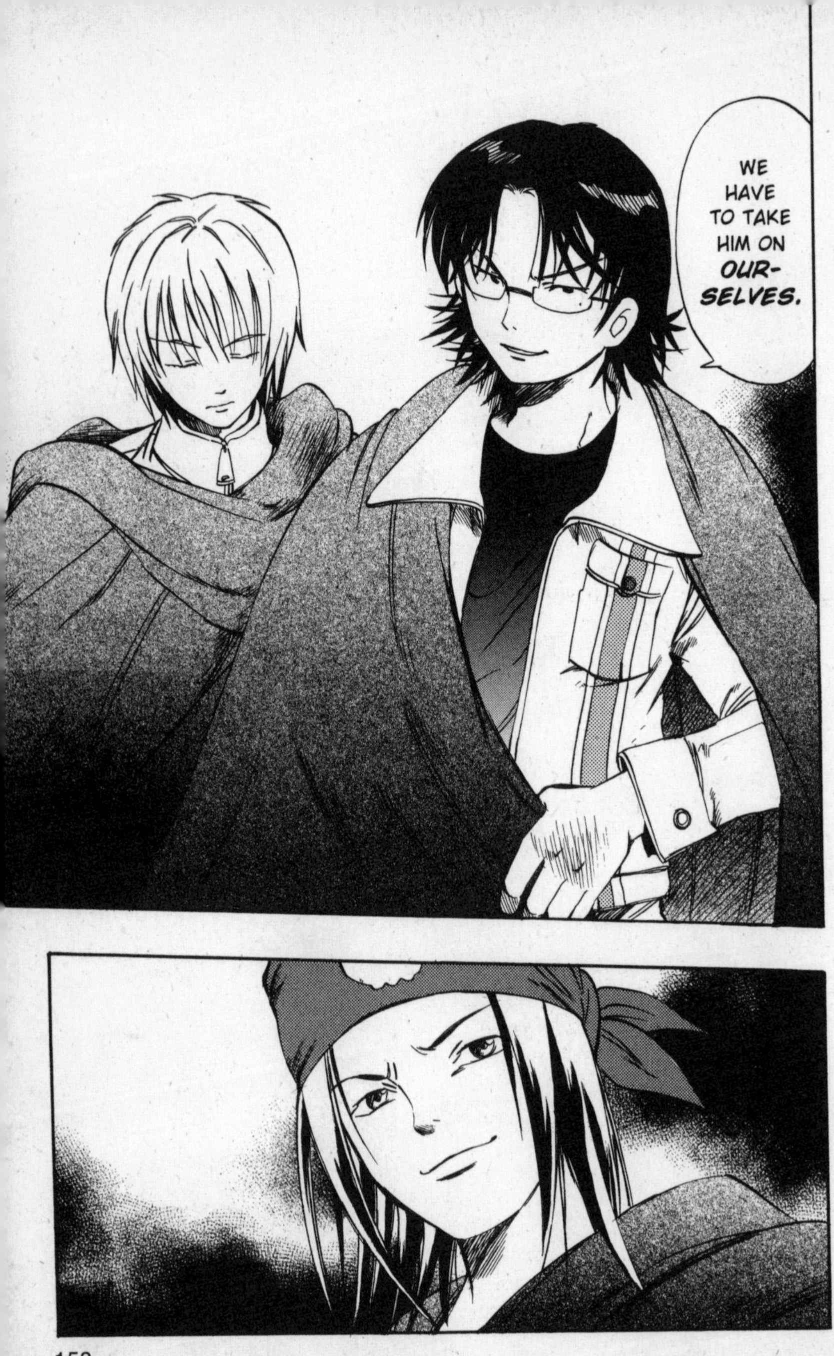
WE HAVE TO TAKE HIM ON OUR-SELVES.

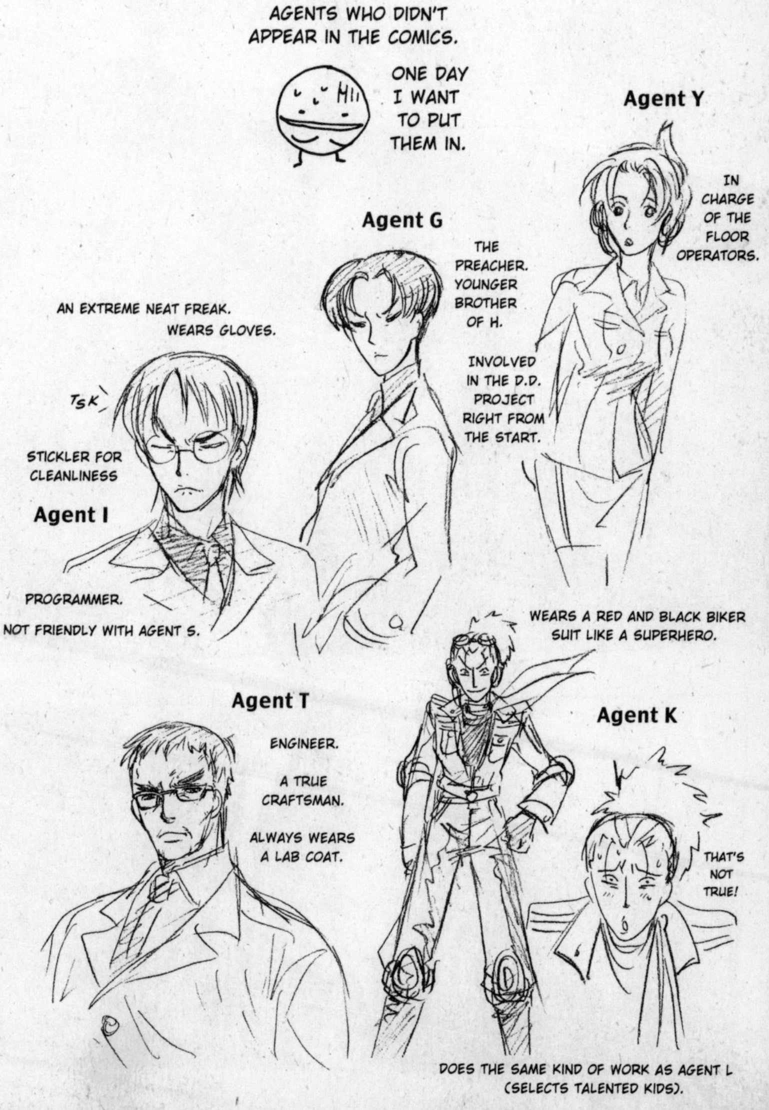
AGENTS WHO DIDN'T APPEAR IN THE COMICS.
ONE DAY I WANT TO PUT THEM IN.
HII
Agent Y
IN CHARGE OF THE FLOOR OPERATORS.
Agent G
THE PREACHER. YOUNGER BROTHER OF H.
INVOLVED IN THE D.D. PROJECT RIGHT FROM THE START.
AN EXTREME NEAT FREAK.
WEARS GLOVES.
TSK
STICKLER FOR CLEANLINESS
Agent I
PROGRAMMER.
NOT FRIENDLY WITH AGENT S.
WEARS A RED AND BLACK BIKER SUIT LIKE A SUPERHERO.
Agent T
ENGINEER.
A TRUE CRAFTSMAN.
ALWAYS WEARS A LAB COAT.
Agent K
THAT'S NOT TRUE!
DOES THE SAME KIND OF WORK AS AGENT L (SELECTS TALENTED KIDS).

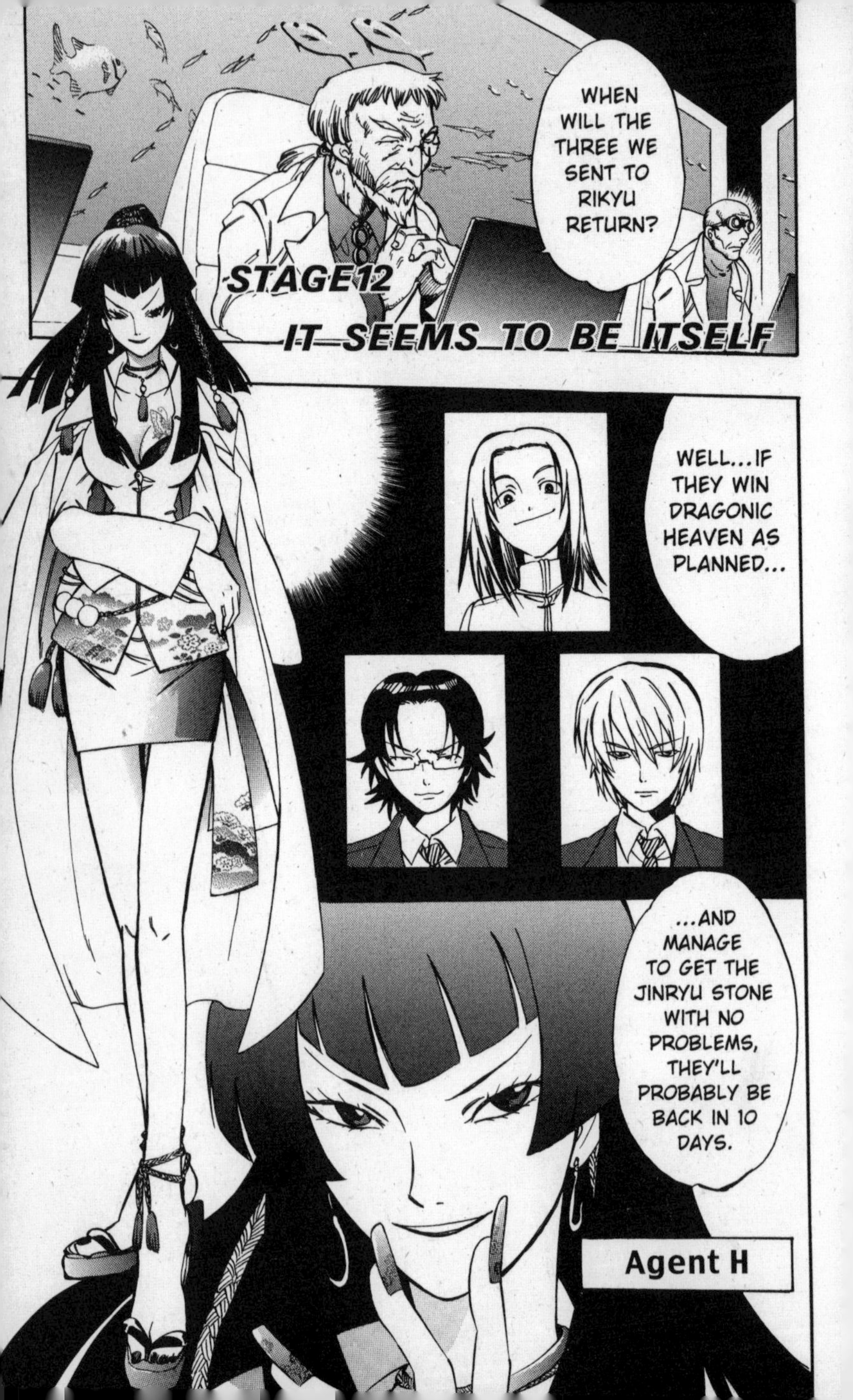
WHEN WILL THE THREE WE SENT TO RIKYU RETURN?
STAGE12
IT SEEMS TO BE ITSELF
WELL...IF THEY WIN DRAGONIC HEAVEN AS PLANNED...
...AND MANAGE TO GET THE JINRYU STONE WITH NO PROBLEMS, THEY'LL PROBABLY BE BACK IN 10 DAYS.
Agent H

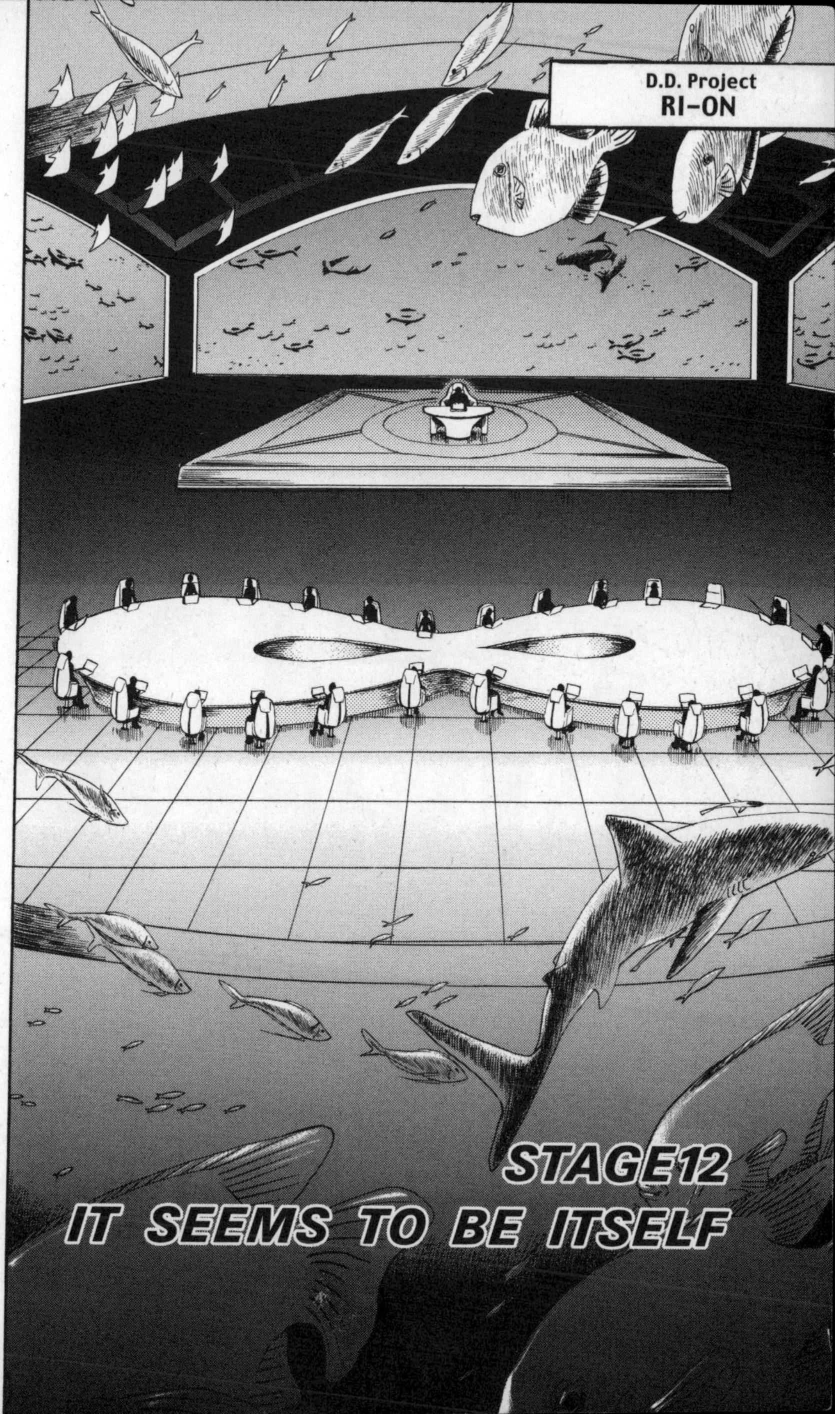
D.D. Project
RI-ON
STAGE12
IT SEEMS TO BE ITSELF

READ THIS WAY

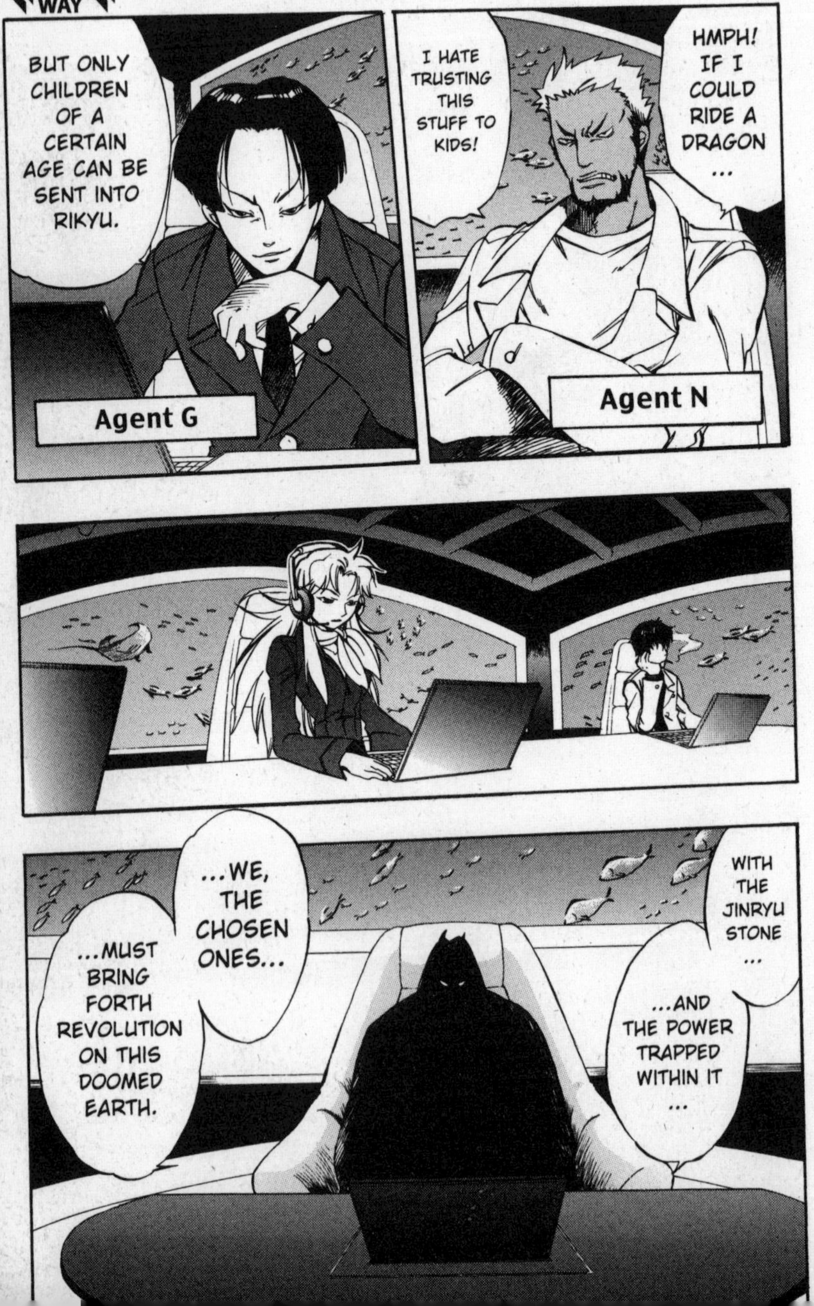
HMPH! IF I COULD RIDE A DRAGON ...
I HATE TRUSTING THIS STUFF TO KIDS!
Agent N
BUT ONLY CHILDREN OF A CERTAIN AGE CAN BE SENT INTO RIKYU.
Agent G
WITH THE JINRYU STONE ...
...AND THE POWER TRAPPED WITHIN IT ...
...WE, THE CHOSEN ONES...
...MUST BRING FORTH REVOLUTION ON THIS DOOMED EARTH.

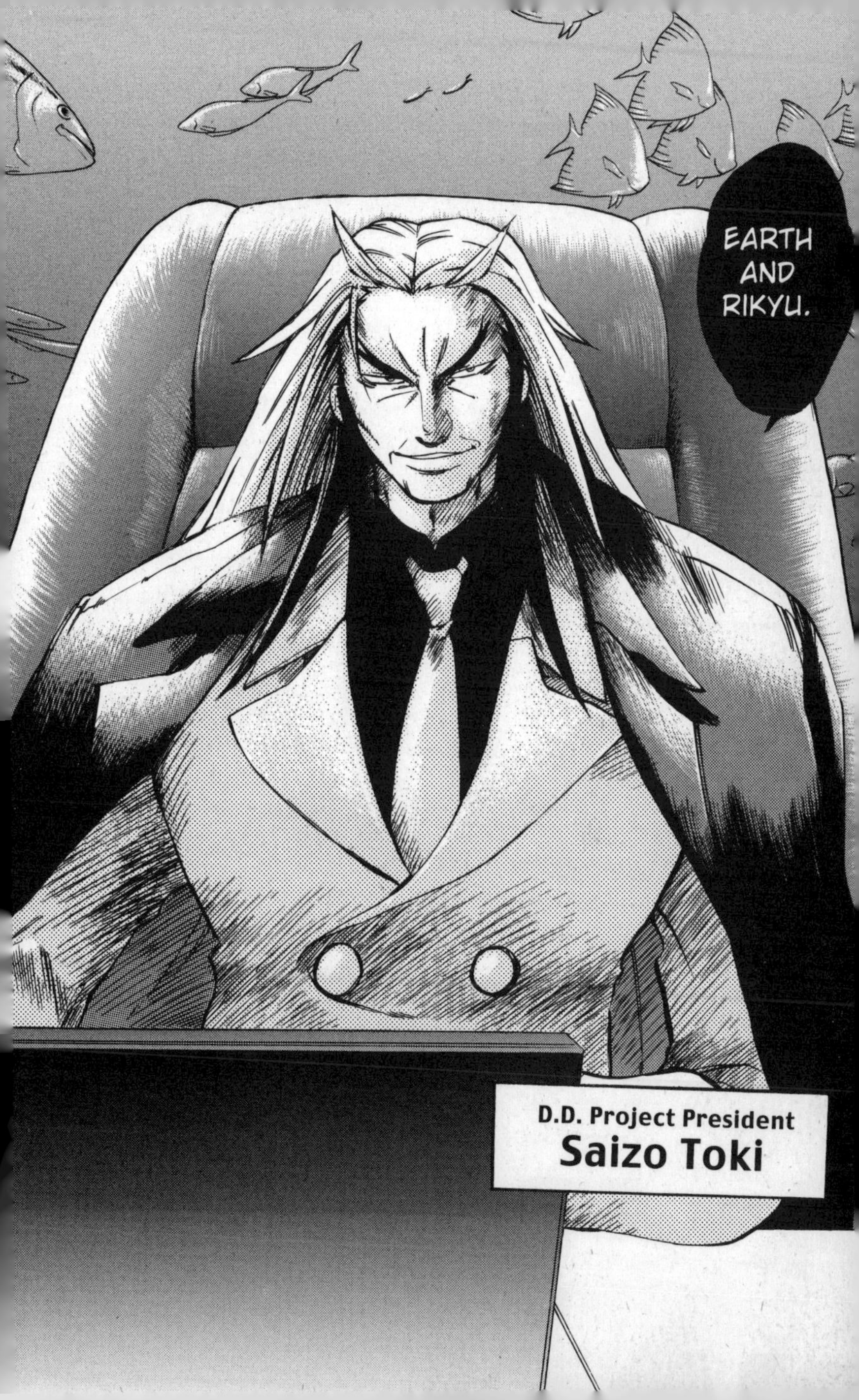
EARTH AND RIKYU.
D.D. Project President
Saizo Toki

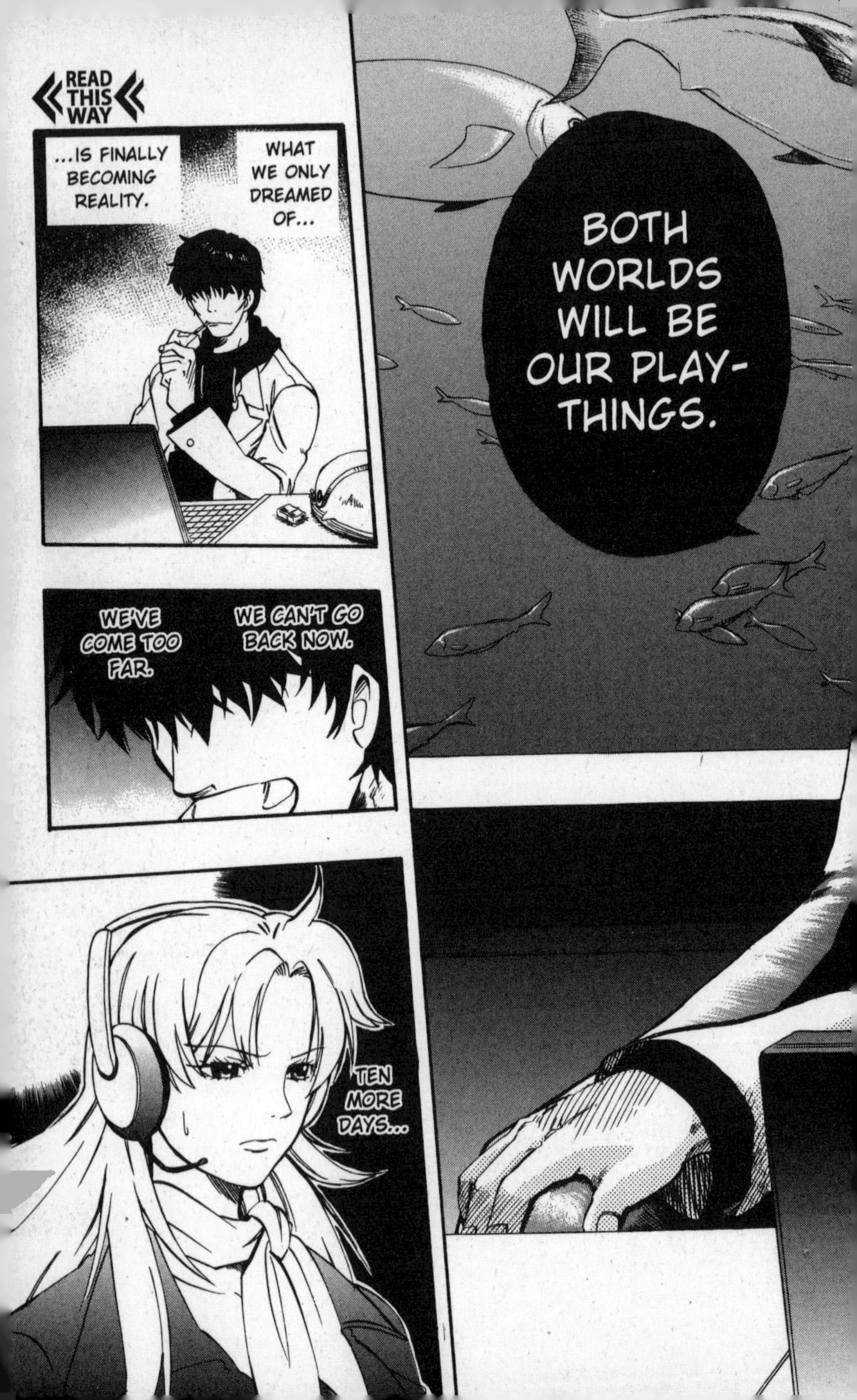

BOTH WORLDS WILL BE OUR PLAYTHINGS.
READ THIS WAY
WHAT WE ONLY DREAMED OF...
...IS FINALLY BECOMING REALITY.
WE CAN'T GO BACK NOW.
WE'VE COME TOO FAR.
TEN MORE DAYS...

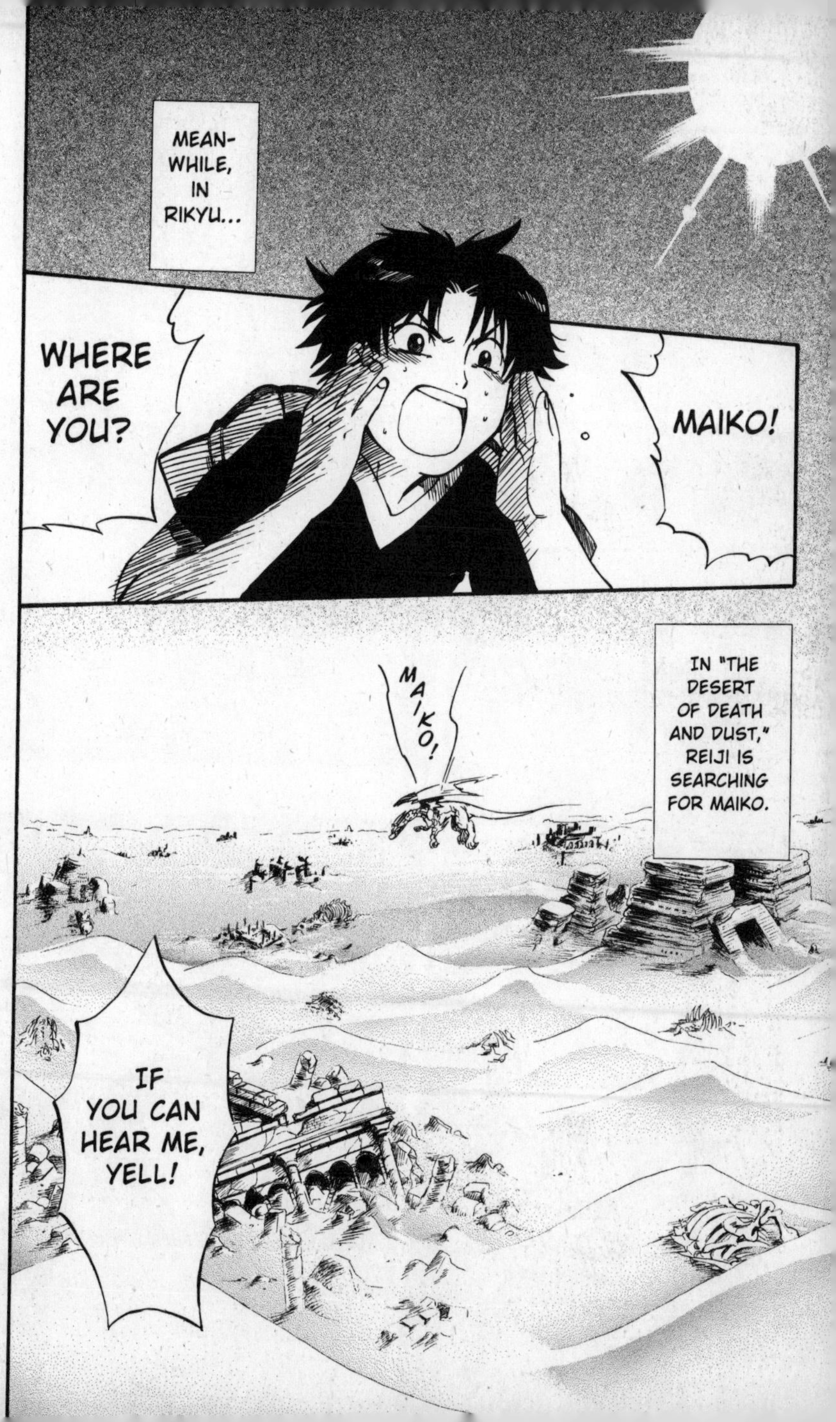
MEAN-WHILE, IN RIKYU...
MAIKO!
WHERE ARE YOU?
IN "THE DESERT OF DEATH AND DUST," REIJI IS SEARCHING FOR MAIKO.
MAIKO!
IF YOU CAN HEAR ME, YELL!

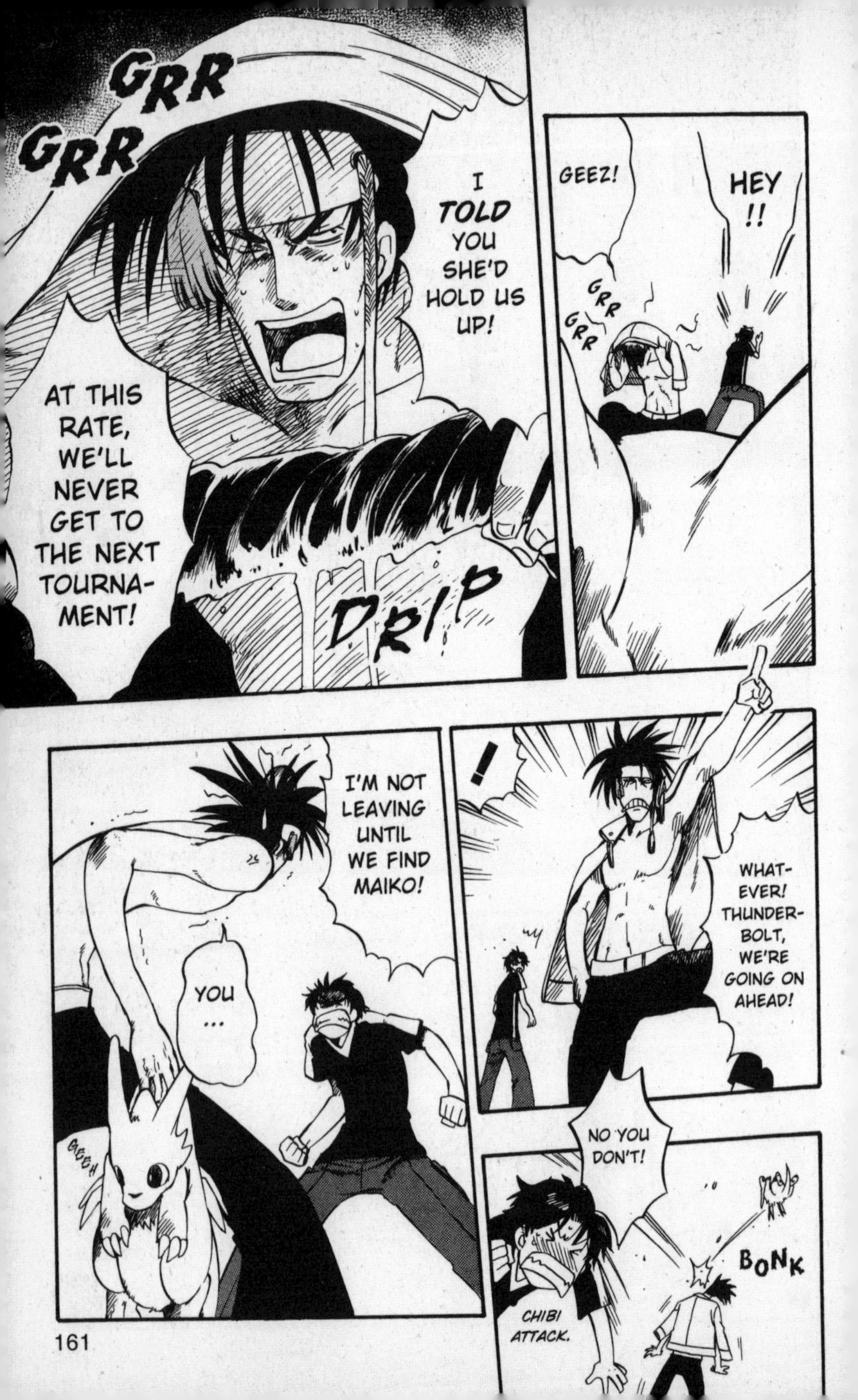
HEY !!
GEEZ!
GRR GRR
I TOLD YOU SHE'D HOLD US UP!
GRR GRR
AT THIS RATE, WE'LL NEVER GET TO THE NEXT TOURNA-MENT!
DRIP
!
WHAT-EVER! THUNDER-BOLT, WE'RE GOING ON AHEAD!
NO YOU DON'T!
BONK
CHIBI ATTACK.
I'M NOT LEAVING UNTIL WE FIND MAIKO!
YOU ...
GEEH

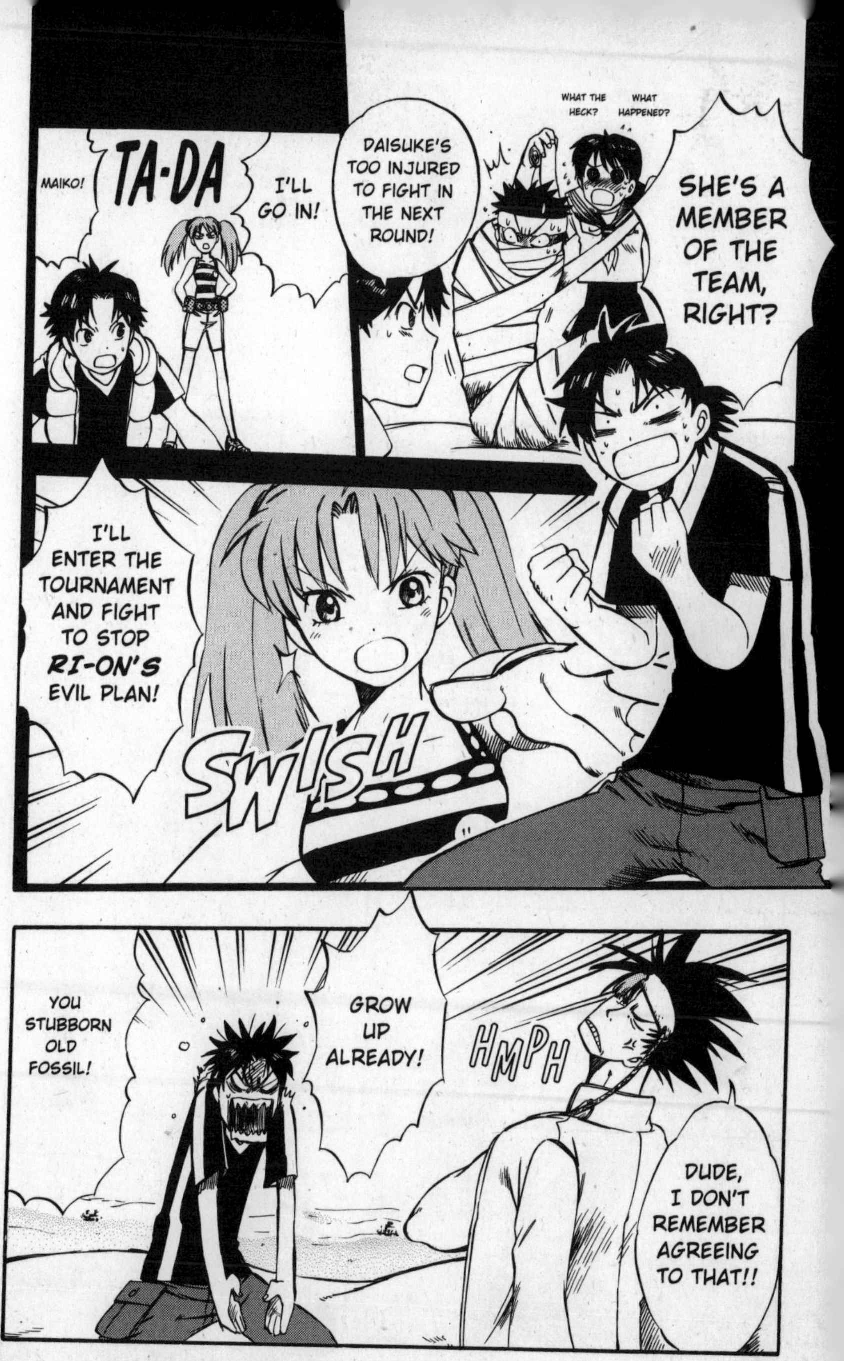
WHAT HAPPENED?
WHAT THE HECK?
SHE'S A MEMBER OF THE TEAM, RIGHT?
DAISUKE'S TOO INJURED TO FIGHT IN THE NEXT ROUND!
I'LL GO IN!
TA-DA
MAIKO!
I'LL ENTER THE TOURNAMENT AND FIGHT TO STOP ***RI-ON'S*** EVIL PLAN!
SWISH
DUDE, I DON'T REMEMBER AGREEING TO THAT!!
HMPH
GROW UP ALREADY!
YOU STUBBORN OLD FOSSIL!

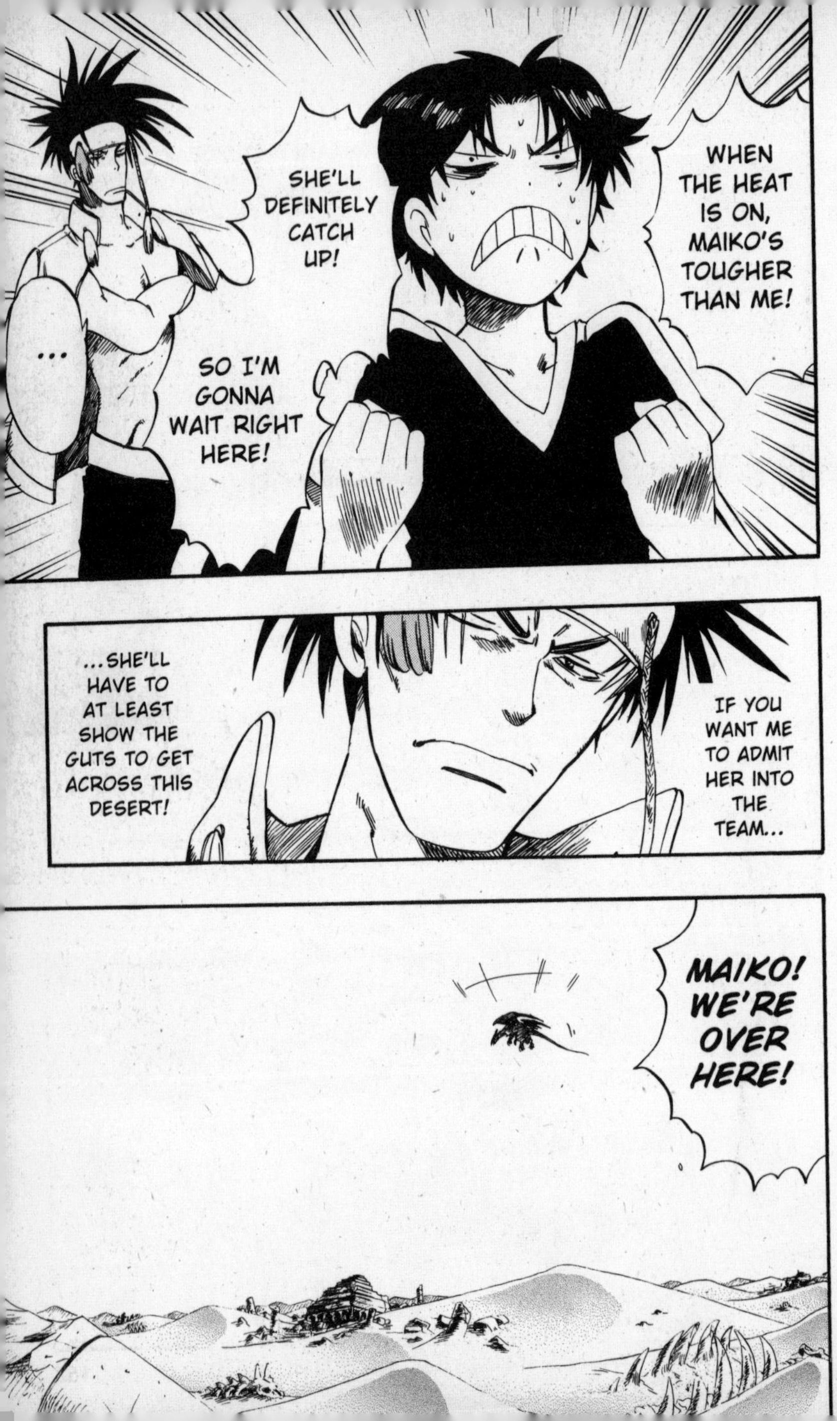
WHEN THE HEAT IS ON, MAIKO'S TOUGHER THAN ME!
SHE'LL DEFINITELY CATCH UP!
SO I'M GONNA WAIT RIGHT HERE!
...
IF YOU WANT ME TO ADMIT HER INTO THE TEAM...
...SHE'LL HAVE TO AT LEAST SHOW THE GUTS TO GET ACROSS THIS DESERT!
MAIKO! WE'RE OVER HERE!

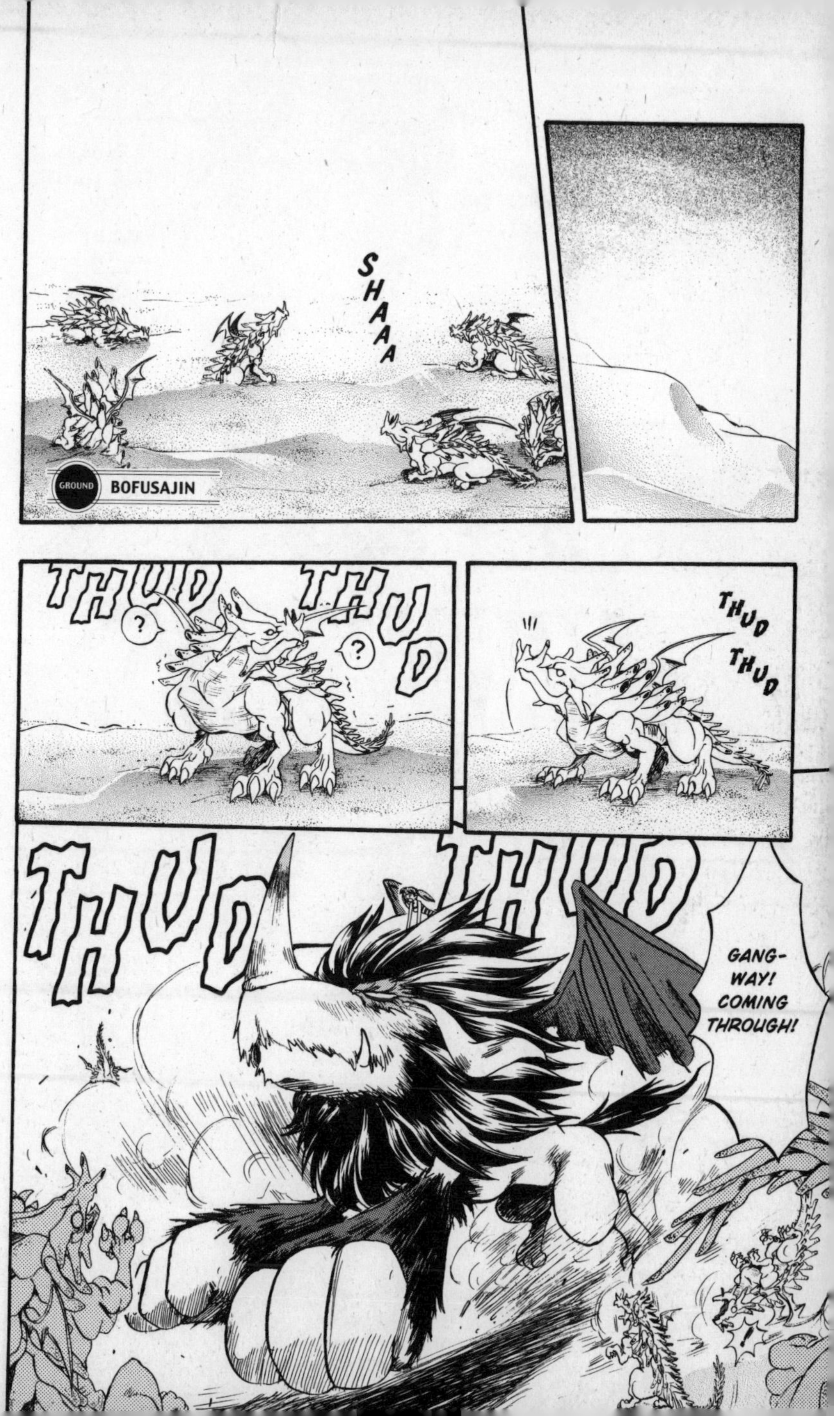
SHAAAA
GROUND
BOFUSAJIN
THUD THUD
THUD
THUD
?
?
GANG-WAY! COMING THROUGH!
THUD
THUD
!

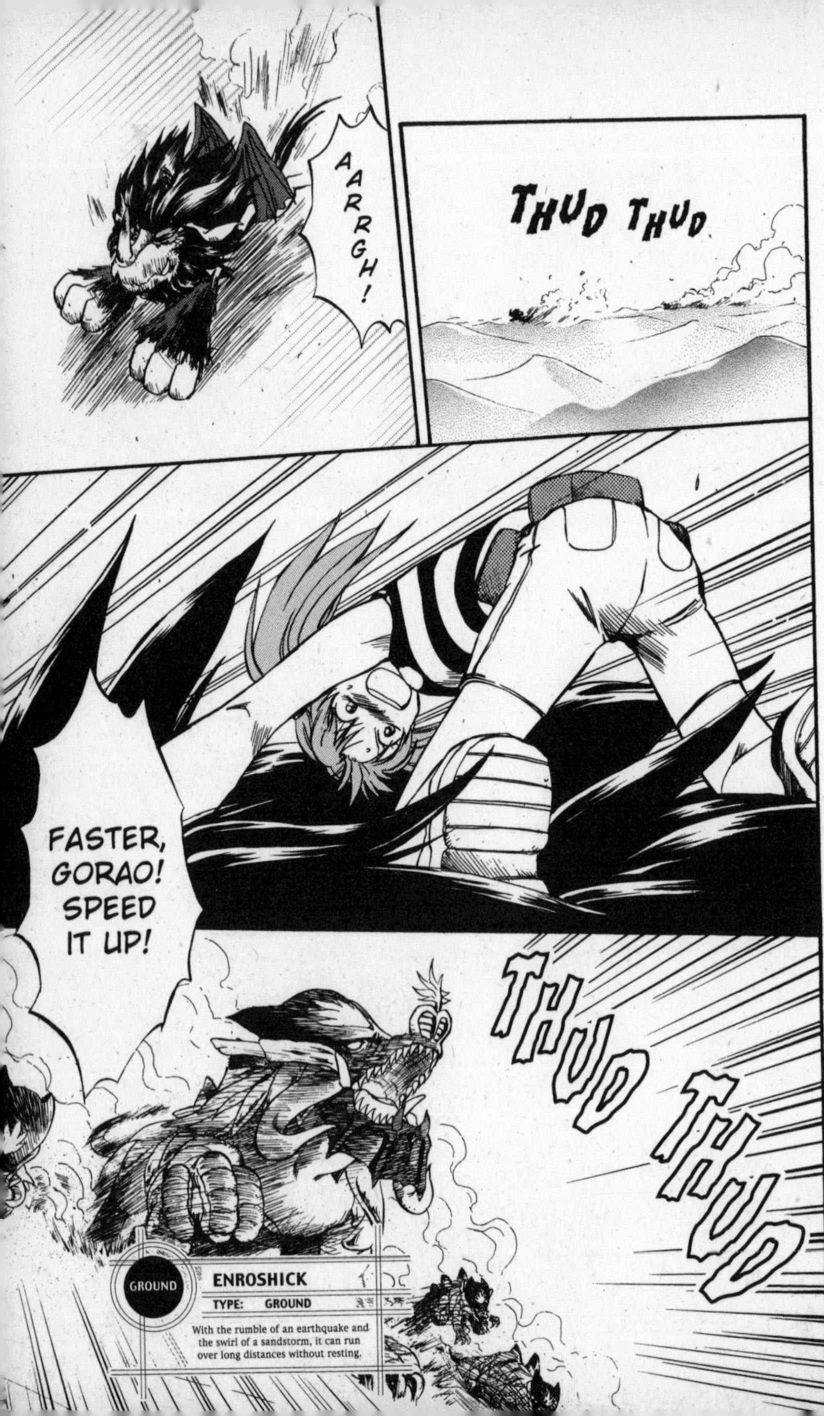
THUD THUD
AARRGH!
FASTER, GORAO! SPEED IT UP!
THUD THUD
GROUND
ENROSHICK
TYPE: GROUND
With the rumble of an earthquake and the swirl of a sandstorm, it can run over long distances without resting.

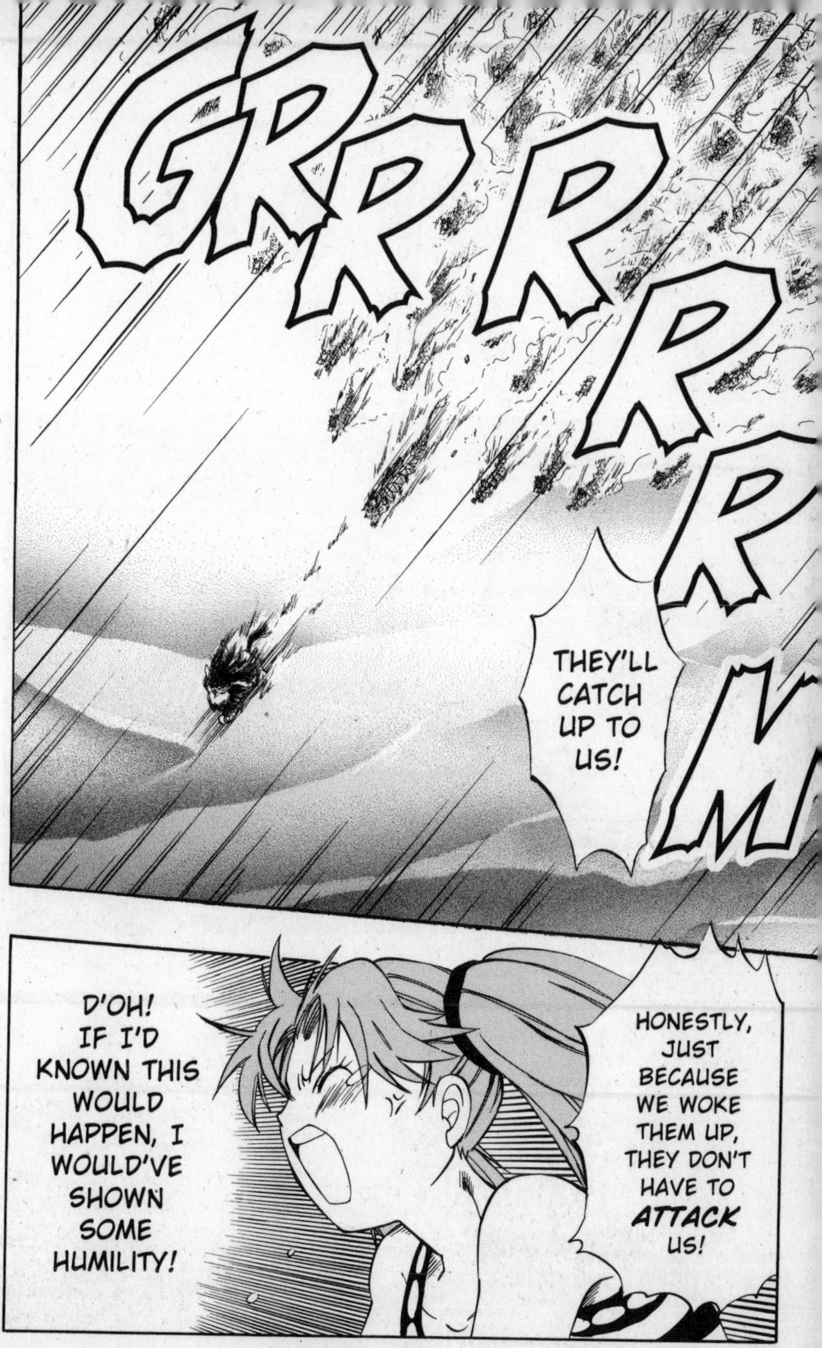
GRRRRM
THEY'LL CATCH UP TO US!
HONESTLY, JUST BECAUSE WE WOKE THEM UP, THEY DON'T HAVE TO ATTACK US!
D'OH! IF I'D KNOWN THIS WOULD HAPPEN, I WOULD'VE SHOWN SOME HUMILITY!

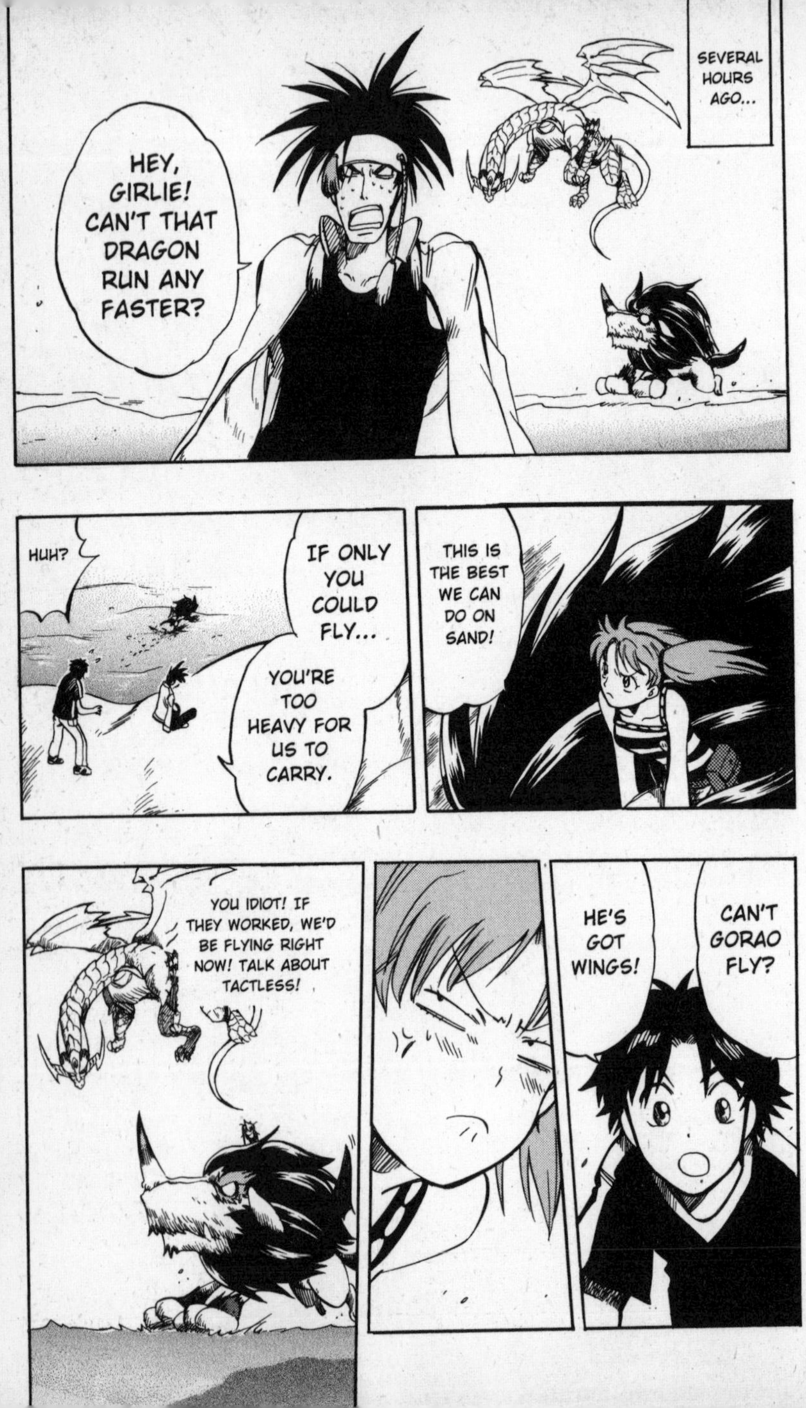
SEVERAL HOURS AGO...
HEY, GIRLIE! CAN'T THAT DRAGON RUN ANY FASTER?
THIS IS THE BEST WE CAN DO ON SAND!
IF ONLY YOU COULD FLY...
YOU'RE TOO HEAVY FOR US TO CARRY.
HUH?
CAN'T GORAO FLY?
HE'S GOT WINGS!
YOU IDIOT! IF THEY WORKED, WE'D BE FLYING RIGHT NOW! TALK ABOUT TACTLESS!

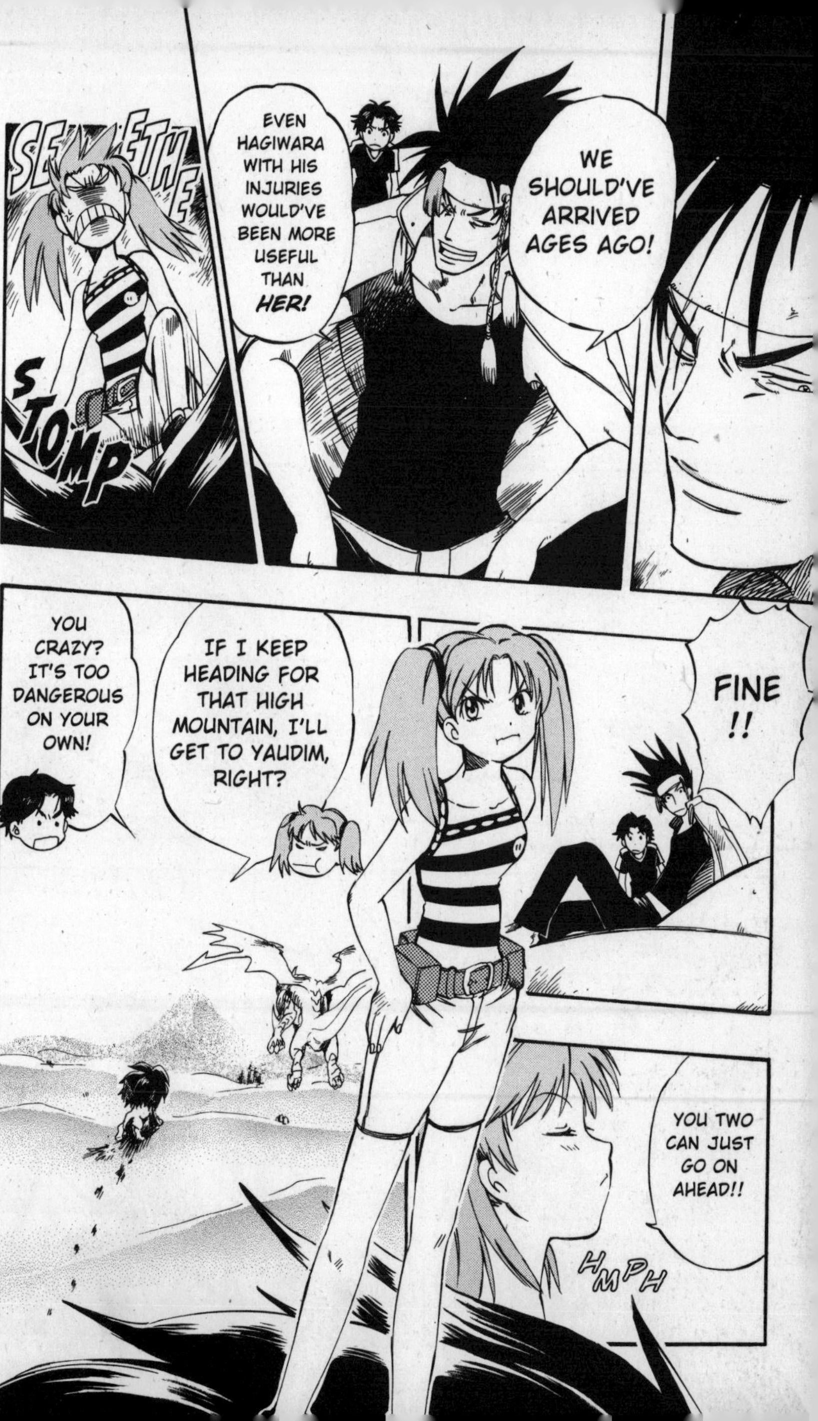
WE SHOULD'VE ARRIVED AGES AGO!
EVEN HAGIWARA WITH HIS INJURIES WOULD'VE BEEN MORE USEFUL THAN *HER!*
SEETHE
STOMP
FINE!!
IF I KEEP HEADING FOR THAT HIGH MOUNTAIN, I'LL GET TO YAUDIM, RIGHT?
YOU CRAZY? IT'S TOO DANGEROUS ON YOUR OWN!
YOU TWO CAN JUST GO ON AHEAD!!
HMPH

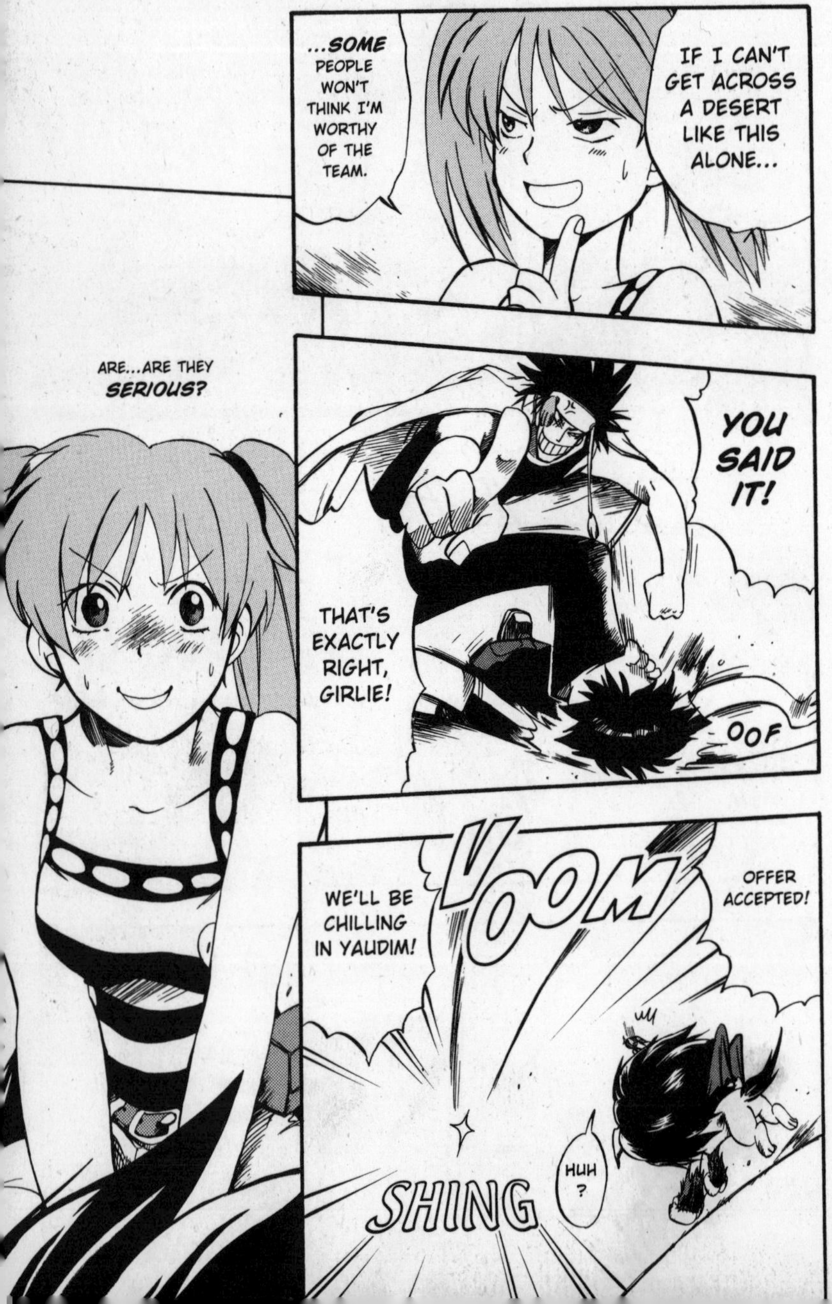
IF I CAN'T GET ACROSS A DESERT LIKE THIS ALONE...
...SOME PEOPLE WON'T THINK I'M WORTHY OF THE TEAM.
YOU SAID IT!
THAT'S EXACTLY RIGHT, GIRLIE!
OOF
OFFER ACCEPTED!
VOOM
WE'LL BE CHILLING IN YAUDIM!
HUH?
SHING
ARE...ARE THEY SERIOUS?

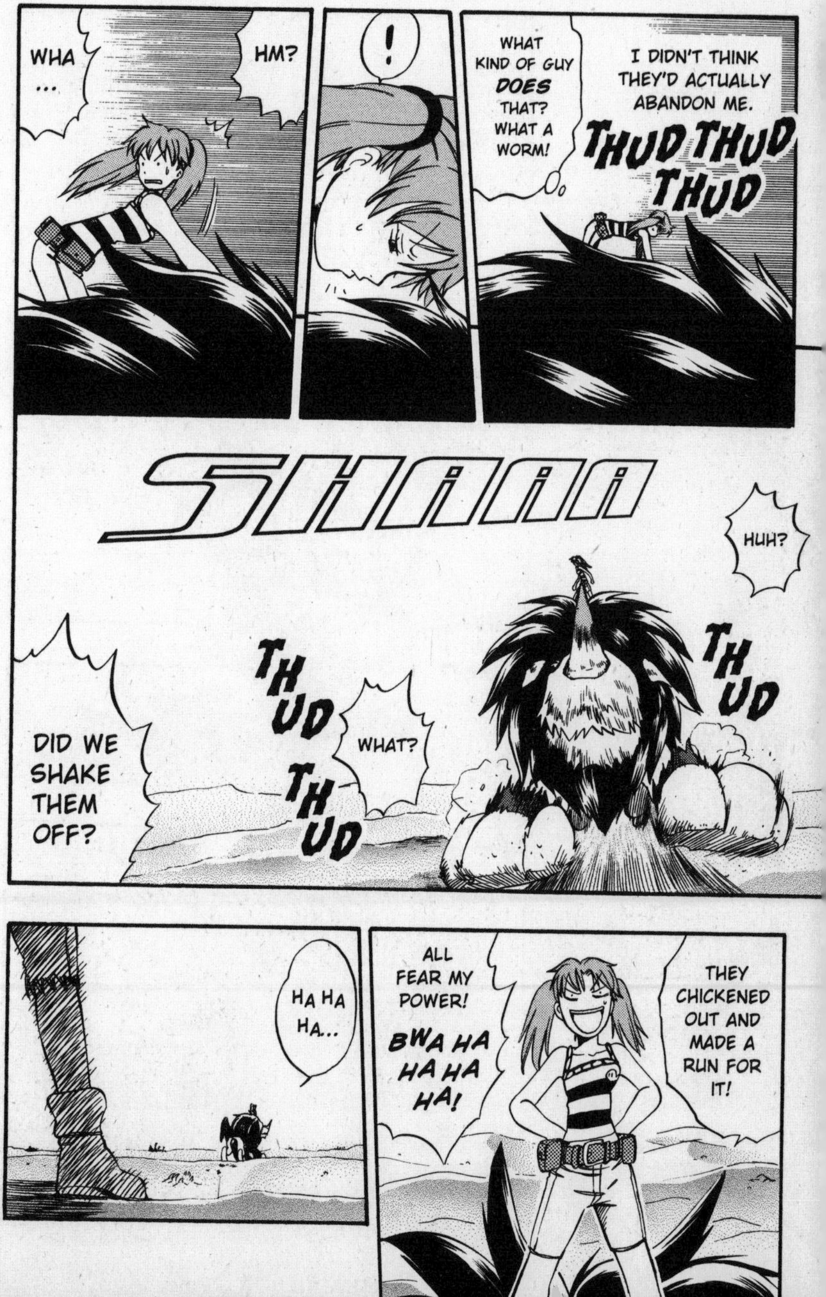
I DIDN'T THINK THEY'D ACTUALLY ABANDON ME.
THUD THUD THUD
WHAT KIND OF GUY DOES THAT? WHAT A WORM!
!
HM?
WHA ...
SHAAA
HUH?
THUD
WHAT?
THUD THUD
DID WE SHAKE THEM OFF?
THEY CHICKENED OUT AND MADE A RUN FOR IT!
ALL FEAR MY POWER!
BWA HA HA HA HA!
HA HA HA...

READ THIS WAY

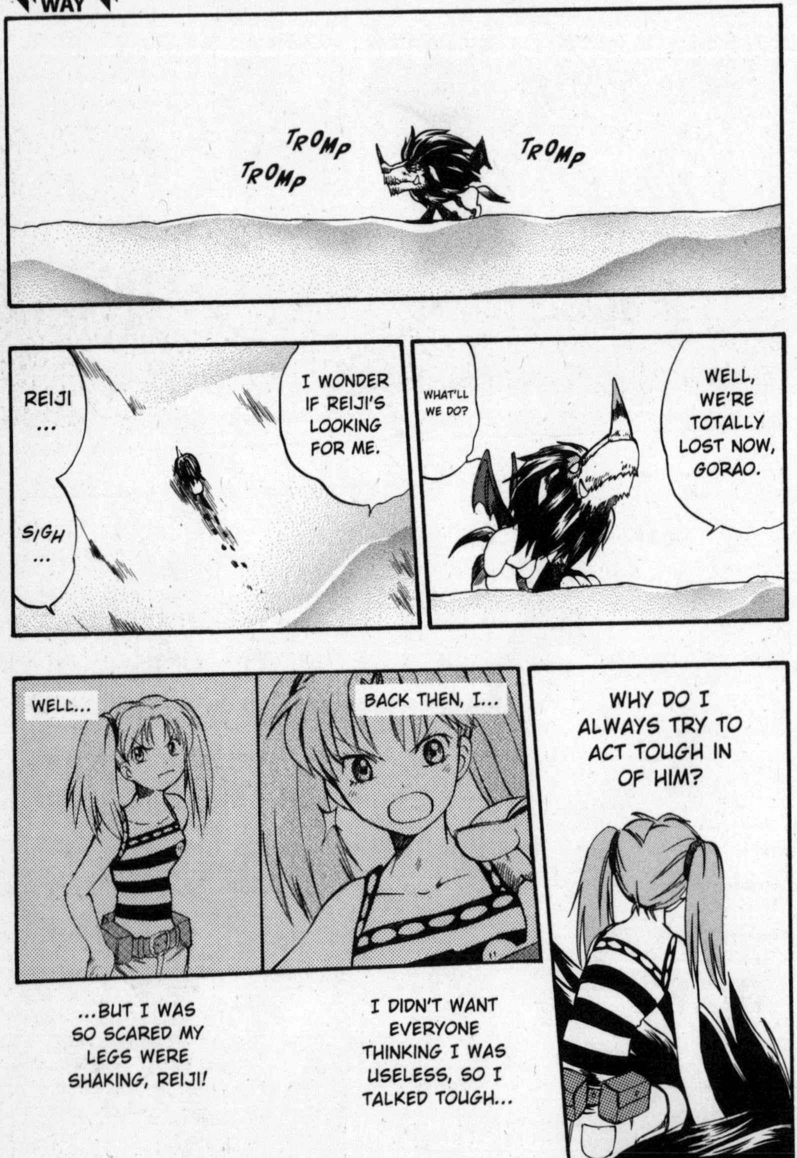
TROMP
TROMP
TROMP
WELL, WE'RE TOTALLY LOST NOW, GORAO.
WHAT'LL WE DO?
I WONDER IF REIJI'S LOOKING FOR ME.
REIJI...
SIGH...
WHY DO I ALWAYS TRY TO ACT TOUGH IN OF HIM?
BACK THEN, I...
I DIDN'T WANT EVERYONE THINKING I WAS USELESS, SO I TALKED TOUGH...
WELL...
...BUT I WAS SO SCARED MY LEGS WERE SHAKING, REIJI!

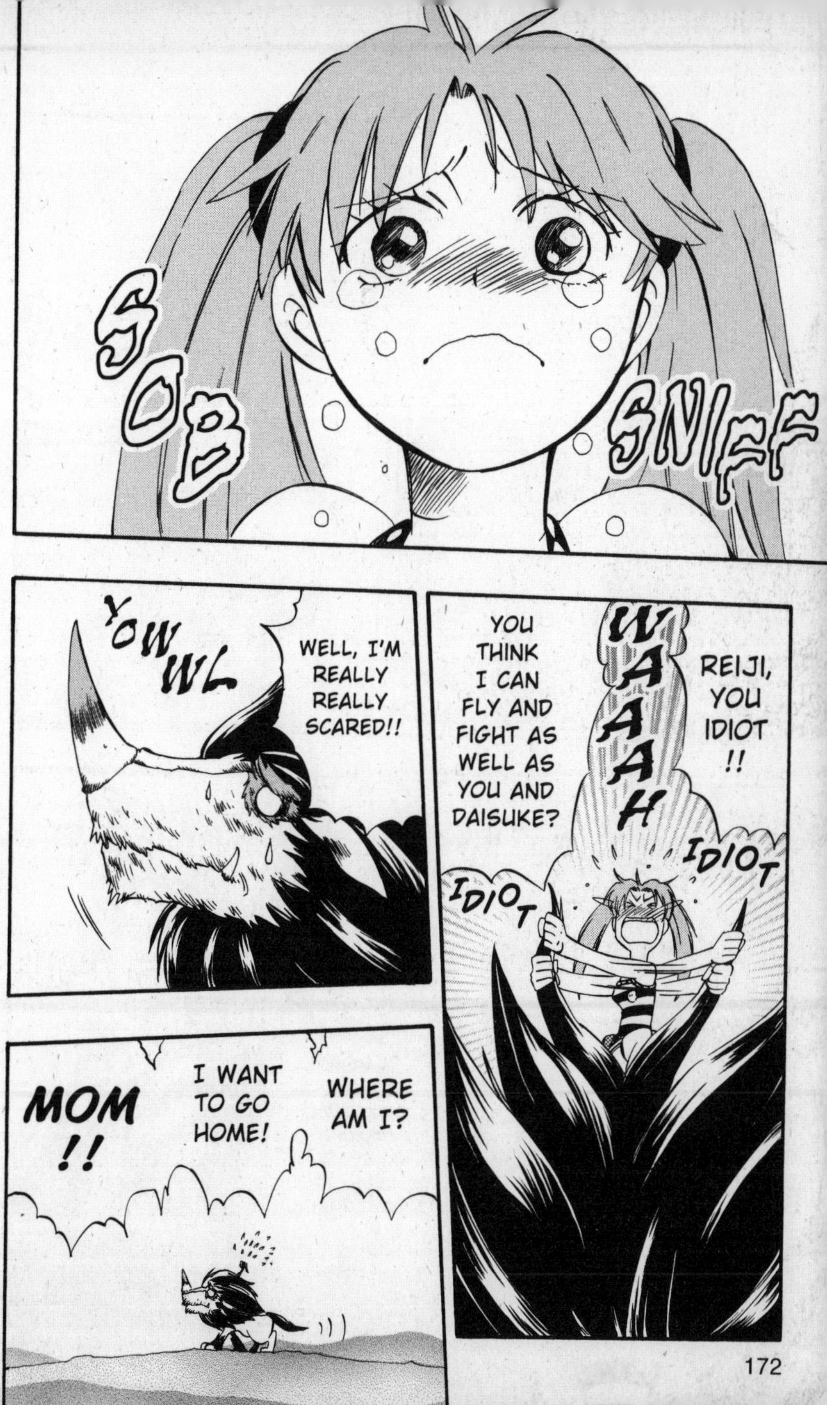
SNIFF
SOB
REIJI, YOU IDIOT!!
WAAAAH
YOU THINK I CAN FLY AND FIGHT AS WELL AS YOU AND DAISUKE?
IDIOT
IDIOT
WELL, I'M REALLY REALLY SCARED!!
YOWWL
WHERE AM I?
I WANT TO GO HOME!
MOM!!

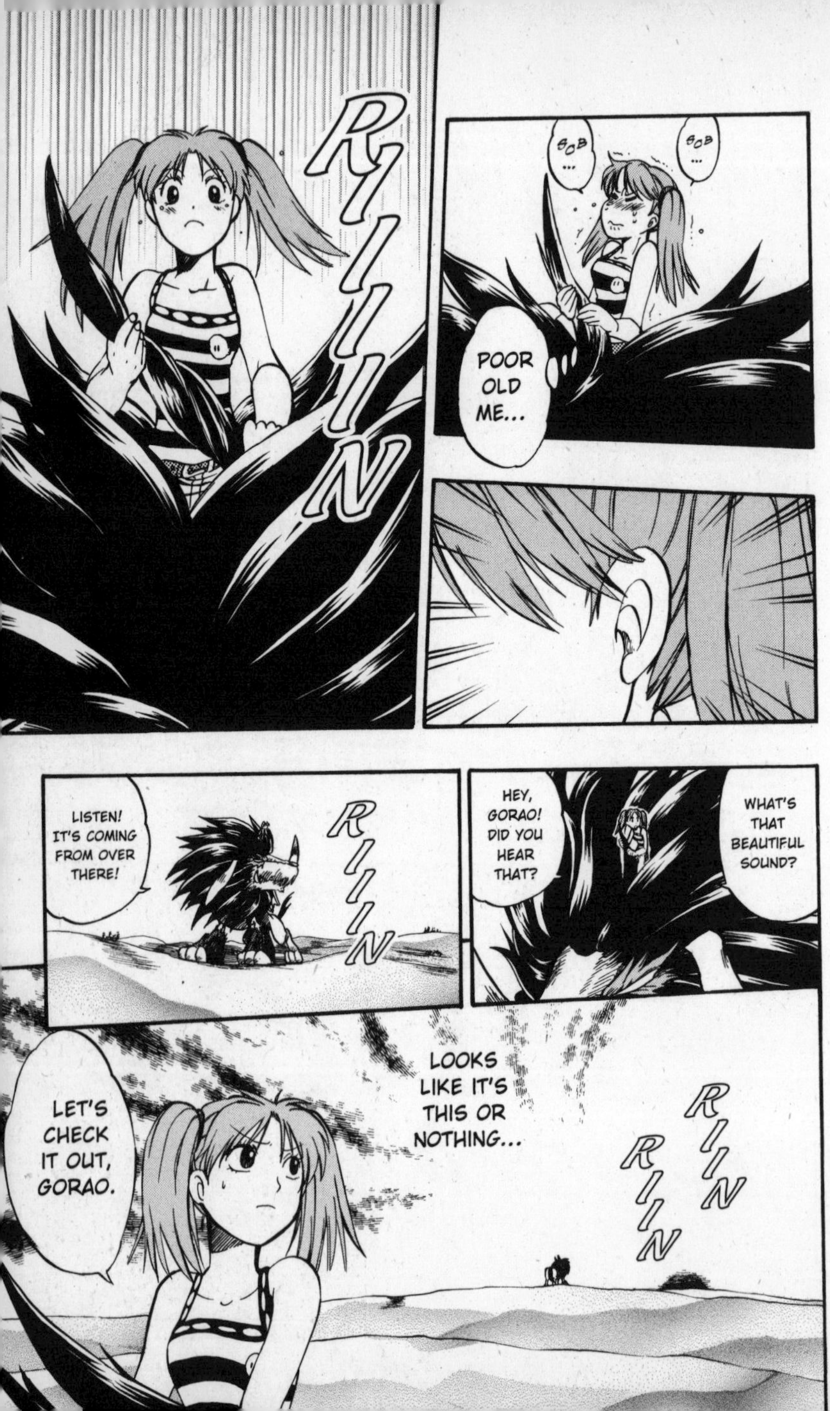
SOB...
SOB...
POOR OLD ME...
RIIIN
WHAT'S THAT BEAUTIFUL SOUND?
HEY, GORAO! DID YOU HEAR THAT?
LISTEN! IT'S COMING FROM OVER THERE!
RIIIN
RIIN
RIIN
LOOKS LIKE IT'S THIS OR NOTHING...
LET'S CHECK IT OUT, GORAO.

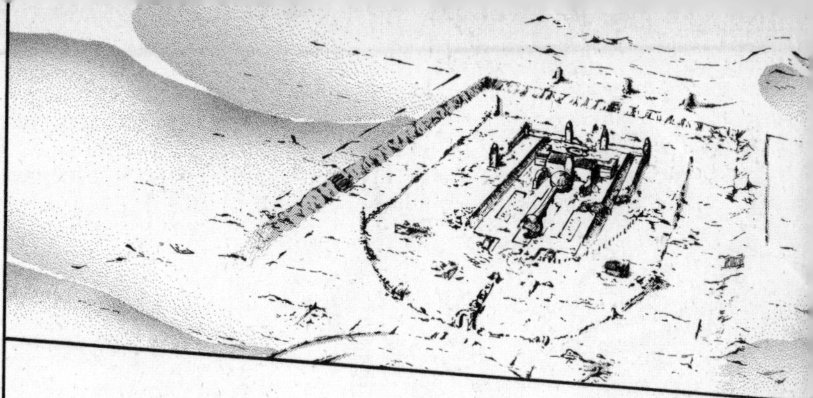
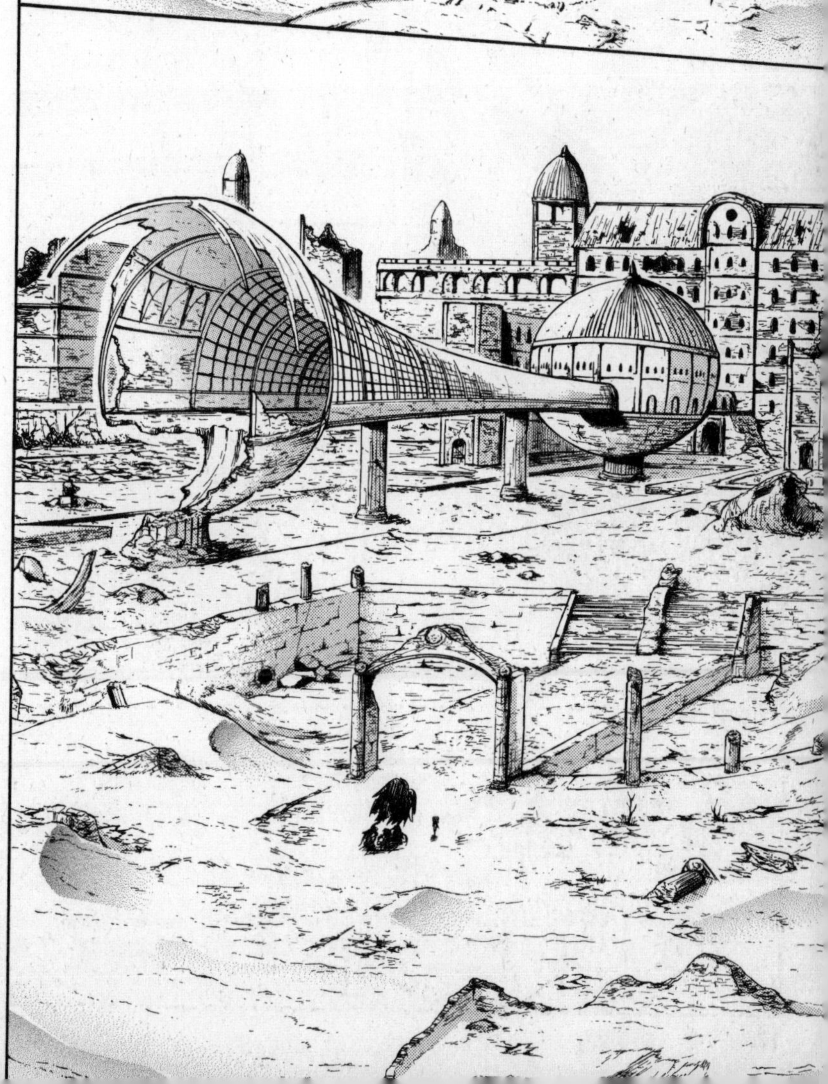

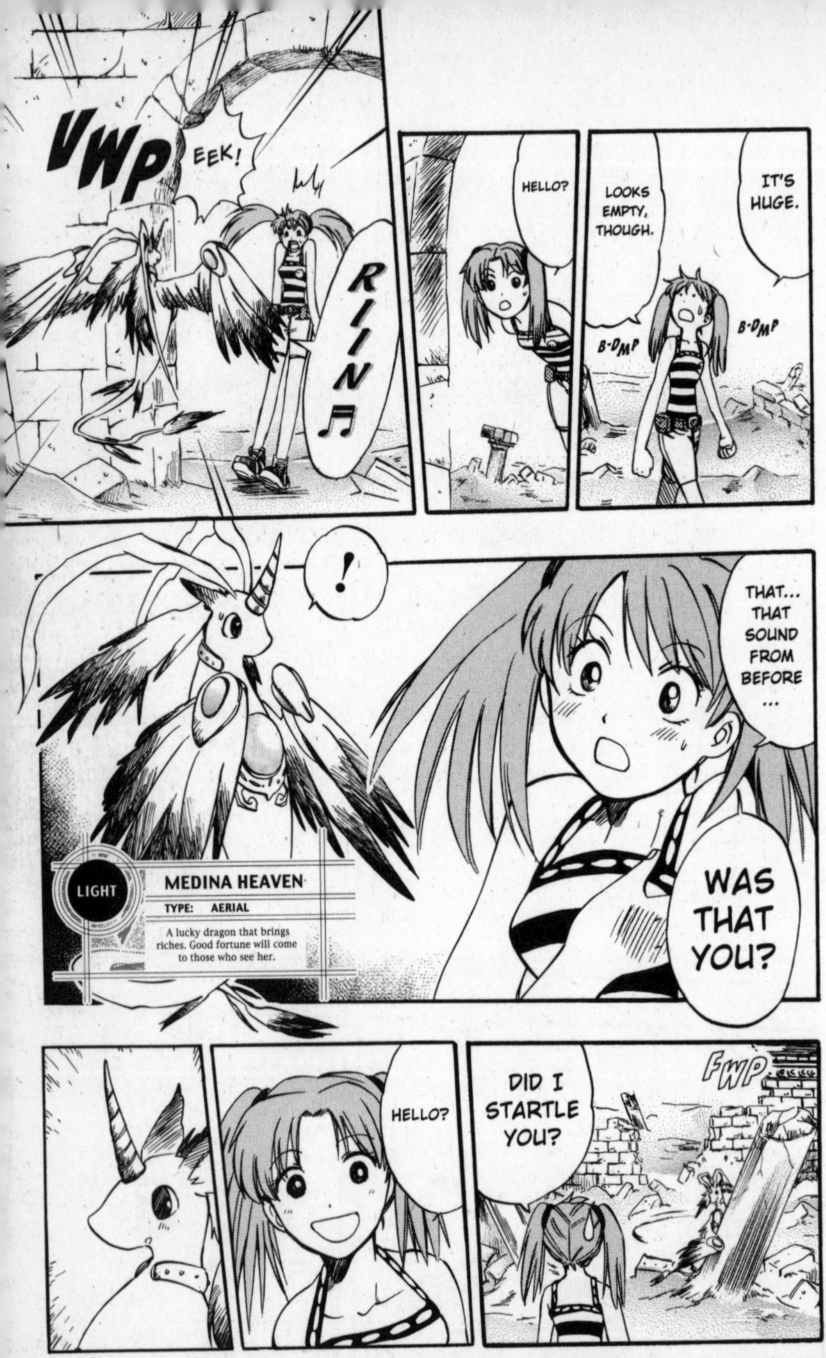
IT'S HUGE.
LOOKS EMPTY, THOUGH.
B-DMP
B-DMP
HELLO?
RIIIN♫
VWP
EEK!
THAT... THAT SOUND FROM BEFORE...
WAS THAT YOU?
!
LIGHT
MEDINA HEAVEN
TYPE: AERIAL
A lucky dragon that brings riches. Good fortune will come to those who see her.
FWP
DID I STARTLE YOU?
HELLO?

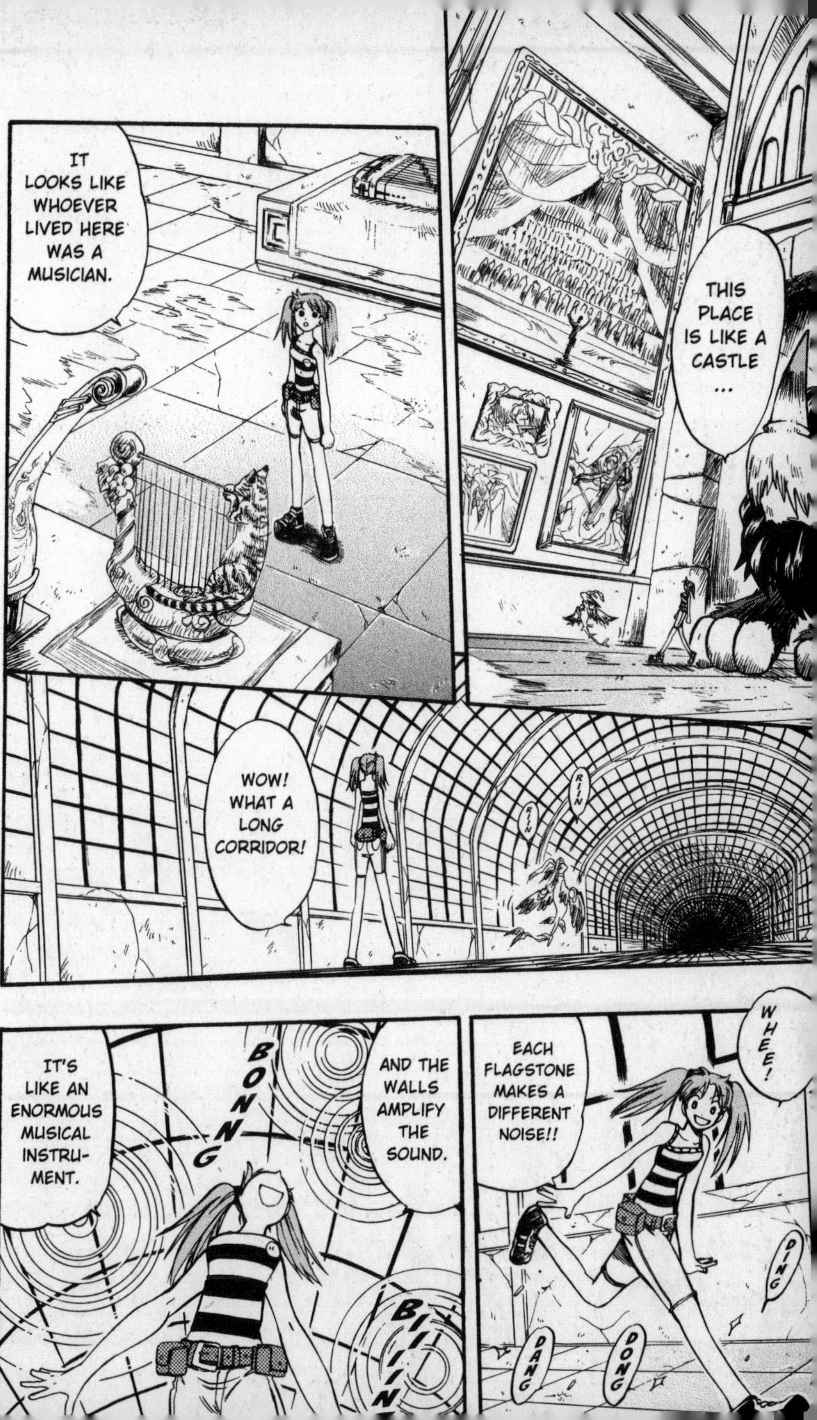

THIS PLACE IS LIKE A CASTLE ...
IT LOOKS LIKE WHOEVER LIVED HERE WAS A MUSICIAN.
RIIN
RIIN
WOW! WHAT A LONG CORRIDOR!
WHEE!
EACH FLAGSTONE MAKES A DIFFERENT NOISE!!
DING
DONG
DANG
BONNG
AND THE WALLS AMPLIFY THE SOUND.
IT'S LIKE AN ENORMOUS MUSICAL INSTRU-MENT.
BIIIN

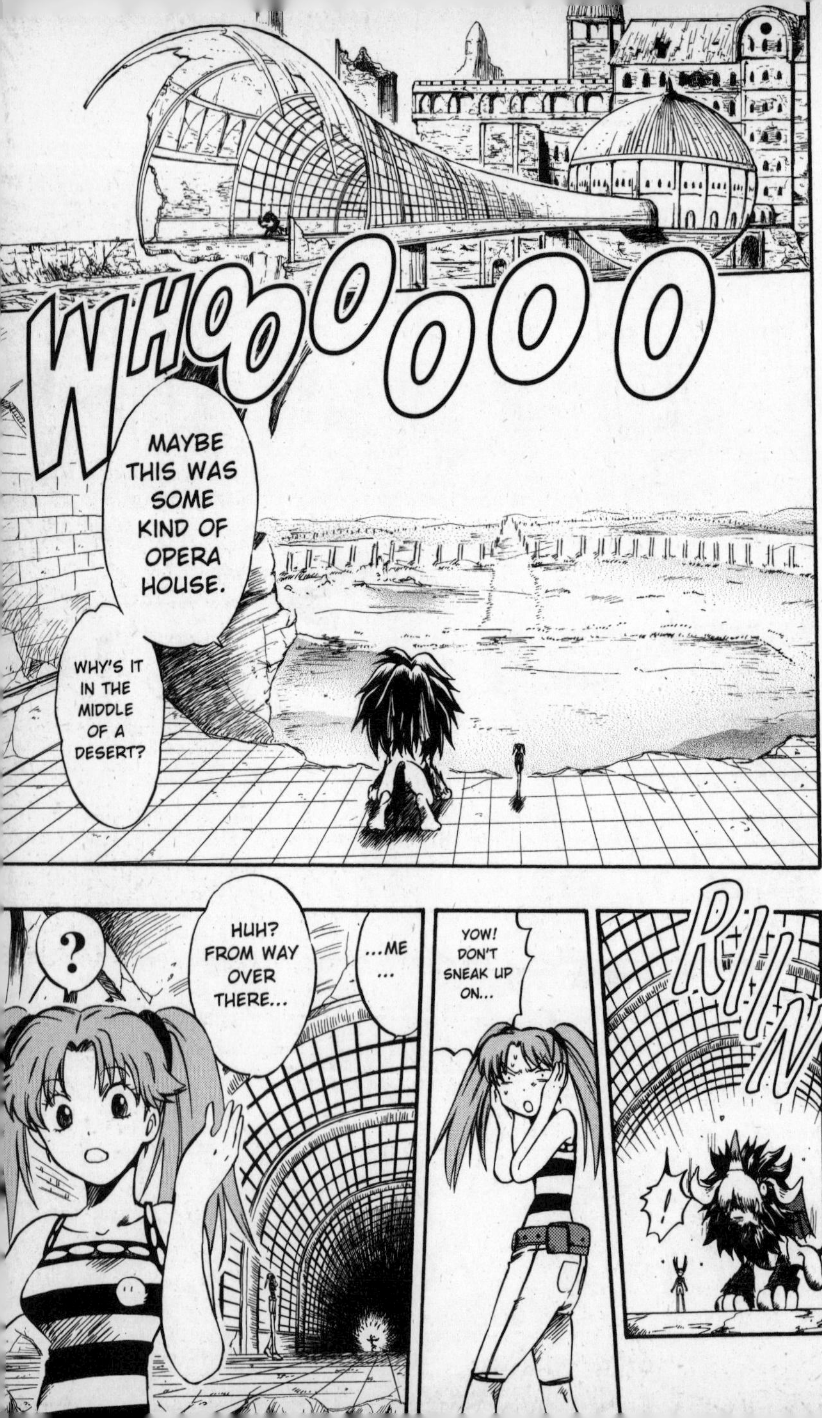
WHOOOOOOO
MAYBE THIS WAS SOME KIND OF OPERA HOUSE.
WHY'S IT IN THE MIDDLE OF A DESERT?
RIIN
!
YOW! DON'T SNEAK UP ON...
...ME ...
HUH? FROM WAY OVER THERE...
?

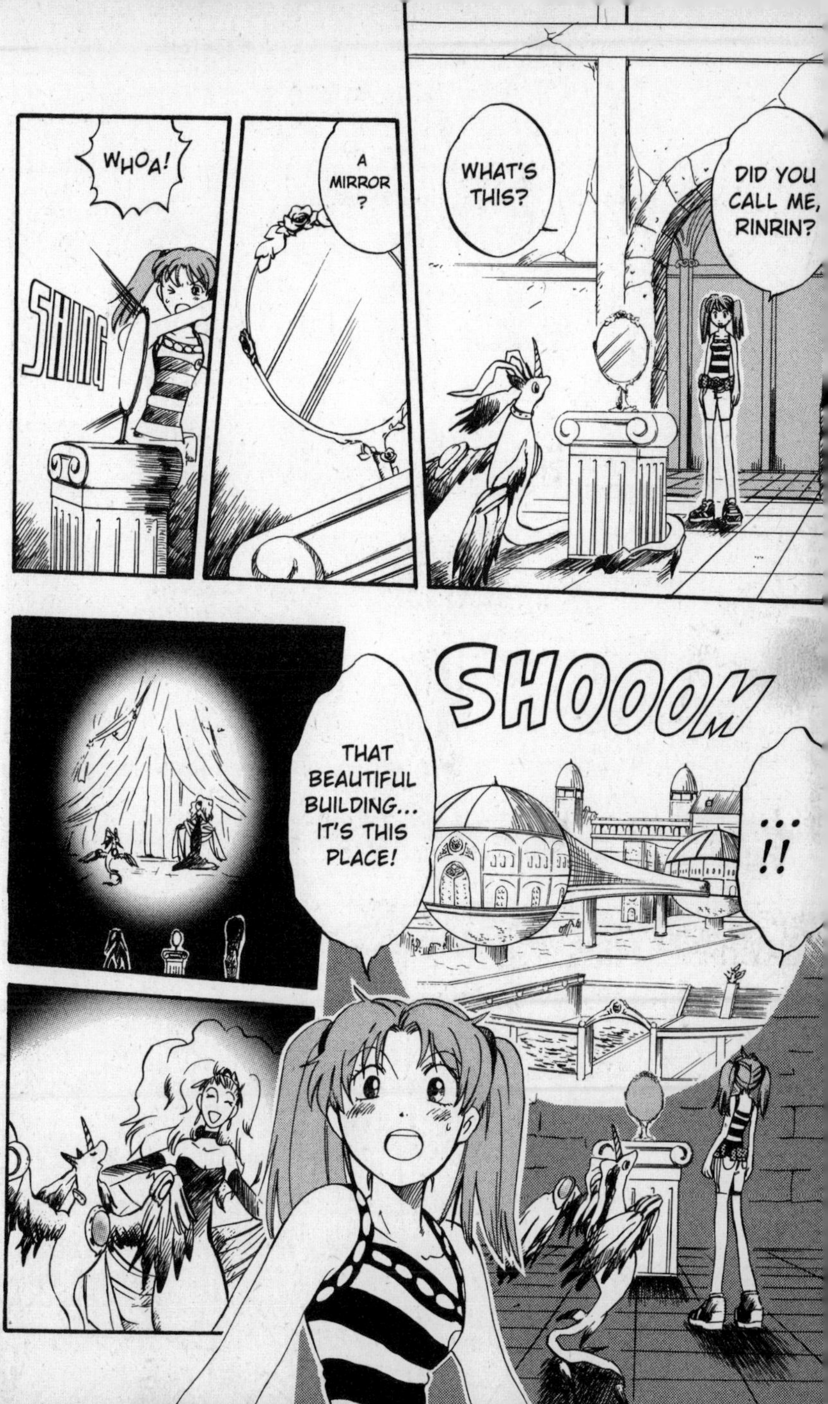
DID YOU CALL ME, RINRIN?
WHAT'S THIS?
A MIRROR?
WHOA!
SHING
SHOOOM
...!!
THAT BEAUTIFUL BUILDING... IT'S THIS PLACE!

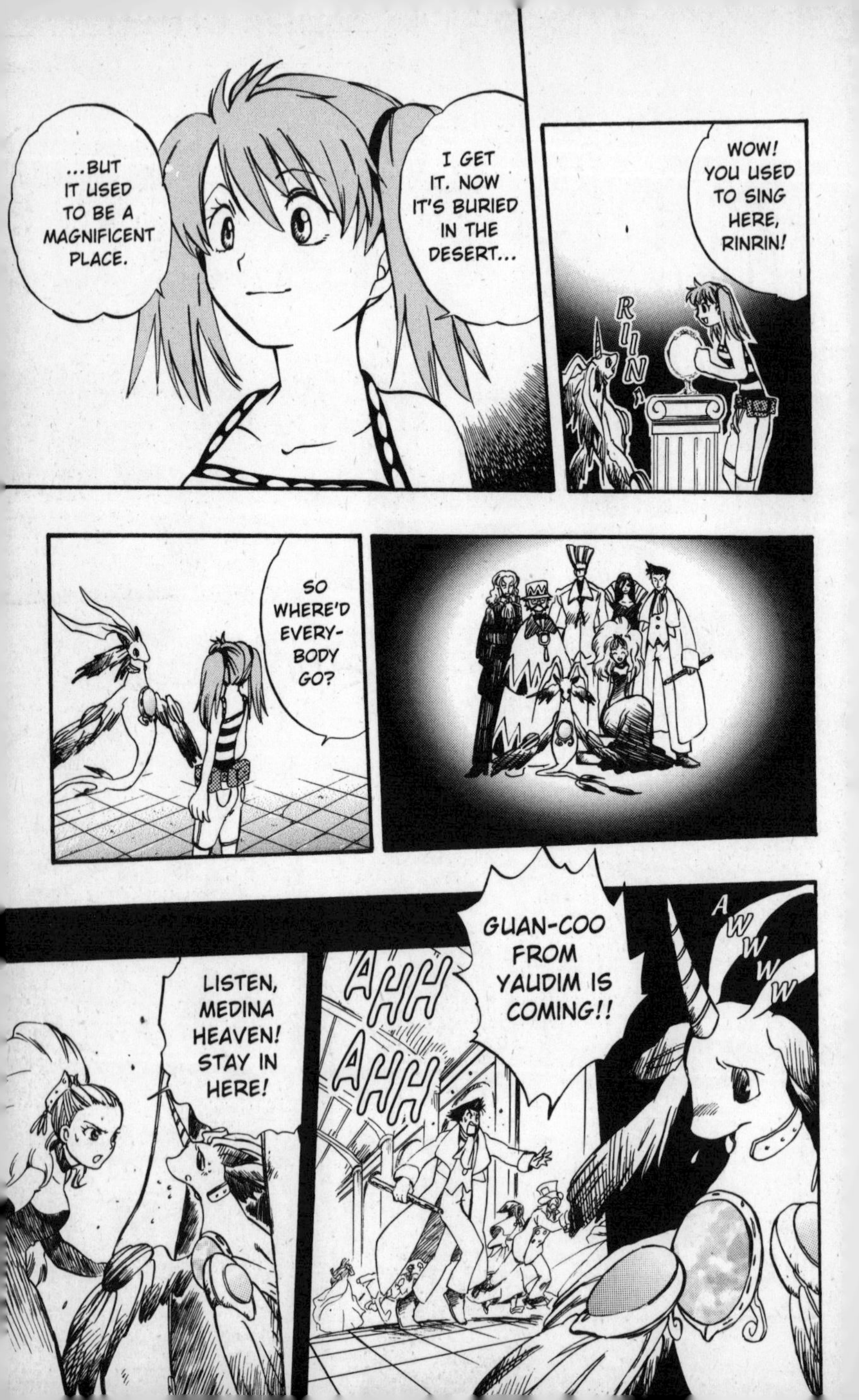
WOW! YOU USED TO SING HERE, RINRIN!
RIIN
I GET IT. NOW IT'S BURIED IN THE DESERT...
...BUT IT USED TO BE A MAGNIFICENT PLACE.
SO WHERE'D EVERY-BODY GO?
AWWWW
GUAN-COO FROM YAUDIM IS COMING!!
AHH AHH
LISTEN, MEDINA HEAVEN! STAY IN HERE!

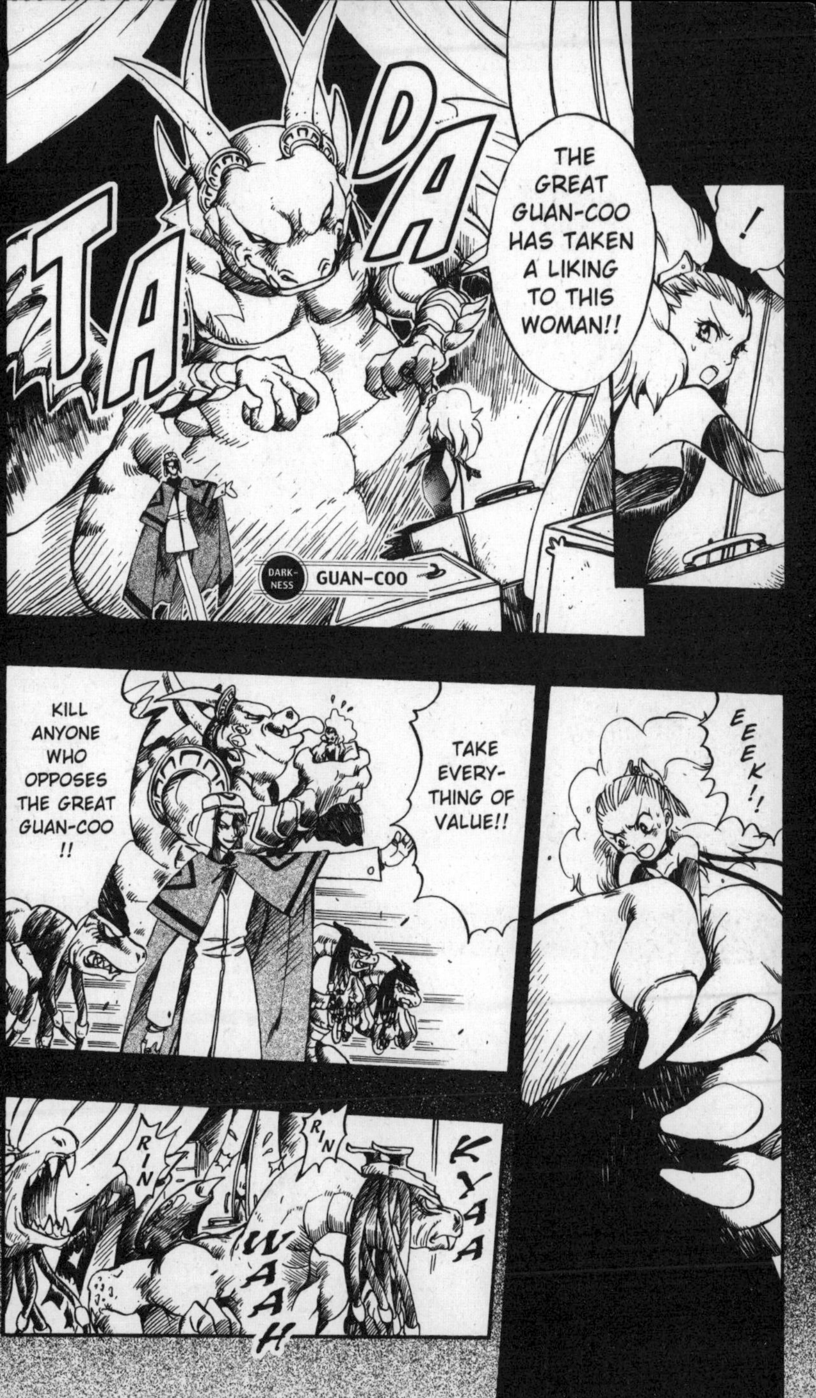
TA DA
THE GREAT GUAN-COO HAS TAKEN A LIKING TO THIS WOMAN!!
DARK-NESS GUAN-COO
!
EEEK!!
TAKE EVERY-THING OF VALUE!!
KILL ANYONE WHO OPPOSES THE GREAT GUAN-COO !!
KYAAA
RIN
WAAAH
RIN

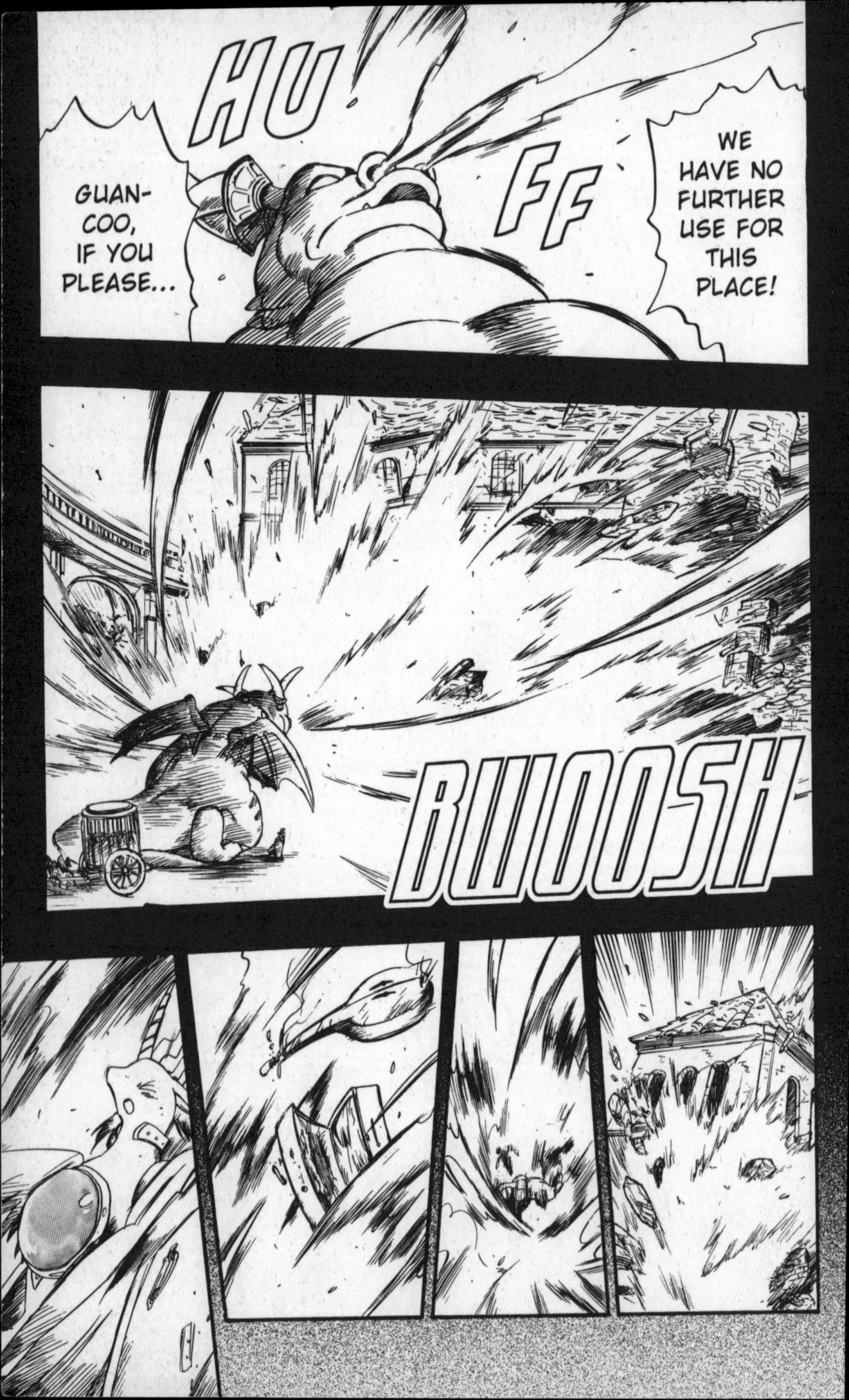
WE HAVE NO FURTHER USE FOR THIS PLACE!
HU! FF
GUAN-COO, IF YOU PLEASE...
BWOOSH

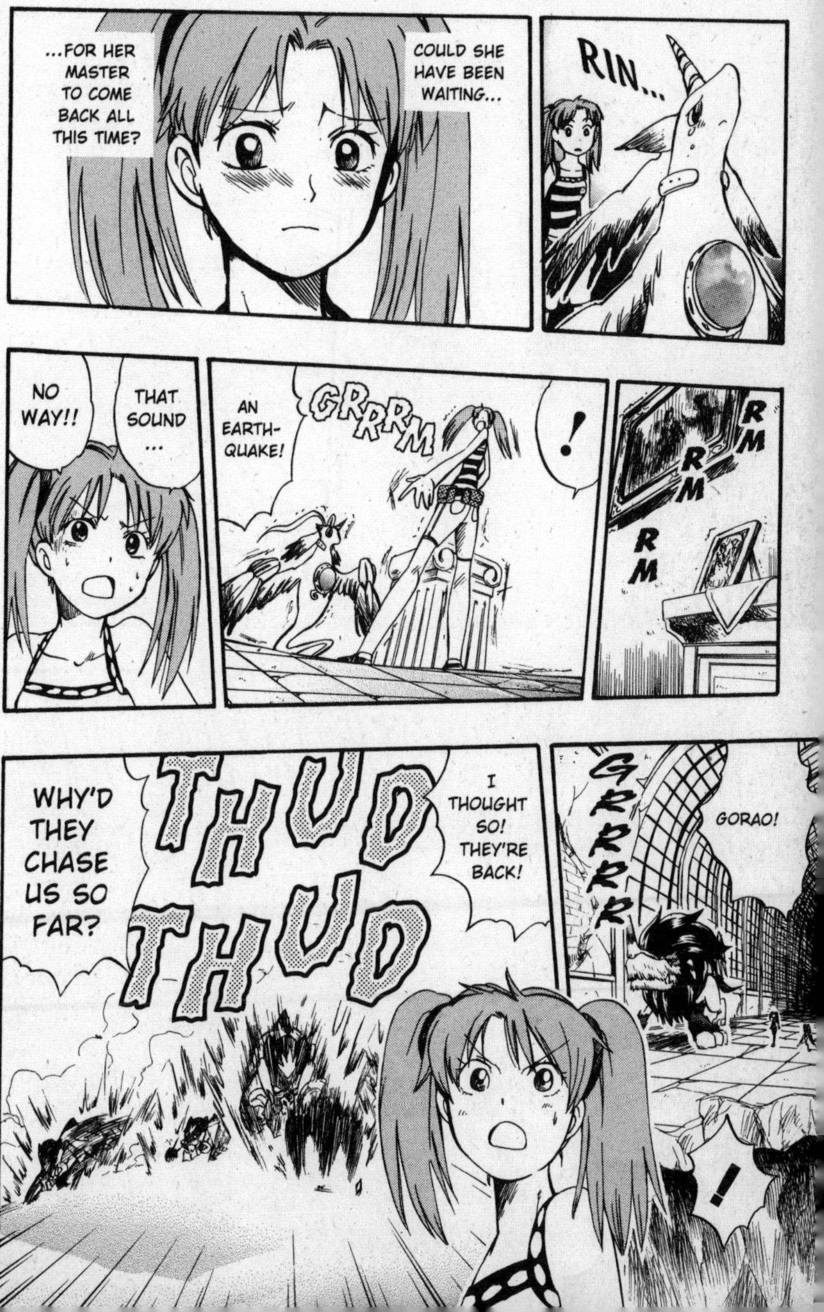
RIN...
COULD SHE HAVE BEEN WAITING...
...FOR HER MASTER TO COME BACK ALL THIS TIME?
RM RM RM RM
!
GRRRM
AN EARTH-QUAKE!
THAT SOUND ...
NO WAY!!
GORAO!
GRRRRR
!
I THOUGHT SO! THEY'RE BACK!
THUD THUD
WHY'D THEY CHASE US SO FAR?

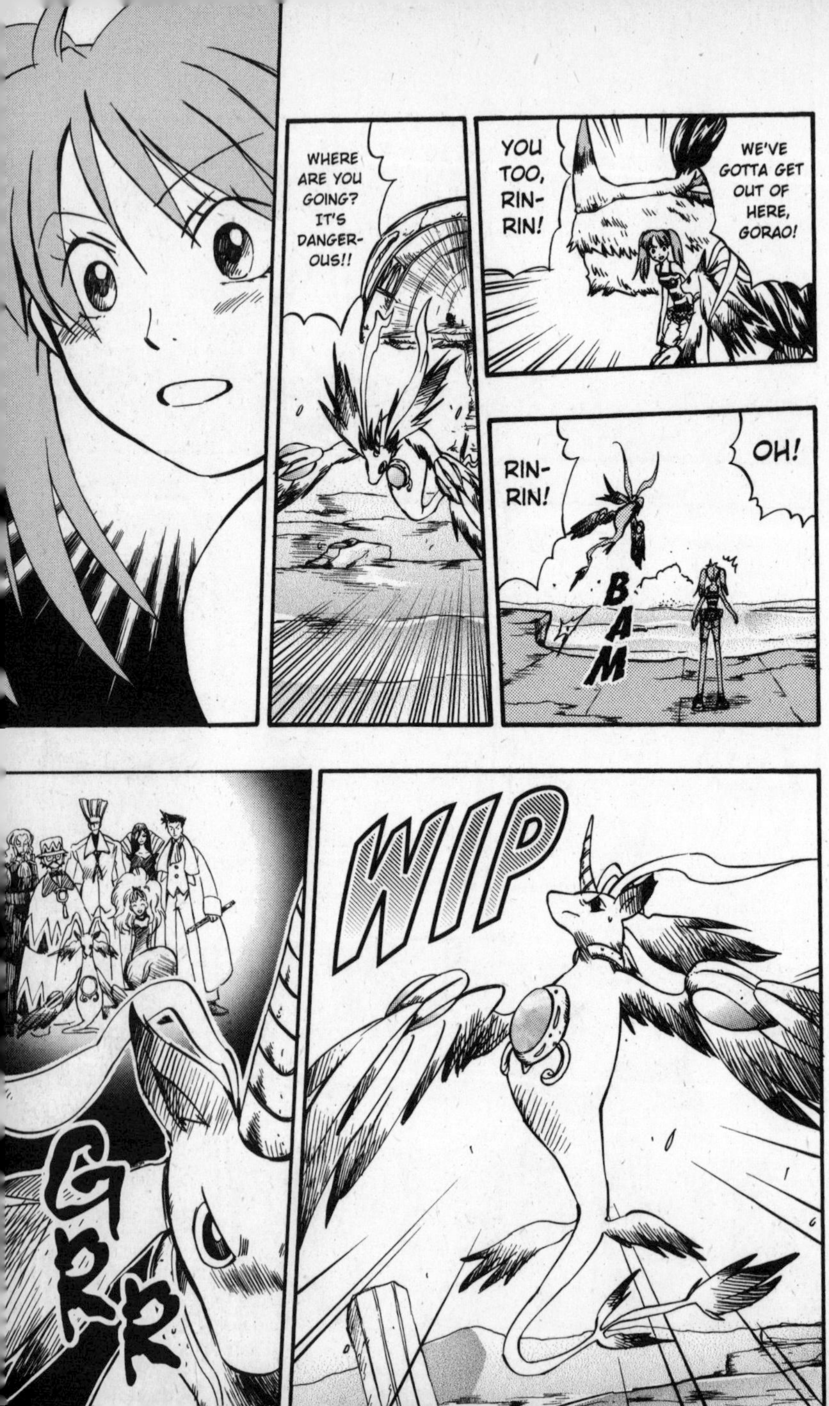
WE'VE GOTTA GET OUT OF HERE, GORAO!
YOU TOO, RIN-RIN!
OH!
RIN-RIN!
BAM
WHERE ARE YOU GOING? IT'S DANGER-OUS!!
WIP
GRRR

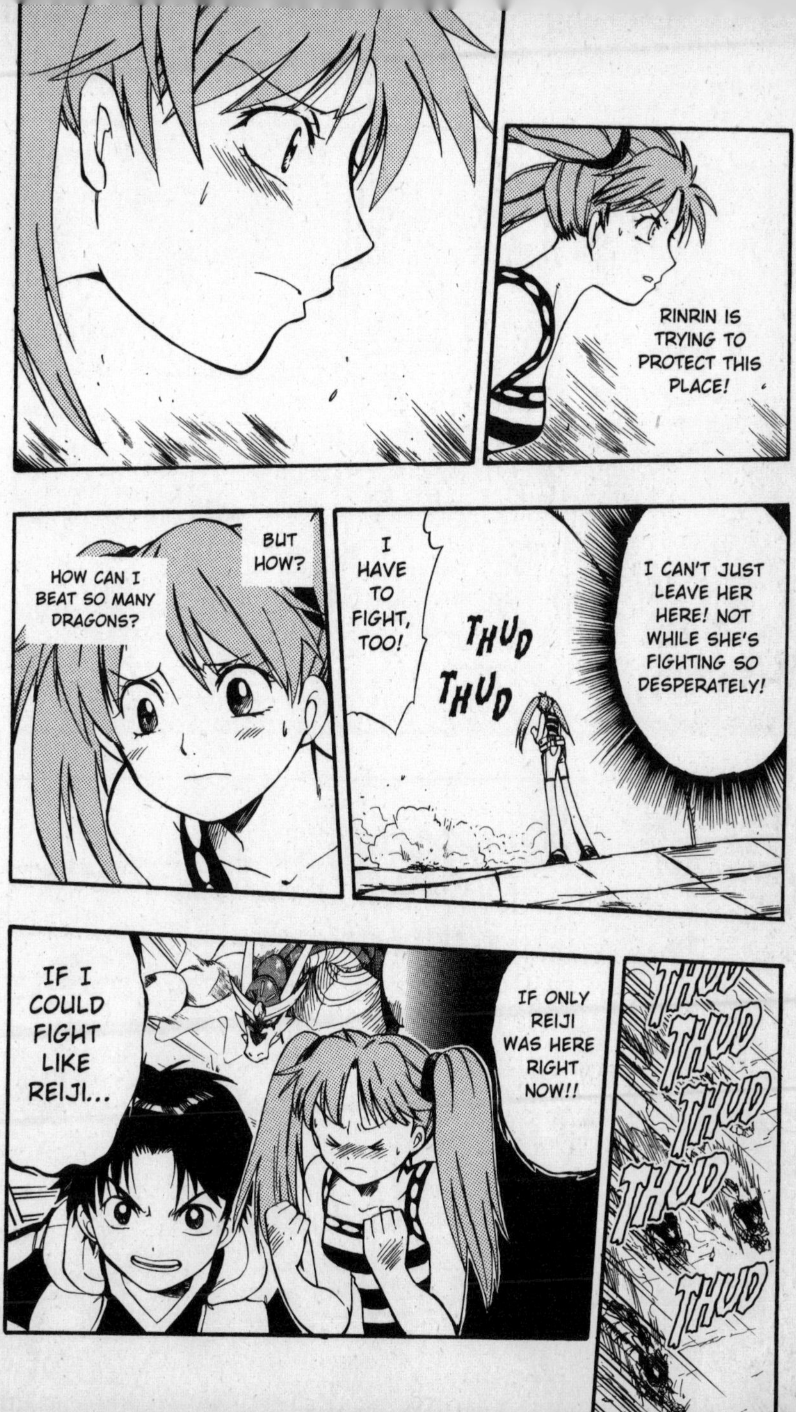
RINRIN IS TRYING TO PROTECT THIS PLACE!
I CAN'T JUST LEAVE HER HERE! NOT WHILE SHE'S FIGHTING SO DESPERATELY!
THUD
THUD
I HAVE TO FIGHT, TOO!
BUT HOW?
HOW CAN I BEAT SO MANY DRAGONS?
THUD
THUD
THUD
THUD
THUD
IF ONLY REIJI WAS HERE RIGHT NOW!!
IF I COULD FIGHT LIKE REIJI...

READ THIS WAY

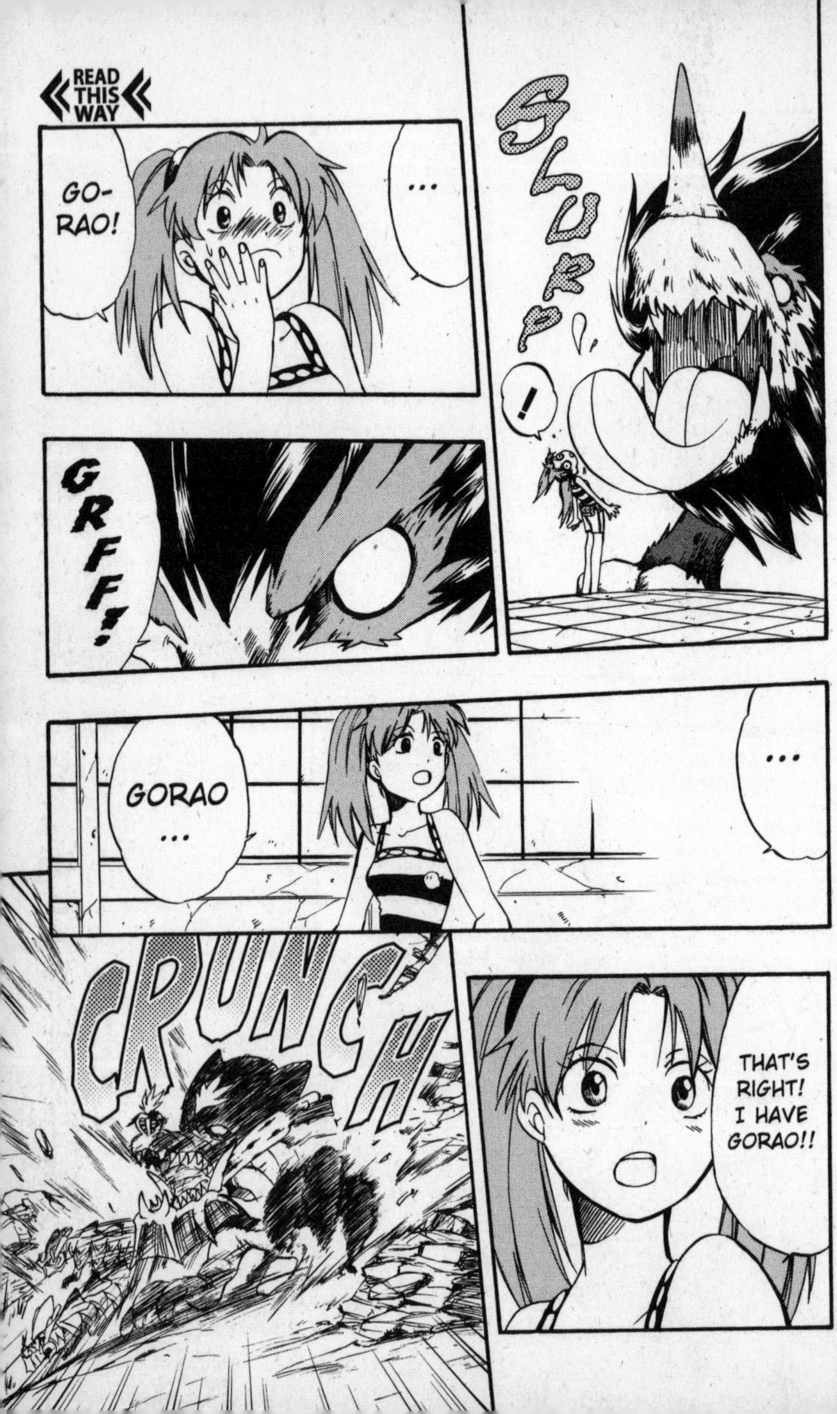
SLURP
!
...
GO-RAO!
GRFF!!
...
GORAO ...
THAT'S RIGHT! I HAVE GORAO!!
CRUNCH

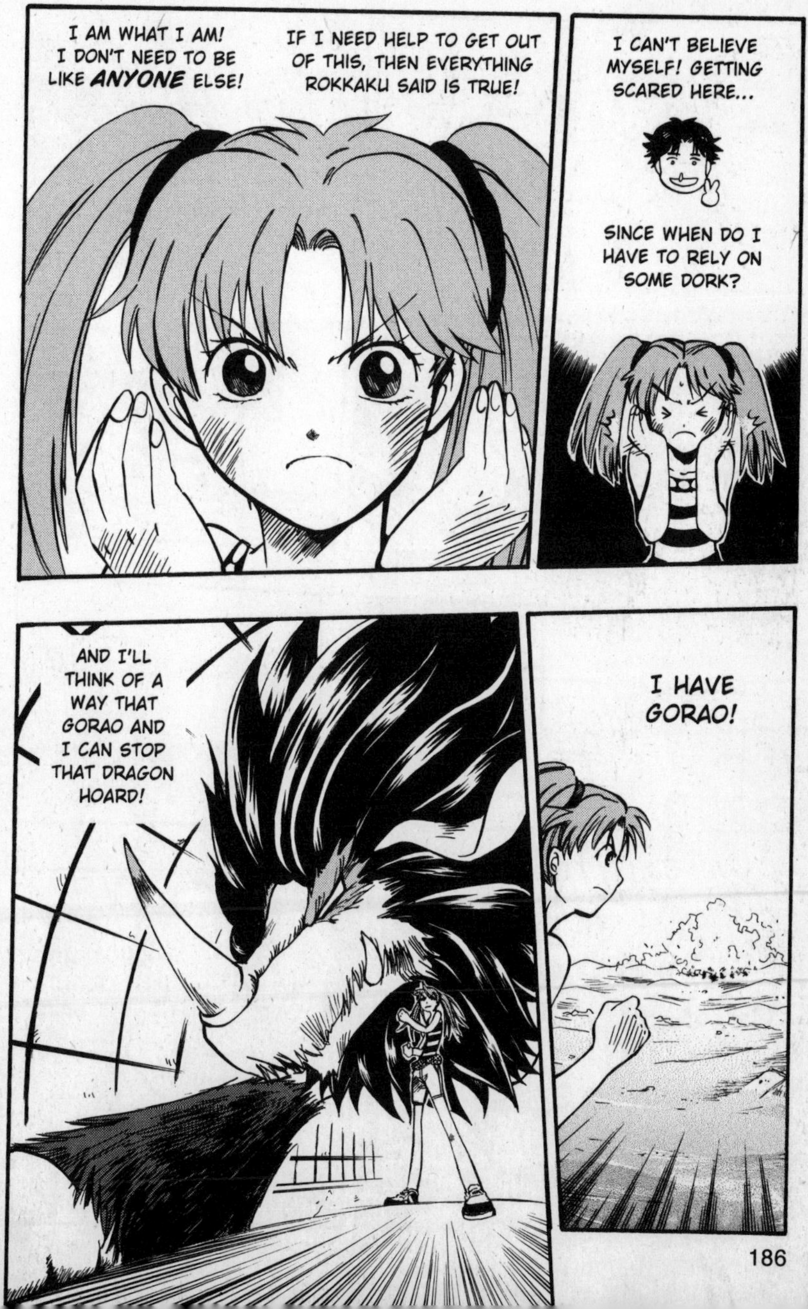
I CAN'T BELIEVE MYSELF! GETTING SCARED HERE...
SINCE WHEN DO I HAVE TO RELY ON SOME DORK?
IF I NEED HELP TO GET OUT OF THIS, THEN EVERYTHING ROKKAKU SAID IS TRUE!
I AM WHAT I AM! I DON'T NEED TO BE LIKE ANYONE ELSE!
I HAVE GORAO!
AND I'LL THINK OF A WAY THAT GORAO AND I CAN STOP THAT DRAGON HOARD!

READ THIS WAY

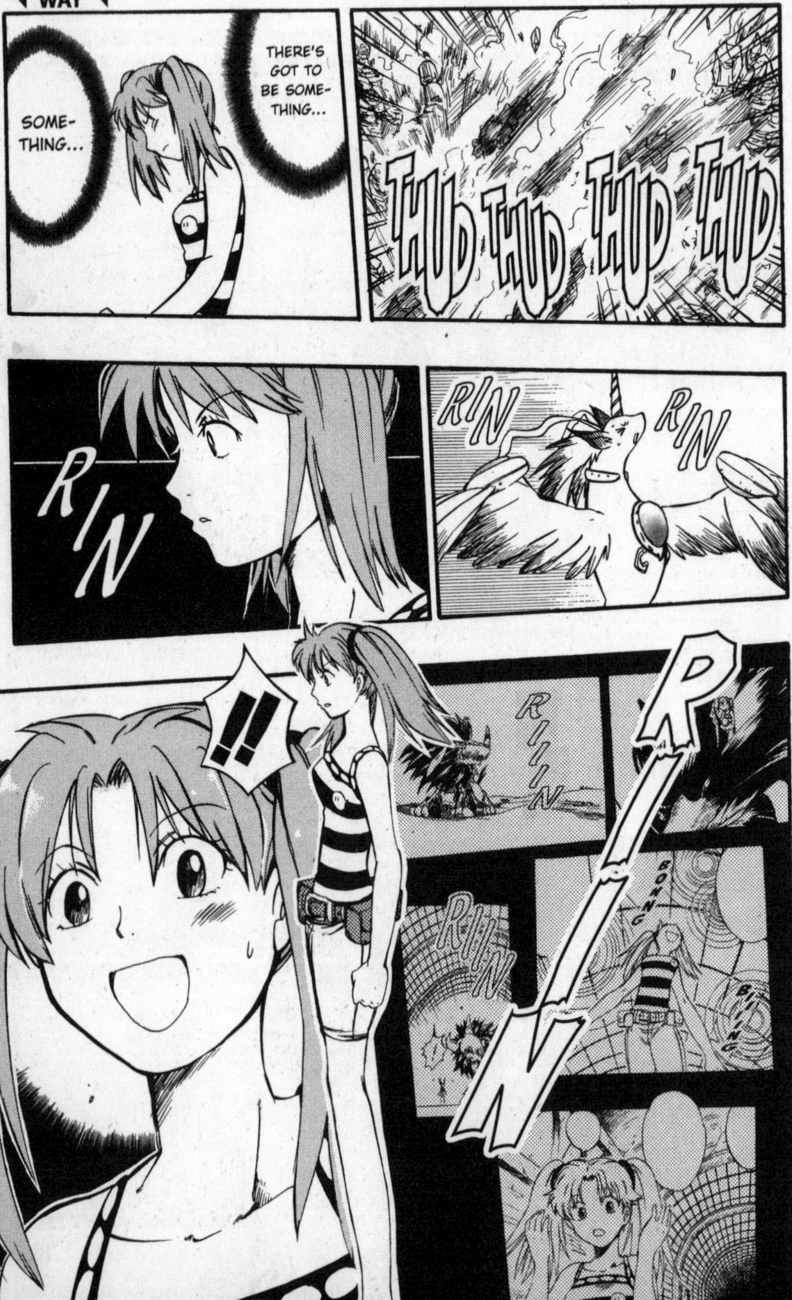
THUD THUD THUD THUD
THERE'S GOT TO BE SOME-THING...
SOME-THING...
RIN RIN
RIN
!!
RIN
RIIIN
BONNG
BIIING
RIIN

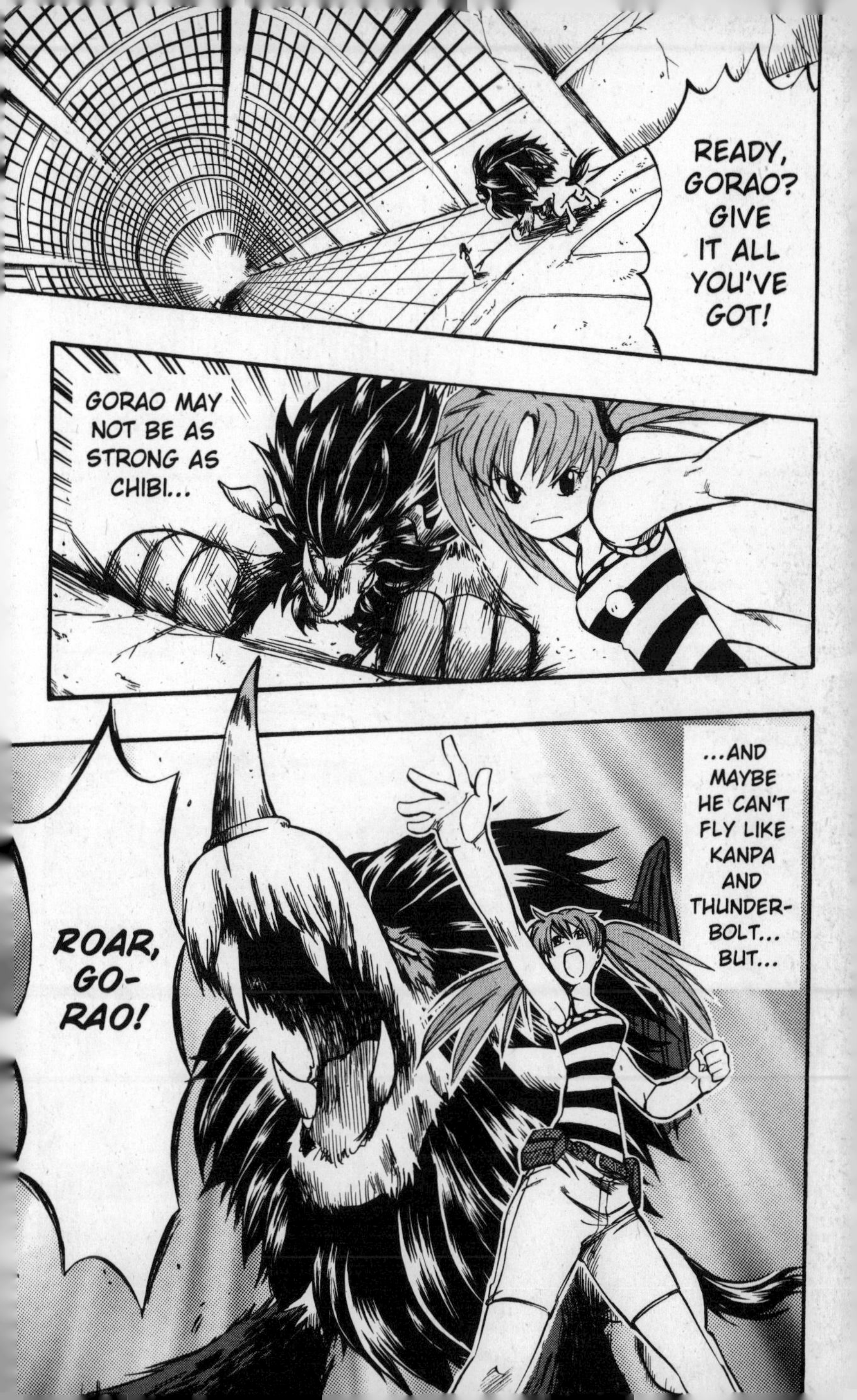
READY, GORAO? GIVE IT ALL YOU'VE GOT!
GORAO MAY NOT BE AS STRONG AS CHIBI...
...AND MAYBE HE CAN'T FLY LIKE KANPA AND THUNDER-BOLT... BUT...
ROAR, GO-RAO!

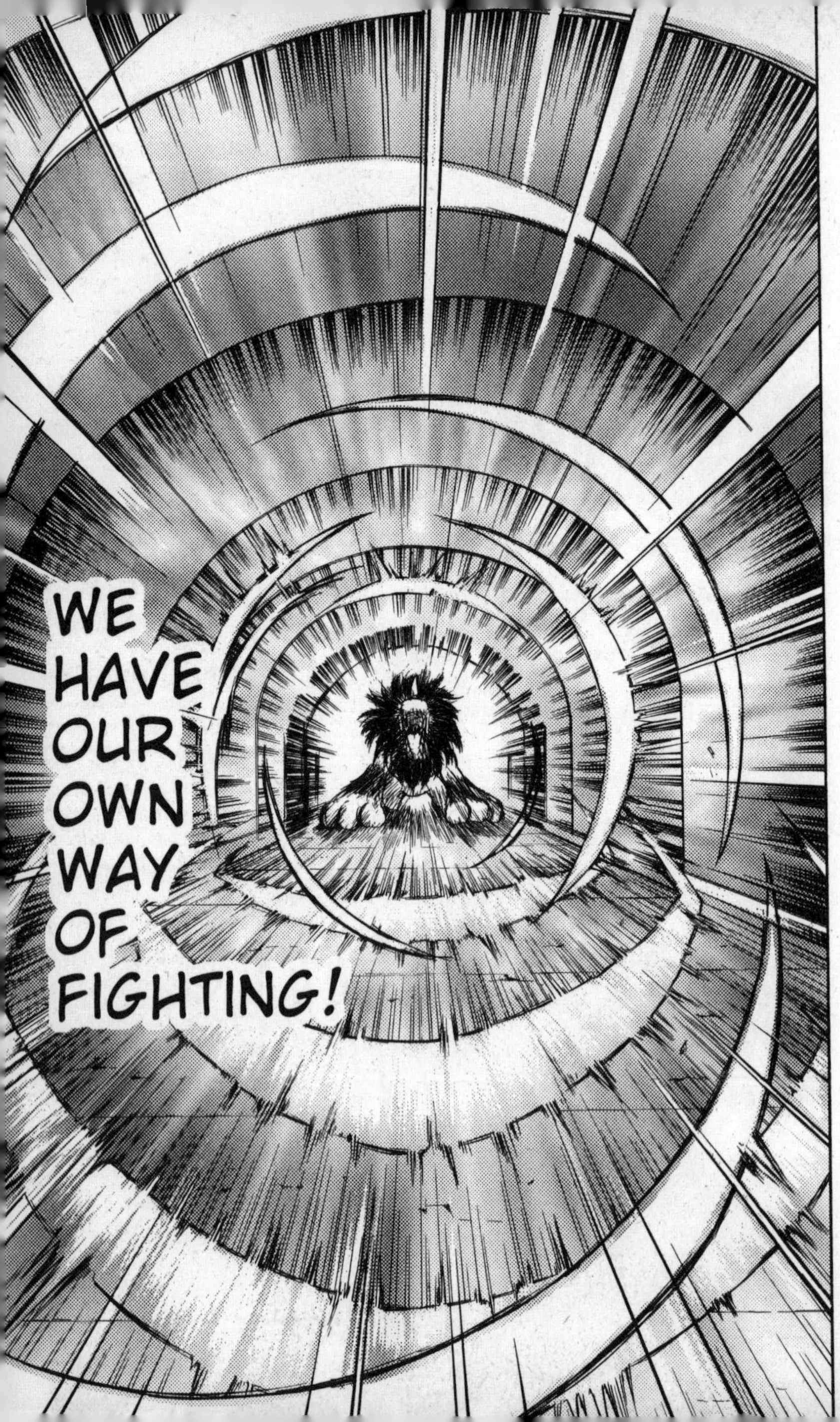
WE HAVE OUR OWN WAY OF FIGHTING!

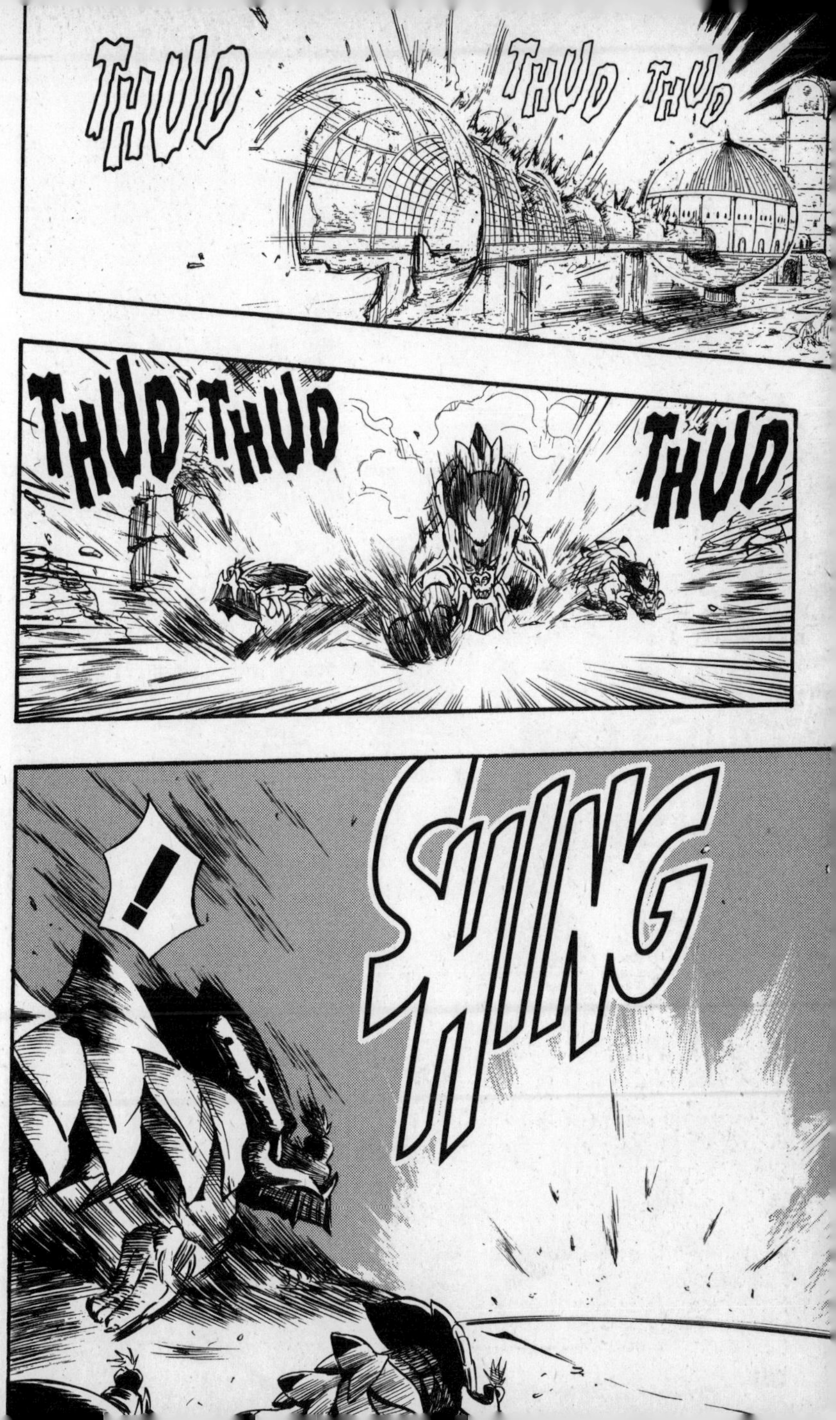
THUD
THUD
THUD
THUD
THUD
THUD
SHING
!

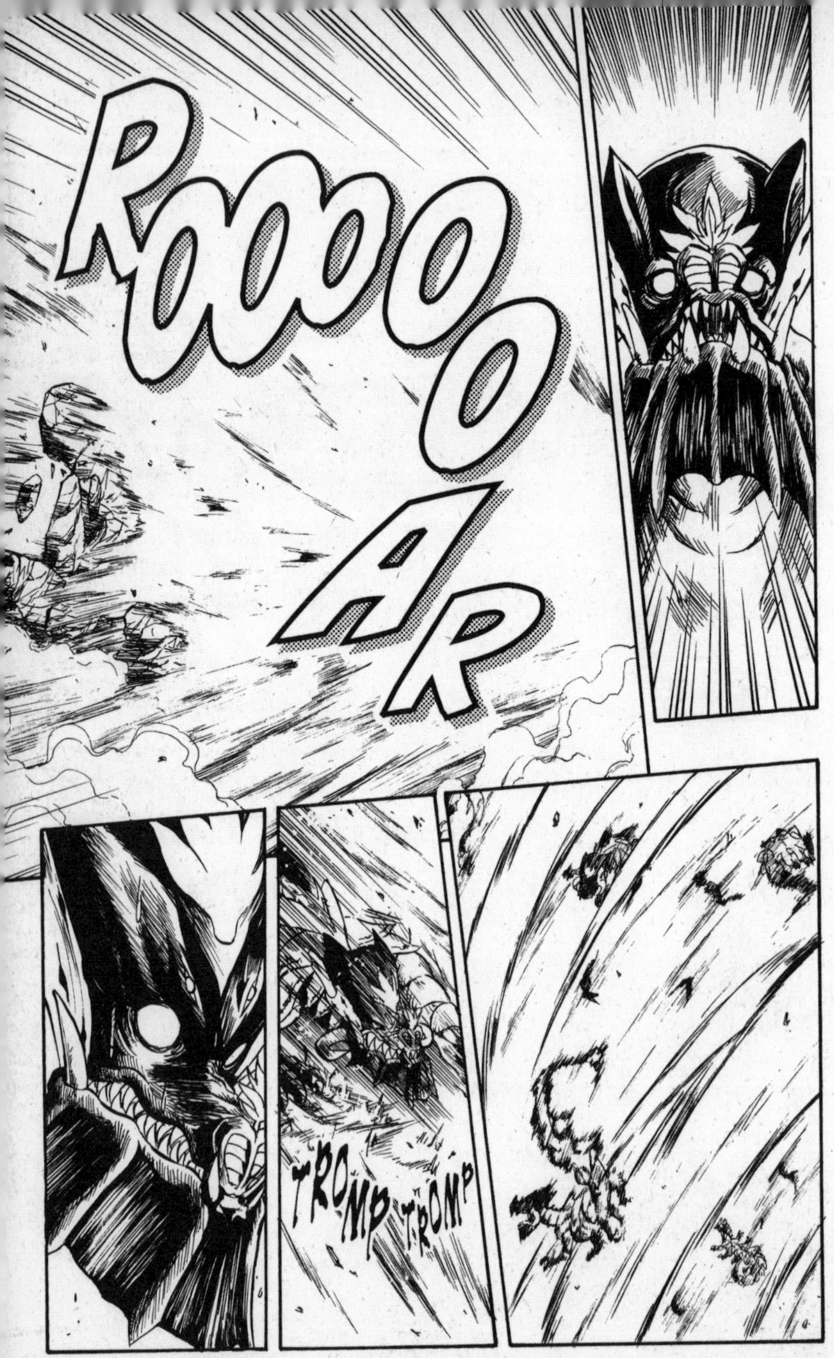
ROOOOOAR
TROMP TROMP

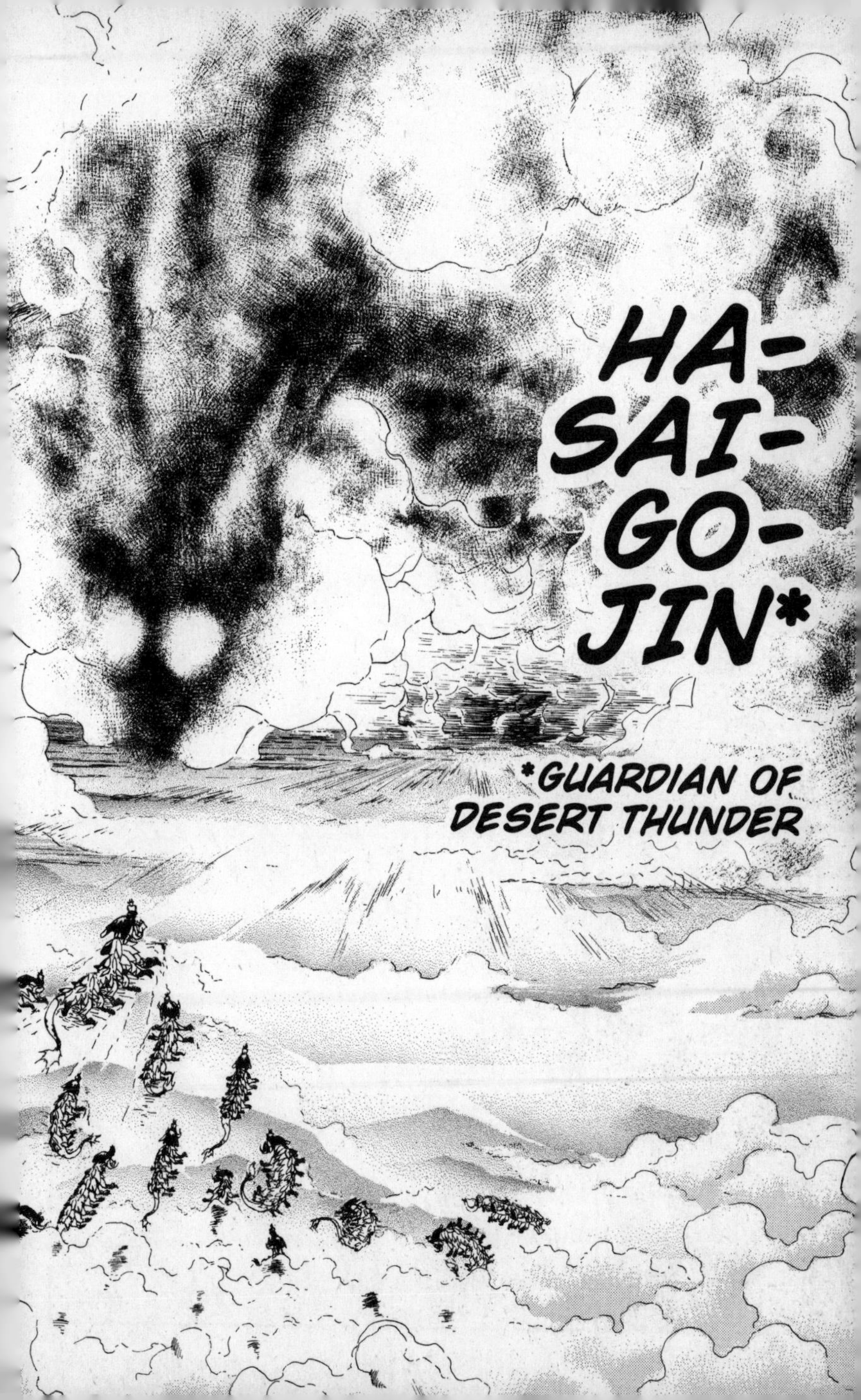
HA-
SAI-
GO-
JIN*
*GUARDIAN OF
DESERT THUNDER

READ THIS WAY

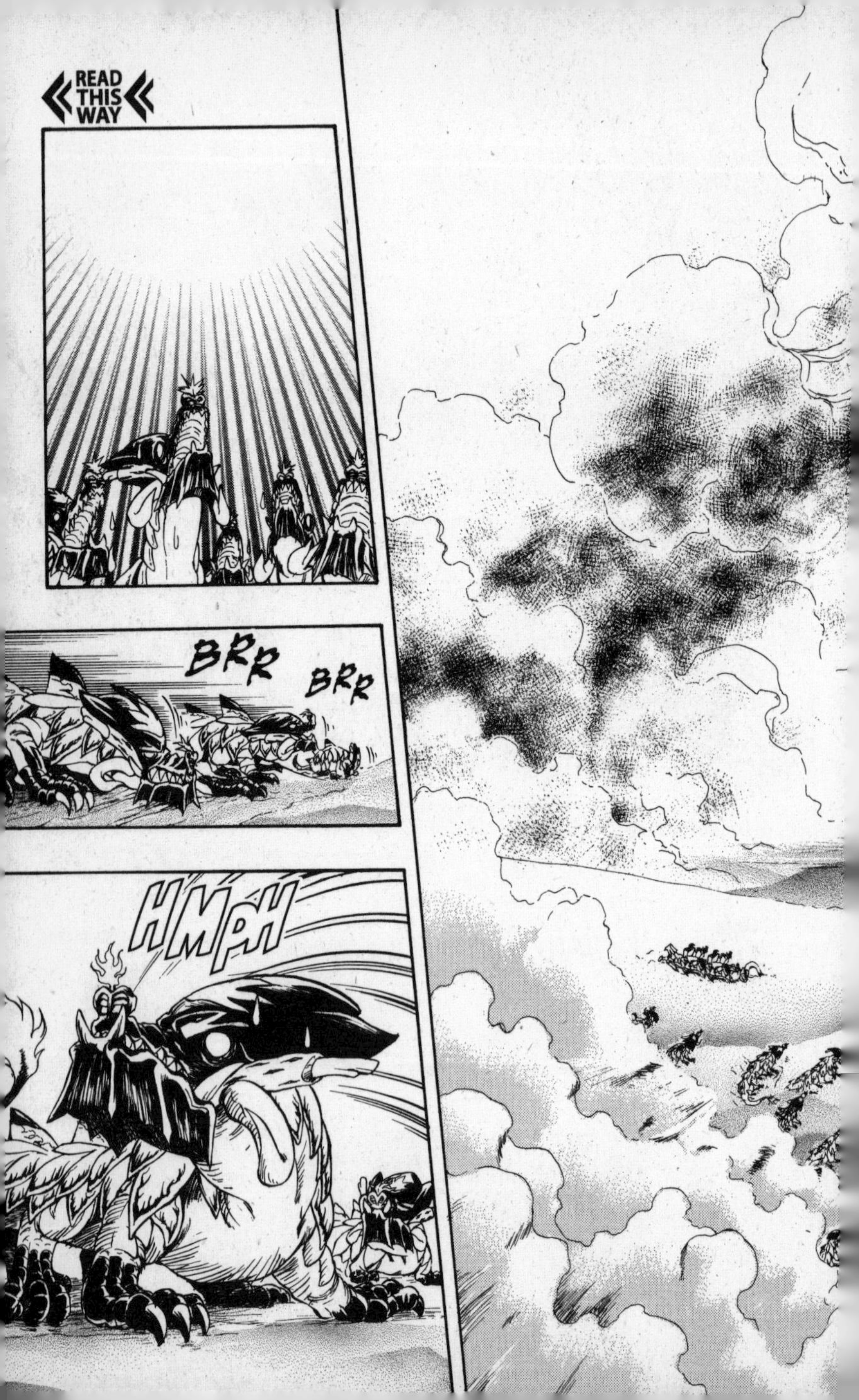
BRR
BRR
HMPH

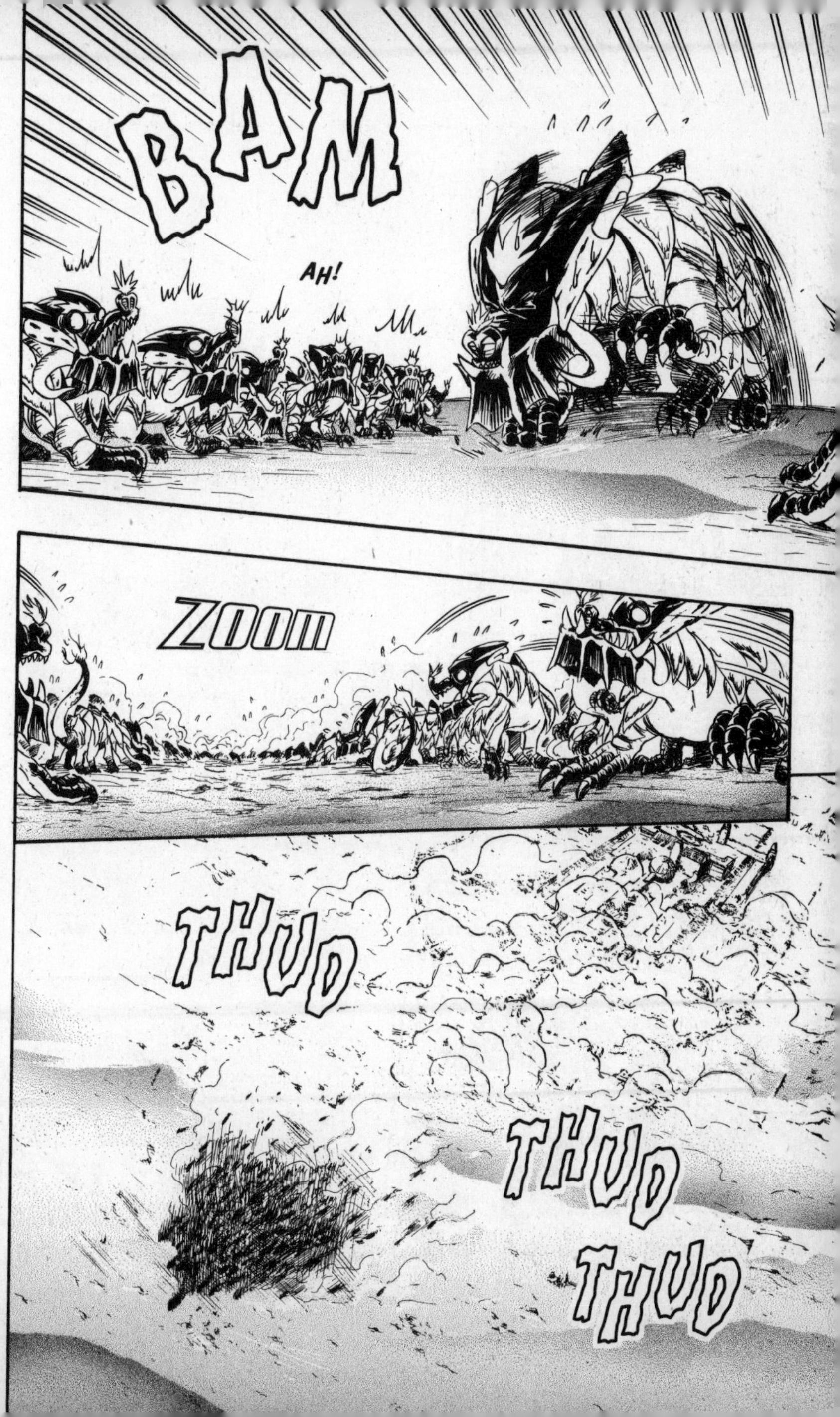
BAM
AH!
ZOOM
THUD
THUD
THUD

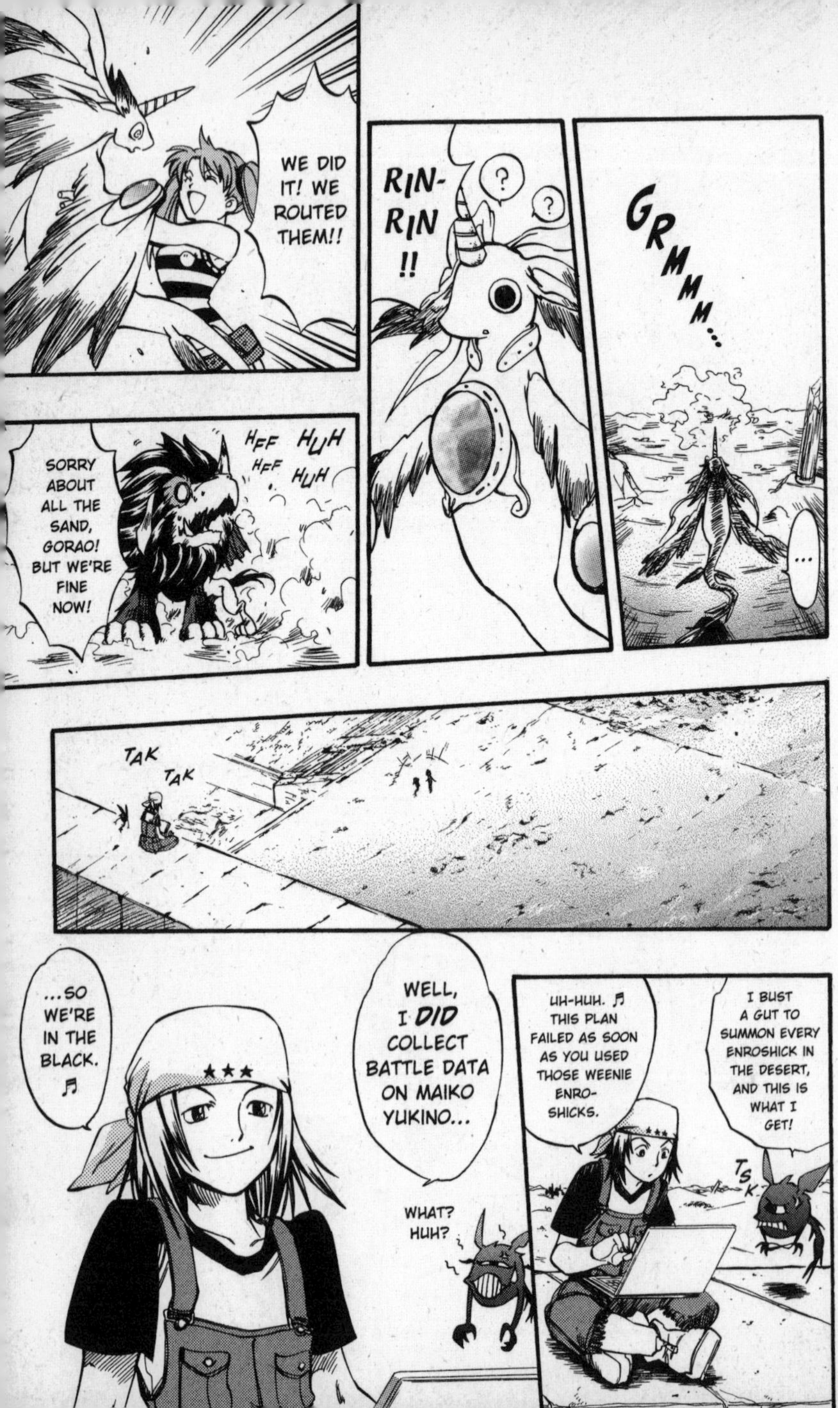
WE DID IT! WE ROUTED THEM!!
SORRY ABOUT ALL THE SAND, GORAO! BUT WE'RE FINE NOW!
HFF HFF
HUH HUH
RIN-RIN !!
?
?
GRMMM...
...
TAK TAK
I BUST A GUT TO SUMMON EVERY ENROSHICK IN THE DESERT, AND THIS IS WHAT I GET!
UH-HUH. ♬ THIS PLAN FAILED AS SOON AS YOU USED THOSE WEENIE ENRO-SHICKS.
TSK
WELL, I DID COLLECT BATTLE DATA ON MAIKO YUKINO...
WHAT? HUH?
...SO WE'RE IN THE BLACK. ♬

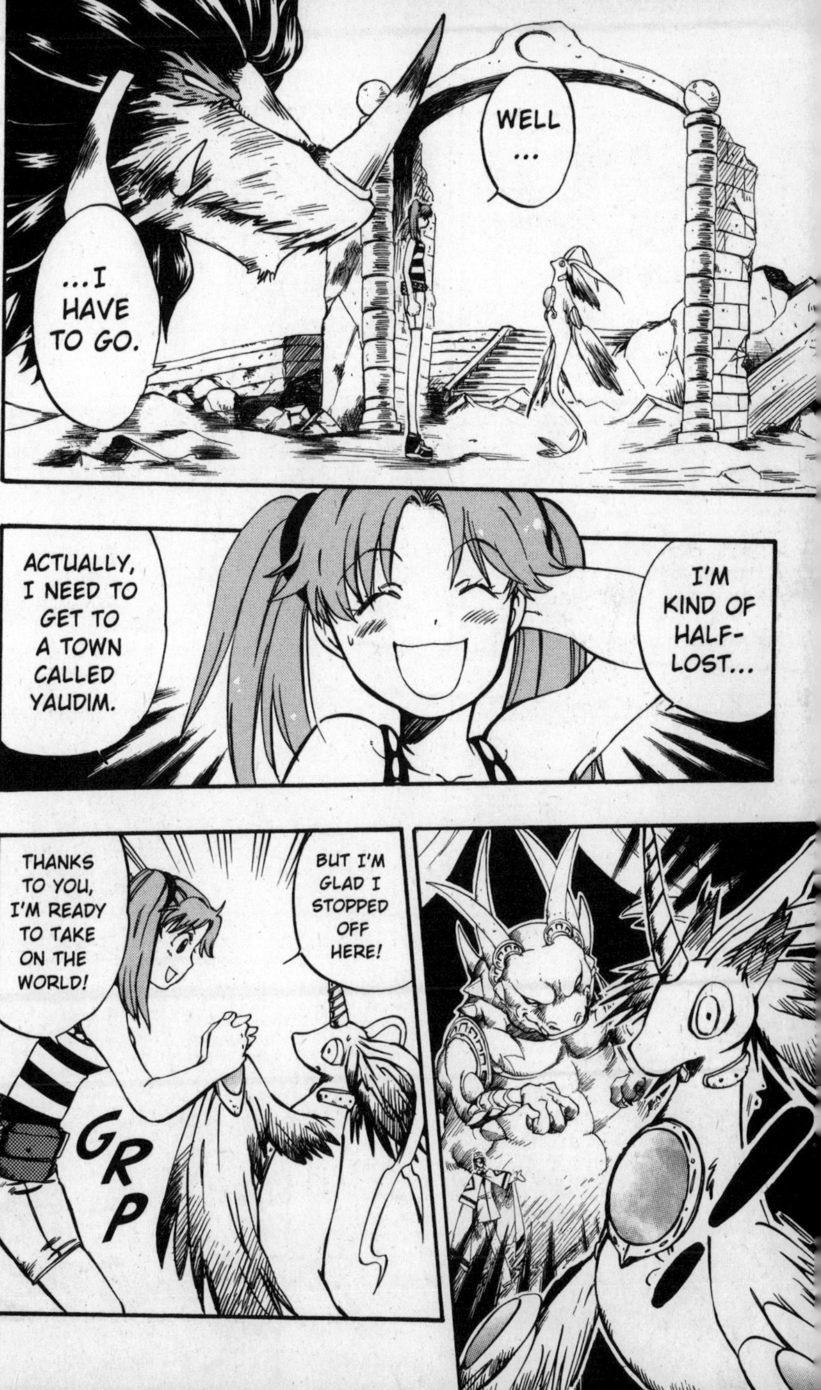
WELL ...
...I HAVE TO GO.
I'M KIND OF HALF-LOST...
ACTUALLY, I NEED TO GET TO A TOWN CALLED YAUDIM.
BUT I'M GLAD I STOPPED OFF HERE!
THANKS TO YOU, I'M READY TO TAKE ON THE WORLD!
GRP

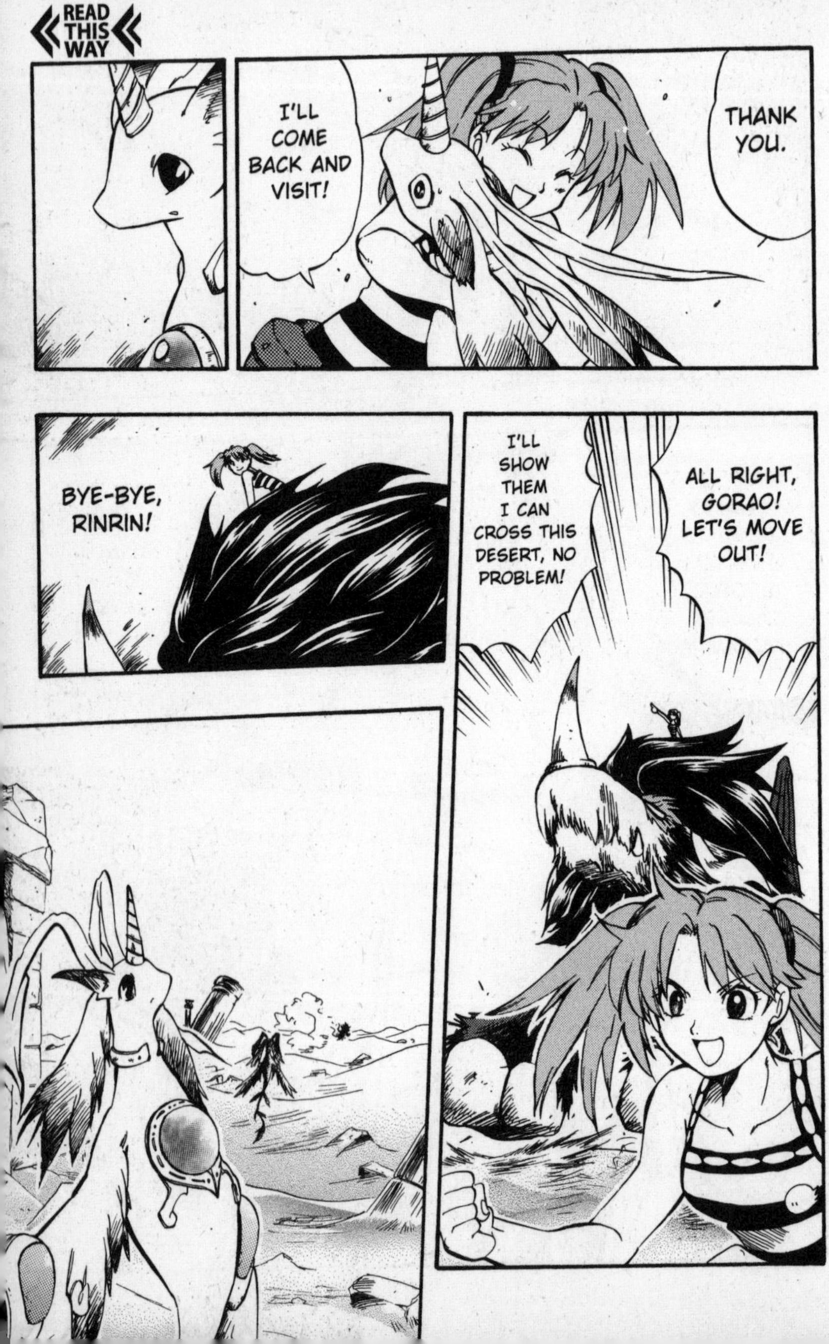
READ THIS WAY
THANK YOU.
I'LL COME BACK AND VISIT!
ALL RIGHT, GORAO! LET'S MOVE OUT!
I'LL SHOW THEM I CAN CROSS THIS DESERT, NO PROBLEM!
BYE-BYE, RINRIN!

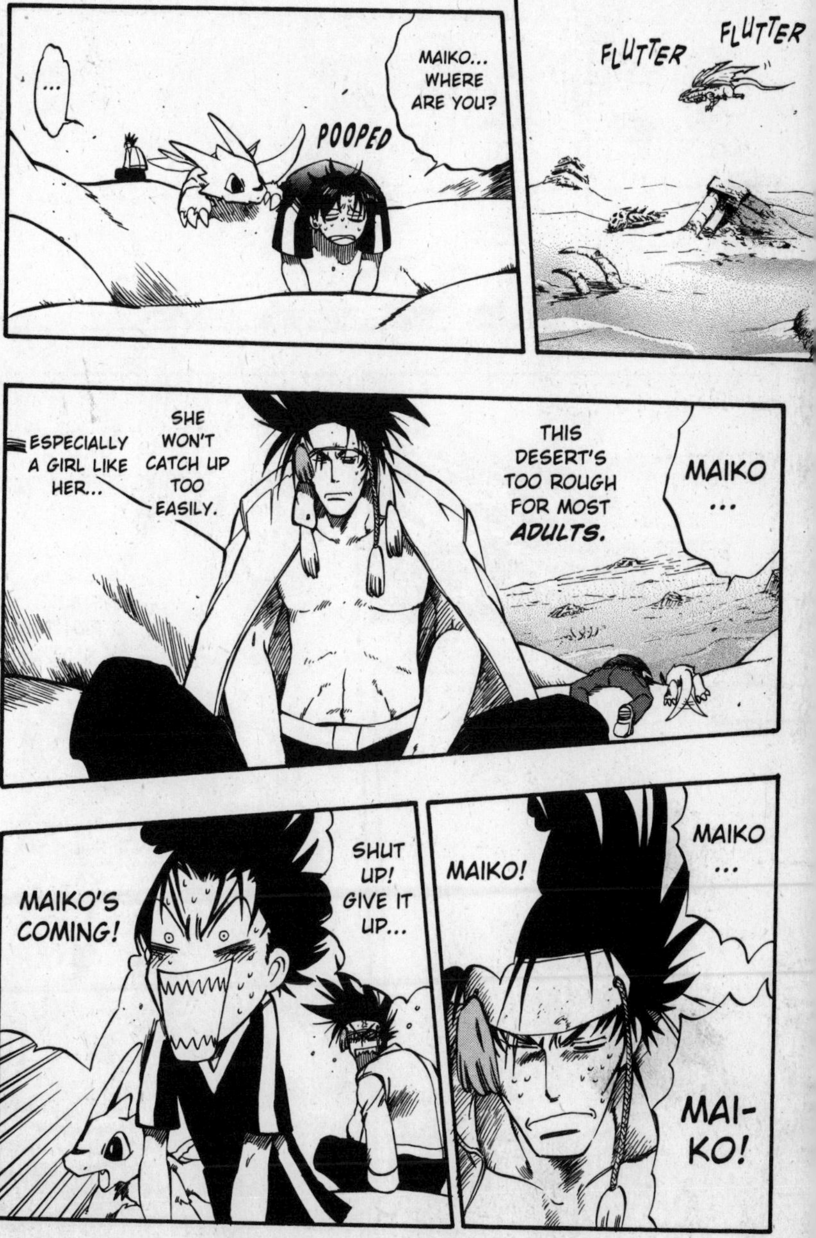
FLUTTER
FLUTTER
MAIKO... WHERE ARE YOU?
POOPED
...
MAIKO ...
THIS DESERT'S TOO ROUGH FOR MOST ADULTS.
SHE WON'T CATCH UP TOO EASILY.
ESPECIALLY A GIRL LIKE HER...
MAIKO ...
MAIKO!
MAI- KO!
SHUT UP! GIVE IT UP...
MAIKO'S COMING!

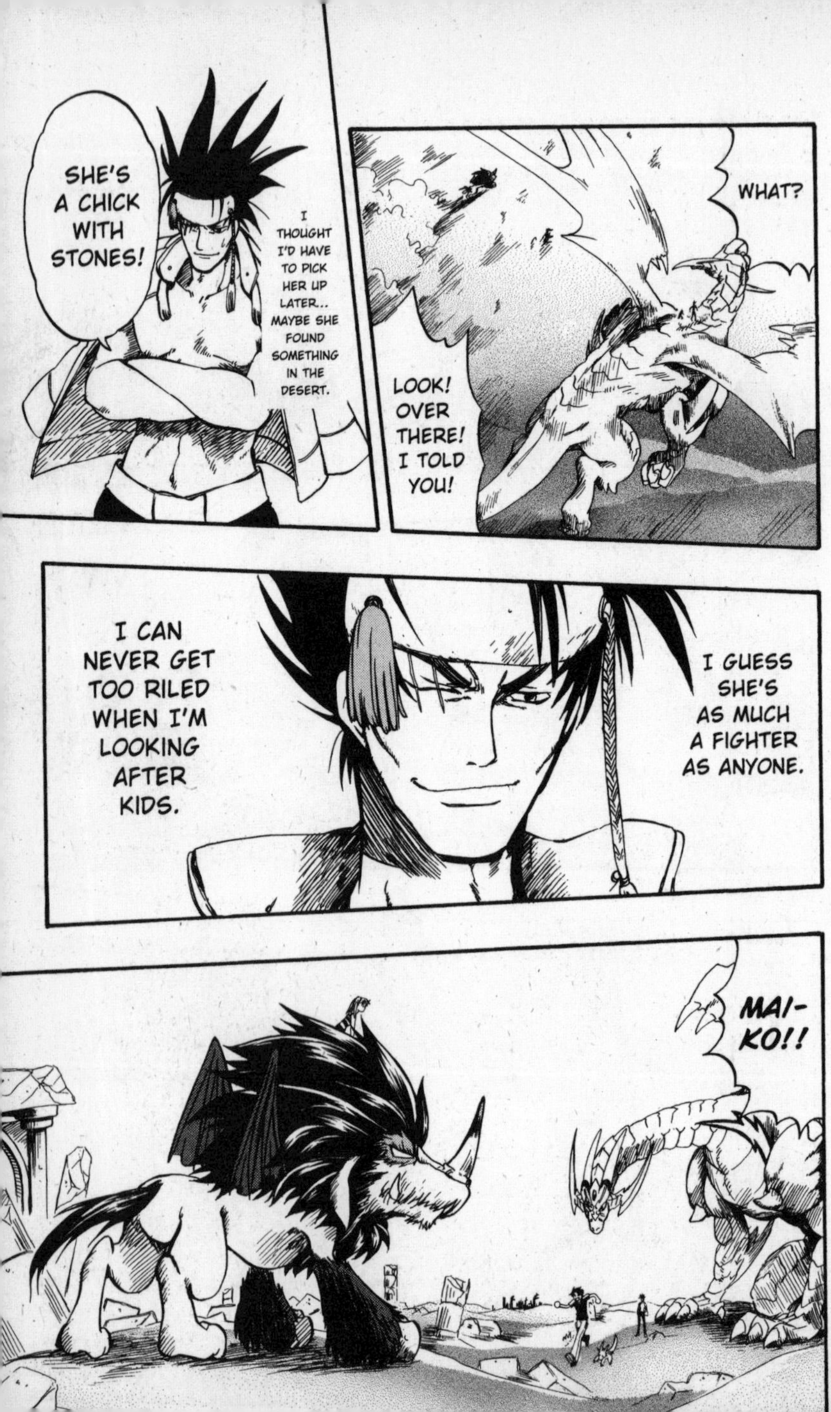
WHAT?
LOOK! OVER THERE! I TOLD YOU!
I THOUGHT I'D HAVE TO PICK HER UP LATER... MAYBE SHE FOUND SOMETHING IN THE DESERT.
SHE'S A CHICK WITH STONES!
I GUESS SHE'S AS MUCH A FIGHTER AS ANYONE.
I CAN NEVER GET TOO RILED WHEN I'M LOOKING AFTER KIDS.
MAI-KO!!

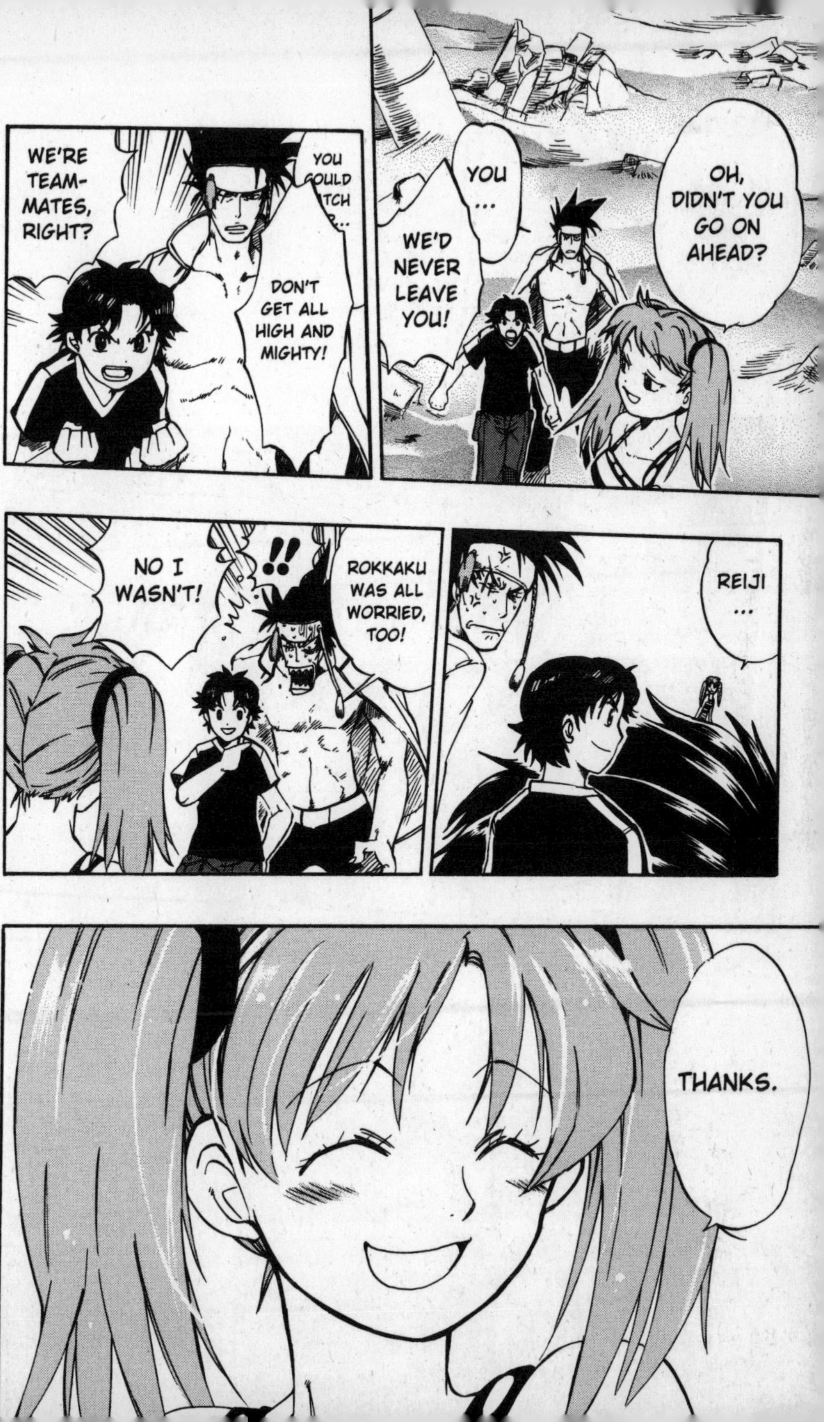

OH, DIDN'T YOU GO ON AHEAD?
YOU ...
WE'D NEVER LEAVE YOU!
YOU COULD
DON'T GET ALL HIGH AND MIGHTY!
WE'RE TEAM-MATES, RIGHT?
REIJI ...
ROKKAKU WAS ALL WORRIED, TOO!
!!
NO I WASN'T!
THANKS.

READ THIS WAY

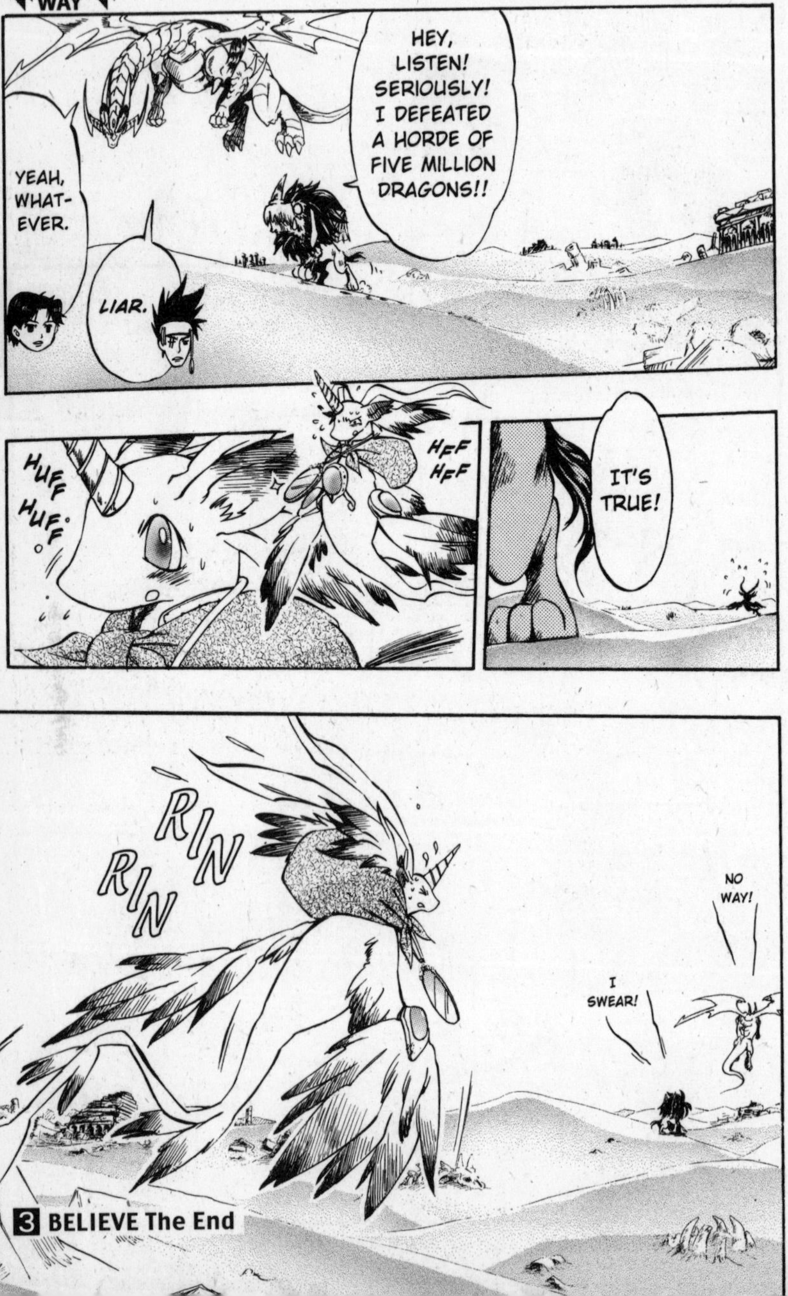
HEY, LISTEN! SERIOUSLY! I DEFEATED A HORDE OF FIVE MILLION DRAGONS!!
LIAR.
YEAH, WHATEVER.
IT'S TRUE!
HFF HFF
HUFF HUFF
NO WAY!
I SWEAR!
RIN RIN

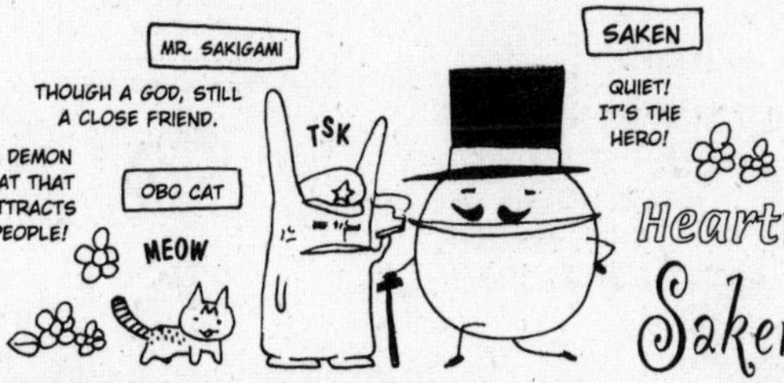
SAKEN
QUIET! IT'S THE HERO!
MR. SAKIGAMI
THOUGH A GOD, STILL A CLOSE FRIEND.
TSK
OBO CAT
A DEMON CAT THAT ATTRACTS PEOPLE!
MEOW

Heartwarming Saken Theater

BY KEN-ICHI SAKURA

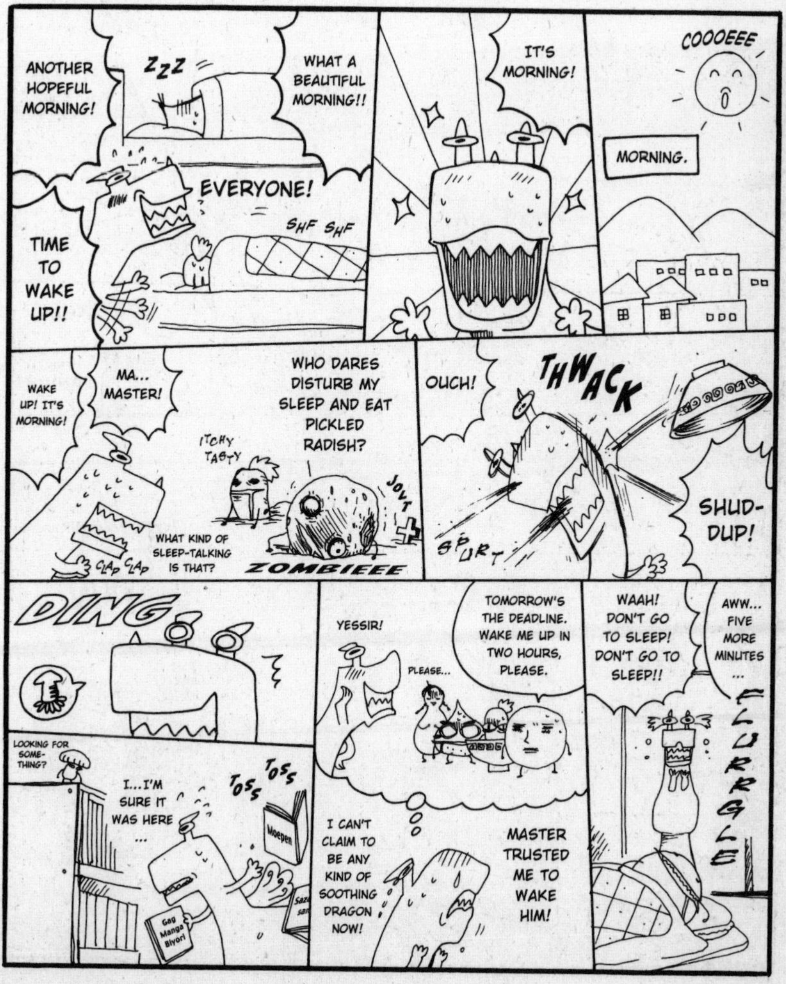
COOOEEE
MORNING.
IT'S MORNING!
WHAT A BEAUTIFUL MORNING!!
ANOTHER HOPEFUL MORNING!
ZZZ
EVERYONE!
TIME TO WAKE UP!!
SHF SHF
OUCH!
THWACK
SHUD-DUP!
SPURT
WHO DARES DISTURB MY SLEEP AND EAT PICKLED RADISH?
MA... MASTER!
WAKE UP! IT'S MORNING!
ITCHY TASTY
JOLT
WHAT KIND OF SLEEP-TALKING IS THAT?
ZOMBIEEE
CLAP CLAP
AWW... FIVE MORE MINUTES ...
WAAH! DON'T GO TO SLEEP! DON'T GO TO SLEEP!!
FLURRGLE
TOMORROW'S THE DEADLINE. WAKE ME UP IN TWO HOURS, PLEASE.
YESSIR!
PLEASE...
MASTER TRUSTED ME TO WAKE HIM!
I CAN'T CLAIM TO BE ANY KIND OF SOOTHING DRAGON NOW!
DING
LOOKING FOR SOME-THING?
TOSS TOSS
I...I'M SURE IT WAS HERE ...
Moepen
Gag Manga Biyori

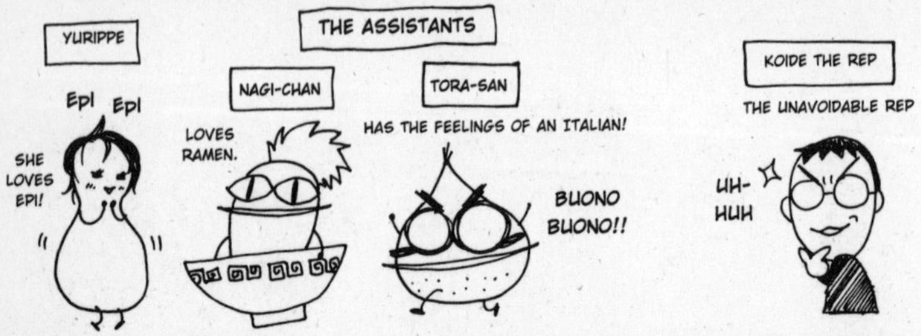
KOIDE THE REP
THE UNAVOIDABLE REP
UH-HUH
THE ASSISTANTS
TORA-SAN
HAS THE FEELINGS OF AN ITALIAN!
BUONO BUONO!!
NAGI-CHAN
LOVES RAMEN.
YURIPPE
Epi Epi
SHE LOVES EPI!

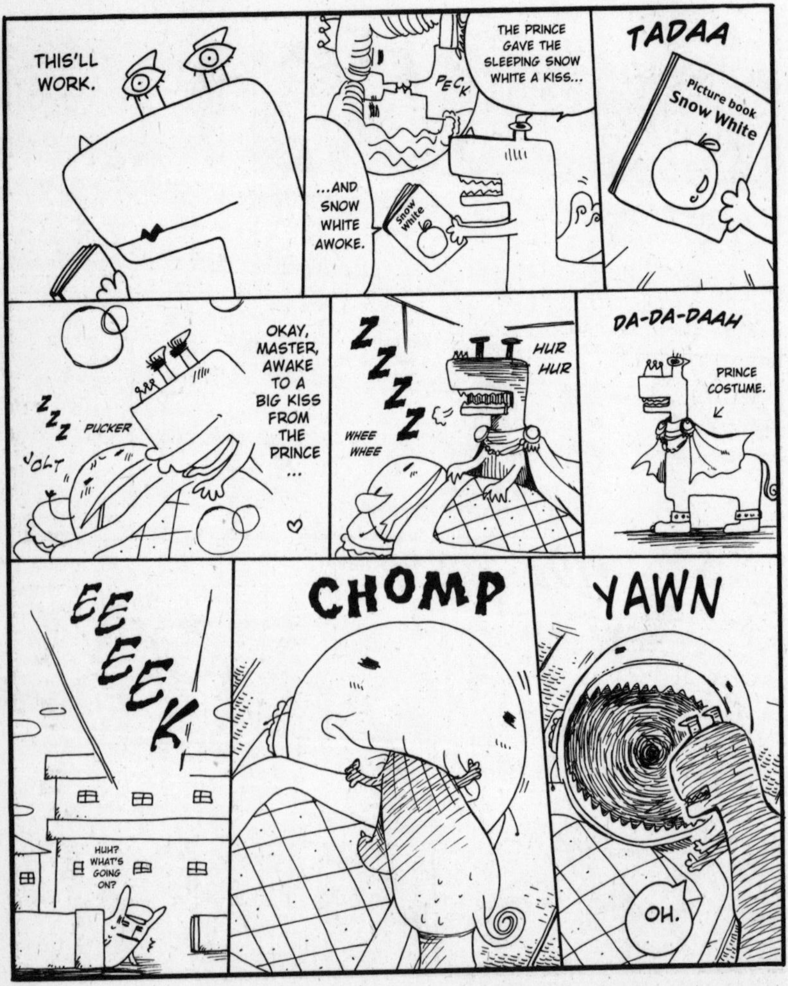
TADAA
Picture book
Snow White
THE PRINCE GAVE THE SLEEPING SNOW WHITE A KISS...
PECK
...AND SNOW WHITE AWOKE.
Snow White
THIS'LL WORK.
DA-DA-DAAH
PRINCE COSTUME.
HUR HUR
ZZZZ
WHEE WHEE
OKAY, MASTER, AWAKE TO A BIG KISS FROM THE PRINCE...
PUCKER
ZZZ
JOLT
YAWN
OH.
CHOMP
EEEEEK
HUH? WHAT'S GOING ON?

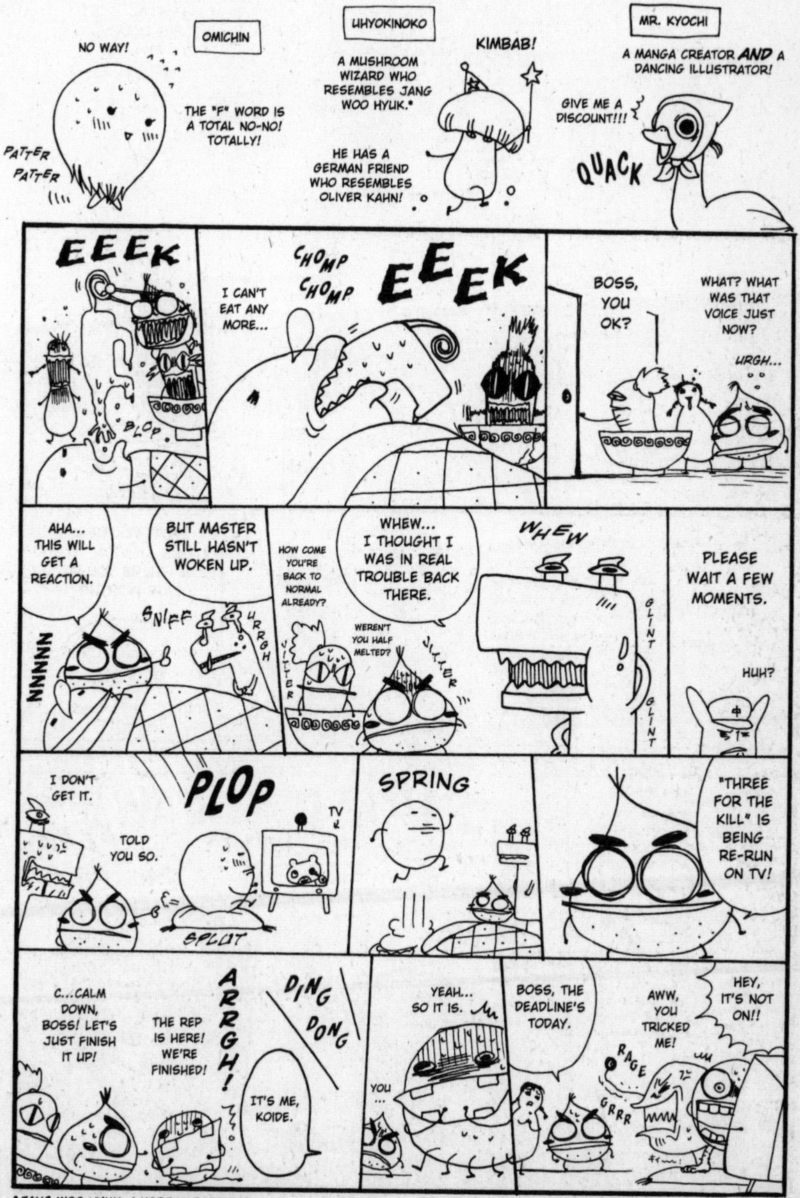
MR. KYOCHI
A MANGA CREATOR AND A DANCING ILLUSTRATOR!
GIVE ME A DISCOUNT!!!
QUACK
UHYOKINOKO
A MUSHROOM WIZARD WHO RESEMBLES JANG WOO HYUK.*
KIMBAB!
HE HAS A GERMAN FRIEND WHO RESEMBLES OLIVER KAHN!
OMICHIN
THE "F" WORD IS A TOTAL NO-NO! TOTALLY!
NO WAY!
PATTER PATTER
WHAT? WHAT WAS THAT VOICE JUST NOW?
BOSS, YOU OK?
URGH...
EEEK
CHOMP CHOMP
I CAN'T EAT ANY MORE...
EEEK
BLOP
PLEASE WAIT A FEW MOMENTS.
HUH?
WHEW
GLINT GLINT
WHEW... I THOUGHT I WAS IN REAL TROUBLE BACK THERE.
HOW COME YOU'RE BACK TO NORMAL ALREADY?
WEREN'T YOU HALF MELTED?
JITTER JITTER
BUT MASTER STILL HASN'T WOKEN UP.
AHA... THIS WILL GET A REACTION.
SNIFF
URRGH
NNNNN
"THREE FOR THE KILL" IS BEING RE-RUN ON TV!
SPRING
PLOP
TV
I DON'T GET IT.
TOLD YOU SO.
SPLUT
HEY, IT'S NOT ON!!
AWW, YOU TRICKED ME!
RAGE
GRRR
BOSS, THE DEADLINE'S TODAY.
YEAH... SO IT IS.
YOU...
DING DONG
ARRGH!
THE REP IS HERE! WE'RE FINISHED!
C...CALM DOWN, BOSS! LET'S JUST FINISH IT UP!
IT'S ME, KOIDE.

*JANG WOO HYUK: A KOREAN POP STAR.

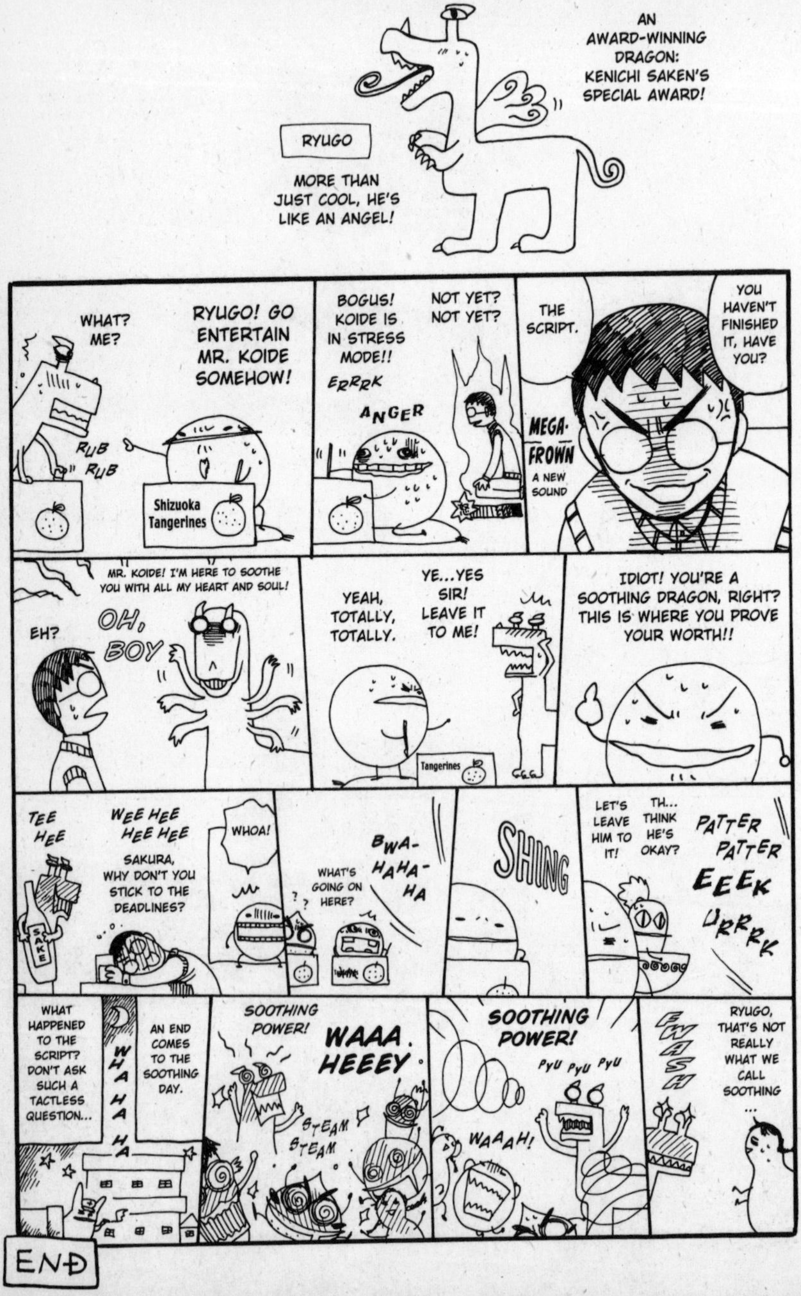
AN AWARD-WINNING DRAGON: KENICHI SAKEN'S SPECIAL AWARD!
RYUGO
MORE THAN JUST COOL, HE'S LIKE AN ANGEL!
YOU HAVEN'T FINISHED IT, HAVE YOU?
THE SCRIPT.
MEGA-FROWN
A NEW SOUND
NOT YET? NOT YET?
BOGUS! KOIDE IS IN STRESS MODE!!
ERRRK
ANGER
RYUGO! GO ENTERTAIN MR. KOIDE SOMEHOW!
WHAT? ME?
RUB RUB
Shizuoka Tangerines
IDIOT! YOU'RE A SOOTHING DRAGON, RIGHT? THIS IS WHERE YOU PROVE YOUR WORTH!!
YE...YES SIR! LEAVE IT TO ME!
YEAH, TOTALLY, TOTALLY.
Tangerines
MR. KOIDE! I'M HERE TO SOOTHE YOU WITH ALL MY HEART AND SOUL!
OH, BOY
EH?
PATTER PATTER
TH... THINK HE'S OKAY?
LET'S LEAVE HIM TO IT!
EEEK
URRRK
SHING
BWA-HAHAHA-HA
WHAT'S GOING ON HERE?
WHOA!
WEE HEE HEE HEE
TEE HEE
SAKURA, WHY DON'T YOU STICK TO THE DEADLINES?
SAKE
RYUGO, THAT'S NOT REALLY WHAT WE CALL SOOTHING ...
FWASH
SOOTHING POWER!
PYU PYU PYU
WAAAH!
WAAA. HEEEY
SOOTHING POWER!
STEAM STEAM
AN END COMES TO THE SOOTHING DAY.
WHAHAHAHA
WHAT HAPPENED TO THE SCRIPT? DON'T ASK SUCH A TACTLESS QUESTION...
END

COMING NEXT VOLUME...

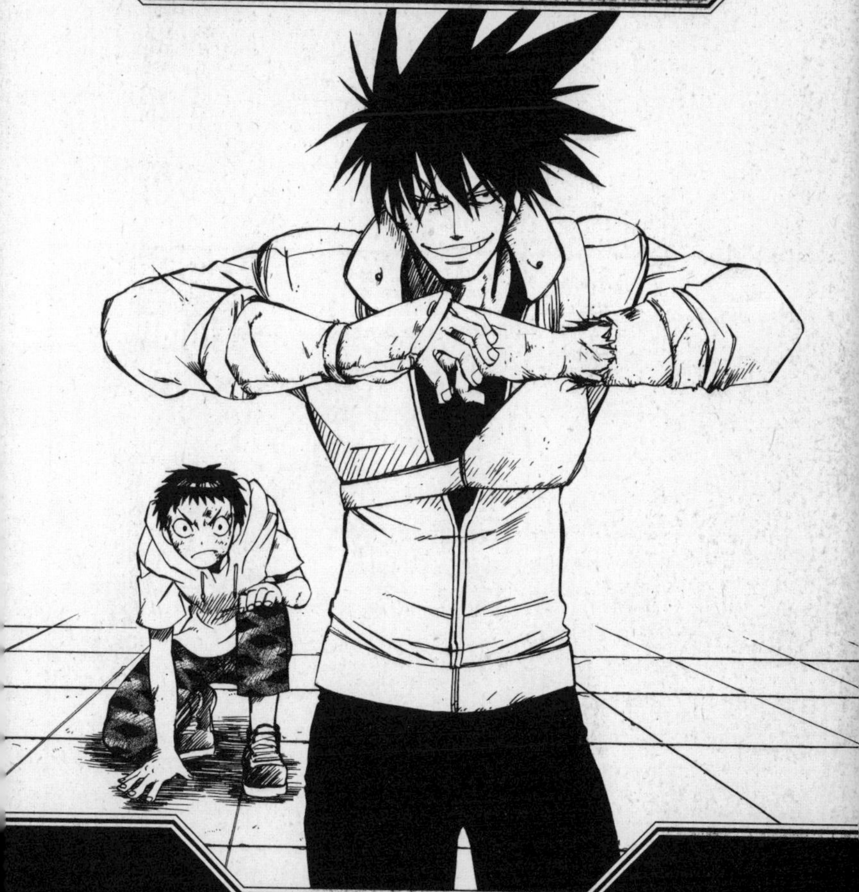

After a tough journey, Reiji and friends arrive in Yaudim, a dangerous place ruled by a huge dragon called Guan-Coo. Upon arrival they befriend a youth named Taiyo, who says that Reiji reminds him of his old mentor. It turns out this mentor was none other than Sun Wols, the champion of the last Dragonic Heaven! Then it's off to the tournament where some unexpected foes await them—foes that cost Rokkaku his right eye. And since he can't get his eye back, he'd like the next best thing—revenge!

AVAILABLE NOW!

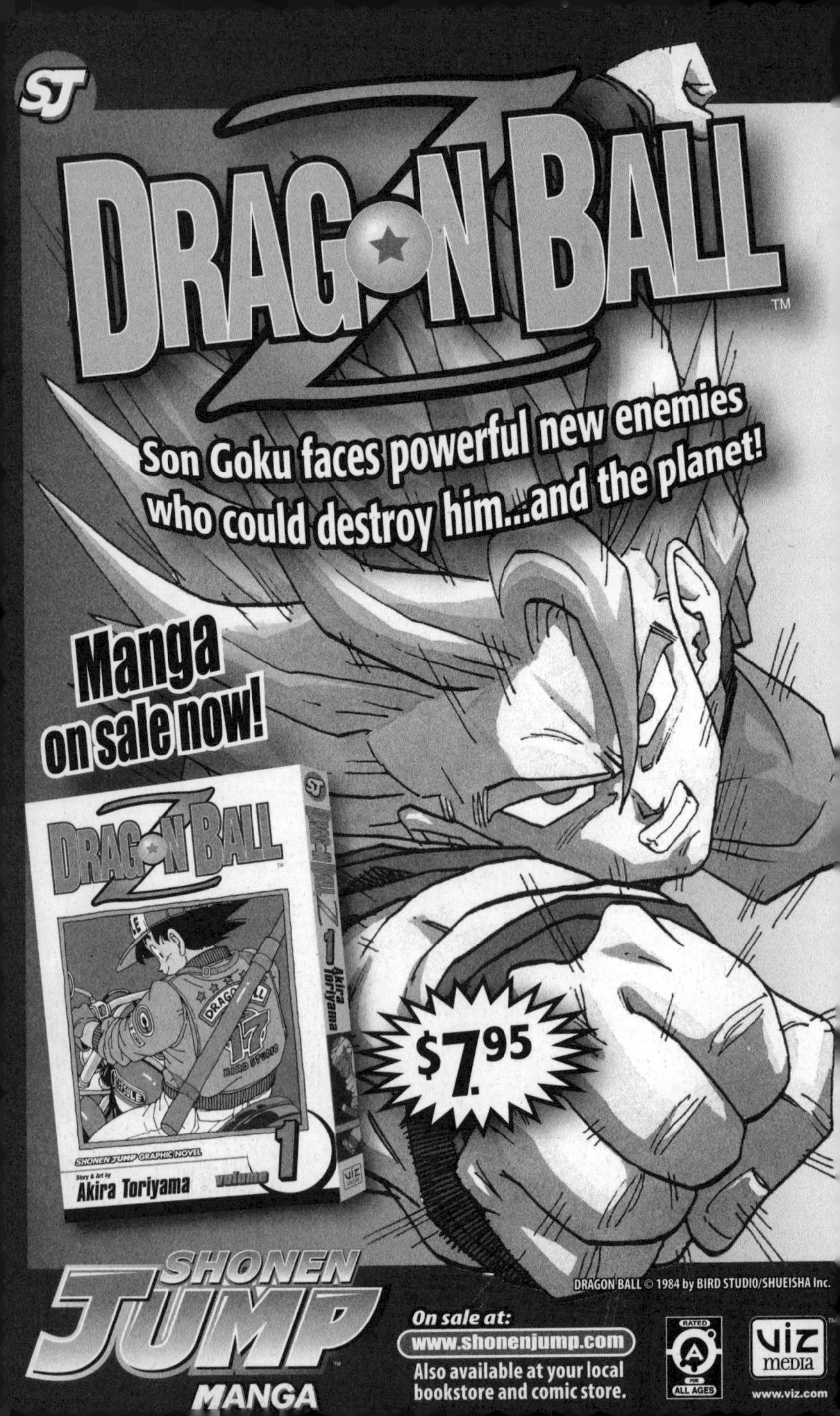
SJ
DRAGON BALL Z
TM
Son Goku faces powerful new enemies who could destroy him...and the planet!
Manga on sale now!
$7.95
SHONEN JUMP GRAPHIC NOVEL
Story & Art by
Akira Toriyama
volume 1
DRAGON BALL © 1984 by BIRD STUDIO/SHUEISHA Inc.
SHONEN JUMP MANGA
On sale at:
www.shonenjump.com
Also available at your local bookstore and comic store.
RATED A FOR ALL AGES
VIZ media
www.viz.com

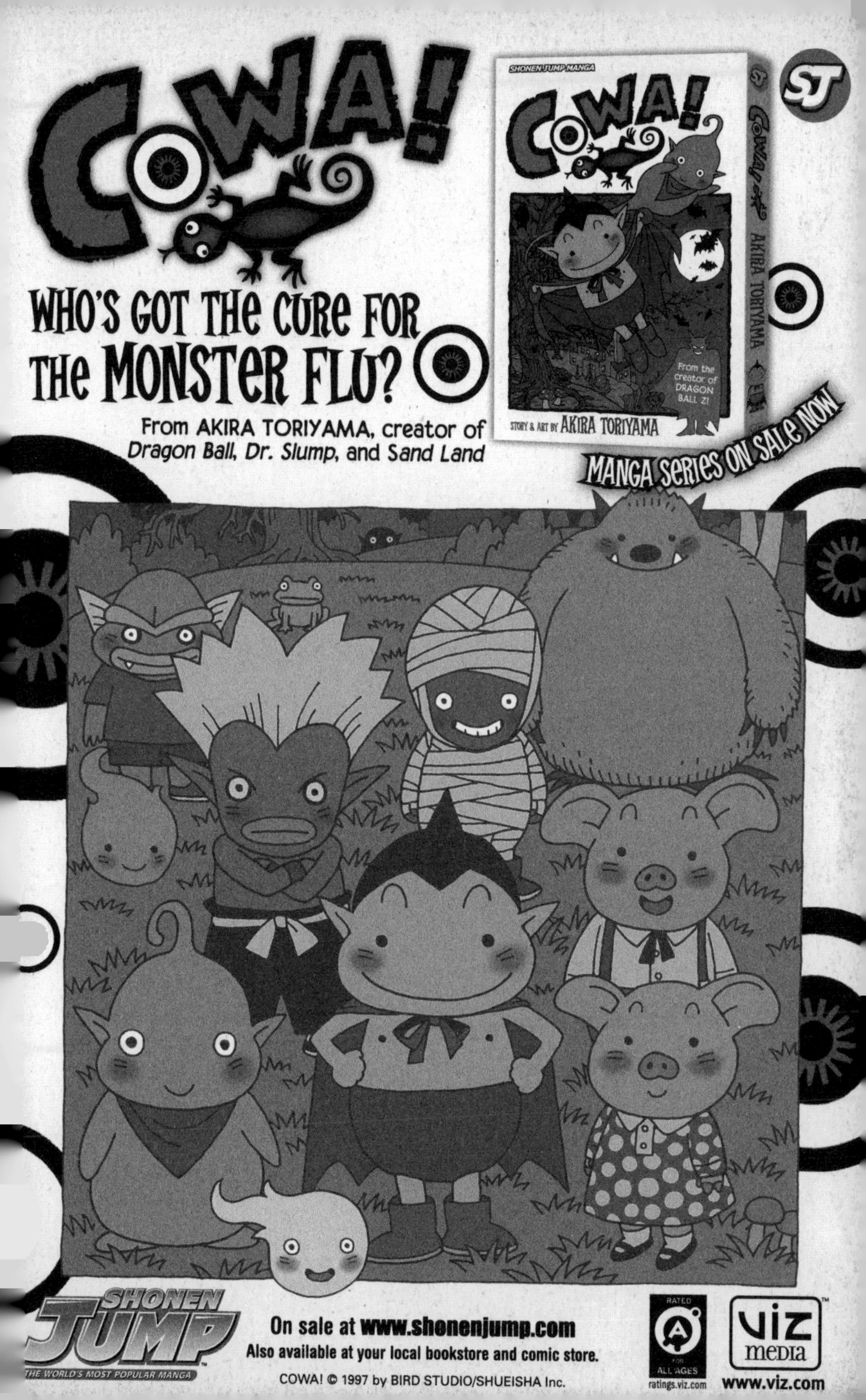
COWA!
WHO'S GOT THE CURE FOR THE MONSTER FLU?
From AKIRA TORIYAMA, creator of *Dragon Ball, Dr. Slump*, and *Sand Land*
SHONEN JUMP MANGA
COWA!
SJ
AKIRA TORIYAMA
From the creator of DRAGON BALL Z!
STORY & ART BY AKIRA TORIYAMA
MANGA SERIES ON SALE NOW
SHONEN JUMP
THE WORLD'S MOST POPULAR MANGA
On sale at www.shonenjump.com
Also available at your local bookstore and comic store.
COWA! © 1997 by BIRD STUDIO/SHUEISHA Inc.
RATED A FOR ALL AGES
ratings.viz.com
VIZ media
www.viz.com

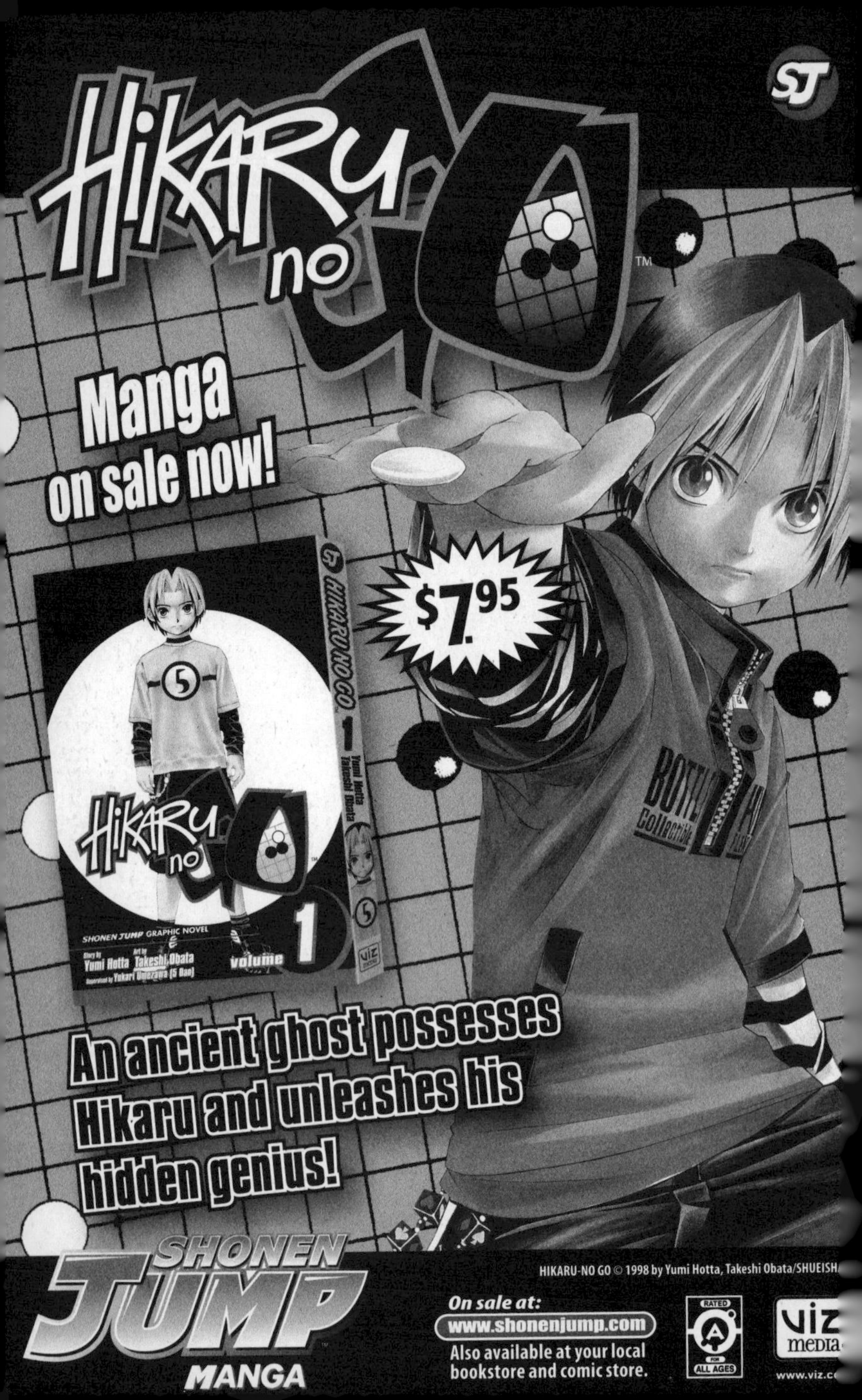
SJ
HIKARU no GO™
Manga on sale now!
$7.95
SJ HIKARU NO GO 1 Yumi Hotta Takeshi Obata
HIKARU no GO
SHONEN JUMP GRAPHIC NOVEL
Story by Yumi Hotta
Art by Takeshi Obata
volume 1
An ancient ghost possesses Hikaru and unleashes his hidden genius!
SHONEN JUMP MANGA
HIKARU-NO GO © 1998 by Yumi Hotta, Takeshi Obata/SHUEISH
On sale at:
www.shonenjump.com
Also available at your local bookstore and comic store.
RATED A FOR ALL AGES
viz media
www.viz.c

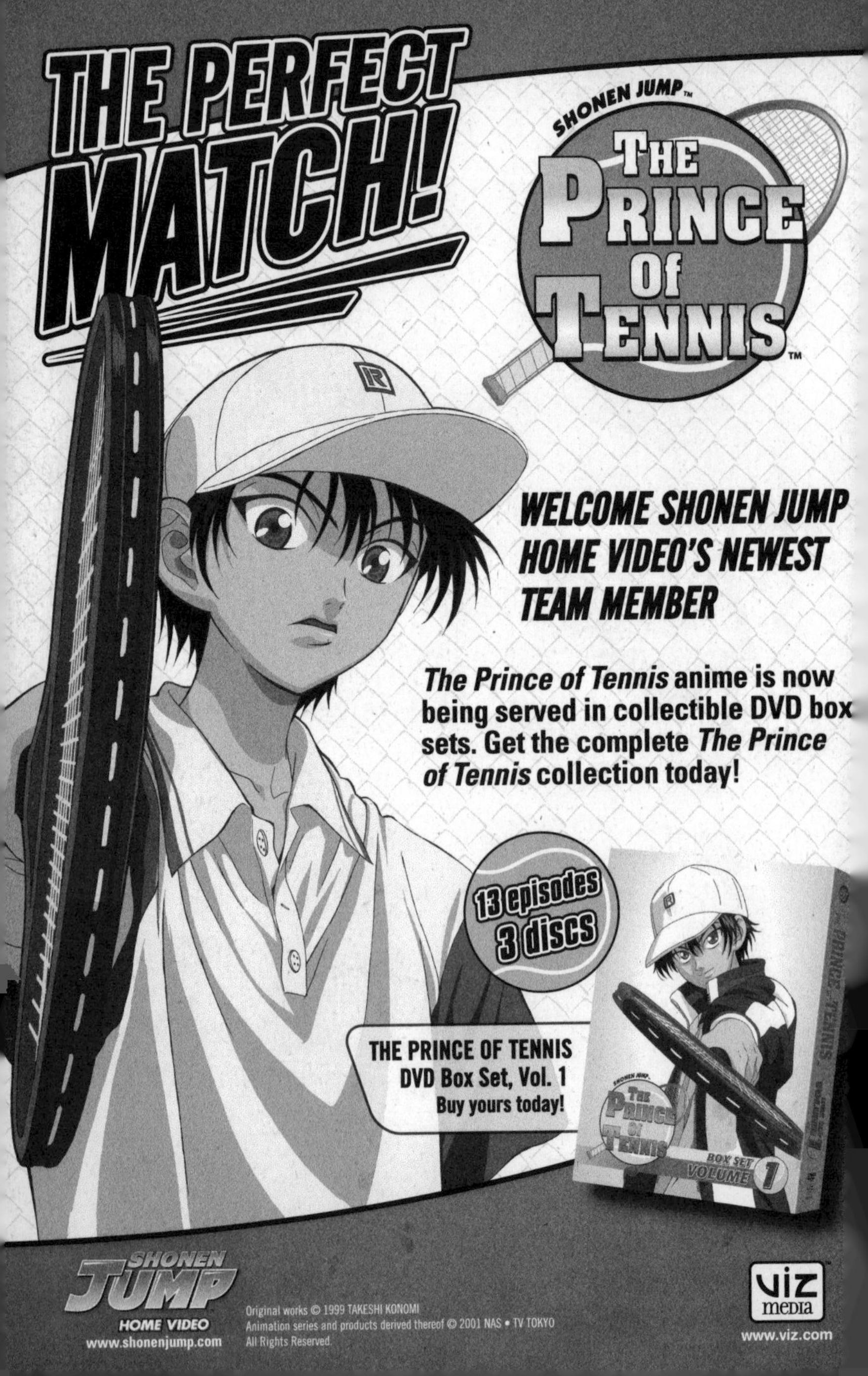

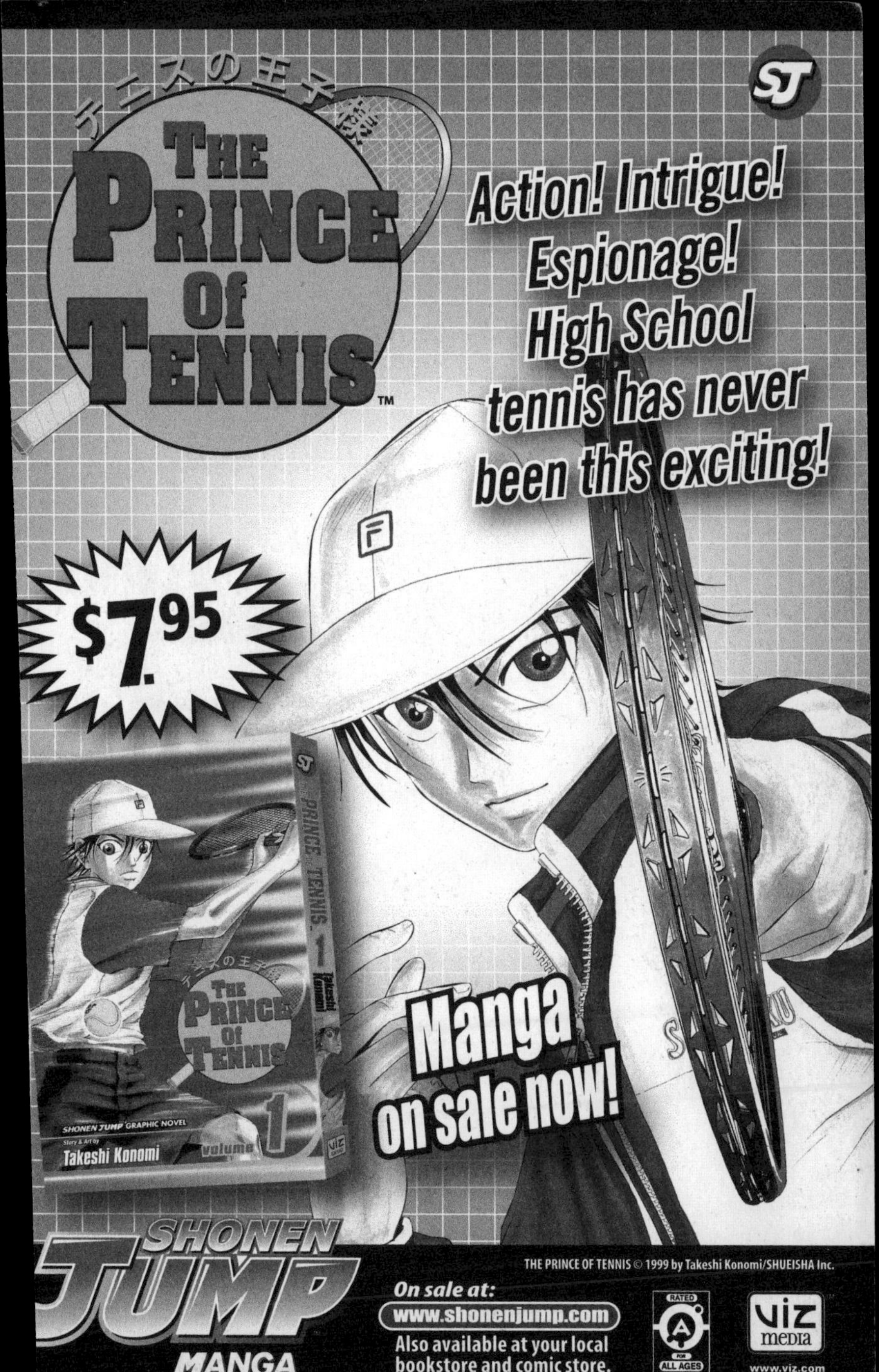
SJ
テニスの王子様
THE PRINCE OF TENNIS™
Action! Intrigue! Espionage! High School tennis has never been this exciting!
$7.95
THE PRINCE OF TENNIS
SHONEN JUMP GRAPHIC NOVEL
Story & Art by
Takeshi Konomi
volume 1
Manga on sale now!
SHONEN JUMP MANGA
THE PRINCE OF TENNIS © 1999 by Takeshi Konomi/SHUEISHA Inc.
On sale at:
www.shonenjump.com
Also available at your local bookstore and comic store.
RATED A FOR ALL AGES
VIZ media
www.viz.com

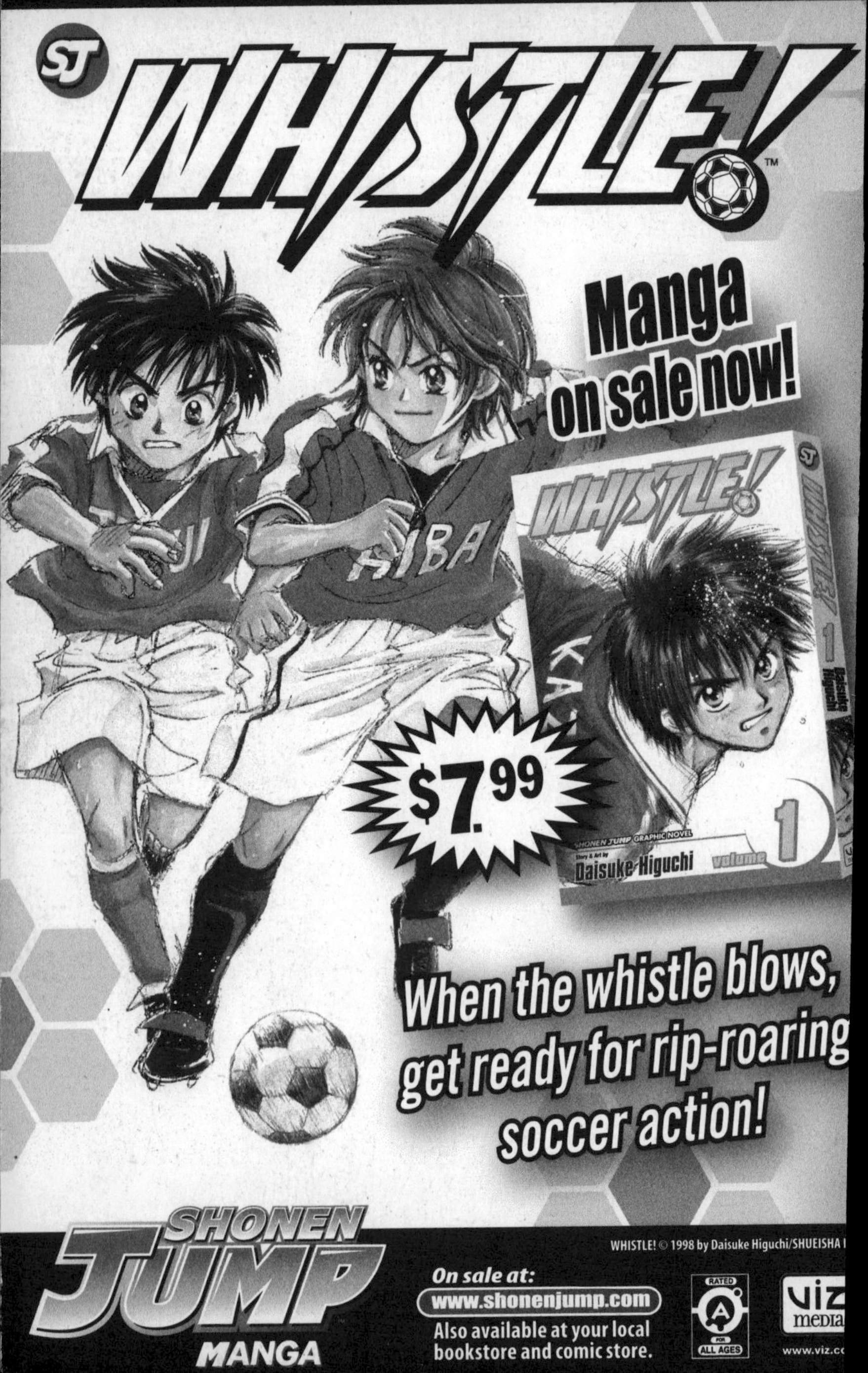
SJ
WHISTLE!™
Manga on sale now!
WHISTLE!
SJ WHISTLE! 1 Daisuke Higuchi
SHONEN JUMP GRAPHIC NOVEL
Story & Art by Daisuke Higuchi
volume 1
$7.99
When the whistle blows, get ready for rip-roaring soccer action!
SHONEN JUMP MANGA
WHISTLE! © 1998 by Daisuke Higuchi/SHUEISHA
On sale at:
www.shonenjump.com
Also available at your local bookstore and comic store.
RATED A FOR ALL AGES
viz media
www.viz.co

SHONEN JUMP

THE WORLD'S MOST POPULAR MANGA

BLEACH

**STORY AND ART BY
TITE KUBO**

ONE PIECE

**STORY AND ART BY
EIICHIRO ODA**

Tegami Bachi
LETTER · BEE

**STORY AND ART BY
HIROYUKI ASADA**

JUMP INTO THE ACTION BY TELLING US WHAT YOU LOVE (AND WHAT YOU DON'T)

LET YOUR VOICE BE HEARD!

SHONENJUMP.VIZ.COM/MANGASURVEY

HELP US MAKE MORE OF THE WORLD'S MOST POPULAR MANGA!

www.viz.com

SAVE 50% OFF
THE COVER PRICE!

IT'S LIKE GETTING 6 ISSUES
FREE!

OVER **350+** PAGES PER ISSUE

THE WORLD'S MOST POPULAR MANGA

This monthly magazine contains 7 of the coolest manga available in the U.S., PLUS anime news, and info about video & card games, toys AND more!

❏ **I want 12 HUGE issues of SHONEN JUMP for only $29.95*!**

_____

NAME

_____

ADDRESS

_____

CITY/STATE/ZIP

_____

EMAIL ADDRESS   **DATE OF BIRTH**

❏ YES, send me via email information, advertising, offers, and promotions related to VIZ Media, SHONEN JUMP, and/or their business partners.

❏ **CHECK ENCLOSED** (payable to SHONEN JUMP)   ❏ **BILL ME LATER**

CREDIT CARD: ❏ **Visa** ❏ **Mastercard**

_____

ACCOUNT NUMBER   **EXP. DATE**

_____

SIGNATURE

CLIP&MAIL TO:
SHONEN JUMP Subscriptions Service Dept.
P.O. Box 515
Mount Morris, IL 61054-0515

P9GNC1

* Canada price: $41.95 USD, including GST, HST, and QST. US/CAN orders only. Allow 6-8 weeks for delivery.
ONE PIECE © 1997 by Eiichiro Oda/SHUEISHA Inc. BLEACH © 2001 by Tite Kubo/SHUEISHA Inc.
NARUTO © 1999 by Masashi Kishimoto/SHUEISHA Inc.

www.viz.com